# *Pound/The Little Review*

## THE CORRESPONDENCE OF EZRA POUND

*Pound/Ford: The Story of a Literary Friendship*
Edited by Brita Lindberg-Seyersted

*Pound/Joyce: Letters & Essays*
Edited by Forrest Read

*Pound/Lewis: The Letters of Ezra Pound and Wyndham Lewis*
Edited by Timothy Materer

*Pound/The Little Review:*
*The Letters of Ezra Pound to Margaret Anderson*
Edited by Thomas L. Scott and Melvin J. Friedman,
with the assistance of Jackson R. Bryer

*Ezra Pound and Dorothy Shakespear: Their Letters 1909–1914*
Edited by Omar Pound and A. Walton Litz

*Pound/Zukofsky: Selected Letters of Ezra Pound and Louis Zukofsky*
Edited by Barry Ahearn

THE CORRESPONDENCE OF EZRA POUND

# *Pound /The Little Review*

## The Letters of Ezra Pound
## to Margaret Anderson:
## *The Little Review*
## Correspondence

EDITED BY

THOMAS L. SCOTT,

MELVIN J. FRIEDMAN,

WITH THE ASSISTANCE OF

JACKSON R. BRYER

A NEW DIRECTIONS BOOK

Manufactured in the United States of America
New Directions Books are printed on acid-free paper.
First published clothbound by New Directions in 1988
Published simultaneously in Canada by Penguin Books Canada Limited

**Library of Congress Cataloging-in-Publication Data**

Pound, Ezra, 1885–1972.
    Pound/The Little Review: the letters of Ezra Pound to Margaret
Anderson: the Little Review correspondence / edited by Thomas L.
Scott, Melvin J. Friedman, and Jackson R. Bryer.
    p.   cm.—(The Correspondence of Ezra Pound)
Bibliography: p.
Includes index.
ISBN 0–8112–1059–6
    1.  Pound, Ezra, 1885–1972—Correspondence.    2.  Poets,
American—20th century—Correspondence.    3.  Editors—United States—
Correspondence.    4.  Anderson, Margaret C.—Correspondence.
5.  Little Review (Chicago, Ill.)    I.  Scott, Thomas L.
II.  Friedman, Melvin J.    III.  Bryer, Jackson R.    IV.  Title.
V.  Series: Pound, Ezra, 1885–1972. Correspondence.
PS3531.082Z483   1988
811'.52—dc 19
[B]                                                                          88–341
                                                                              CIP

New Directions Books are published for James Laughlin
by New Directions Publishing Corporation,
80 Eighth Avenue, New York 10011

# Contents

Notes on the Editing     ix

Introduction, by Thomas L. Scott and Melvin J. Friedman     xiii

The Letters     1

Appendix     321

Selected Bibliography     331

Index, prepared by Edi Bjorkland     344

For
Ralph M. Aderman
Scholar,
Editor,
and Friend

# Notes on the Editing

Timothy Materer remarks in *Pound/Lewis* that "Pound from the late thirties on refers familiarly to events and personalities that are so private or obscure that even his correspondents do not recognize them" (vii). Although Pound's letters to Margaret Anderson are mainly from an earlier period (spring 1916 through spring 1923), they also present certain difficulties. For one thing, Anderson's letters to Pound have not survived and one can only guess as to their contents. Secondly, the references to obscure people, events, or works which become so disturbing in later letters are here also, if only to a lesser degree. Finally, the appearance of the letters suggests that they were written in haste: omitted words, incomplete sentences, irregularities in spelling and punctuation are typical.

We have dealt with these difficulties in several ways. Explanations in Margaret Anderson's autobiography, *My Thirty Years' War,* and in other texts dealing with the period supply some of the background necessary to approximate her attitudes and the events of her life. Then, too, her writings in *The Little Review* help to create something of a profile of her at the time these letters were written. These sources, therefore, are useful in constructing the missing half of the correspondence, and we have referred frequently to them. (Brief citations within the notes to the letters or the Introduction are keyed to the Selected Bibliography at the end of the volume.)

Notes at the end of each letter provide information about persons, events, or works when they are first mentioned; thereafter, brief identifications are supplied within brackets in the text. When a person is referred to frequently, the bracketed information is not repeated each time. Pound's references to items which are to appear in *The Little Review* or to those which have already been published are identified in the notes when necessary; if these selections are not readily available outside the pages of *The Little Review,* we have provided explanations or summaries of the material. When helpful, cross-references to other letters have also been supplied.

Most of these letters were typewritten, at apparently great speed, with comments or clarifications added interlinearly and marginally. These authorial insertions are indicated by angled brackets. (Editorial intervention is identified by squared brackets.) Canceled material, when it seems significant, is provided in squared brackets with the word *crossout* preceding the omitted words. At the beginning of each letter, a designation indicates the form and number of pages: TLS—typed letter signed by author; ALS—autograph letter signed by author; PC—post card. The number following these abbreviations indicates the number of pages in the original. Descriptions of the headings are also provided. Most of the letters were dated by Pound, often below his signature. For the convenience of the reader, we have supplied these dates within brackets at the head of each letter. If the letter is undated, we have supplied a probable date, accompanied by a question mark. Salutations, indentations, and paragraphing conform as nearly as possible to Pound's practices in the originals.

Misspellings have been silently corrected when they have seemed trivial (e.g., *lable* for *label; calender* for *calendar*) or are obviously typographical inversions (e.g., *hte* for *the*). Misspellings which appear intentional or characteristic of Pound have been reproduced as in the original. *Sic* has been provided in those instances where confusion or misreading might result from the misspelling. Since Pound's spelling of proper names may be an indication of how well he knew the person he was referring to, misspellings of this kind have been allowed to stand with the correct version given in brackets or in the notes at the end of the letter. For frequently mentioned names, we have not repeated the correct version each time.

Pound's punctuation was at times erratic. To suggest the character of the original letters, we have reproduced the punctuation as it stands, except that we have silently added closing quotation marks and parentheses where Pound had omitted them. When misreading seemed a possibility, we have supplied punctuation in brackets. Pound's characteristic omission of apostrophes in contractions and possessives has been retained as have his capitalization irregularities.

Parts of these letters have been published previously. Excerpting and rearranging passages within a letter and at times combining these with passages from other letters, Margaret Anderson included thirteen of Pound's letters in *My Thirty Years' War,* first published in 1930 (159–72 and 216–18 of the 1969 edition). For example, the letter which appears on pages 163 and 164 of the autobiography is, in fact, comprised of passages from Letters 34 and 43 as we have numbered them. Some of Miss Anderson's alterations involve deletions of material of a mundane nature and rearrangements aimed at achieving a thematic unity. Passages from several letters, for example, may be combined when they deal with similar subject matter. At other times, however, one has the uncomfortable feeling that her gestures may have been prompted by less admirable motives—a desire on her part, perhaps, to show Pound in a negative way or to soften his criticism of her. In any case, the letters—abridged and rearranged as they are in *My Thirty Years' War*—are not accurate representations of what Pound had indeed written. Unfortunately, working no doubt from Miss Anderson's autobiography, D. D. Paige included eleven of these versions in *The Letters of Ezra Pound, 1907–1941* (Letters 120, 124, 126, 127, 133, 135, 140, 142, 144, 147, and 150). *The Letters of Ezra Pound to Margaret Anderson:* The Little Review *Correspondence* will, we hope, set the record straight.

Something needs to be said about the lists some of these letters contain. Pound forwarded to Margaret Anderson the names of people to whom he wanted sample copies sent, a list of those to whom free copies should be regularly mailed, and the names of subscribers. These listings are revealing because they indicate who was reading *The Little Review* during Pound's tenure as foreign editor—or, at least, who had an acquaintance with it. More generally, they suggest the efforts Pound expended in advancing the work he now was involved in publishing. The sample-copy lists, for example, include the names of people of the London literary establishment, prominent hostesses who would "talk about" the magazine (Lady Cunard, Lady Tredegar, Natalie Barney), American college professors, and editors of other magazines. The lists, therefore, have some value, and we have reproduced them as they appear in the originals.

Finally, it should be mentioned that the originals of Pound's *The Little Review* letters are housed at the Golda Meir Library of the University of Wisconsin–Milwaukee. The letters from 1953–54 are part of the Yale Pound Center collection of the Beinecke Library; Margaret Anderson's letters are in the Beinecke Rare Book and Manuscript Library, Yale University. Donald Gallup alerted us to the existence of the 1953–54 letters; he also read through our manuscript with scrupulous care and offered many helpful suggestions. Ruth M. Alvarez assisted with the transcription of the letters. Jackson R. Bryer's work on the project was supported by grants from the National Endowment for the Humanities, and we are grateful also for the help of the following people: William C. Roselle, Stanley I. Mallach, Mark L. Krupnick, Herbert Blau, and Ralph M. Alderman—all connected with the University of Wisconsin–Milwaukee. Finally, we should like to acknowledge our gratitude to Peter Glassgold of New Directions and to Deans Jessica Wirth and William F. Halloran of the University of Wisconsin–Milwaukee for continued support of research.

# Introduction

Little magazines have played an essential role in the development of modern literature. Even a glance at the biographies of such central figures as Joyce, Eliot, and Pound confirms this fact. What becomes clear is that, had there not been these little magazines—periodicals in which so many of the major and minor modernist writers first broke into print and in which they continued to publish—the direction of this literature might have taken a different turn. In fact, without these "trial-track[s] for racers" (to borrow a phrase Jane Heap coined to describe *The Little Review*), we can hardly imagine how or where an avant-garde in literature would exist; its antagonistic stance toward "mass" culture often made its work unwelcome in the popular media. Little magazines, therefore, became the places where the avant-garde could undermine the status quo and experiment with new forms. And so, in manifestos, proclamations, articles, and critical discussions, the avant-garde ridiculed the stale or sentimental and called for a new art for a new age. For an admittedly small number of readers, the little magazines published the fiction, poems, and plays of the new breed of experimental writer. Because unevenness of quality is an almost inherent characteristic of these magazines, some of the selections were ephemeral, hardly worth the first reading, while others later proved to be literature of enduring consequence. Underlying it all were the notions that Western culture had come to a turning point and that a renewed art could provide a coherence for a world in which the center could no longer hold. The form such a coherence would take was a matter of disagreement among the various factions of the avant-garde; little magazines provided the forums in which the issue could be argued.

Given the economics of publishing and the comforting role mass-circulation magazines usually play within society, the new and the experimental have little chance of being published in commercial magazines; and so the unfamiliar, the assaultive, is doomed to remain in manuscript until a more adventurous publishing enterprise (often one which is blithely indifferent to economics) agrees to set the type. At the turn of the century in America, the established publishing avenues were frequently, and for varying reasons, closed to the experiments of the avant-garde. In an article written in 1930, Pound, looking back, described the publishing situation as he saw it. In the latter part of the nineteenth century, he says, "[t]he elder magazines, the *Atlantic, Harper's, Scribner's, Century,* had even in their original titles more or less and in varying degrees abjured the pretentions [*sic*] of London 'Reviews,' i.e., to serious and consecutive criticism of literature. They had grown increasingly somnolent, reminiscences of General Grant being about their maximum effort toward contemporaneity" ("Small Magazines" 690). Then, toward the beginning of the twentieth century,

> there was a new and livelier current in the trade. The methods of Armour's meat business were introduced into distribution. A commercial talent blossomed in the great firm of Condé Nast. A bright young man observed a leakage in efficiency. The advertising men had to collect such ads as the contents could attract. In the new system the contents were selected rigorously on the basis of how much expensive advertising they would carry. Hence the sameness in impression given by successive numbers of these bright and snappy periodicals. . . . These things . . . ultimately leave a vacuum. They leave a need for intellectual communication unconditioned by considerations as to whether a given idea or a trend in art will "git ads" from the leading corset companies. ("Small Magazines" 690)

Pound's assessment that economic considerations were exerting an uncomfortable control over intellectual and aesthetic expression is no doubt valid. Putting the matter succinctly, Frederick J. Hoffman, Charles Allen, and Carolyn F. Ulrich suggest the basic impulses that generated the founding of little magazines: "rebellion against traditional modes of expression and the wish to experiment with novel (and sometimes unintelligible) forms; and a desire to overcome the commercial or material difficulties which are caused by the introduction of any writing whose commercial merits have not been proved" (Hoffman, Allen, and Ulrich 4–5).

Ezra Pound's involvement with little magazines—both as a contributor and an editor—shaped not only his own career but that of others as well: Eliot and Joyce, to name the most obvious. A systematic study of Pound's relationship with little magazines is beyond the scope of this introduction. To suggest the range of such an enterprise, one has only to notice that, through 1923 (the year by which the majority of Pound's *The Little Review* letters had been written), Donald Gallup's standard bibliography lists some 654 entries of Pound's contributions to periodicals. Most of these cite publications that could be classified as little magazines. This listing, of course, does not indicate the extent of Pound's involvement in editorial duties. Some salient facts, however, may help to show the nature of his activities.

Pound had arrived in London in (about) September 1908, having just privately published in Venice *A Lume Spento,* his first book of verse; he was nearly penniless and more or less unknown. When *A Quinzaine for this Yule* was published in December 1908, followed by *Personae* in April 1909, Pound's career was launched. However encouraging it must have been for him to see his work printed in individual volumes, perhaps even more gratifying was having "Sestina: Altaforte"—the first of his poems to appear in a British magazine—included in the June 1909 issue of Ford Madox Ford's *The English Review.* Ford's journal had already published established writers such as Thomas Hardy, Henry James, William Butler Yeats, Walter de la Mare, John Galsworthy, W. H. Hudson, and Norman Douglas. To be published in this company provides just the kind of encouragement a young writer needs. Although not in the strict sense "a little magazine" and its big-name contributors scarcely part of the avant-garde, yet, during the year and a half in which Ford Madox Ford exercised editorial control, *The English Review* was receptive to the new and the experimental. As Pound saw it, "Part, and by no means the smallest part of the glory of the first year and a half of the English Review, is that in that time Hueffer printed not only Anatole France, Swinburne, Tho. Hardy, Henry James but also work by all the young men who have since come off. Lewis, Lawrence, Cannon [Gilbert Cannan], myself etc." (see Letter 24). "Printing all the young men," *"les jeunes"* as he called them, was a lesson Pound was not soon to forget. The letters in this volume illustrate vividly Pound's insistence that *les jeunes* (John Rodker and Iris Barry, for example) should be published, even though Margaret Anderson often objected and he himself knew their work was not genuinely first-rate. Their "stuff" was a "bet," not a compromise (Letter 24).

In 1911, Pound met Alfred Richard Orage, the editor of the socialist weekly *The New Age.* Convinced that everything cultural suggested solutions to social problems, Orage had begun editing the magazine in 1907 with the intention of transforming it from a narrowly socialist journal to one that included the discussion of art, literature, and other aspects of culture and thought. Orage offered Pound the opportunity to publish a series of his translations from Anglo-Saxon, Provençal, and Tuscan poetry, along with prose commentary, an invitation Pound eagerly accepted. His association with *The New Age* thus established, Pound continued to publish regularly in it, and he met frequently with the journal's other contributors, people such as T. E. Hulme, Sturge Moore, Rupert Brooke,

Allen Upward, John Middleton Murry, Llewellyn Powys, Katherine Mansfield, and A. E. Randall. Pound's relation with these writers was valuable
to him not only for the entryway they provided to the literary world of
London, but also for the interplay of ideas afforded by such a diverse
group. What is more, his work for *The New Age* provided him with badly
needed income. Noel Stock points out the impact the involvement with
*The New Age* had on Pound's career: ". . . it was not only the contact
with new and dissimilar views which for Pound was important, there was
the matter of money: during the next ten years [through 1921] Orage
published nearly three hundred of his articles and this regular payment
was the biggest single factor in keeping the wolf from the door" (106).

Another British periodical with which Pound became involved during
his London years was *The Egoist: An Individualist Review,* a journal
founded in June 1913 by Dora Marsden and Harriet Shaw Weaver as
*The New Freewoman: An Individualist Review.* (The name was changed
with the January 1914 issue, and Harriet Shaw Weaver became its principal editor in July 1914.) In August 1913, shortly after the magazine
began appearing, the editors asked Pound to take charge temporarily of
the literary department, an invitation that initiated a long-term involvement. During these years, Pound supplied numerous pieces to the magazine, some under pseudonyms like "Bastien von Hemholtz," "Baptiste
von Hemholtz," or "Hermann Karl Georg Jesus Maria." In addition, he
used his association with the journal to promote the work of writers and
of artists he was interested in. For example, he persuaded Harriet Shaw
Weaver to publish serially Joyce's *A Portrait of the Artist as a Young
Man* (in 1914), and Wyndham Lewis's *Tarr* (in 1916)—services typical
of the kind he would perform on many occasions for Joyce and for Lewis;
he drew attention to the work of young writers (Edgar Lee Masters, Robert Frost) and extolled the merits of the paintings of Wyndham Lewis and
the sculpture of Henri Gaudier-Brzeska and Jacob Epstein; he even secured for T. S. Eliot a position as assistant editor on the magazine. There
is no question that his efforts on behalf of others were selfless and persistent, as the letters in this volume also amply demonstrate. Except for
1915, when his contact with the magazine was minimal, Pound continued
to contribute to *The Egoist* until 1919, the year in which it ceased publication as a periodical to begin functioning exclusively as a publishing house,
The Egoist Press.

Pound's growing friendship with Wyndham Lewis in 1914 led to his
collaboration with this combative artist and writer on the magazine *BLAST,*
the official organ of Lewis's and Pound's new movement, which Pound

had named "Vorticism." The first issue of *BLAST: A Review of the Great English Vortex* (there were only two) came out on 20 June 1914 and contained assaults on anyone and anything the editors felt smacked of the old, the sentimental, the middle-class, and "also the Aristocracy and Proletariat." The issue was oversized, approximately nine by twelve inches, and its cover was a shocking pink, with "BLAST" printed diagonally across it in bold black letters. The typography used for the selections was no less bold than on the cover, some of the type a half-inch tall. The second number of *BLAST,* its War Number, was issued in July 1915 and maintained much the same tone as the first. The public's reaction to the belligerence of *BLAST,* particularly to the first issue, was, not surprisingly, mixed: some liked it; others, like G. W. Prothero, the editor of *The Quarterly Review,* were outraged.

Pound's most sustained—and, in some senses, most frustrating—experience with an American little magazine during this period grew out of his association with Harriet Monroe's *Poetry: A Magazine of Verse.* Miss Monroe had purchased copies of Pound's *Personae* and *Exultations* while in London in 1910 and had read and reread them on her return to Chicago via Russia, impressed with the qualities she found in the poems. In the late summer of 1912, when her plans to publish a journal devoted to poetry neared completion, she wrote to Pound, asking if he would collaborate with her and send her his own verse and that of others he thought worthy of publication. Pound agreed to serve as the magazine's foreign correspondent, and immediately started to send her material. In *The Life of Ezra Pound,* Noel Stock suggests that Pound saw his responsibilities as twofold: "to gather contributions worth publishing and to educate or if necessary to bully the editor into publishing them" (121). The first he did, and the second often became necessary.

At the time Harriet Monroe's proposal arrived, Pound, along with others, was developing the new principles of poetry he had named "Imagism." It is not surprising, then, that the first poems he sent to *Poetry* were those by Richard Aldington and himself that had been written according to those principles. To subsequent issues of *Poetry,* Pound made frequent contributions—reviews, essays, poems—and supplied the work of others. He sent to the magazine selections by Yeats, Tagore, Aldington, H.D., Eliot, and his own translations—or, more accurately, transformations— of Chinese poems based on the notes of the Sinologist Ernest Fenollosa, whose papers had been entrusted to him by Fenollosa's widow. But collaboration with Harriet Monroe was not without its difficulties for Pound, and he offered his resignation on more than one occasion. One particularly exasperating experience occurred after he had sent Miss Monroe T. S. Eliot's "The Love Song of J. Alfred Prufrock" in October 1914. Just a few weeks earlier, Pound had met Eliot, who had recently arrived in London after the War had forced his departure from Germany. When Eliot showed him "Prufrock," Pound was enthusiastic, marveling that Eliot had, on his own, "trained himself and modernized himself" (*Letters,* Letter 50). He sent the poem to *Poetry.* When Harriet Monroe received it, however, she was not entirely taken with it, objecting to what she felt to be a certain negativism toward American culture, and she wrote Pound expressing her view. Pound, of course, was irritated with her objection and responded: "I will not ask Eliot to write down to any audience whatsoever. I dare say my instinct was right when I volunteered to quit the magazine quietly about a year ago" (*Letters,* Letter 58). But Harriet Monroe continued to resist, and Pound had to nag her repeatedly before she finally relented, publishing "Prufrock" in the June 1915 issue—discreetly, at the *end* of the poetry selections. For Eliot, this was his first appearance in print since his Class Ode had been included in the *Harvard Advocate* and in two Boston newspapers on 24 June 1910. But for Pound, the experience underscored his dissatisfaction with his relationship with *Poetry.*

These then, briefly, were characteristic of Pound's experiences with little magazines when, in June 1916, he wrote a letter to Margaret C. Anderson, the editor of *The Little Review,* asking her to publish two poems, in French, by the Belgian poet-artist Jean de Bosschère. They were too long for *Poetry,* he pointed out to Miss Anderson, and besides "they are more in your tone"; "it will be difficult to find anybody else sporting enough to print them in French" (Letter 1). In his words we glimpse his perception of *The Little Review* and its editor: "sporting"; willing to risk the irritation of those readers who were unable to read French; open to the experimental; flexible enough to adjust the magazine's format to the material to be printed; and indifferent to accusations of appearing "too European." And his assessment was, for the most part, accurate.

In her autobiography, *My Thirty Years' War,* Margaret Anderson describes how she came to Chicago as a young woman fresh out of college (she had been living with her family in Columbus, Indiana), ready to absorb the music and art of the city—concerts at Orchestra Hall, visits to the Art Institute. She had come with her sister Lois, and the two had settled in at the Y.W.C.A. Margaret got a job writing book reviews for a religious weekly called *Interior* and for the *Chicago Evening Post.* Her stay this time, however, was short-lived because her parents, worried about reports they had received of their daughters' spendthrift and daring ways (they had developed a taste for cigarettes), decided the girls should return home. The two were brought back to Columbus, but Margaret, headstrong and determined to live in Chicago, returned a few months later to the city she called her "enchanted ground." This time she found a job as a book clerk at Browne's Bookstore, which was in the Fine Arts Building (designed by Frank Lloyd Wright) on Michigan Boulevard. This building also housed the offices of *The Dial,* edited at the time by Francis F. Browne. One day Browne walked into the Bookstore, upset because he couldn't remember a word in one of Matthew Arnold's poems. When Margaret supplied the word—"lovely"—a friendship began. Shortly after this incident and perhaps because of it, she landed a position on the staff of *The Dial,* where she was "initiated into the secrets of the printing room—composition (monotype and linotype), proofreading, make-up" (*My Thirty Years' War* 28)—practical knowledge she would find indispensable when she began to publish *The Little Review.* Anderson remained with *The Dial* until the summer of 1912, when she left to become the literary editor of the *Interior,* now called the *Continent,* the religious magazine for which she was still writing book reviews. During her stint as literary editor, she came to know Floyd Dell, who was then literary editor of the *Chicago Evening Post.* Dell arranged social gatherings in his home, and through him Margaret Anderson met the literary figures of Chicago—people like Theodore Dreiser, Sherwood Anderson, John Cowper Powys, Jerome Blum, George Cram Cook, Susan Glaspell, Edna Kenton, Llewellyn Jones, Arthur Davison Ficke—the writers, in other words, we now associate with the "Chicago Renaissance."

Margaret Anderson stayed at her job on the *Continent* "for a year" (dates in her autobiography are often hazy and sometimes contradictory) until she began to "chafe" under the restrictions of its editorial policies. One incident that demonstrated to her the reality of these constraints happened when she favorably reviewed Dreiser's *Sister Carrie,* but "forgot" to mention that its subject matter was "immoral." Actually, it never occurred to her that the novel was "immoral." Her omission, she writes, raised protests from some of her readers—particularly from fathers who had bought the book for their daughters on her recommendation—and the magazine's editor called Anderson to his office to express his unhappiness. At the time, however, she was tiring of reviewing books written in "execrable style but well adapted to family fireside reading" (34). She was twenty-one years old, and she had come to feel "it was time to confer upon life that inspiration without which life is meaningless" (35). She was in this mood when the notion of *The Little Review* surfaced:

I had been curiously depressed all day. In the night I wakened. First precise thought: I know why I'm depressed—nothing inspired is going on. Second: I demand that life be inspired every moment. Third: the only way to guarantee this is to have inspired conversation every moment. Fourth: most people never get so far as conversation; they haven't the stamina, and there is no time. Fifth: if I had a magazine I could spend my time filling it up with the best conversation the world has to offer. Sixth: marvelous idea—salvation. Seventh: decision to do it. Deep sleep. (35)

Such was the way Anderson in 1930, looking back at a moment probably in 1913, remembered her decision to found a magazine.

Typical of her personality and of her youth was her indifference to the financial considerations of such an enterprise: "Someone would give the money . . . . Someone would have to" (36). Her prediction became a reality when she met, at Floyd Dell's, DeWitt C. Wing ("Dick" of the autobiography), a staff member of the agricultural journal *The Breeder's Gazette*. After hearing her describe her plans "in gasps, gaps, and gestures," he offered to finance the renting of an office and the printer's fees during the first months of publication. With this assurance, Margaret Anderson set off for New York to solicit advertising. Having raised $450, she returned to Chicago triumphant and leased an office in the Fine Arts Building. There she prepared the first number of *The Little Review*.

The first issue, March 1914, announced the magazine's "ambitious aim":

to produce criticism of books, music, art, drama, and life that shall be fresh and constructive, and intelligent from the artist's point of view. For the instinct of the artist to distrust criticism is as well founded as the mother's toward the sterile woman. More so, perhaps; for all women have some sort of instinct for motherhood, and all critics haven't an instinct for art. Criticism that is creative—that is one high goal. And criticism is never merely an interpretive function; it is creation; it gives birth! It's not necessary to cite the time-worn illustration of DaVinci [*sic*] and Pater to prove it. (2)

For the material in the first number, Miss Anderson turned to the people she knew in Chicago. Floyd Dell (who had recently moved to New York to work on *The New Masses*), Llewellyn Jones, George Burnam Foster, George Soule, and Sherwood Anderson, along with Margaret Anderson herself, contributed articles; Margery Currey and Cornelia Anderson, Sherwood Anderson's wife, provided book reviews; and Vachel Lindsay, Eunice Tietjens, and Arthur Davison Ficke supplied poetry. The first number suggested the interests that were to be repeatedly expressed in subsequent early issues: Nietzsche, particularly his insistence on individual freedom and self-expression; feminism; and the importance of the arts. Music—particularly piano music—was one of Margaret Anderson's most persistent enthusiasms, and the discussion and criticism of literature were central to her purposes: "Books register the ideas of an age; this is perhaps their chief claim to immortality . . . . [C]riticism must be a blend of philosophy and poetry. We shall try very hard to achieve this difficult combination" (2). And underlying everything was Miss Anderson's devotion to two principles: the inseparableness of Art and Life (both with capitals) and the intrinsic value of "conversation"—talking about and around ideas from many points of view. Her welcoming of diverse viewpoints is expressed explicitly in her opening "Announcement": "Our point of view shall not be restrictive; we may present the several judgments of various enthusiastic contributors on one subject in the same issue. The net effect we hope will be stimulating and what we like to call releasing" (2).

This spirit of open-mindedness was accompanied by an interest in "the new," and the early numbers of *The Little Review* published articles entitled "Futurism," "The New Paganism," "Futurism and Pseudo-Futurism," and "The Meaning of Bergsonism." In an essay "Dostoevsky's Novels" (July 1914), Martin Lazar speaks of a modern aesthetic, expressing a viewpoint that was perhaps also Anderson's:

Chiefly concerned with the fester of civilization, literature, music, painting, all the modern forms of individual expression are elliptical in the sense that the old aesthetic values of emotional beauty seem to have become nullified, or else congealed, in the artist's direct application of his instrument to the repudiation of fixed social values or moralities, to the expansion of life-interests. We today want more than beauty of external form; we want the beauty of depth. (44)

For Margaret Anderson, championing the new in the political arena meant propounding the tenets of Emma Goldman's anarchism. Beginning with the May 1914 issue, anarchism as a means of radical change—a personal as well as political liberation—becomes a recurring motif. In an article entitled "The Challenge of Emma Goldman" (May 1914), Anderson points out what she believes to be the "substance" of Goldman's "gospel":

Radical changes in society, releasement from present injustices and miseries, can come about not through *reform* but through *change;* not through a patching up of the old order, but through a tearing down and a rebuilding. This process involves the repudiation of such "spooks" as Christianity, conventional morality, immortality, and all other "myths" that stand as obstacles to progress, freedom, health, truth and beauty. (6)

But Jackson R. Bryer, in his unpublished University of Wisconsin dissertation, " 'A Trial-Track for Racers': Margaret Anderson and *The Little Review*," draws an important distinction between Margaret Anderson's attraction to anarchism and the type of devotion to its tenets exemplified by Emma Goldman and Alexander Berkman:

> [A]t the outset and for some time, although Miss Anderson seemed aware of some of these implications of anarchism [indicated in the passage quoted above], she pursued the cause purely on the intellectual, philosophical level, which Emma Goldman advocated and which coincided, again abstractly, with her own sense of the liberated individual; and she was aroused by Miss Goldman herself just as she was by other forceful personalities who impressed on her the strength of their positions. (89–90)

During its early years *The Little Review* became increasingly committed to the publishing of poetry. Championing the new in this arena meant promoting the Imagists. Even before she began publishing her magazine, Margaret Anderson must have been aware of the movement that was calling for a greater precision in verse. After all, *Poetry* had been printing the work of the Imagists almost from its inception, a fact which could not have escaped Anderson's attention. Then, in February 1914, as the first number of *The Little Review* was being prepared, Alfred Kreymborg published *Des Imagistes* as the fifth number of his journal *Glebe*. (The small anthology—containing nine poems by Richard Aldington, six by Pound, five by F. S. Flint, and one each by Ford Madox Ford, William Carlos Williams, Skipwith Cannell, Allen Upward, John Cournos, James Joyce, and Amy Lowell—was issued as a book by Albert and Charles Boni in April 1914 and later by Harold Monro of London's Poetry Bookshop.) *The Little Review* took up the Imagists' cause in its July 1914 issue: Charles Ashleigh provided a review of the *Glebe* anthology, and Margaret Anderson reprinted from it three of Pound's poems, one of Flint's, one of Aldington's, and the one by Amy Lowell. Although Pound by this time had lost interest in Imagism as a movement—he felt the strength of the new vision had been diluted by Amy Lowell's usurpation of the group and was turning his attention to Vorticism and the work of Wyndham Lewis and Henri Gaudier-Brzeska—Margaret Anderson was becoming increasingly convinced of the merits of Imagist verse. Having met Amy Lowell, she joined the battle of the Imagists for a new clarity of expression and freedom in verse form, a battle Anderson waged in the pages of *The*

*Little Review* during most of 1915 and 1916. The work of Aldington, Lowell, John Gould Fletcher, H.D., and others often appeared during these years.

In February of 1916, Margaret Anderson met Jane Heap, a meeting which was to result in a lifelong friendship and one which would have an impact on *The Little Review*. To Anderson, Jane Heap was "the world's best talker"; she "made ideas":

> We talked for days, months, years. . . . We formed a consolidation that was
> to make us much loved and even more loathed. We talked every place, to all
> sorts and conditions of people. I made up quarrels of opinion so that Jane
> could show her powers. . . . [H]ere was my obsession—the special human
> being, the special point of view. I never let anyone escape her psychological
> clairvoyance. (*My Thirty Years' War* 107–08)

Understandably, Anderson wanted her new friend to contribute to *The Little Review,* but Jane Heap was reluctant to do so. After enduring several months of Anderson's coaxing, however, she finally consented. Beginning with the November 1916 issue, her contributions signed "jh" became a regular feature of the magazine, and from then on, she functioned, more or less, as coeditor. Eventually, Anderson came to think of her relationship with Jane Heap as "the most interesting thing that had happened to the *Little Review*—the most interesting that ever happened to it" (*My Thirty Years' War* 102).

In the summer of 1916, Jane Heap and Margaret Anderson went to California, where they stayed in a small, isolated ranch house in Mill Valley. During this summer, Anderson underwent a number of shifts in attitude. First of all, she lost faith in the anarchist doctrines of Emma Goldman. According to Anderson's autobiography (126–27), she parted ways with Emma Goldman and Alexander Berkman following an argument about aesthetics and revolution: they maintained that art should appeal to the masses and be readily understandable to the common man, whereas Anderson argued that art should powerfully express the "eternal human emotions." "Eternal poppycock!" was Emma Goldman's terse response.

Then too Anderson was growing increasingly dissatisfied with the inferior quality of the manuscripts she was receiving and with what she felt to be an overall lack of "Art" in previous issues. In "A Real Magazine," an article she wrote for the August 1916 number, she maintained that during the past two years *The Little Review* had never come "near its ideal" and declared, "We shall have Art in this magazine or we shall stop publishing it." What had been published had been the result of compromise, she said, the selections being "almost good" or "interesting enough"; but she promised, "If there is only one really beautiful number it shall go in and the other pages will be left blank." True to her word, she published the September issue, leaving blank the first thirteen pages after the caption, *"The Little Review* hopes to become a magazine of Art. The September issue is offered as a Want Ad." The second page quoted the August editorial: "The other pages will be left blank." The remainder of the issue carried a centerfold of cartoons, done by Jane Heap, showing the "Light occupations of the editor when there is nothing to edit" (e.g., swimming, practicing the piano, attending an Emma Goldman lecture); an essay by Robert Minor on a bombing during an anarchist parade in San Francisco, along with Margaret Anderson's comments on the subject; Jane Heap's observations under the title "And—"; a New York letter by Allan Ross MacDougall; and "The Reader Critic." The issue clearly signaled Margaret Anderson's feeling that a change in direction for *The Little Review* was needed. Perhaps out of this sense, coupled with a less defined and more personal restlessness, she decided that the magazine should move to New York (see Letter 3n). The editors took their journal there at the end of 1916.

During this period of transition, then, Pound sent off the de Bosschère manuscripts to Margret Anderson. He had, however, been aware of *The Little Review* for some time. Jackson Bryer points out that, in an unpublished letter to Harriet Monroe, dated as received by her on 5 August 1914, Pound had written, "I'm glad the Small Review has started. . . . A jolly place for people who aren't quite up to our level" (" 'Trial-Track for Racers' " 224; the letter is among the *Poetry* papers at the University of Chicago Library). Whether Pound had read *The Little Review* with any frequency is hard to say, but in the April 1916 issue, Margaret Anderson published "A Letter from London" by Pound which complained about the tariff on books (7–8), and another letter of his in "The Reader Critic" (36). In the latter, he thanks Anderson for sending him complimentary copies of her magazine. That he should, therefore, send her the de Bosschère manuscripts in June 1916 is not surprising.

In the November 1916 issue, Margaret Anderson published a second article by Pound about the tariff on books ("Das Schone [*sic*] Papier Vergeudet"), a regulation which Pound maintains "has contributed more than any other cause, and perhaps more than all other causes, to the intellectual isolation of America, to her general ignorance, to her sodden parochialism" (16). Just when Pound sent off this article to *The Little*

*Review* is not revealed in the correspondence—our guess is either July or August—but that he did so suggests his growing interest in *The Little Review* as a place for publishing his own material. Given, moreover, his on-going frustrations in working with Harriet Monroe on *Poetry*—she, for example, balked at publishing the "shorter" de Bosschère poem he had sent her because "it [was] a good deal of space for a French poem"— Pound's search for another way of reaching American readers, of having access to a periodical over which he could exercise editorial control, is understandable. When Margaret Anderson published the blank pages of the September 1916 issue as a "Want Ad," Pound no doubt sensed the opportunity and wrote to her "to ask whether there [was] any use [in his] trying to help the Little Review" (Letter 3). We can imagine the enthusiasm of Anderson's response, and on 26 January 1917 (Letter 4), Pound set down for her the conditions for his collaboration: the regular appearance of Eliot, Joyce, Lewis, and himself; a guarantee of a certain number of available pages; a "minimum of obstructionism" from her; and the publication of at least eight issues per year. What in fact he wanted was his own magazine comfortably housed within hers. For his part, he would approach his friend John Quinn ("my prospective guarantor"), a New York lawyer and patron of the arts, to provide the money to pay the contributors he, Pound, was able to recruit. (*The Little Review* to date had not paid for contributions.) Pound admitted to Miss Anderson that his conditions must sound "very dictatorial," but pointed out that "one must settle this thing clearly in advance." The terms were acceptable to her, and in the March 1917 issue she promised "a special editorial surprise for the next issue (a gorgeous surprise)." In the April 1917 number, she announced Pound's new affiliation with the magazine and quoted liberally from his 26 January 1917 letter. The May 1917 issue carried Pound's editorial in which he explained his reasons for joining *The Little Review* and clarified his irritations with *Poetry* (see Letter 8n).

Pound's influence on the magazine was immediate and profound; the years he was associated with *The Little Review*—1917 until the spring of 1919 and then again in 1921 through the spring of 1923—proved to be the high points in the magazine's history. Furthermore, it was through Pound's efforts that *The Little Review* provided its single most important service for modern literature, the serial publication of Joyce's *Ulysses* (March 1918 through September-December 1920)—a venture that resulted in, on four separate occasions, the suppression of the magazine by the New York Post Office. The last of these incidents had its climax in a courtroom. The letters Pound wrote to Margaret Anderson chronicle these most important years of *The Little Review*. This was the period in which Pound made the journal into what Hoffman, Allen, and Ulrich see as the first magazine to give Americans "an adequate cross-section view of European and American experimentalism" (66). As a behind-the-scenes record of how Pound accomplished this feat, the letters are invaluable.

As a partial chronicle of a portion of Pound's London years, the letters are also notable. This was the period in which Pound began his work on the *Cantos,* was growing increasingly interested in modern French poetry, and was continuing his explorations of the ways in which Oriental literature could vitalize English poetry. He was writing such poems as "Homage to Sextus Propertius" and was coming to the position he was to assume in "Hugh Selwyn Mauberley." The letters complement the views we get of him in biographies and in studies of his *oeuvre*. They also dramatize Pound's growing sense of frustration during the last several years he spent in London. Perhaps most intriguing, however, is the insight the letters give us into Pound's functioning as an editor and into his conception of how a little magazine could contribute to the revitalization of literature.

Certain passages within Pound's letters to Margaret Anderson indicate that, when he began his association with *The Little Review,* he saw the magazine as a vehicle for creating a "Vortex." In Letter 46, for example, he told Margaret Anderson, "We want all the available energy poured into our vortex." *Vortex*—the image helps to define Pound's hopes for *The Little Review* and to give a sense of his editorial strategies. Hugh Kenner, in *The Pound Era,* points out that what Pound had in mind when he coined the word *Vorticism*

> is traceable to [his] figure, in the ninth "Osiris" article of early 1912, of words as electrified cones, charged with "the power of tradition, of centuries of race consciousness, or agreement, of association, an image . . . for all that the artist does not invent but must know." It assimilates also his "Osiris" term, *virtu,* for the individuating energy by reason of which "we have one Catullus, one Villon." And as for "centuries of race consciousness," they localize in capitals, and in 1913 he had likened London to Rome, "a vortex, drawing strength from the peripheries." . . . The Future [hence, Futurism] has no locale, an Image [Imagism] or a Cube [Cubism] may turn up in anyone's pocket, but any Vortex is somewhere on the map. (238)

Among these manifestations of the Vortex, it is possible to conceive of a magazine creating a type of Vortex itself, setting up, in accordance with Kenner's definition, "a circulation with a still center: a system of energies drawing in whatever comes near" (239). Along these lines, then, a magazine could function in two ways: (1) as a component of a larger "National Vortex," as one of the energies drawn into the still center; and (2) as a small Vortex in and of itself, as a center into which other energies could be drawn. Conceptions such as these may have been operating behind what Pound saw as the role *The Little Review* was to play in the cultural renaissance he had envisioned.

Just where "on the map" Pound had imagined the Vortex is not easy to discern. Chicago? At first, perhaps—*Poetry* and *The Little Review* were being published there—but Margaret Anderson had determined to move her magazine to New York. New York must have seemed a more likely center. After all, John Quinn was there—he had underwritten the Vorticist Show of July 1916 and was buying the work of Wyndham Lewis and Gaudier-Brzeska—and the New York publisher Alfred A. Knopf, early in 1917, had agreed to publish Pound's *Lustra*. But when Margaret Anderson informed Pound that her magazine was moving to New York, he asked, "Why stop at New York? London and Paris are quite as interesting, even in war time" (Letter 3). More than likely, Pound still hoped that London would fulfill its promise of becoming the Vortex that *BLAST* had announced it as being. The lists of people to whom Pound wanted sample copies of the May 1917 number sent included many Londoners—*les jeunes* as well as establishment figures. But he also sent Anderson the names of professors at the University of Pennsylvania, and those of a host of acquaintances living in such places as Cambridge, Massachusetts; New York; and Paris. His doing so suggests— apart from the obvious motive any editor has of expanding a magazine's readership—his conviction that, for a Vortex to be created in any locale, energies must be drawn into it from "the peripheries."

How then should a magazine be edited so that a variety of energies could work together to produce a powerful dynamism? When Pound explained to Margaret Anderson that he wanted "a place where [he] and T. S. Eliot [could] appear once a month . . . and where James Joyce [could] appear when he likes, and where Wyndham Lewis [could] appear if he comes back from the war" (Letter 4), he was asking for a place where the writers of the London Vortex could appear regularly, but also *together,* a site for the *circulation* of energies. Much has been made of Pound's selfless promotion of the work of other writers, and undeniably there was selflessness in much of what he did for Eliot, for Joyce, and for others. The letters in this volume reveal that. But Pound was also selective in choosing whom he helped, aware perhaps that he was orchestrating "the new sensibility, decisive and blocked and faceted, a vortex of vortices" (*The Pound Era* 246). Essentially his concern was not only for the writers as individuals—as sincere as that concern no doubt was— but also for the energizing effect created by publishing each with the others. Orchestration, after all, involves playing one instrument off against another, the effect of the whole achieved by the interplay of the parts. Pound's plans for his first number of *The Little Review* suggest this or- chestrating strategy:

> I want to start off the new order of things with a bang. Decent (or indecent) tale by me, something from Eliot, something from Joyce, etc. good wodge of 16 pages of new "blood".
>
> (Pages of blood! wot a expresshun.) anyhow, a good cubic hunk of BLAST, to catch edgeways on the public ivory. . . .
>
> It would only be a waste of energy to bring in the new set of contributors one by one. Must use fire-controll. BOMM! Simultaneous arrival of new force in pages of "Little Review." (Letter 5)

Passages from Letter 24 also illustrate the point:

> . . . certain elements must be combined in a book, or in a number of a magazine or of a paper. . . . [The] May [number] needed a poem. The lack in May, can not be remedied in June . . . Sept. being in the main harsh, acid, satiric needs a certain amount of atmosphere, or 'beauty' (whatever that is.) . . . [I]t is a defect, even a defect of ART not to make each number of the magazine an entity; an indication of the necessity of a certain number of elements in one's scheme of things.

But it was not only the *ensemble* effect Pound was after; he was aware that certain selections would in themselves set off volatile reactions. One of the merits of his translation of a Laforgue poem, he wrote, was that "it will irritate a number of people" (Letter 8), and the Yeats poems published in the June 1917 issue were worth the "all-fired lot of room" they would take to print because they were "a big score for the magazine, and several nails in the coffins of the 'Atlantic' and the other decrepit snobs" (Letter 11). And Lewis's "Cantleman's Spring-Mate" he called "a vol- cano" (Letter 21).

Another strategy for creating the Vortex was to set before *The Little Review* readers the work of recent French writers, the idea being to ener- gize American literature by bringing it in touch with French literature. In one of his first letters to Margaret Anderson, Pound told her, "A Bet- ter understanding with France is one; if not the first step toward better art conditions in america" (Letter 3). *The Little Review* need not become a " 'propagandist' affair," he pointed out, but "French individual-ism, french realism, abolition of ⟨at least the material⟩ impediments to the circulation of thought [e.g., the import tariff on books]. Learning to enrich the individual, not to be merely an enslaving system, as now arranged in our universities. These things can perfectly well be a not very perceptible under-current" (Letter 3). One does perceive this "undercurrent," however, in the first issue of *The Little Review* Pound organized (May 1917). In it, he included his translation of Jules Laforgue's "Pierrots: Scène courte mais typique," a translation Pound was "not wholly satisfied" with but one which had "the merit of NOT being like every second page of 'Poetry' " (Letter 8).

By the summer of 1917, Pound was planning a French number, his original intention being simply to print as an anthology the selections of the poets who had published in the *Mercure de France*. Alfred Val-lette of the *Mercure,* however, had pointed out that doing so would raise copyright difficulties and suggested that it would be legally simpler to publish the poems as part of a study, reproducing them to illustrate the critical commentary. This, therefore, Pound proposed to do and, in Sep-tember, he wrote to Margaret Anderson (Letter 46), "I can be all the more vigorous and free, simply because the critical function is imposed by circumstance." But he warned her to "keep the little French anthology quiet until it is launched. Especially on account of dear Amy [Lowell]. I think I can get about as much in one number as there is in her vol-ume [*Six French Poets: Studies in Contemporary Literature*]." In October 1917, Pound's manuscript was complete and he sent it to Miss Anderson, telling her not to worry about additional costs because of the length of the manuscript, but to "consider that the number will be a definite prop-erty, like a book and there should be a steady demand for it." Further-more, he was convinced it had "more in it than Amy's $2.50 ⟨volume⟩, and there is no other French anthology in English to compete with it" (Let-ter 50). "A Study in French Poets," running nearly sixty pages, was pub-lished in the February 1918 issue of *The Little Review* and was later in-cluded in *Instigations* (1920).

And so Pound worked at editing *The Little Review,* securing for its pages such diverse items as Ford Madox Ford's *Women and Men;* Lady Gregory's "Hanrahan's Oath"; Wyndham Lewis's stories, essays, and "Imaginary Letters"; poems by Yeats, Eliot, and others; selections from *les jeunes*—Iris Barry and John Rodker; and, most exciting, Joyce's *Ulys-ses*. He organized and contributed to special issues: the French number noted above; a Henry James number, August 1918, for which he reread all of James's work; and a Remy de Gourmont tribute, the February-March 1919 issue. He offered his own work, much of which was specifically written for the magazine: editorials, book reviews, essays, dialogues, pseudonymous squibs, "Imaginary Letters," and poetry ("L'Homme Moyen Sensuel," "Cantico del Sole," "Homage à la langue d'oc," "Moeurs contemporaines," etc.).

Yet he was not content with simply supplying copy. His letters demonstrate his efforts to secure subscribers and to arrange the magazine's finances through John Quinn. They show his concern with typography, proofreading (always a *bête noire* for *The Little Review*), and the quality of paper. We see him suggesting schemes to Margaret Anderson for absorbing other magazines or for securing "chronicles," what Pound called "rubrics," written by people living in cities other than New York. (Even Amy Lowell might be useful!) All this while he continued to contribute to *Poetry, The New Age, The Egoist,* and other periodicals, and fought to find time and energy to work on his own poetry. It is no wonder that by 20 February 1918 he was writing rather wearily to Anderson, "I have only a certain amount of energy . . . . I am ageing rapidly . . . . I am, for the time being, bored to death with being any kind of an editor. I desire to go on with my long poem [the *Cantos*]" (Letter 73). But toward the end of this letter, Pound's remarks suggest that something other than fatigue was bothering him; it is as though he were beginning to sense that the Vortex had lost its energy: "Hueffer is dead, absolutely dead with army. Eliot is dead with his bank. Lewis wanders about interrupting, and he thinks he is hunting for a studio (only he isnt) in which to paint his picture for the Canadian govt." The letter sounds two notes which gain in intensity as one reads through the remaining correspondence: Pound's growing recognition of (1) his need to find more time to devote to his own poetry, and (2) the deadness, the lack of energy, of a London drained by the War. The first recognition led to a break with *The Little Review;* the second, to a break with London.

Money was a continuing concern for *The Little Review,* a troublesome worry which John Quinn's (and Quinn's friends') contributions only temporarily relieved. Reading Margaret Anderson's *My Thirty Years' War* makes clear just how acute the problem often was; the complications created by running *The Little Review* on a shoestring are frequently discussed in these letters. But the need for money—or, more accurately, for the time money could buy—was a reality in Pound's personal life as well. By the end of April 1918, Pound realized that his situation required a change. He needed to "buy," as he says in the "plebiscite" he sent to

Anderson (the full text of which is included in the notes to Letter 89), "leisure sufficient for whatever creative processes are possible to me." Published in the July 1918 issue, the "harangue," as he called this editorial, ended with an ultimatum: "either the *Little Review* will have to provide me with the necessities of life and a reasonable amount of leisure, by May 1st. 1919, or I shall have to apply my energies elsewhere." Although Pound had given *The Little Review* readers nine months to uncover the resources to meet his needs and to keep him with the magazine, they failed to do so; true to his word, in the spring of 1919, Pound resigned as foreign editor and John Rodker replaced him. A year and a half later, Pound left London. The reason? Noel Stock suggests that Dorothy Pound's explanation is as good as any: "the London climate, physical and mental, did not suit Ezra; he was searching for 'mental life' and thought he would find it in Paris" (234). A Vortex perhaps?

In any case, the history of Pound's involvement with *The Little Review* did not end in 1919. While he was still in London in October 1920, he wrote Margaret Anderson after he had heard that charges had been brought against the editors of *The Little Review* for publishing an episode of *Ulysses* (see Letter 119). That he wrote only one letter to her about "the trouble"—and that one rather noncommittal—may be explained by something he wrote to Joyce at about the same time. The letter to Joyce shows clearly that Pound was irritated with the editors and that he felt serial publication was damaging the chances of publishing *Ulysses* in book form, a worry that John Quinn also had expressed. Pound's letter reads as follows:

> Dear Joyce: I enclose a letter from Quinn, which you need not of necessity read. Point is that "Nausikaa" has been pinched by the PO-lice. Only way to get *Ulysses* printed in book form, will be to agree not to print any more of it in the *L.R.*
>
> I had already made this suggestion on other ground[s], namely that the expensive private edition planned by Quinn wd. have wider sale if it contained final chapters which had not already appeared in the *L.R.*
>
> Also in Paris I did, I think, explain to you that M.A. and j.h. had not spent any money on you. I got the original trifle that was sent you, and the printing deficits were paid by J.Q., and in general the editrices have merely messed and muddled, NEVER to their own loss.
>
> The best thing to do, now that things have come to present pass is to turn the whole matter over to Quinn. He is on the spot and both will and can deal with local conditions better than we can from here.
>
> The excuse for parts of *Ulysses* is the WHOLE of *Ulysses;* the case for

publication of bits of it serially is weak; the editrices having sent copy to someone who hadn't asked for it further weakens case.

ANYHOW, the only thing to be done now is to give Quinn an absolutely free hand. . . . (*Pound/Joyce* 184–85)

Whatever repugnance Pound felt for "clause 211" and the operations of the New York Post Office, the Society for the Prevention of Vice, and the U.S. courts, his letter to Joyce shows he also saw the situation as a way of extricating *Ulysses* from serial publication in *The Little Review*. Interesting also is the pique he expresses at the "messing" and "muddling" of the editors and at their not having adequately paid Joyce.

But Pound's personal irritations with Margaret Anderson and Jane Heap did not prevent him from re-establishing a connection with *The Little Review* in the spring of 1921, an association which seems to have been suggested by Anderson. At the time, he was living in Paris and was serving as the foreign correspondent for *The Dial* (New York), which was being edited then by Scofield Thayer. Pound had served as *The Dial*'s foreign correspondent since March 1920, but as his comments in Letter 123 indicate, his connection with *The Dial* was to come to an end on 1 July 1921. (In fact, Pound remained with *The Dial* until May 1923.) Pound's motives for taking up with *The Little Review* again are only hinted at in Letter 124. His irritation that the magazine could not afford to pay him and his sense that editing—promoting the work of other writers—deprived him of the time and energy to work on his own poems were as strong as ever:

> Point I never can seem to get you to take is that I have done more log rolling and attending to other people's affairs, Joyce, Lewis, Gaudier, etc. (dont regret it) But I am in my own small way, a writer myself, and as before stated. I shd. like (and wont in any case get) the chance of being considered as the author of my own poems rather than as ⟨literary politician, &⟩ a very active stage manager of rising talent. ⟨ = = at least during periods when I see nothing of 1st order in need of launching.⟩
>
> It is bad enough to have to look forward to Christ knows what means of paying ⟨for⟩ precisely my (as jh puts it) cup of coffee and shoes (say rather re-soles). . . . ⟨can't spend whole life jawing about other people's work⟩

Joyce, he points out, "has the sense, or grit, or sheer imbecility to DO nothing but his Ulysses and let the world go hang." That the United States and Britain should be indifferent to the financial struggles of its writers—

Pound by this time had become immersed in the economic theories of Major C. H. Douglas—was a source of bitter resentment:

> . . . why the HELL shd. I deform my bloomin thoughts by being reminded of the existence of the ang-sax race in any or either of its branches, both of which are probably superfluous.

> If either or both nations were worth saving they wd. raise 1000 dollars per yr. for me, 2000 for Joyce, Eliot and Lewis (who has less practical sense or more expensive habits than I have). (Letter 124)

Nevertheless, Pound does agree to "give a heave at the axle when [his] unspeakable temper . . . permits" (Letter 124). One reason for his willingness, no doubt, was that Francis Picabia had consented to be the French editor of the magazine, and it would be he rather than Pound himself who would have the major responsibility. Another reason seems to have been the satisfaction he felt he would derive from lending his name to *The Little Review*, as an indication of, as he puts it, "the extent to which I regard Sumner and the N.Y. courts as the dung of ignoble animals." But surely the prime motive for his agreeing to cooperate lay in his sense of what *The Little Review* had been, what it had in the past achieved: "The L.R. accomplished more in six months than the Dial has in a year, en fait de littérature" (Letter 124). What was true once for *The Little Review* could be true again.

And so Pound resumed his efforts on behalf of *The Little Review,* this time as a "collaborator." Because the magazine had suspended publication following its January-March 1921 issue, the plan being to reorganize as a quarterly, Pound saw a chance for a new start: "number must be a clean break. = a wholly new burst of something the public don't expect" (Letter 125). There is a sense of enthusiasm here, and Pound went to work. He polished Jean Hugo's English translation of Cocteau's "Le Cap de Bonne Espérance"; wrote a number of articles for the magazine, the most significant being one on Brancusi's sculpture; sent off manuscripts—Paul Morand's, Clement Pansaers', and others; proposed plans for future issues; and attempted, without success, to arrange a Wyndham Lewis number. But the excitement was short-lived; many of Pound's suggestions were never implemented in the revived magazine and Margaret Anderson botched others (e.g., the publication of his supposed death mask). The tone of the final letters of this period reaches exasperation. Then, in the spring of 1923, Margaret Anderson and Jane Heap made their pilgrimage to Paris, and Anderson decided to stay in Europe. Pound's correspondence with her ended (resuming only briefly between 1953–54 upon publication of *The Little Review Anthology*). So did his association with *The Little Review*. In 1930, Pound claimed he had been "ejected" from the magazine's staff "for frivolity" ("Small Magazines" 696).

In *My Thirty Years' War* Margaret Anderson writes, "[Pound's] letters alone would have made a good magazine" (159). They make a good book. Their liveliness, the insights they offer into those important years in Pound's life and the publishing of one of America's influential little magazines, make these letters eminently worth reading. The St. Elizabeths group offers something of a coda.

Thomas L. Scott
Melvin J. Friedman

# The Letters

**1. TLS–1.** On stationery embossed: 5, Holland Place Chambers/ Kensington. W. [30 June 1916]

Editor
Little Review.

Dear Madam

    I enclose two sketches by Jean de Bosschère. In normal times they would appear in La Nouvelle Revue Francaise or in "L'Occident". ⟨Both of which have stopped publishing during the war.⟩ I don't think they are translatable. At least I shouldn't want to attempt translation. I am sending a shorter poem to "Poetry". These are I think too long for H.M. [Harriet Monroe], and also they are more in your tone. I have recommended De Bosschere to let you have them, as it will be very difficult to find anybody else sporting enough to print them in french.

    De Bosschere is a man of parts, many vols. of his have appeared. Am doing a note in Poetry, I dare say H.M. will give you data if you go to press before she does. De B. has been translated into russian by Veselofsky. etc. He is undoubtedly about the most "modern" writer Paris can boast, not excluding Apollonaire [Guillaume Apollinaire].

    I think some of his french dam'd hard. Am trying to get some english equivalent for some of his "Metiers Divins". He is certainly not like anyone else. verb. sap. etc.

      Yours
      E. Pound
    30–6–'16

*two sketches by Jean de Bosschère:* Jean de Bosschère (1878–1953) was a Belgian painter, illustrator, poet, and novelist. Born in Brussels, he began his career by writing historical-archaeological criticism of painting, sculpture, and the arts of printing and book-making. As a young man, de Bosschère made frequent trips to Paris, where he became acquainted with the literary circles surrounding the journals *L'Occident, La Phalange,* and *Vers et Prose,* and formed friendships with Paul Claudel, Adrien Mithouard, André Saurès,

Francis Jammes, and Charles Péguy. In 1909, his first book of poems and illustrations *Béâle-Gryne* was published by the Occident Press. In 1911, Occident also published *Dolorine et les ombres*, an experimental book illustrated with the author's own drawings. In 1913, *Métiers divins*, a collection of poems, was published, again by Occident. It too was illustrated with the author's drawings and woodcuts. (*Twelve Occupations*, published in London in 1916, is a version of *Métiers divins* with English translations by EP.) The following year, 1914, de Bosschère wrote and published a critical study on the Flemish poet Max Elskamp.

Early in 1915, de Bosschère fled from Belgium to London, where he was introduced to the figures of the Anglo-American literary world living there or passing through. His influence on the English and American Imagists has been noted by several critics, among them René Taupin in *L'Influence du symbolisme français sur la poésie américaine.*

In 1917, London publisher John Lane put out a volume of de Bosschère's poetry entitled *The Closed Door.* May Sinclair wrote the introduction to the collection, and F. S. Flint provided English translations to accompany each of the twelve poems. Two of the poems included were the ones EP had sent to the *LR,* the "sketches" to which EP refers in Letter 1: "Ulysse Fait Son Lit" and "L'Offre de Plebs." Each of these poems was published in French in the *LR,* the former in the August 1916 issue (6–8) and the latter in the November 1916 number (12–15).

*La Nouvelle Revue Francaise: La Nouvelle Revue Française; revue mensuelle de littérature et de critique* was a French review of literature and the arts founded by Jean Schlumberger, Jacques Copeau, and André Gide in November 1908 (regular publication beginning in February 1909). The journal published the work of Giraudoux, Claudel, Péguy, Valéry, and of Gide himself, little known writers at the time they first appeared in the *Revue.* Although it suspended publication from September 1914 to May 1919, its influence was particularly strong in the years preceding and following the First World War. In 1943, the *Revue* ceased publication except for a special number issued in the fall of 1951 as a tribute to Gide. The journal was revived as the *Nouvelle Nouvelle Revue Française* in 1953.

*L'Occident:* a journal published monthly in Paris between December 1901 and January 1914, except for 1911.

*shorter poem to "Poetry":* In late September of 1912, *Poetry: A Magazine of Verse* began monthly publication in Chicago under the editorship of Harriet Monroe (1860–1936). Alice Corbin Henderson, Eunice Tietjens, and Helen Hoyt served at various times as assistant editors, and EP was the foreign correspondent from 1912 to 1917. The magazine published the early work of many neglected young poets, some of whom later became significant literary figures: T. S. Eliot, Robert Frost, Vachel Lindsay, Wallace Stevens, Richard Aldington, H.D., and William Carlos Williams. EP served as the magazine's foreign correspondent.

The importance of *Poetry*'s contribution to the development of twentieth-century verse has often been noted. Hoffman, Allen, and Ulrich, for example, suggest that the "first issue of *Poetry* marks the turning point in American

poetry of the twentieth century" (*The Little Magazine: A History and a Bibliography* 241).

The poem to which EP refers is de Bosschère's "Homère Mere Habite Sa Maison des Planches." Harriet Monroe, however, delayed publication of this poem, and, on 3 July 1917, eventually wrote EP saying, "I rather like his poem, and still intend to use it—but it's a good deal of space for a French poem when we have so much waiting" (qtd. in Williams 182). Although the poem never did appear in *Poetry*, it was published, with an English translation by F. S. Flint entitled "Homer Marsh Dwells in His House of Planks," in de Bosschère's *The Closed Door*. This poem has been noted as a specific influence on T. S. Eliot's "Mélange adultère de tout" (see, for example, Taupin 219–220, 235).

*Veselofsky:* Alekseĭ Nikolaevich Veselovskii (1843–1918) translated both *Béâle-Gryne* and *Dolorine et les ombres* into Russian.

**2. TLS–1.** On stationery embossed: 5, Holland Place Chambers/ Kensington. W. ⟨8⟩ [9 July 1916]

Dear Margaret:

Please note subscriptions:
Begin May number.
Miss Marion Thomson, 26 Oxford Rd. Kilburn, London. N.W. 6.
C.R. Hollway, Red Cross Hospital for Officers,
　　　　　　9 Eastern Terrace, Brighton. Eng.
E.R. Brown, Penketh School, Warrington, England.

/ / /

　　I think you might try sending me 20 copies per month, beginning with May. The thing is so small, that in two packets of ten each I doubt if there would be any objection. I get 6 copies [of] Poetry, which are as large in bulk, and the regulation isn't intended for us, but for things like Vogue, which ship themselves by the ton.

　　　　　　　　yours　　E.
Ezra Pound,　　Ezra Pound
　　　　　　　　9/7/'16

*the regulation:* A wartime postal regulation restricted the importation of magazines into England.

**3. TLS–2.**   On stationery embossed: 5, Holland Place Chambers/ Kensington. W. [29 November 1916]

Dear Miss Anderson:

Why stop at New York? London and Paris are quite as interesting, even in war time.

I am writing really to ask whether there is any use [in] my trying to help the Little Review. If you want me to try, etc.?

I shall have to know what your circulation (paid and unpaid) is, also how much you lose or can afford to lose, and whether you would make the magazine a "pays its contributors magazine" if that were possible. And whether you want capital, or on what terms. Foreign correspondents, ditto.

I have done so much work for "love" that I have about come to the end of making free contributions to anything, still. . . . . .

One does not want to see the country sink back into the arms of Harpers and the Atlantic.

It is, on the other hand, very hard to get interested in an unpaying magazine whose nerve centre is so far off.

I should think you might absorb "Others" or at least all that was worth while in it.

There are still people here who could be drummed up to sending you stuff unpaid, if they felt you were sufficiently a centre and that the stuff would reach the right people.

One would want to be sure that the review went to certain people in France.

So far as propaganda is concerned I dont think we greatly disagree.

French individualism, french realism, abolition of ⟨at least the material⟩ impediments to the circulation of thought. Learning to enrich the individual, not to be merely an enslaving system, as now arranged in our universities. These things can perfectly well be a not very perceptible undercurrent. One need not turn the paper into a "propagandist" affair.

This note is private, to you, not to "The Editor". (aside: try DeGourmont instead of, or in addition to Clive Bell. I think you'll enjoy him if you strike the right books)

⟨A Better understanding
with France is one; if not
the first step     Yours
toward better art conditions   Ezra Pound
 in america.
  29–11–'16⟩


*Why stop at New York?:* Since its founding in 1914, the *LR* had been based in
Chicago. As early as the spring of 1916, however, MCA talked of moving
her operations to New York. In the June–July issue, she announced that "by
the first of the year we plan to establish ourselves in New York, where all
good things seem to turn at last." In her autobiography *My Thirty Years'
War,* MCA gave the following explanation for her decision:

> Chicago had had all it wanted from us, we had had all that it could give. It
> was time to touch the greatest city of America. It would then be time for
> Europe. The only way to make the L.R. the international organ I had planned
> was to publish it from New York where our position would be more command-
> ing. We hadn't yet met all the interesting people in the world. Some of them
> were in New York. Some were in London and Paris—the greatest artists of the
> modern age. I loved Chicago forever, I could never forget it, I would come back
> to it . . . but I must go on. (136–37)

*"Others":* Others: *A Magazine of New Verse* was a little magazine published
in Grantwood, New Jersey; New York; and Chicago. Edited by Alfred
Kreymborg, William Saphier, and William Carlos Williams, it published verse,
plays, criticism, and fiction. Its contributors included Amy Lowell, William
Carlos Williams, Wallace Stevens, T. S. Eliot, John Rodker, EP, Richard
Aldington, Marianne Moore, Carl Sandburg, Edgar Lee Masters, Conrad
Aiken, Iris Barry, H.D., Sherwood Anderson, and Djuna Barnes.
*DeGourmont:* Remy de Gourmont (1858–1915) was a French novelist, critic,
poet, and playwright. Along with Alfred Vallette, he was one of the founders
of the *Mercure de France* in 1889, the aim of which he later told EP, "has
been to permit any man, who is worth it, to write down his thoughts frankly—
this is a writer's sole pleasure. And this aim should be yours" (qtd. in Stock
184–85). Although they had never met, EP and de Gourmont were correspondents. In two published articles, EP had high praise for de Gourmont,
calling him "a symbol of so much that is finest in France" and saying that
from him proceeded a personal, living force, a "personal light" [see *Fortnightly Review* (1 December 1915) and *Poetry* (January 1916)].
*Clive Bell:* (1881–1964), Bloomsbury art and literary critic. A close follower
of Roger Fry, Bell coined the term "significant form" as a criterion of value
in art and, in his criticism, insisted that the most important elements of art
were its form and design. Bell was married to Vanessa Stephen, the elder
sister of Virginia Woolf. From 1933 to 1943, he was the art critic of the
weekly magazine *The New Statesman and Nation.*

**4. TLS–12.**    On stationery embossed: 5, Holland Place Chambers/ Kensington. W. [26 January 1917]

Dear Miss Anderson

Your letter came last night. I had in the interval since writing to you, mentioned the matter ⟨of my wanting some space⟩ to the Egoist, that is to say I mentioned it three days ago, and Miss Weaver's reply came this morning. She also wants to make some arrangement. There are some advantages in having ones printing house near one, and in being sure of 12 issues per year.

ON THE OTHERHAND, the Little Review is perhaps temperamentally closer to what I want done ???????? At any rate I will try to state what I want as clearly as possible, and if you will reply fairly soon and state clearly just what you want to give me, I will refrain from concluding anything with the Egoist until I hear from you.

I don't mean that I am going to drive a jew bargain ⟨for⟩ "inches per month", but that it will be best for all concerned that I should join in where there can be the most good will and cooperation and the minimum of obstructionism.

DEFINITELY then:

I want an "official organ" (vile phrase). I mean I want a place where I and T. S. Eliot can appear once a month (or once an "issue") and where James Joyce can appear when he likes, and where Wyndham Lewis can appear if he comes back from the war.

Definitely a place for our regular appearance and where our friends and readers (what few of 'em there are) can look with assurance of finding us.

((E.G. I persuade people to subscribe to Poetry, a few, and then they blame me for there being nothing by me in a given number, etc, etc, and they don't pass it on or recommend it.))

Also copy ⟨(a certain amount of it)⟩ would have to go in "at once", i.e. in the next number after you received it.

That is not a demand, it is simply the only condition on which collaboration would be of any practical use to either of us, or be enjoyable to me.

The question is: how much stuff per month, by me, Eliot, Joyce, Lewis, or let us say, how much stuff chosen by me can you use in each number ????

If the Egoist gave me four or five pages that would be from 6000 to 7500 words. ⟨or about that, I think.⟩ I don't know quite how much your pages carry. I don't want to swamp you.

If your pages take 300 words, 16 pages would hold 4800, or a little less with headings.

Could you manage 5000 words per issue, and could you be reasonably sure of bringing out at least eight numbers per year.

I have to ask these questions very clearly and get very clear answers before I can tackle my prospective guarantor.

I say "prospective", he has already offered me money for some sort of magazine venture, ⟨but⟩ as a business man, he wants to ⟨know⟩ what he is spending it on.

I am afraid he won't offer you and ???? the other of you the ten dollars per week each that you suggest. What I can offer you is only the full amount of whatever new subscriptions you get from having a new paid section to the magazine.

That is to say Mr X. will give me money £120 or £150 per year to pay a few contributors and myself. ⟨($600–$750)⟩

Neither I, Eliot, nor Joyce or Lewis can afford to work for nothing. I have done a deal of unpaid work during the last six years and a deal of underpaid work. It only keeps down ones prices and earning capacity.

ALSO it would do the paper no good to have me on it if every time I did something I could sell elsewhere I had, for fiscal reasons, to try to place it elsewhere.

I must have a steady place for my best stuff ⟨apart from ⟨original⟩ poetry, which still must go to "Poetry" unless my guarantor is to double his offer. Even so I oughtn't to desert "Poetry" merely because of convenience.

I have only three quarrels with them: Their idiotic fuss over christianizing all poems they print, their concessions to local pudibundery, and that infamous remark of Whitman's about poets needing an audience.⟩

I wonder, now, can I make my proposition. That you agree to print (??? 5000 or some number of words per issue ⟨chosen by me, & publish⟩ at least eight issues a year.

That I agree to pay the contributors of said number of words, including myself,.

I may not send that number some months, in which case I shouldn't mind paying for some contribution selected by you, provided I liked it.

All money from new subscriptions to go to you. I to have no responsibility about printing. I to provide this address as London address of Little Review.

My name to appear on the magazine as "regular contributor", or "London Editor", or whatever label you like. (I don't care a hang about this, but it should be worth doing) or "Contributing London Editor". ⟨It oughtn't to be "foreign correspondent" as I'm that on "Poetry" for all the good it does⟩ (n.b. also the stuff I choose should go in a solid lump, not be scattered among other things.)

I should try to get a London imprint on the Review, ⟨IF YOU WISH IT,⟩ though I doubt if that can be done till after the war, as I know that "Vogue" has had to print a special edition here, because the freight people, or someone won't guarantee to deliver sheets, etc.

Single subscriptions, of course, go all right by mail.

Is all this clear? It sounds very dictatorial, but I don't mean it that way.

Now about permanency. My guarantor would go on for several years I think, at the moderate rate mentioned. He would not go on forever unless there were some prospect of the magazine becoming self supporting. By self supporting under this new scheme, it would mean
> a. that it pay its printing, postage, and office expenses,
> b. that it pay you two, at least ten dollars per week each.
> c. that it should pay or begin to pay a further annual profit sufficient to pay me and my block of contributors at the same rate we start with under the guarantee. ⟨& thereby make it possible for the guarantor to stop his payment gradually.⟩

///////

My suggestion therefore is, that all money from the magazine go to you, until you both pay all running expenses and get a steady salary of not less than ten dollars per week each.

2. that ⟨the next⟩ profit beyond that, up to an annual sum equal to the

£ 120, or £ 150 provided at first by the guarantor, shall come to me, so that the guarantor can little by little be relieved of his annual expense.

3. in the improbable event of there ever being as much or more than this, there should be some share of profit to each of us, (⟨???⟩ say 25% coming to me), part or all of which I should spend on the magazine,

⟨actually⟩ I should get 25 dollars a month out of the subsidy or out of the profit that might replace it, at the end of some years I <u>might</u> feel I had earned a rise.

At any rate I might want to draw up to ten per week, after that any profit coming to my share should go to increasing the pay of contributors, or to establishing payment for all contributions.

Until a vaguely impossible time, all of ⟨us⟩ aged and bent (there having been, of course, NO turmoils, rows and scraps in that unthinkable interval . . . . . . ) when there should be still further surplus and the grandchildren of our cousins be gathering about our knees and bedsides and we be as dull as Harpers and the Century.

All of these details are a bore, perhaps, but one must settle this sort of thing clearly and in advance. I am afraid they dont, however, conduce to ecstasy but to knitting of brows.

I wish one could talk instead of writing such preliminaries.

As to what I have in mind to put in. There is at the moment a simple tale of indian life ("Jodindranath's Occupation") very brief.

There ⟨would be⟩ a lot of Fenollosa stuff, Chinese and Japanese, I suppose it is of interest. The Times gave two aimable [*sic*] columns to the new book on Jap Noh Plays ⟨yesterday.⟩ Mrs Fenollosa promises to send another great batch of Chinese notes.

As to policy, I don't think I am particularly propagandist. I have issued a few statements of fact, labeled two schools, and there has been a lot of jaw about 'em. But an examination of files will show that I have done very little preachy writing.

The American copyright regulations, the tariff on books imported into

America, are both scandals. I should want to feel free to say so. Not more than half a page per issue. Probably the repetition of one or two lines. now and again.

e.g.

. . . . . . . . . .

. . . . . . . . . .
The Tariff on books is an INFAMY.

. . . . .
Eliot is, I suppose, going to France after the war. I shall go to Paris for a while.

A monthly should keep some tab on the few interesting books that DO appear in London and Paris.

I should count on Eliot a good deal for such ⟨current⟩ criticism and appreciation. He is in touch with various papers here and sees what is going on.

I don't know how much Joyce would send in. He is working on another novel.

Lewis is not to be counted on, NOW, by the grace of God he may come back in due season.

The young stuff here that hasn't a home, would be an occasional poem from Rodker or Iris Barry ⟨& the unknown.⟩

The rest are clustered to the Egoist. I got Aldington that job some years ago. He hasn't done quite as well as I expected, BUT he was very young. H.D. is all right, but shouldn't write criticism.

The Lawrence-Lowell-Flint-Cournos contingent give me no active pleasure. Fletcher is all right now and again, but too diffuse in the intervals.

You advertise "new Hellenism". Its all right if you mean humanism, Pico's "De Dignitate", the Odyssey, the Moscophorus.
                Not so good if you mean Alexandria, and worse if you mean the Munich-sham-greek. "Hellas" with a broad swabian brogue.

Confucianism is not propagandist, and polytheism would only be misunderstood, so I shant offer any ⟨or much,⟩ competition on these lines. ⟨(Perhaps an essay on Confucius? on approval)⟩

I would send in (?5000 ???? ) or thereabouts words per number, or per month as the case may be. This to be printed straight off. (Bar of course libels, and the usual thing, or the printers refusing ABSOLUTELY to set it up, because of its inflammability)

If there happened to be more copy it ⟨the excess⟩ would be submitted to you as any other contribution. No hard feelings if you chuck it.

I think we might criticize each other's selections in confidence with some freedom and directness ????
       (as you like . . . it is sometimes amusing . . . . I dont insist . . . . .)
          Miss A.   "Mr P. you will annihilate ALL our subscribers."
          Mr P.   "Sorry."
          Mr P.   "Your dear Powys is a wind-bag lacking both balance
                  and ballast"
          Miss A.   "DO wind bags have ballast !!!"
              etc.
IN A NUT SHELL.
The suggestion is this.
You provide a certain number of pages.
I fill, and pay for contributions to, said pages.

Some hope to be held out to the guarantor that the drain on his pocket need not go on forever, and that it may lead to the magazines being a permanent self supporting, contributor-paying publication.

I dont know whether you want to ask any further questions
         ???????
About anything ?????????

Will you answer this with a letter in full saying what you can, or care to, do. A letter I can forward to my guarantor, or quote to him. Covering: space available, my freedom in choice of stuff ⟨for said space,⟩ (I dont imagine this would entail your using much that you wouldn't have chosen yourself), your first claim on profits, the possibility of the guarantor being able to draw out and leave me, Eliot etc. still in a position to ⟨make⟩ a small sum per month.

Amitiés! I don't believe I can get it clearer than that. Perhaps if the Review goes back to 48 or 64 pages you could offer more space, as much, for example as five pages of Egoist. I dont know that I want it.

Simply, a story, or a Noh play oughtn't of necessity to crowd out all articles and notes in the London-Paris section. I dont suppose it would. If it was worth printing you'd want it anyhow.

Do say quite clearly if there is anything in this you object to, and suggest alterations of the proposal that occur to you.

I to use my best stuff (after the 20 pages or thereabouts that goes to Poetry each year),
to get "creative" stuff when there is any that is any good,
to use a certain amount of criticism, or chronicle of London and Paris, and of other furrin parts on occasion.

For example, first month, my indian story or sketch or whatever it is, second month, probably a noh play, third month perhaps some chinese, or an essay with translations to illustrate it.

Eliot to do criticism each month, save when he has something original.

Both he and I would ⟨or could⟩ send poem now and again, I think.

I should probably want you to take on a few more exchanges and have certain of them sent here.

Good luck, and let me know what you think of it.

> Yours ever
>
> 26–1–17                 Ezra Pound

*Egoist: The Egoist: An Individualist Review* was a little magazine published in London from 1914 to 1919. See Introduction for further detail.
*Miss Weaver:* Harriet Shaw Weaver (1876–1961) financed and edited *The Egoist*. In addition to serving as the principal editor of the magazine, Miss Weaver had a special interest in the career of James Joyce. The Egoist Ltd. brought out the first English edition of *A Portrait of the Artist as a Young Man,* using sheets supplied by B. W. Huebsch in New York, and helped to

bring out Sylvia Beach's first edition of *Ulysses*. She was generous to Joyce during his lifetime and eventually served as his literary executor.

*My prospective guarantor:* John Quinn (1870–1924), a New York lawyer, practiced financial law and was a major collector of art, books, and manuscripts. Quinn had agreed to pay EP $750 a year for two years to help finance a magazine. $300 was to go to EP for his editorial duties and $450 was to be spent on the magazine's contributors. Later Quinn increased his own backing and secured contributions from three patrons: Mrs. James Byrne, Otto Kahn, and Max Pam.

*???? the other of you:* Jane Heap (?–1964), coeditor of the *LR*. In February 1916, MCA had met Jane Heap and a close friendship was formed between the two women almost immediately. By the summer of 1916, Miss Heap was involved in editing the *LR*, and, beginning with the November 1916 issue, she became a regular contributor. She maintained her connection with the *LR* until its demise in 1929.

*infamous remark of Whitman's:* "To have great poets there must be great audiences too," the motto of *Poetry*.

*"Jodindranath's Occupation":* "Jodindranath Mawhwor's Occupation," a prose sketch by EP on India and the Indian attitude toward sex, was first published in the *LR* (May 1917) and later included as one of the selections in *Pavannes and Divisions* (New York: Knopf, 1918).

*Fenollosa stuff:* Ernest Fenollosa (1853–1908), after having studied at Harvard, became an instructor in rhetoric at the Imperial University in Japan, and eventually was appointed Imperial Commissioner of Art in Tokyo. He wrote *Epochs of Chinese and Japanese Art,* a two-volume work which was published posthumously in 1911. After having read EP's "Contemporania," Fenollosa's widow, Mary, decided that EP should be the person to act as executor of her husband's literary papers.

*Jap Noh Plays:* EP published two books of Noh plays. The first of these was a small volume (*Certain Noble Plays of Japan*) published by the Cuala Press in Dublin on 16 September 1916. The title page of this edition described the plays as being "From the Manuscripts of Ernest Fenollosa, Chosen and Finished by Ezra Pound." The second book, which included a larger collection of the Fenollosa material, was published in London by Macmillan on 12 January 1917 (although dated 1916) under the title *"Noh" Or Accomplishment: A Study of the Classical Stage by Ernest Fenollosa and Ezra Pound.* The *Times Literary Supplement* of 25 January 1917 gave the book a long and favorable review, mentioning EP's "mastery of beautiful diction" and saying that, in general, "his versions [of the plays] are spirited and graceful, and the lover of exquisite curios will be glad of these jewels, which he has polished and set in cunningly rhythmical prose" (41).

*labeled two schools:* Imagism and Vorticism. Noel Stock suggests that EP coined the phrase *Les Imagistes* sometime in April 1912 (perhaps a month or so later). "The first use of this title in print was in Pound's *Ripostes,* in a note he placed at the back to accompany the publication in book-form of [T. E.] Hulme's 'Complete Poetical Works' " (115). *Ripostes* was published in October 1912.

In the spring of 1914, Wyndham Lewis established the Rebel Art Centre in London and began to edit *BLAST,* the journal of the movement EP named "Vorticism." EP and Lewis were its chief spokesmen.

*Rodker:* John Rodker (1894–1955), British author and founder of the Ovid Press, took over the London editorship of the *LR* from EP in the spring of 1919.

*Iris Barry:* (1895–1969), English poet who turned film critic before moving to the United States. In the United States, she became the curator of the Film Library at the Museum of Modern Art in New York. EP began his correspondence with Iris Barry in April 1916 after he had read some of her work in *Poetry and Drama.* The two met in July 1916 when Barry came from her home in Birmingham to London.

*Aldington:* Richard Aldington (1892–1962), British poet, novelist, and biographer, worked with EP to promote the first phase of Imagism and was, for a time, an editor of *The New Freewoman* and its successor, *The Egoist.*

*H.D.:* Hilda Doolittle (1886–1961), American-born poet and novelist, was one of the original Imagists. EP promoted her early career.

*Lawrence-Lowell-Flint-Cournos contingent:* D. H. Lawrence (1885–1930), English novelist, praywright, poet and critic whose work EP promoted in 1913.

Amy Lowell (1874–1925), American Imagist poet and critic.

F. S. Flint (1885–1960), English poet, translator, and critic who was prominent in the Imagist movement and with whom EP conducted a running argument over Imagism.

John Cournos (1881–1966), Russian-born poet, playwright, novelist, reviewer, and translator who came to the United States at the age of ten, where he first learned English. He lived in London from 1912 to 1930, where he met EP. One of his poems was included by EP in *Des Imagistes* (1914).

The poetry of Lawrence, Lowell, and Flint appeared in *Some Imagist Poets* of 1915, 1916, and 1917, all of which were edited by Lowell. EP refused to participate in Lowell's venture, believing that she would create a less exclusive movement with lower standards. Annoyed with her, EP renamed the Imagist movement "Amygism."

*Fletcher:* John Gould Fletcher (1886–1950) was an American poet from Little Rock, Arkansas, who lived in London from 1909 to 1914. EP met Fletcher when each of them happened to be in Paris in April of 1913.

*Pico's "De Dignitate":* Giovanni Pico Della Mirandola (1463–94) was an Italian nobleman, scholar, and writer. He held many unorthodox views, several of which he expressed in a set of 900 theses on a wide variety of topics. When Pope Innocent VIII declared some of his notions heretical, however, he abandoned the project.

*Moscophorus:* EP's reference is to a life-size Greek sculpture, the Mos*c*hophorus (the "calf-bearer") located at the Acropolis. The sculptor's name is probably Rhonbus, but his signature is preserved only in part. Dating from *c.* 560 B.C., the sculpture depicts a male figure carrying a calf across his shoulders. In a letter to John Quinn on 24 January 1917, EP mentions the sculpture: "I don't believe there's much 'oil' of lucre in Pisistratan sculpture, but the blighted Greeks did a few things before Phidias, and it would be amusing to point out Greek art as one continuous decadence. The Moscophorus (alias 'The chap with the calf') is, I think, a good job (possibly better than Yakob)" (Letter 117, *Letters,* Paige 104).

*Powys:* John Cowper Powys (1872–1963), English critic, educator, novelist, and poet. MCA was enthusiastic about Powys and advertised a number of his lectures in the *LR.* When she and Jane Heap went on trial 14 February 1921 on obscenity charges stemming from the *LR*'s serial publication of Joyce's *Ulysses,* the editors' lawyer, John Quinn, called on Powys to testify. In his testimony, Powys contended that *Ulysses* was too obscure and philosophical a work to be corrupting and that he personally considered it "a beautiful piece of work in no way capable of corrupting the minds of young girls" (Anderson, *My Thirty Years' War,* 220).

**5. TLS–5.** On stationery embossed: 5, Holland Place Chambers/ Kensington. W. [8 February 1917, incomplete item]

Dear Margaret Anderson

Dont think me a pig for not enclosing poem at once. The fact is I aint got no pome, and I've only one "story" ready for printing. AND if we are going to coöperate, along the lines of my long letter, which you will have rec'd by now, OR along other lines to be outlined by you in reply,

I want to start off the new order of things with a bang. Decent (or indecent) tale by me, something from Eliot, something from Joyce, etc. good wodge of 16 pages of new "blood".

(Pages of blood! wot a expresshun.) anyhow, a good cubic hunk of BLAST, to catch edgeways on the public ivory.

Take note that within three weeks of the opening of the Vorticist show in New York, even that codfish of a president, burst in something almost like action.

It would only be a waste of energy to bring in the new set of contributors one by one. Must use fire-controll. BOMM! Simultaneous arrival of new force in pages of "Little Review"

I have just written to my capitalist [John Quinn], explaining about the L.R., so there need be very little time wasted. Dont jump, he is not really a capitalist, only a man who works like hell and makes a large income.

When I say, I ain't got no pome, I don't think I am confessing to a complete sterility. the "Gaudier Brzeska" came out early in 1916. Then I compiled a huge prose book "This Generation", all my essays and a lot of connecting matter. Fortunately the publisher in N.Y. absconded. "FORTUNATELY" as the book was too bloody long, and t.b. dull.

Then "Lustra", then a few more poems which have been printed in "Poetry", then the big book of Japanese plays finished up, and put through the press, just out this fortnight.

Also three cantos (5000 words) of an endless poem, dispatched to "Poetry", and during the intervals the "Vorticist" pictures selected and shipped to N.Y., mostly by me, as all the various painters are serving in the army, etc.

Also one story, a few bad one act plays (DAMN BAD) and three or four unimportant translations.

Also Coburn and I have invented the "vortoscope" a

[*pages three and four of this letter are missing*]

I do not want to go Tagoring all over the place with bad copies of Cathay as he does with ⟨dilutations of⟩ diluted Gitanjali., or to eke out Cathay-light as the Celtic Twilight has been eked out.

Yours
Ezra Pound

You'll do much better to wait and use them, if they are used at all, as part of a series of Chinese things, which will have some interest and not be a mere stray thread of embroidery.

*BLAST:* EP's reference is to the rebellion and iconoclasm expressed in Wyndham Lewis's *BLAST,* "A Review of the Great English Vortex."
*the opening of the Vorticist show:* After learning of Gaudier-Brzeska's death in the First World War, John Quinn had written to EP on 27 July 1915 that he would underwrite the expenses for a New York show of the Vorticist group, an exhibition which would feature the work of Wyndham Lewis and Gaudier-Brzeska. Quinn's intentions were to arrange the showing, probably at the Montross Gallery, for late spring of 1916. In addition to Lewis and Gaudier, the artists to be represented were Edward Wadsworth, Frederick Etchells, Helen Saunders, and Jessie Dismorr. When Sophie Brzeska proved

to be difficult and shipping complications arose, the show had to be delayed. By late June, Montross had backed out of the venture and an alternate site had to be found. The show finally opened, however, in July 1916 at the Penguin Club at 8 East 15th Street with Horace Brodzky in charge. From London, EP handled the dealings with Sophie Brzeska as well as the other arrangements and shipping responsibilities. For further discussion of the events surrounding this affair, see Reid 204, 247–54.

*the "Gaudier-Brzeska":* On 5 June 1915, sculptor Henri Gaudier-Brzeska was killed in action at Neuville St. Vaast. Upon learning of Gaudier's death, EP began to put together a memorial volume. The book *Gaudier-Brzeska: A Memoir,* which included "the published writings of the sculptor, and a selection from his letters with thirty-eight illustrations, consisting of photographs or his sculpture, and four portraits by William Bennington, and numerous reproductions and drawings," was published by John Lane in London and by the John Lane Company in New York on 14 April 1916.

*publisher in N.Y. absconded:* EP had given the manuscript of *This Generation,* which had originally been entitled *The Half Decade* and included articles and reviews he had written along with an occasional letter and other explanatory material, to the New York publisher John Marshall. John Quinn believed that Marshall had little capital for running a publishing company and warned EP about the dangers. When Quinn tried unsuccessfully to contact Marshall, he got in touch with Alfred Kreymborg, who informed him that the publisher had gone to Canada with his young bride who was dying of tuberculosis. Apparently, Marshall had taken the manuscript with him and *This Generation* was never published (see Reid 255).

*"Lustra":* A private edition of two hundred copies of EP's *Lustra* was printed by Elkin Mathews in London in September 1916. See Letter 17n.

*the big book of Japanese plays: "Noh,"* Or *Accomplishment.* See Letter 4n.

*three cantos:* Harriet Monroe published these cantos consecutively in the June, July, and August 1917 issues of *Poetry.*

*Coburn and I have invented the "vortoscope":* Alvin Langdon Coburn (1882–1966) was a pioneer photographer who is credited with making the first non-objective photographs. A founding member of the Photo-Secession group of New York City (in 1902), Coburn took a number of photographs which emphasized the abstract patterns created by streets, parks, and buildings within the city. In 1912, he moved to London, where he met EP and Wyndham Lewis and became involved with Vorticist ideas. The "vortoscope" which he and EP invented consisted of a triangle lined with mirrors (pieces of EP's old shaving mirror) through which pictures could be taken and complete abstraction achieved. EP himself described the vortoscope as "a simple device which frees the camera from reality and lets one take Picasso's [*sic*] direct from nature." In February 1917, an exhibition of "vortographs" was held at the Camera Club, 17 John Street, London, and EP spoke at the opening. George Bernard Shaw attended the exhibition.

*Tagoring . . . Gitanjali:* EP's allusion here is to Rabindranath Tagore (1861–1941), the Indian poet, novelist, and short-story writer. Tagore had moved to London in 1878 and wrote prolifically, mostly in Bengali. The *Gitanjali,* the English version of his songs and poems, was published with an introduction by W. B. Yeats in 1912 and helped win for Tagore the Nobel Prize in 1913.

*Cathay: Cathay*, published 6 April 1915 by Elkin Mathews, was EP's book of poems, which the title page describes as being "Translations by Ezra Pound, for the most part from the Chinese of Rihaku [i.e., Li Po], from the notes of the late Ernest Fenollosa, and the decipherings of the professors Mora and Ariga."

*the Celtic Twilight: The Celtic Twilight* is the title of a collection of stories by W. B. Yeats, published in 1893. The stories tell of the mysticism of the Irish and of their belief in fairies, ghosts, and spirits. The term "Celtic Twilight" has since become, as EP's use here illustrates, a slightly ironical way of referring to the Irish Literary Renaissance.

**6. TLS–1.** On stationery embossed: 5, Holland Place Chambers/ Kensington. W. ⟨8⟩ [23 March 1917]

⟨London⟩

Dear Miss Anderson

Mails leaving New York, or rather collected in N.Y. between Feb. 14 and Feb. 18. were on that boat that was sunk.

This is just a line to say that if you answered any of my notes on those days I wont receive your letter.

Yours of Jan 25. I have answered. That is the last rec'd.

⟨March 23rd
Rec'd copies of Little Review for March but as yet no letter.⟩

Yours
Ezra Pound

**7. TLS–2.** On stationery embossed: 5, Holland Place Chambers/ Kensington. W. ⟨8⟩ [26 March 1917]

March 26. ⟨1917⟩

Dear Margaret Anderson:

Your letter of Feb 27 has just come. I can not, therefore, expect to get manuscript to you by March 28, day after ⟨for

April number⟩ tomorrow, so have cabled you, at the Brevoort Hotel, as follows:

Margaret Anderson, Lafbrevort, N.Y.
Letter received will try for May number

Pound.

My next act will be to endite an epistle to my prospective guarantor [John Quinn]. As he offered to do as much for me some months ago, and as, so far as I know, his heart hath not turned in wroth against me since that date. Speriamo. I trust you may hear "la bonne nouvelle", with no chinks and uncertainties, before many more hours elapse.

I dont think there's much to add. Lewis' copy is on the premises. Shall see Eliot tonight if possible. And get mss. together, to be sent off via. special permit etc.

Joyce is laid up with his eyes again, but the worst of the attack is over.

He is doing another novel. I think a sort of continuation, or at least a second phase of his "Portrait of the Artist".

Whether we can enlarge the format soon enough to be able to print it as a serial, heaven knows.

I dont know whether we can get much short stuff from him in the interval, or whether it is fair to ask him for it until he gets the big job done. However he will be with us in spirit ⟨at once⟩. And in some sort of "copy" before long.

enough of this now.
Will prepare announcements, editorials etc.

yours ever.
Ezra Pound

*As he offered . . . some months ago:* As early as the spring of 1915, EP had been looking for a journal of his own, or, at least, one over which he could exert editorial control. He was in touch with John Quinn about the idea, and, in a letter dated 21 May 1915, told Quinn he could get hold of the *Academy*, a London journal. Quinn encouraged EP, but the arrangement failed to materialize. Later, Quinn passed on to EP the news that Mitchell Kennerly in New York was about to abandon his sponsorship of the *Forum*. Quinn's idea was that EP take over the magazine and retitle it *The International Forum*. EP, however, had reservations and Kennerly eventually changed his own mind about the arrangement. EP and Quinn then discussed the possibility of EP's starting his own magazine.

In February of 1916, EP re-established his connection with *The Egoist*. (During 1915, he had published little in it.) On 15 March 1916, Quinn wrote to EP offering £100 or £120 to subsidize EP in his editorial duties and to pay contributors if EP were to become the editor of *The Egoist*. Quinn also indicated that he was willing to guarantee this subsidy for two years, and, in a letter dated 5 April 1916, raised the sum to £150. EP explored the possibility of such an arrangement, but wrote to Quinn on 10 April 1916 that, although Harriet Shaw Weaver seemed favorably disposed to the idea, Dora Marsden offered reservations and so he was calling things off.

*another novel:* Joyce was at work on *Ulysses*.

**8. TLS–4.**   On stationery embossed: 5, Holland Place Chambers/ Kensington. W. ⟨8.⟩ [29 March 1917]

Dear Miss Anderson

I have just sent off one letter to you and another to my proposed guarantor [John Quinn] ⟨now March 29. This was three days ago.⟩. As he is in America I have asked him to communicate with you direct. So you will know the result very shortly after the receipt of these letters. Please cable me, if he does not do so himself.

I enclose my opening manifesto. The other mss. I am sending to him, as I want him to see them.

If for any reason he does not approve the scheme, you can have my own stuff for the L.R. anyhow. That by the others will have to be sold elsewhere.

I think I'd better be called the "Foreign Editor" if the new arrangement goes through. ⟨Or if you prefer some other title for me, change it in the "Editorial" enclosed.⟩

It will always be impossible to send me proofs, and as we won't be able to "talk things over" at the last moment, I think you had better simply add M.C.A. footnotes when you disagree.

I hope the "Editorial" is all right. At least it is a fairly simple statement.

I wonder would you begin the London section ⟨on⟩ page 15, or what comes as page 15 in the March number. Or whether that would be inconvenient ??????

I am sending my story ⟨"Jodindranath"⟩, three things by [Wyndham] Lewis, for May, June, July,. A translation from LaForgue [Jules Laforgue] ⟨poem⟩ (enclosed in this letter), something by [T. S.] Eliot, which he hopes to bring in by Sunday.

I am ⟨sending⟩, or rather have just sent [John] Rodker out to see what he can find. Iris Barry may have a few lines of decent verse ready.

[James] Joyce is ill with his eyes, but I hope he can find something.

My "Anachronism at Chinon" is typed, but needs a few things put into place. That's for June. And probably a Noh play for July.

I am not wholly satisfied, or really satisfied with the LaForgue translation, but it has the merit of NOT being like every second page of "Poetry", and also is I think, about the first LaForgue in English. All sane people, myself included, having always supposed that LaForgue was "utterly untranslatable". Also I believe it will irritate a number of people.
Ergo. I think my list of contents, for my "chunk" of May runs as follows. ⟨in this order⟩

> Editorial⟨————————————————⟩E.P.
> "Pierrots, Scene courte mais typique"
>      after the French of J.LaF.⟨————⟩John Hall
> Jodindranath's Occupation⟨————⟩Ezra Pound
> ‥‥‥‥                    ⟨————⟩T.S. Eliot
> The First of SIX Letters from
>      William Bland Burn to his wife.
>                    ⟨————⟩by Wyndham Lewis

plus a word from Joyce if it comes in time. And possibly a story by Rodker and a verse by Iris Barry if there is room.
⟨more anon.
also list of my friends to whom sample copies or announcements, or better[,] sample copies with bundles of announcements should go.⟩

Malhereusement [sic] there can be no importation in bulk into England until after the war, but I'll send on a couple of dozen names of the people who

really matter and they can have single copies. If the thing is GOOD
ENOUGH we can dispose of bound vols. post bellum.

       enough for the moment. I must get the rest of the typescript
ready for the printer.

          yours ever     E.P.
                        Ezra Pound
29/3/17


*opening manifesto:* EP's "manifesto" was published in the opening pages of the
    May 1917 *LR.* In it, he explained why he accepted the position of Foreign
    Editor: "chiefly because: . . . I wished a place where the current prose
    writings of James Joyce, Wyndham Lewis, T. S. Eliot, and myself might ap-
    pear regularly, promptly, and together, rather than irregularly, sporadically,
    and after useless delays" (3). He also made clear the nature of his quarrel
    with *Poetry:*

> *Poetry* has done numerous things to which I would never have given my personal
> sanction, and which could not have occurred in any magazine which had con-
> stituted itself my "instrument." *Poetry* has shown an unflagging courtesy to a
> lot of old fools and fogies whom I should have told to go to hell tout pleine-
> ment and bonnement. . . .
>     Had *Poetry* been in any sense my "instrument" I should years ago have
> pointed out certain defects of the elder American writers. Had *Poetry* been my
> instrument I should never have permitted the deletion of certain fine English
> words from poems where they rang well and soundly. Neither would I have felt
> it necessary tacitly to comply with the superstition that the Christian Religion is
> indispensable, or that it has always existed, or that its existence is ubiquitous or
> irrevocable and eternal. (3–4)

*"Jodindranath":* "Jodindranath Mawhwor's Occupation" was published in the
    May 1917 issue (12–18).
*three things by Lewis:* the first three of Wyndham Lewis's "Imaginary Letters
    (Six Letters of William Bland Burn to His Wife)." They were published con-
    secutively in the May (19–23), June (22–26), and July (3–7) issues of 1917.
    Letters IV through VI, "Walter Villerant to Mrs. Bland Burn," were written
    by EP as responses to the first three letters and appeared in the September,
    October, and November numbers. Two letters (VII and VIII) written by
    Lewis appeared together in the March 1918 issue, and "Imaginary Letter,
    IX" (by Lewis) was published in the April 1918 issue. An edited version
    of the Lewis series was reprinted in *The Little Review Anthology* (110–28).
    These letters were numbered I–V.
*translation from LaForgue:* The poem entitled "Pierrots: Scène courte mais
    typique (After the 'Pierrots' of Jules LaForgue)" and signed by "John Hall
    [i.e., EP]" appeared in the May 1917 issue (11–12). The French Symbolist
    poet Jules Laforgue (1860–87) was an inaugurator of *vers libre.*
*something by Eliot:* Part I of Eliot's sketch "Eeldrop and Appleplex" was pub-
    lished in the May 1917 issue (7–11). (Part II did not appear, however, until

the September 1917 issue.) "Eeldrop and Appleplex" was included in *The Little Review Anthology* (102–09).

*"Anachronism at Chinon":* EP's selection, which appeared in the June 1917 issue (14–17), is a dialogue between François Rabelais and a young, twentieth-century American student. Each speaks of the stupidity and repression of his own world. Rabelais complains of the monastery and of the Church's repressive measures taken against art; the student, of the university and the repressiveness of modern democracies. Both find stupidity and an obsession to censor artistic expression endemic in their societies.

In one of his speeches the student claims, "I have had a printer refuse to print lines 'in any form' private or public, perfectly innocent lines, lines refused thus in London, which appeared and caused no blush in Chicago; and vice-versa, lines refused in Chicago and printed by a fat-head prude—Oh, most fat-headed—in London, a man who will have no ruffling of anyone's skirts, and who will not let you say that some children do not enjoy the proximity of their parents."

"An Anachronism at Chinon" was reprinted in EP's *Pavannes and Divisions* and again in *Pavannes and Divagations*.

**9. TLS–2.**   On stationery embossed: 5, Holland Place Chambers/ Kensington. W. ⟨8.⟩ [3 April 1917]

Dear Miss Anderson

You may announce:

"Eight poems by W.B. Yeats, for the June number."

The mss for the May number, i.e. mine, [T. S.] Eliot's, [Wyndham] Lewis, plus Lewis for June and July, went off yesterday via the Chief Censor and our, let us hope, guarantor [John Quinn].

I hope by now you will have got word of his financial sanction.

At any rate, now that I have got started I am going ahead, whether I get any financial sanction or not.

I have sent revised order of May contents with the mss.

The announcement for June can be:
Eight poems, Yeats
An Anachronism at Chinon, by me

Second of Imagin. Letters. by Lewis
Second part of Eliot's, "Eeldrop and Appleplex".
I am doing another dialogue for July, presenting Poggio at a sixteenth century bath. dont, however announce it until June number. If I dont finish in time, I'll use a Noh play.

The Yeats poems ought to "help". I haven't seen them together, and dont quite know which they are but he says they include some of the best he has done. I am expecting them in a day or so.

more anon, yours ever

Ezra Pound

3/4/1917

*Eight poems by W. B. Yeats:* See Letter 10n.
*his financial sanction:* See Letter 8.
*another dialogue for July:* EP's "Aux Étuves de Wiesbaden [misspelled "Weis-baden" in the *LR*], A. D. 1451" was published in the July 1917 issue (12–16). The selection is a dialogue between Poggio, whom EP modeled after the fifteenth-century Italian cleric Gian Francesco Poggio Bracciolini (1380–1459), and Le Sieur de Maunsier, both of whom are at Wiesbaden to enjoy the baths.

The dialogue was reprinted in *Pavannes and Divisions* and in *Pavannes and Divagations*.

**10. ALS–4.**   On stationery embossed: 5, Holland Place Chambers/ Kensington. W. ⟨8⟩ [4 April 1917]

Chere M.C.A.

The Yeats' poems are ripping. No one else could have turned out such a bunch. Various people might have done one as good as any one of these but no one would have done six running so even.

——Still I don't see how he expects six and one to make eight. ⟨which is the number he mentioned Monday.⟩ He has sent me six, or nine, according as one counts four little ones in a sequence as one poem or as four.

————

However if you have set up an announcement of "eight poems" as per yesterday's letter. ——leave it.——he may have two more anyhow.

Will send the June stuff soon.

Have already mss. running on for July, Aug, possibly Sept.

—

—

Note 1. Don't forget to put —(on cover ?) notice.

=

"Foreign subscriptions received at English Office of Little Review"
5 Holland Place Chambers.
Kensington, London W. 8.

We'll have to pack the pages rather tighter. less space between lines of verse. etc.—after the May number.

—

—

Rodker has sent in bundle of stuff some interesting, will start his shortest allotment in July.

—

June will be a tight squeeze with Yeats, my long "Chinon", Eliot & Lewis.

There'll be no more blank half pages for some time. I am glad to get W.B.Y. for June. a second number always ought to be stronger than a first—

Yours
Ezra Pound

4 April. 1917.

—

—

It may amuse you to know that ⟨our⟩ W.B.Y.'s poems are his newest & that the lot now with "Poetry" have been in reserve for some time—

This is a private glut & you are to keep it to "ourselves". It is just chance & no Macchiavellian [sic] devilment on my part. it so happens.

The Yeats' poems: These Yeats poems were published in the June 1917 issue (9–13). Each, with the exception of the last, appears with a date: "The Wild Swans at Coole" (October 1916), "Presences" (November 1915), "Men Improve with the Years" (July 19, 1916), "A Deep Sworn Vow" (October 17,

1915), "The Collar-Bone of a Hare" (July 5, 1915), "Broken Dreams"
(November 1915), and "In Memory."

*Rodker . . . his shortest allotment in July:* John Rodker (1894–1955). The
July 1917 issue (16–18) contains three short prose sketches by Rodker entitled "Night Pieces."

**11. TLS–2.**   On stationery embossed: 5, Holland Place Chambers/ Kensington. W. ⟨8⟩ [11 April 1917]

⟨April 11
    1917⟩

Dear Miss Anderson:

Yeats' poems ⟨enclosed⟩ are going to take up an all-
fired lot of room. BUT they're worth it, and they are a big score for the
magazine, and several nails in the coffins of the "Atlantic" and the other
decrepit snobs. One cant put them in smaller print, or save space by trying double column, but I think the printers might get a few more lines
on the page than they have done in the March number.

I think it particularly important to have a strong second
number, under the new scheme. So I dont want to leave out much. If there
simply isn't room, then please print my "Chinon" and [T. S.] Eliot, as
follows: First page of each in large type, and following pages in the
smaller type which you have used for correspondence. Same with [Wynd-
ham] Lewis' second installment. If any of the four things have to be postponed till July, then postpone the Lewis. I think it would be worth while
getting in all four, IF possible. AS the Yeats' stuff ought to give the magazine a boost, and as the unused reader will know there cant be ⟨seven⟩
Yeats' poems every month, he will be more likely to subscribe if the rest of
the thing looks fibrous and full of meat.

Besides the Yeats is an extra, my "staff" stuff is well within
10,000 words (I think), and it is just possible that you might have devoted
some of your own particular part of the issue to W.B.Y. if he had turned
up on his own.

I've a more cheery dialogue for July. Had to get this ⟨set of⟩ basic propositions off my chest first. Also three things of [John] Rodker's, shall begin
with the weakest and progress to the more forte. July, Aug, Sept,

Hope you like at least my opening paragraphs on the old man. ⟨(this

Rabelais dialog.)⟩ My next Dialogue is "Aux Etuves de Wiesbaden", it can't be announced until I have actually finished it, if its not done in time I'll use a "Noh". All of which I have written you three times already?

I enclose also Rodker's first mss. for July, if there is room.

Do be careful in getting Yeats' proofs correctly corrected.

> more anon.
>             Yours
>                 Ezra Pound

⟨1.                            ⟨s.v.p.
Enclosures.                    Let Quinn see the Yeats &
Yeats.  Seven Poems.           my Rabelais as soon as
        2.                     possible.
E.P.    Anachronism at         John Quinn 31 Nassau St.⟩
        Chinon.
        3.
J.R. night pieces.⟩

*Yeats' poems:* See Letter 10n.
*my "Chinon":* "Anachronism at Chinon." See Letter 8n.
*and Eliot:* Eliot did not complete the second part of "Eeldrop and Appleplex" for the June issue. See Letter 8n.
*Lewis' second installment:* See Letter 8n.
*more cheery dialogue:* "Aux Étuves de Wiesbaden, A.D. 1451" appeared in the July 1917 issue. See Letter 9n.
*Rodker's first mss.:* "Night Pieces." See Letter 10n. Rodker's series of poems "Theatre Muet" appears in the August 1917 number, but nothing of Rodker's is in the September issue.

**12. TLS–2.**   On stationery embossed: 5, Holland Place Chambers/ Kensington. W. ⟨8⟩ [22 April 1917]

Dear Miss Anderson:

Received your card saying my cablegram had arrived. But as yet no cablegram from you to say that the financial side of things has been finally settled. I shall have a large meal when said cable arrives, and feel more luxuriant.

However, am going on with something or other.

Eliot has not yet finished his second installment of "Eeldrop", so, if he dont finish in time, go ahead with Yeats, Lewis and me, for June.

Eliot has turned in a good bunch of poems, for July. Three french and one english, announce simply "a group of poems by T.S. Eliot will appear in the July number"

S.V.P. I dare say there'll be one or two more by then. Getting his book into print seems to have set him off again.

The actual cash don't, in one way matter, only I shall probably die of famine if it aint, or are not forthcoming. Also T.S.E. will be less blithe in spirit. both of which conditions would be "adverse".

I have sent on Joyce's letter to [John] Quinn, a short formal letter and a long gay one. Perhaps you had better announce simply "James Joyce has written to say that he will be among the early contributors to the magazine",.

The only real question now is whether I use up my personal credit in getting contributions, or whether the guarantor [John Quinn] approves and I use his hard cash.

The next step will be to tackle someone for increase in format. There is [Jean] DeBosschere, likewise Waley, the best Chinese scholar in England, with an eye for good poems (but unfortunately defects in his translatorial style). Also I should like room for more prose from Yeats, AND for Joyce's next novel [*Ulysses*], when finished. ⟨and possibly some extracts from old J.B. Yeats letter[s]. I have just edited a vol of them for the Cuala press.⟩

All this is however looking long ahead, and none of this can be even attempted until we have got out several numbers of the You, plus me-Joyce-Eliot-Lewis, plus the Yeats' poems, arrangement.

However the stuff is to be got as soon as we can hold it.

And if I have a row with "Poetry" there will also be my own poems (and my certain starvation).

Good luck
Yours ever
Ezra Pound
22 april
1917

*the financial side of things:* See Letter 8.

*Eliot . . . a good bunch of poems:* The Eliot poems which appeared in the July 1917 issue were "Le Directeur," "Mélange adultère de tout," "Lune de Miel," and "The Hippopotamus."

*Getting his book into print:* The Egoist Press was in the process of publishing *Prufrock and Other Observations.*

*Joyce's letter:* The "short formal" letter was printed in the June issue of the *LR* (26):

> I am very glad to hear about the new plans for The Little Review and that you have got together so many good writers as contributors. I hope to send you something very soon—as soon, in fact, as my health allows me to resume work. I am much better however, though I am still under care of the doctor. I wish The Little Review every success.

For the "long gay one," see *Letters of James Joyce,* I, 101–02.

*Waley:* Arthur David Waley (1889–1966) was a prominent British orientalist. Self-taught in both Chinese and Japanese, he published many translations of oriental literature, among them being *A Hundred and Seventy Chinese Poems* (1918) and Murasaki Shikibu's *The Tale of Genji* (6 vols., 1925–1933).

*I have just edited a vol of them: Passages from the Letters of John Butler Yeats: Selected by Ezra Pound.*

**13. TLS–4.**   On stationery embossed: 5, Holland Place Chambers/ Kensington. W. [5 May 1917]
Dear M.C.A.

At last the cable, saying the scheme is financed, has come.

Please therefore send sample copies of the May number to the following people. They should contain announcement of Yeats poems, etc. "to appear". Perhaps a single-leaf announcement might also be printed and sent to the [*crossout:* starred] names in this list for further distribution.

Distribute May number as follows. marked
SAMPLE COPY

1. to my father

H.L. Pound, Wyncote. Pa. 12 copies, with request for subscription, and that he drum up a few dozen more subscriptions at once.

one copy to the following.
Fred. Vance, Vance Studios, Crawfordsville, Ind.

Prof. Felix Schelling, Univ. of Penn. Philadelphia, Pa.
Dr. C.G. Child                ditto.
Prof. W.P. Shepard, Hamilton College, Clinton. N.Y.
Prof. H.A. Rennert, Univ. of Penn. Philadelphia, Pa.


Mrs. Chas. Wadsworth. Upland Farms, Chatham, N.Y.
Miss C.N. Perkins, 413 S. Broad St. Philadelphia.
F.R. Whiteside, Chelten Hills, Wyncote. Pa.
G.C. Woodward    1304 Pine St. Philadelphia.


Mrs. E.F. Fenollosa co/ Grant Thompson Co.
    280 Madison Ave. New York. with a note asking IF copy reaches
    her, and requesting her to BOOST.
ditto. to W.C. Williams, 9 Ridge Rd. Rutherford N.J.


The following should——
receive copies and a note, from you, saying you hope Mr. Pound's friends
will help you to convince him that America is not a blasted wilderness in-
capable of supporting a magazine devoted to good letters.
Mrs G.M. Smith, 266 Belmont St. Watertown, Mass.
Mrs. J.F. Cross, 32 Elmwood Ave. East Orange. N.J.
Milton Bronner    310 Windsor Place, Brooklyn. N.Y.
Mrs. V.B. Jordan    81 Palisades Ave. Bogota, N.J.
Miss K. Buss, 44 Bradlee Rd. Medford, Mass.
Chas. Grinnell, co/ Hale and Grinnell, 16 Central St. Boston


C.A. Hand, Law Offices of S.J. Murphy, 26 Broadway. N.Y.
L.B. Hessler    727 Packard St. Ann Arbor, Mich.


((Also find Charlotte Hirsch, (Mrs. Gilbert Hirsch) and get her to work.
    A letter sent in care of that Pig Lippmann, on the New Republic,
    might reach her.))


copies with NO comment to.
H. Hagedorn, Sunny Farm, Fairfield, Conn.
Basil King, 1 Berkley St.    Cambridge, Mass

W.G. Long    2254 N. 18th St. Philadelphia,
Mrs. J.P. Marks, 192 Brattle St. Cambridge, Mass.


H.L. Mencken (exchange with the Smart Set,)
Robert Mountsier, Adams Newspaper Service, co N.Y. Sun.
    naturally give John Quinn ALL the copies he wants.


Jas. Walter Smith, co/ Boston Transcript
Rev. DeF. Snively, St Philips Rectory, East Hampton, Mass.
    (if he dont subscribe AT ONCE, send him the June number too, and
    tell him he's GOT to.)


Gilbert Welsh (possibly at)
        15 W. 36th St. New York.
    (I think a copy co/ of the evening Globe or some such paper might
    reach him. poet and dramatic "critic", good chap.)


Mrs. M.W. Palmer, 6 Patchin Place. N.Y.
Carey C. Stevens, Taylor-Critchfield Co. Brooks Bld. Chicago.
Nicholas Brown. House of Books, 1720 Chestnut St. Philadelphia.
Glenn Palmer    29 Beeckman Place. N.Y.


Miss K.R. Heyman    "The Judson"    53 Washington Sq. New York.


Mrs L.U. Wilkinson    co/ G.A. Shaw
    1735 Grand Central Terminal. N.Y.


at least some of these people ought definitely to help you work up subscription list.
some should be made to send on announcements etc. Eliot will send a
small list also.

Free Copies ⟨subscriptions⟩ go regularly to
Miss G. Baxter    561 W. 180 St. New York
J.B. Yeats, whose address I have mislaid, Quinn will know it.

As I have written, we can't do anything in England until after the war. I
want you, however, to send the May and June number, together, when the
June is ready to about a dozen people who may help later.

English free list, to start at once.
Edmond Dulac, 72 Ladbroke Rd., London W. 11.
Wyndham Lewis, in my care,
J. Rodker, ditto.
Miss Iris Barry, 20 Glebe Place, Chelsea, London. S.W.3.
T.S. Eliot, 18 Crawford Mansions, Crawford St. London W.1.
W.B. Yeats, 18 Woburn Bld[g]s., London. W.C. 1.
Jean de Bosschere, in my care.
                    these are all contributors.
Foreign.
James Joyce, Seefeldstrasse 73, III. Zurich VIII
                    Switzerland.

///////////////
Sample Copies of May number.

La Baronne A. DeBrimont, 40 rue de Monceau, Paris.
Miss Natalie Barney, 20 Rue Jacob, Paris,
Miss I.B. Mapel, 8 bis. Rue Campagne Premier, Paris,
Joseph Campbell, Kilmolin, Ennisberry, Co. Wicklow, Ireland
Miss May Sinclair, 1 Blenheim Rd. St. Johns Wood, London N.W.8.
Maurice Hewlett, 7 Northwick Ter. London. N.W. 8.
E. Heron-Allen   33 Hamilton. Ter. London. N.W. 8
P.J. Jouve, 73 Rue de la Iranchee, Paris,
Chas. Vildrac.   (regular free copies)
        11 rue de Seine, Paris.
Frank Rummel, 6 Rue Nicolo, Passy, Paris.

I'll send a few more names when I have their subscriptions safe in my
pocket. they may as well begin to pay for the May number as the June.
H.M. Barzun, 7 rue de la Tour.
Mlle. Clare de Pratz, Hotel de Calais, 5 Rue de Capucines.
        (till the end of the war).
better send her copies regularly , whether she pays or not.
also.
Fritz Vanderpyl, co/ Mercure de France.
also, request exchange copies to be sent to me by LA VIE,
        G. Cres   116 Boulevard Saint-Germain, Paris.
        I will make out an exchange list later. I get the Mercure from "Poetry".

Father would help with clerical work if he were in N.Y.. Whether you could get Mrs [M. W.] Palmer, or Gwen Baxter to help you with correspondence, I dont know. I dont know whether they are worked to death or not. At any rate you can ask 'em if you want help.

Gwen might drum up some one who could if she couldn't[.] Bill [William Carlos] Williams ought to do something, but his doctoring in the country is an obstacle.

It is only the people who are worked to death who ever WILL do anything.
       ///////

SAMPLE COPIES, May number.
J.R. Henderson, Patomac Farm, Brooke, Va.
            (I'll forget my head next)
C.T. Chester, Lebanon. Pa.
Mrs D.P. Young, possibly at 504 E. Wabash. Ave.
     Crawfordsville, Ind.
Ford Madox Hueffer, (regular free list)
     South Lodge, Campden Hill. London W.8.


          /////
Saw H.D. [Hilda Doolittle] yesterday. she expressed her liking for Little Review. We can count on pretty full cooperation from the Egoist.

This list will do for May number.
Various other things I want tried as soon as we can display three numbers of new series.

This will give you enough for one afternoon.
more later.
                    Yours
                         Ezra Pound
                         5-5-1917

*At last the cable:* See Letter 8.
*Pig Lippmann, on the New Republic:* Walter Lippmann (1889–1974), associate
   editor of the *New Republic*. At least part of EP's animosity toward Lippmann
   must have resulted from a luncheon the two had together (along with Conrad
   Aiken) several years earlier at the Hotel Russell in London. According to
   Aiken, EP apparently had been under the impression that during the luncheon
   Lippmann would be interviewing him for a position on the *New Republic*.

Toward the end of the meal, however, when Lippmann had said nothing about the job, EP inquired about it and Lippmann said he was indeed looking for a general correspondent. EP offered his services, but Lippmann declined them. In a letter to John Quinn (8 March 1915), EP referred to the incident: "About the *New Republic,* I am afraid it is not much use.——I saw and lunched with Lippmann when he was over here, but he didn't seem disposed to take any of my stuff. A poet, you know! ! ! Bad lot, they are. No sense of what the public wants. Even [John] Cournos, who isn't exactly modern, met Lippmann and said: 'You've heard of English stodge? Well, there's one stodge that's worse. That's American stodge' " (*Letters,* Paige 54). For a fuller account of EP's encounter with Lippmann, see Norman 166.

**14. TLS–1.**   On stationery embossed: 5, Holland Place Chambers/ Kensington W. ⟨8⟩ [6 May 1917]

Dear M.C.A.

Here is Eliot's list of people for sample copies of May number:

Prof. Wm. Allen Nielson, Harvard University, Cambridge, Mass.
Oswald Bacchus, Rome. N.Y.
Boston Herald.
Harvard Advocate, Cambridge, Mass
Mrs Ralph Barton Perry, Cambridge, Mass
Miss Margaret Norton, Cambridge, Mass
Mrs George Lawrence Smith, Chaworth Farm, Mielis, Mass
Mrs John Lowell Gardner, Green Hill, Warren St. Brookline, Mass.
Miss Adelene Moffat, 179 Marlboro St. Boston. Mass
B.A.G. Fuller Esq. Farm St. Sherborne, Mass
Miss Eleanor Hinkley, 1 Berkeley Place, Cambridge, Mass.

The Rev. Arthur Galton, Edenham Bourne. Lincs. England.

//////

Recd. 7/ for one years subscription from
              Mrs H.H. Shakespear, 12 Brunswick Gdns.
                                    London. W.8.

I'll send over a lump sum to cover subscriptions as soon as the amiable guarantor [John Quinn] tells me I've something to my credit. I've asked him to put some of it in an American bank to facilitate matters.

Too busy to write much more than necessary data, just now.

Yours ever
Ezra Pound
6–5–1917

15. **TLS–4.** On stationery embossed: 5, Holland Place Chambers/ Kensington. W. ⟨8⟩ [7 May 1917]

May 7.
Dear M.C.A.

I may not have been explicit about postal regulations. You can not send the Little Review into England in bulk during the rest of the war, only single copies are permitted to come in. ("Poetry" does as a matter of fact send me packets of six, and they get through, though they shouldn't.). Hence my request for copies to various roving males, in my care.

I will meander after subscriptions during the next few weeks, may as well wait till I meet people. In the mean time please send May number to the following (mostly middle aged gossips, ⟨i.e. the first few.⟩) who will "talk about it" rather than subscribe. One number will oil 'em up. Those who subscribe will have the subscription counted "from May" so dont mark the copies "sample".

Miss Phyllis Bottome, 15 Brunswick Gdns. London W. 8
Miss Ethel Coburn Mayne, 11 Holland Road, London W. 14
> (get these new system numeral[s] right
>> for the London postal districts, there
>> are six Holland Roads.)

Mrs Clifford, 7 Chilworth St. London W.2.
Miss G. Hyde-Lees 30/13 Bramham Gdns. London S.W.5
R.B. Cunninghame-Graham Esq. 14 Washington House
> Basil St. Knightsbridge, London.
> S.W.

Wilfred Scawen Blunt, Esq.
                    Southwater, Sussex, Eng.
Antonio Cippico, 27 Landsdowne Rd. Holland Park.
                    London W. 11
Miss Ella Coltman, Netherhampton House, Salisbury, Eng.
Mrs Caird, 34 Woronzow Rd. St Johns Wood, London N.W. 8.
M. Henri DeRegnier, 24 rue Boissiere, Paris.
Mlle. Marcella Du Cros, 30 Holland Park Rd. London W. 14
Godfrey Elton, Ovington Park, Alresford, Hants. Eng.
Mrs Emery, Ramanathan College, Chunnakan, Ceylon.
Mrs. Fenollosa, Spring Hill, Mobile Co. Alabama.
          (try this address in case the other one I sent you dont work. She
          ought to help.)
Mrs Fowler, 26 Gilbert St. London W. 1.
W.L. George Esq. 3 Pembridge Crescent, London W. 11.
E. Gosse Esq. 17 Hanover Terrace, London. N.W.1.
P. Gaskell Esq. 35 Acacia Rd. London N.W.8.
E. Heron-Allen Esq. Hamilton Ter. London N.W.8.
Mrs Herbert    35 Avonmore Rd. London W. 14

Edgar Jepson Esq. 36 Priory Rd. Bedford Park. London W.
          (send the magazine to him regularly, whether he subscribes or
          not.)
Mrs Kibblewhite    67 Frith St. London W.1.
Murray Kendall, Scotland House, Victoria Embankment, London. S.W.1.
Edward Knoblock    G.2. The Albany, London W.1.
Sir Thomas Beecham, Bart, The Albany, London W.1.
P.G. Konody Esq. L.5. The Albany, London W.1.

Prof. E. Legouis, 98 Ave. Emile Zola, Paris XVe.
B. Lynch Esq. 207 Lauderdale Mansions, ⟨Maida Vale⟩ London N.W. 9
B. Moir Esq. M.D. 93a. Harley St. London W.1.
T. Sturge Moore, 40 Well Walk, Hampstead, N.W.3.

G.R.S. Mead Esq. 47 Campden Hill Rd. London W.8.
          (ask him to send you "The Quest" as an exchange, but dont be-
          lieve anything he says in it. He gets one interesting article every
          five years. sometimes more often.)

The Rt. Hon. C.F.G. Masterman, 46 Gillingham St. London S.W.1.

X. Mayer Esq. 34 Walpole St. London S.W.3.

L. J. Maxse, 33 Cromwell Rd. London S.W.7.

The Honble. Mrs Nicholson, 182 Ebury St. London S.W.1.

Victor Plarr Esq. 28 Fitzgeorge Ave. London W. 14

G.W. Prothero Esq. Edtr. The Quarterly Review,
    51 a. Albermarle St. London W.1.
    (ask him to exchange for the "Quarterly" just for the sake of a lark.
    see "wot comes o' 't")

Miss Ada Potter, 21 Trevor Sq. Knightsbridge, London S.W.7.

Mrs Rawlinson, Hill Lodge, Campden Hill Rd. London W.8.

Grant Richards, 7 Carlton St. Regents St. London S.W.1.

G.B. Shaw Esq. 10 Adelphi Terrace. London. W.C.2.
    (put him on the free list, permanent.)

Madame Sartoris, 17 Boulevard Delessert, Paris.

Miss Thomas, Royal South London Dispensary,
    St. Georges Cross, London. S.E.

Miss H.S. Weaver, 29 Queensborough Terrace. London W.2.
    (this is not the H.S. Weaver of the Egoist)

Mrs Derwent Wood, 284 Kings Road, Chelsea, London S.W.

That'll do for now. When I can display a set of three or four achieved numbers, I will plug for the outer and higher regions.

Joyce is in hospital with small chance of doing much. I want however to be able to enlarge format WHEN his next novel [*Ulysses*] is ready, and also to pay him at least £50 for it.

Ditto. IF Hueffer is invalided out of the army. His best work has lain half written for the past five years. It is not like his other work or like anybody's. I want to be able to print it, and to pay, or rather to be able to say to him "Damn you get the job through", here is the postdated cheque, and here are the waiting pages.

There is enough good stuff IF one knows where to root, and whom to agitate.

Yeats is in Ireland. He sent me a request to find a mss. in his rooms, didn't find it, but noted stacks of his father's [John Butler Yeats's] letters NOT yet used. If they are half as good as those I have edited for the Cuala Volume. We should get some excellent stuff from them.

Better put Lady Gregory on the free list.

Coole Park, Gort, Co Galway, Ireland.

At least we will "inspire" opinion, even if we dont make a living.

More as it comes to mind. I feel I ought to supply you with a shipping clerk, but you ought to find an enthusiast in N.Y.

Yours

Ezra Pound

7–5–'17

*various roving males, in my care:* i.e., Wyndham Lewis, John Rodker, and Jean de Bosschère. See subscription list in Letter 13.

*try this address in case the other one . . . .* : See subscription list in Letter 13.

*"The Quest":* Edited by George Robert Stow Mead (1863–1933), *The Quest* was a journal devoted, for the most part, to speculative essays on topics dealing with mysticism. Mead, however, did have a tolerant viewpoint and published essays on a variety of topics. EP's essay "Psychology and Troubadours" was published in *The Quest* (October 1912); the essay was reprinted as Chapter V of *The Spirit of Romance* (in editions published in 1932 and later).

*Joyce is in hospital:* Joyce was living in Zurich in 1917 and was suffering from glaucoma and synecchia, eye problems which had begun when he was in Trieste. In February, he had already suffered an attack that lasted four weeks; at the end of April the glaucoma again flared up and his doctor suggested an operation. Hesitant to undergo an operation which would remove bits of the iris, Joyce contacted EP. EP consulted American specialists and sent Joyce their suggestions—to have the surgery. Eventually, after suffering a severe attack of glaucoma on 18 August 1917, Joyce did have the recommended eye operation on August 24 (see Ellmann, 412–13, 417).

*Hueffer . . . His best work:* Ford Madox Hueffer, later Ford Madox Ford (1873–1939). In 1908, Ford founded *The English Review,* a monthly he edited until the end of 1909. Under his astute editorship, the magazine published not only the work of established writers—Conrad, Hardy, Henry James, etc.—but also that of authors who were as yet unknown—D. H. Lawrence, Wyndham Lewis, and EP.

EP is perhaps referring to Ford's *Women & Men,* which EP had called "Hueffer's best ms." The work was published in six installments in the *LR* in 1918. Ford had begun working on *Women & Men* in 1911, and, according to Arthur Mizener, the "fragment" that was published in the *LR* was all he ever managed to write, which implies that Ford had intended the work to be longer than the six parts actually published (see Mizener 296–97).

Whether the selections serialized in the *LR* represent the whole of *Women & Men* as Ford had conceived it is a matter for conjecture. EP apparently did not think the series complete and said so in an obituary he wrote for Ford [see "Ford Madox Ford: Obit," *Nineteenth Century and After,* 127 (August 1939): 178–81, rpt. in *Furioso* (Spring 1940); and in *New Directions: Number Seven,* 1942, 479–83]. But, in 1923 (while Ford was still alive), three hundred copies of *Women & Men* were printed by Three Mountains Press in Paris, an edition which contained the same selections as the *LR* serialization. Ford must have approved the selections standing independently whether or not he had originally intended to expand the work. Moreover, in a bibliography of Ford's work and criticism, David Dow Harvey refers to a letter now in the Deering Library, written by O. K. Mann to the literary agent J. B. Pinker and dated 24 January 1912. Mann asks to see the "complete manuscript" of *Women & Men,* a request Harvey takes as meaning the manuscript was complete as it stood. Harvey concluded that "Ezra Pound's obituary [for Ford] . . . assumes, apparently wrongly, that *Women & Men* was never finished" (56).

*Cuala Volume:* i.e., *Passages from the Letters of John Butler Yeats: Selected by Ezra Pound.*

**15a. TLS–2.** On stationery embossed: 5, Holland Place Chambers/ Kensington. W. ⟨8⟩ [7?–8 May 1917; see note]

Dear M.C.A.

Please send the May number to
The Hon. Evan Morgan, 45 Grosvenor Sq. W.1.
A. Clutton-Brock Esq. Farncombe Lodge, Farncombe, Surrey, Eng.
  (send him the review regularly. He is responsible for at least two of
  the good reviews of me in the "Times". You might also ask him on
  your own to arrange an exchange with the Times Literary Supplement. It is dull, but it is the only weekly publication here that is in
  any way fair and complete.)
Miss Abbot, ⟨73⟩ Church St. London W.8.
  full year.
  (she keeps a cake shop, is enthusiastic reader of BLAST, and the
  moderns. I've told her she can have a free subscription if she gets me
  15 subscribers. If she dont she'll pay up on her own. She is quite
  willing to help, and rather objects to selling lunch or confections to
  anyone who isn't at least a hanger on of the arts. Age 49 to 57 ??????)
"The people one forgets to put in ones address book."

Subscription recd. from

Mrs. E. Wadsworth, 1a. Gloucester Walk. London W.8.

Tuesday May 8.

Harriet [Monroe] has made a fool of herself again and we shall probably have another fine lot of Yeats' poems for August or Sept.

It will absolutely declass "Poetry" and we shall be THE IT.

However for God's sake dont breathe until it is fait accompli.

I expect a subscription from

Guy Little, 33 Tite St. Chelsea, London S.W.

you might send him the May number on chance.

As I have said before, I'll send you a lump sum on

subscriptions etc. as soon as cash arrives in my account

from the noble guarantor [John Quinn].

I dont want to be spiteful about "Poetry", but a little HEALTHY competition will be good for Chicago.

⟨Tuesday 1 30

Lost Lewis mss. discovered part of it.

better than anything of his we've had.

May as well send this off⟩

yours ever<br>Ezra Pound

8–5–19

---

*7?–8 May 1917:* Although EP has written "8–5–19" at the end of this letter, the contents make clear the year must have been 1917.

*Clutton-Brock . . . at least two of the good reviews:* English critic and essayist Arthur Clutton-Brock (see also Letter 98 and 98n) was an art critic for the London *Times* and a frequent contributor of reviews and essays to the *Times Literary Supplement.* One of the reviews to which EP refers is Clutton-Brock's of *Cathay,* entitled "Poems of Cathay," in the 29 April 1915 issue (144). The other is most likely one of the following unsigned reviews: "The New Sculpture," rev. of *Gaudier-Brzeska: A Memoir,* (27 April 1916): 199; "The Poems of Mr. Ezra Pound," rev. of *Lustra,* (16 November 1916): 545; or "Japanese Mysteries," rev. of *"Noh,"* or *Accomplishment,* (25 January 1917): 41.

*Miss Abbot:* Ella Abbott ran a small tea shop EP frequented on Holland Street in London.

*BLAST:* See Letter 24n.

*another fine lot of Yeats' poems:* See Letter 24n.

*Lost Lewis mss.:* See Letter 16.

**16. TLS–2.** On stationery embossed: 5, Holland Place Chambers/ Kensington.W. ⟨8⟩ [9 May 1917]

Dear M.C.A.

Please send May, June and July numbers to Horace DeV. Cole, 34 Cheyne Row, Chelsea, London S.W. It will take that long to get it into him that the Review exists, but if he once starts subscribing he will I think continue for life.

I wish too that you would let me know how much, or how many, cash or new subscribers it will take to pay for increase to 48 pages a month, (ditto to 64 pages.)

IF I get the second bunch of Yeats poems and follow on with it in Aug. or Sept. I think we should be warranted in trying to increase the number of pages. There is good stuff to be printed. AND a larger format is much sounder as a "business" proposition. "Business" matters only because the arts have to be "kept up" and people fed, AND if we can pay them enough they can give us their full time. ONE good page is worth ten thousand bad pages, and if it takes a man one month to do one good page, he should not need to starve in the interim.

The essay of [Wyndham] Lewis' that I dug out of the receivers of a defunct publishing house, is the best-muscled bit of prose he has done. The story he is going to rewrite, parts of it are excellent.

There IS the stuff. I haven't touched [Arthur] Waley or [Jean] DeBosschere at all yet. And if or when [Ford Madox] Hueffer comes out, there is, as I think I wrote, his best prose book, lying half done this five years.

We can perfectly well be what the English Review was during the first 18 months when F.M.H. ran it. It may take a bit of a shove, but it can be done.

I pause to write elsewhere.

Yours ever<br>Ezra Pound

9–5–'17

⟨Let me know what's
needed for increase in size.⟩

*increase to 48 pages:* The *LR* had been running about thirty-six pages per issue.
MCA, however, made a concerted effort to attract new subscribers so that the
format could be enlarged. In May she announced that the June issue would
be at least forty-four pages, but, in fact, it was only forty. In the July issue,
she ran the following announcement:

> It is to the interest of every subscriber to *The Little Review* to get us more sub-
> scribers at once, for the single reason that we have plenty of excellent matter on
> hand waiting to be printed. The larger our subscription list the more we can
> give you each month.

The August number asked potential advertisers to buy space in the magazine
so that the format could be enlarged, and the September issue contained an
appeal to readers to urge their friends to subscribe. With the October 1917
number, the format was expanded to forty-eight pages and the following
announcement ran under the bold headline "WE WANT!":

> We want *monthly* eight pages more for French, eight pages *more* for painting
> and sculpture (when extant), sixteen pages *more* if we are to print both the
> Hueffer prose series and the new novel promised by James Joyce, at the same
> time. We see no reason why we should not publish music (not criticism of
> music) if any happens to be written. Even our most rabid detesters can not
> expect us to double our format unless we can, at about the same time, double
> our list of subscribers. It is, placid reader, up to you. (42)

The November 1917 number contained a notice of a price increase effective
January 1918: yearly subscriptions would be $2.50, an increase of a dollar,
and single copies would be twenty-five cents, an increase of ten cents. The
December 1917 issue ran sixty-four pages.

*essay of Lewis':* A book of Lewis's short stories had been scheduled for publication but, when the First World War broke out and members of the publishing firm lost their lives, the firm was disbanded. EP, apparently, retrieved
the manuscripts for Lewis (who was himself fighting in the War). The essay
to which EP refers was to have served as the introduction to the volume.
When the essay was published in the *LR* in September 1917, it was titled
"Inferior Religions" (3-8). The stories from the intended volume that did
appear in the *LR* were "Cantleman's [misspelled in places "Cantelman"]
Spring-Mate" (October 1917) and the two-part story "A Soldier of Humour"
(December 1917 and January 1918). The October issue containing "Cantleman's Spring-Mate," however, was suppressed by the New York Post Office,
which declared the Lewis story obscene.

*Waley:* See Letters 12n and 32n.

*his best prose book:* See Letter 15n.

*English Review:* Convinced that no existing magazine properly supported the
best that was being written, a group of writers that included Ford Madox
Ford, Joseph Conrad, and Edward Garnett founded *The English Review* in

1908. When the journal was registered as a company on 22 January 1909, Ford was identified as the general partner and Arthur Marwood as a limited partner. From the first, Ford served as its editor.

**17. TLS–6.**   On stationery embossed: 5, Holland Place Chambers/ Kensington. W. ⟨8.⟩ [10 May 1917]

Dear M.C.A.

Received ⟨year's⟩ subscriptions from
Capt. Guy Baker, co/ Mrs Murray, 110 Harley St. London W.1.
Guy Little, 33 Tite St. Chelsea, London S.W.
(also two more, which I shall believe in when they have paid up.)
EDITION DE LUXE
Please send copies of May Number to
Mrs. M.B. Turner, 33 Park Lane, W.1.                    (I'm tired of
Lady Cunard, 2 Upper Brook St. W.1.                    writing "London"
                                                       so often,
                                                       understand it
                                                       wherever letters
                                                       and postal numbers
                                                       are used.)
It is important that you should send the edition on extra fine paper to a certain sort of person. Only a finely got up magazine will strike the eye in certain districts.

Send the edition de Luxe to Lady Cunard regularly. Mrs Turner can go hang, only we wont get a subscription ⟨from her⟩ unless she sees the de luxe format first.

The rough paper is good enough for all the other people whose names I've sent you. The swells in Paris won't expect vellum in war time.

Sample copy May number to
Mrs Herbert Leaf, The Green, Marlborough, Wilts. Eng.
Mervyn Fletcher Esq. 39 Green St. W.1.
Lady Low, 23 De Vere Gdns. .W.8.

                                                       Ezra Pound
                                                       10–5–'17

I think it might be worth while to have some announcements printed on blank post cards. Statement of "reorganization" or something of that sort of "Little Review". and announcement of contributors.

Eng. subs. receivable, 5. H.P.Chambers. (7/)
American subs. receivable, 31 W. 14th. (1.50)

People will more readily put a half-penny stamp on a card than use up an envelope and write a note re/ an enclosure.

Send me 50 cards if you do this. It is cheaper than sending May numbers to the possibly unworthy.

[John] Quinn will probably order his secretary to ship out a few billion cards.

I enclose proposal for announcement on post cards. Shall use it in June Egoist instead of the form used in their current number.

I should be glad if you could scrunch these verses by Iris Barry into the July number. They could be squeezed into a page, unless we have enlarged format by that time. I dont think they are worth more than a page. Even if all but the first poemlet had to be in small type.

I accepted them for August, but I also accepted them before I knew how much stuff there was lying about.

If we are going to have the second great bunch of Yeats for August, these things ought to be out of the way before then. I did want to call on both Iris Barry and [John] Rodker, three of whose things I accepted, but after July I dont think we can stop for things of "promise" and of amateur standing.

PLEASE NOTIFY ME OF RECEIPT OF ALL MSS. at once,. Just drop a post card. I will send fairly early, and if stuff doesn't arrive, there will be time to send on a duplicate.
I have sent, to date.

|  |  |
|---|---|
| Editorial for May. | acknowledged |
| Poem (translation) signed. J. Hall | =" " |

to Quinn:

Jodindranath's Occupation.

Three "Letters" by Lewis.

Eeldrop and Appleplex (one installment) by Eliot.

to you:

An anachronism at Chinon,

three poems by Rodker.

SEVEN poems by Yeats

you might cable if any of these have failed to arrive. (bar the Rodker, which isn't of breathless value) I know you've the J. Hall translation as it was in with the editorial.

I enclose the I. Barry's verse, as said.

Eliot's poems for July I will send soon.

He has not turned in his prose for June. DONT WAIT for it. The "Chinon" and the Yeats, will hold that issue O.K., and I dare say fill or overfill my space. But try to get in the Lewis as well. Yeats is a coup and worth an overlap. I am working to be able to enlarge, and if I encroach ⟨at [a] little⟩ on the rest of the magazine now, forgive me, and hope to make it up later.

Until we can enlarge, we must make it a practice to give the reader the absolute MAXIMUM of reading matter, crowding the page, and printing all but the first page or so of prose articles and stories, and all but the first poem or two of a series, in smaller type when necessary, in my section.

I'll write about your Bookshop when I've time. I could have used it well a few years ago. Now that Knopf is to publish me in N.Y. I dont know that it will be so much use to me.

You can stock me heavily, and take some copies of Eliot's "Prufrock" from the Egoist. Have Joyce's books in the front window.

Communicate with N[icholas]. Brown, of the House of Books
        1720 Chestnut St. Phila.
see if he is any good. Make him start local agency for Little Review.

You might also stock a few sets of the Egoist from the beginning, with fee for binding.

OUR FIRST YEARS VOL. under the new series, MUST and WILL be INDESPENSABLE AND a permanent property[.]

IF it is any use for adv. purposes you may state that a single copy of my first book has just fetched £8. (forty dollars); that the first edition of "Lustra" unabridged is said to be out of print and "advanced" in price. I haven't any official notice to that effect but saw a copy for one guinea in a window recently, and know another sold for 10/6 shortly before.

Our volume May 1917 to ?????, shall also arise in due season if Mercury be propitious. It's SOME LITTERCHURE even if we dont get anything more to put in it.

Failing an increase in size, an improvement in paper ⟨(even a slight imp)⟩ would make a fuller use of the smaller font of type less disagreeable. That might be an intermediate move.

We might aim for 48 pages by September. ne c'est pas [n'est-ce pas]. I think that is soon enough. If we saw our way to it we could make the announcement in August. We must give the effect of a steady augmentation of strength.

We need only the remains of [Thomas] Hardy, and of W.H. Hudson to be "complete" here. After the war we must have the best of the Frenchmen. i.e. as soon as I can get to Paris. One cant get them by letter.

I could get a critical "appreciation" from [Jean] DeBosschere every month. And "Varietés" from Paris by [Fritz-René] Vanderpyl or some one better. And also dig something out of Jules Romains, if he is left alive.

Hueffer's best unfinished work, and Joyce's next novel [*Ulysses*], I have already mentioned. There is plenty before us if we can go to it.

It would in time be advisable to have a very brief set of monthly reports like those at the end of the Mercure de France, but that is a long way off. It might be six pages out of 64, but would go better as 16 out of 80. The writing I can get done very cheaply, but the necessary negotiations for having the review copies of books sent in from the continent will take a lot of time and trouble.

Dont even bother to talk about it YET. Once we can get

that machinery started we are a solid and permanent fact, beyond the throws [throes?] of chance and the jettatura of adversity. Nothing but our own mental atrophy can thereafter annihilate us.

Can Quinn get at the Carnegie library advisory board and INSERT us. (Not just now. Jodindra ["Jodindranath Mawhwhor's Occupation"] wont suit. But beginning with June and the splendour of Yeats' reputation. ??????)

Announcements of the Yeats' poems should be sent to the English depts of ALL american colleges and universities. Etc. enough for the moment.

Yours

Ezra Pound

10–5–1917

EDITION DE LUXE: In a letter to us dated 20 May 1987, Donald Gallup pointed out that perhaps as many as twenty-five copies (as EP later implies) of some issues of the LR were printed on high quality paper. This fact, Gallup notes, "is especially important because the 'rough' paper was of such bad quality that many runs of *The Little Review* have crumbled away and many libraries (including the New York Public Library) have only microfilms."

*verses by Iris Barry:* Six poems by Iris Barry appeared in the August 1917 issue (17–19): "His Girl," "Widow," "At the Ministry: September 1916," "The Black Fowl," "At the Hotel," and "Towards the End."

*second great bunch of Yeats:* The August 1917 issue (3–7) published Yeats's "Upon a Dying Lady," "Certain Artists Bring Her Dolls and Drawings," "She Turns the Dolls' Faces to the Walls" (in four sections), and "Her Friends Bring Her a Christmas Tree." See Letter 24n.

*Rodker, three of whose things I accepted:* i.e., John Rodker's "Three Nightpieces" in the July 1917 (16–18) issue, his poem "Theatre Muet" in August 1917 (12–15), and "Incidents in the Life of a Poet" in January 1918 (31–35).

*your Bookshop:* As a service to the readers of the LR, MCA offered books for sale. The following announcement ran on page 24 of the April 1917 issue:

> We are going to have a book store in connection with The Little Review.
> This is not merely a plan to sell you books through a kind of mail order system, which we tried once before and which did not work out very well, but a regular book shop in the large front room of our office [31 West 14th Street, New York City] where you can sit by a fire and choose your books and perhaps even drink a cup of tea during your selection.
> It will be a beautiful shop to look at and it will have all the books you want; or if you are the kind of person who wants books nobody else wants we can guarantee to get them for you within half a day.
> Also we can supply mail orders promptly to any of our subscribers. By handling this part of the business directly we will avoid all the confusions and delays inherent in our former arrangement. . . .

Some of the titles listed in the May 1917 issue as being available were Joyce's *Portrait;* EP's *Gaudier-Brzeska;* Carl Sandburg's *Chicago Poems;* Maurice Hewlett's *Thorgils;* the works of Freud and Jung; John Cowper Powys' *Confessions, Suspended Judgments;* H.D.'s *Sea Garden;* and Tagore's *Reminiscences* and *Personality.*

*now that Knopf is to publish me:* Early in 1917 Alfred A. Knopf, at John Quinn's prompting, had agreed to bring out an American edition of *Lustra.* The first impression of this edition appeared in October 1917 and was limited to sixty copies for private circulation. Knopf brought out the second impression, the trade edition, in the same month.

*my first book:* i.e., *A Lume Spento.* A hundred and fifty copies of EP's book of poems were printed ("for the author") in Venice by A. Antonini in 1908. It was John Quinn, himself a devoted collector and a friend of EP's, who had paid £8 for a copy of this edition.

*first edition of "Lustra":* Donald Gallup notes the following about this edition:

> The manuscript as submitted had been set in type (by William Clowes and Sons, Ltd., London) and Ezra Pound had received page-proof, when printer and publisher (apparently frightened by the suppression in the previous year of D. H. Lawrence's *The Rainbow*) refused, on grounds of the indecorum of certain poems, to continue with the book as set. It was eventually agreed that 200 copies would be printed "almost unabridged" (i.e. omitting only "The Temperaments," "Ancient Music," "The Lake Isle," and "Pagani's November 8"). These copies, although technically not published, were in fact sold by Elkin Mathews to those who requested the unabridged text when ordering the book. For the second impression, nine additional poems were omitted and one title altered. . . .
> (*Ezra Pound: A Bibliography* 21)

See Letter 5n.

*48 pages by September:* See Letter 16n.

*W. H. Hudson:* William Henry Hudson (1841–1922), naturalist and novelist. Among his best known works are *The Purple Land* (1885), *A Crystal Age* (1887), and *Green Mansions* (1904).

*Vanderpyl:* Fritz-René Vanderpyl (b. 1876), a Dutch writer and art critic whom EP had met on a trip to Paris in the spring of 1913.

*Jules Romains:* Jules Romains was the pseudonym used by Louis Farigoule (1885–1972), a French poet, playwright, essayist, and novelist.

In 1918 EP asked Romains to be "French Editor" of the *LR* and he apparently accepted. In a letter to John Quinn dated 4 June 1918, EP quotes from a letter he has received from Romains: "Jules Romains writes his thanks for 'ouvrir si largement votre revue. Je ne demande mieux que d'être "french editor" comme vous me la proposez. Mais j'aimerais que vous me disiez en quoi au juste consisterait cette fonction, et de quoi j'aurais à m'occuper' " (*Letters,* Paige 136). Romains, however, never did contribute to the magazine although MCA continued to list him as "French Editor."

*Hueffer's best unfinished work:* See Letter 15n.

*Mercure de France:* Founded in 1890 by Alfred Vallette and a group of Symbolist writers (including Remy de Gourmont) who had contributed to the early Symbolist review *La Pléiade, Mercure de France* became, in its early years, the chief periodical to express Symbolist thought. Although it was committed to the Symbolist aesthetic, the review published original work by writers of a variety of "schools" and nationalities.

**18. TL–1.** On stationery embossed: 5, Holland Place Chambers/ Kensington. W. ⟨8⟩ [15 May 1917]

⟨May 15th⟩

Dear Miss Anderson:

⟨Please⟩ Place the following on the list of paying subscribers: s.v.p.

R. Wilenski, 10 Gray's Inn Square, Grays Inn, W.C. 1.
E.W. Sutton, 6 Carlyle Studios, Chelsea, S.W.
Miss Booth, 37 Stanhope Gdns. S.W.7.
/////
I enclose contents for July, i.e. the rest of it.

Note that the two first french poems by [T. S.] Eliot will probably go into double column. My whole aim in format at present is to get the magazine so full of meat that the unsympathetic will have to subscribe, value rec'd being more than cash required.

His (T.S.E.'s) "Hippotamus" ["The Hippopotamus"] must be in full size type, the french can be packed rather close, if necessary. My Dialogue must this time be all in full size type, ⟨I dare say its the best I've done.⟩ Lewis' "Letter" can be small type except the first two pages.

We are definitely to have ⟨the Other⟩ bunch of poems by Yeats, but I don't quite know what date they will go in. Will settle it in a few weeks time, when he gets back to London. ⟨probably for August or Sept.⟩

Proofs of my big American vol. of poems just here and marked "hurry" so I wont write much this a.m.

*two first french poems by Eliot:* "Le Directeur" and "Mélange adultère de tout." See Letter 12n.
*My Dialogue:* "Aux Étuves de Wiesbaden." See Letter 9n.
*Lewis' "Letter":* See Letter 8n.

*my big American vol. of poems:* i.e., the proof pages for the first American edition of *Lustra*. Two impressions of this edition were made. The first, which was limited to sixty copies, was for private circulation and was distributed primarily by John Quinn. The second (number of copies unknown) was pub-lished by Knopf on 16 October 1917.

**19. ALS–5.** On stationery embossed: 5, Holland Place Chambers/ Ken-sington. W. ⟨8⟩ [*This hand-written letter is a continuation of Letter 18.*] [15 May 1917]

May 15th

evening.

Dear M.C.A=

Subscription for 6 months. from Miss H. Saunders.

4 Phené St.

Chelsea. S.W.

Have spent the day correcting the proofs of Knopf's chryselephantine edi-tion of Lustra. dead with it.

This is only a note of evening meditations= Looking over my schedule for the Review. I am inclined to exhort you, IF I have over lapped my space for May. June. July. = go ahead & get the stuff in anythow. I'll pay back the pages out of Aug. Sept. Oct. if you require them. =

Only I do want.&

even need three solid numbers. —before I can make the next attempt to advance.

I sent off the July stuff via special permit. this a.m.

more anon.

Yours

Ezra Pound.

Yeats poems. second lot. mailed probably ⟨for⟩ August. but date not yet fixed.

---

P.S. ref. position of my section in magazine.

It is your magazine & I think you should keep the front half. = You will

have set up May & June before this reaches you—anyhow——so there's
not much point in my mentioning the matter.

I shan't kick up a fuss if you have put the foreign dept at
the front in either or both those numbers. only I shouldn't like you to give
away your front door yard & then wish you hadn't.

——

——

Benedicte.
Yours
E Pound

---

*Knopf's chryselephantine edition of Lustra:* See Letters 15n and 17n.

**20. TLS–3.**   On stationery embossed: 5, Holland Place Chambers/ Kensington. W. [17 May 1917]

⟨May 17th⟩

Dear Miss Anderson:

Have just rec'd long letter from John Quinn.

He seems to like you. At any rate he expresses approval
and says you are intelligent. So that's all right.

He says he has told you to keep guaranty secret, to
conceal any past or future indigence, etc.

He says he dont want the magazine on his shoulders.

Still, I think an occasional, "consultation" or whatever you
choose to call it, might do no harm. He is very much respected in the
painter's world here. He has been extremely intelligent in all the picture
buying he has done through me here.

I haven't seen Kuhn's work, or Davies' for the past few years, but
I imagine they must be good, or at least the best in N.Y.

If Quinn can get them to cooperate in the L.R. it should be
worth while.

I don't know whom else he can turn on. He has a proper and
healthy mistrust of the local-talent and the local hog-wash.

He is the busiest man in New York, and the whitest. He don't,
emphatically don't, want to be bothered. I dont think he will "interfere"

with anything. He is not of a meddlesome disposition. I think that an occasional talk with him about the magazine will, however, do none of us any harm.

Particularly he wants the connection kept secret, because he <u>dont</u> want people bringing him contributions and asking <u>him</u> to get 'em <u>accepted</u>. It is our job to keep <u>out</u> the bores and the <u>weedy</u> and washy, The Hunekers, the New Republicans[,] the SevenArty.

Glad to learn, via his letter, that copy has arrived O.K. "May stuff, and Yeats' poems."
//////////
Have I sent you memo. of following subscriptions <u>paid</u>.

A.E. Ayliffe Esq. 171 Kensington High. St. London W.8.
Miss E.A. Abbot, "A Sprig of Heather", Church St. W.8.

(Begin all subscriptions with May number, unless specially asked not to do so.)
Please put on the free list.
G.S. Street, Esq. 64 Curzon St. W.1.
send sample copy of May to
Edgar Jepson, 36 Priory Rd. Bedford Park. London W.
and to
Wm. Wadsworth, 56 Wall St. New York.

did I write before?
first three numbers, to Rev. A. Galton. Edenham, Bourne, Lincs. ⟨England⟩
Will send you £5 to cover subscriptions etc. as soon as I hear it ⟨part of my fund⟩ has been put in my American bank. Q[uinn]. says it will be on his return from Washington.

Staggered home with four huge folios in a burlap sack yesterday, result of walking about with "subscriptions" loose in my pocket. Cubic capacity 10 by 16 by 10 ½, weight uncertain, and no 'busses running. ¼ inch leather boards, and about 4000 pages. <u>Some</u> raid. The pap that Voltaire was fed on.

                                        Have already gleaned
some data about the Anabaptists that may light some dialogue of the future.

Waal, I am pleased that you and Quinn have got on together.

At least I haven't yet heard from you on Quinn, but I judge the results of the meeting were satisfactory.

I write too often to write much at a time.
This is all for the moment.

July copy has been sent you.
Quinn reports, Yeats' first lot of poems, and mss. for May. had been safely rec'd.

Yours
Ezra Pound
17–5–17

*keep guaranty secret:* See Letter 4n.

*in all the picture buying:* Following Henri Gaudier-Brzeska's untimely death in the War, Quinn had wired EP money to buy what was available of Gaudier's work. EP entered into a long series of negotiations with Sophie Gaudier-Brzeska to obtain the work for Quinn. EP had also brought Wyndham Lewis's work to the attention of Quinn, who subsequently purchased a considerable number of Lewis's paintings.

*I haven't seen Kuhn's work . . . it should be worth while:* The New York artists Walt Kuhn (1877–1949) and Arthur B. Davies (1862–1928) had been close friends of John Quinn even before the two artists were involved in founding the Association of American Painters and Sculptors in 1912. With Davies as its president and Kuhn its secretary, this group was responsible for organizing the famous Armory Show of February and March 1913, an enterprise with which Quinn also had been deeply involved. Later, Walt Kuhn and a few of his artist friends established the Penguin Club at 8 East 15th Street in New York; it was here that, in January 1917, the Vorticist Show, which Quinn and EP had arranged, was put on. See Letter 5n.

Quinn's biographer B. L. Reid indicates that Quinn had tried to interest Kuhn and Davies in taking over the "art side" of the *LR* and had organized a dinner for Kuhn, MCA, and Jane Heap where they could discuss the matter. There were, however, "mutual misgivings" and the idea was abandoned (289).

*The Hunekers:* James Gibbons Huneker (1860–1921), an American music critic, novelist, essayist, journalist, and long-standing friend of John Quinn.

*the SevenArty:* The *Seven Arts* was a monthly journal published in New York from November 1916 to October 1917. James Oppenheim was its editor with Waldo Frank and Van Wyck Brooks as associate editors.

*Staggered home with four huge folios:* EP wrote of this incident in a letter to James Joyce dated 18 May 1917 (*Pound/Joyce* 117).

**21. TLS–4.**   On stationery embossed: 5, Holland Place Chambers/ Kensington. W. [24 May 1917]

⟨May [*crossout:* 25th] 24th⟩

Dear M.C.A.

I have just finished my August editorial, and as the ink of the corrections is not yet dry I now think it is a good one.

I revised and condensed my long poem, i.e. the first three cantos of it, between Saturday 11.15 p.m. and Sunday 8 a.m. . It goes at the end of the volume Knopf is bringing out, and also runs as a serial in Poetry June, July, Aug. (At least that's what they wrote me they were doing with it.) Dont say I have revised it. I want them ⟨i.e. "Poetry"⟩ to go on with the text they've got.

I sent you my July dialogue ⟨on⟩ Poggio "Aux Etuves de Wiesbaden", some days ago.

I have also, etc. etc., this merely to let you know I am in action.

### ////

Yeats came in last evening on his way from Ireland to North Britain. He says we can have Lady Gregory's play "Hanrahan" and that it is one of the best things she has done. One act. He don't know how many pages, thinks it "would play about half an hour".

I have spent all my splurge fund for the first six months on his two lots of poems. Which, BY GORD ought to act as an announcement that the L.R. is a vurry serious magazine.

I suppose it would be worth while to go bust and get the Lady Gregory play for November. Even if it takes most of the next six months spare fund. She certainly has readers, and I should think readers who don't see the L.R.[,] and I think her name might smash it ⟨the L.R.⟩ into their attention.

People certainly should be willing to pay 15 cents for a whole play by her. Of course it will fill all my section. I suppose it will flop over and fill nearly the whole number. Ergo I will try to wait until I hear from you before I take it on.

I think it would be advisable to make the announcement as soon as possible, if you agree.

I think the Nov. number might well be simply your editorial and the Gregory play. . Your's and "jh"s [Jane Heap's] whoever that mysterious entity may be.

I'll write you as soon as I really get the mss. from Lady Gregory and see that it can be got between the covers. Then you can announce it for Nov. (if you agree) as soon as you like.

//// 

You can announce the Yeats second lot of poems for August. He thinks there are seven of 'em. My impression is that there either are or were more in the series. You might announce "⟨Another series, of⟩ At least seven poems, by Mr Yeats will appear in our Aug. number."

//// 

I have discovered a satiric work of my own which should lend life to Sept. At least I experienced a certain pleasure in perusing the half forgotten pages. (I dont mean that it is a work ten years old.)

BY the WAY, do send Yeats the edition de luxe [of the *LR*], he'll fuss and lose interest if he sees his poems on cheap paper.

Twenty five copies on thick paper are probably enough for the present, but there is a certain type of mind that worries about such things. Quant a moi, I am more concerned with what people say than with the ink it is written in.

//// 

Subscriber:

Mrs Deighton Patmore, Baylis House, Slough, Bucks. England
also I think we may assume that

May Sinclair, 1 Blenheim Rd., St. Johns Wood, N.W. 8. is a subscriber. She sent a verbal message to that effect, and is most scrupulous about payments.


a scotchman named Dismorr has sent in seven pence for a sample copy. I think he might have the de luxe, such caution ought to be rewarded. (& my great grandfather was a quaker.)
John Dismorr, Poste Restante, Cannes, France.
one copy L.R. (presumably May. number.) (I am a little inclined to send him one of last year's, but lust for a whole subscription. And fear a back number might only annoy him.)

Your ?? friend or acquaintance, Boyd, the irish pseudocritic who reviewed Joyce in New Ireland, would like to borrow some numbers, says he will pay postage both ways if I'll send them to him in Dublin. I think he may go to hell.


I liked the two articles on Joyce in "April".
Also your remarks on the competition and ⟨on⟩ Bill [William Carlos] Wil-

liams. Alas neither of the lights whom I reared from childhood seem to be possessed of much critical sense.

I am saving Lewis' volcano for October. At least according to my present schedule, that is where it will fit best. There is it, and one story, in my desk; and a longer story which he promises to get rewritten before leaving for France. Possibly a few shorter things, so he will be in the magazine fairly often for the full year. The long story will probably make two installments. Parts of it were excellent in the first version, I think he will be able to pull it together. Hope so.

more anon.

The August editorial will follow as soon as I have had time to reread it.

Yours ever

Ezra Pound

24/5/17

*August editorial:* EP's August editorial offers a commentary on three books: his own *Passages from the Letters of John Butler Yeats* and *"Noh," or Accomplishment,* as well as Joyce's *A Portrait of the Artist as a Young Man.* In the course of his commentary, EP expresses rather harsh criticism of Rabindranath Tagore and Edgar Lee Masters. He takes Tagore to task for writing in English, "a language for which he has no special talent." Tagore's first poems, EP maintains, were praised because they were effectively rendered in Bengali; in other words, "they were written in a precise and objective language, and in a metric full of interest and variety." Now, however, Tagore has been vulgarized by the "babu press" and has become the prey of "religiose nincompoops" who have focused on the "unimportant element." Tagore has become a commercial property and his "disciples may bear the blame as best they may; along with his publishers."

    Edgar Lee Masters also "stands in peril," EP insists. *The Spoon River Anthology* is good to a certain extent, but it needs rewriting: "Masters must go back and take the gobbetts of magazine cliché out of his later work" and "spend more time on *Spoon River* if he wants to last . . ." (8–11).

*the first three cantos of it:* The three cantos which conclude Knopf's edition of *Lustra* (1917) are Cantos II, III, and I, in that order. They differ considerably from their final versions. The June (113–21), July (180–88), and August (248–54) numbers of *Poetry* published other versions of these cantos.

*Lady Gregory's play "Hanrahan":* Lady Isabella Augusta Gregory (1852–1932), a close friend of W. B. Yeats, worked with Yeats in the creation of the Irish National Theatre, for whose productions she wrote many plays. "Hanrahan's Oath" was first published in the *LR* (November 1917): 6–16, 33–38. It was subsequently brought out in her *The Image and Other Plays* (London: Putnam's, 1922).

*Yeats' second lot of poems:* See Letter 24n.

*a satiric work of my own:* EP's "Stark Realism: This Little Pig Went to Market (A Search for the National Type)" appeared in the *LR* (August 1917): 16–17. The piece, a takeoff on the familiar children's rhyme, is an acid description of certain American "types." The selection was subsequently published in *Pavannes and Divisions* and in *Pavannes and Divagations.*

*Boyd, the irish pseudocritic:* Ernest Augustus Boyd (1887–1946) was born in Dublin and educated in Switzerland and Germany. A polyglot fluent in French, Italian, German, Spanish, modern Greek, and several other languages, Boyd worked as a journalist, translator, editor, biographer, and literary critic and historian. His review of Joyce's *A Portrait of the Artist as a Young Man* to which EP refers appeared in the *New Ireland* (3 March 1917).

*two articles on Joyce in "April":* In the April (1917) issue of the *LR*, Jane Heap and MCA wrote comments on Joyce's *A Portrait of the Artist as a Young Man.* Miss Heap's commentary stresses that the novel must be read as a portrait of an *artist* and not simply as one of a youth. She suggests that the story "is told the way a person in a sick room sharply remembers all the overfelt impressions and experiences of a time of fever; until the story itself catches the fever and becomes a thing more definite, closer-known, keener-felt consciousness—and of a restless oblivion of self-consciousness" (8–9). MCA maintains that this "James Joyce book is the most beautiful piece of writing and the most creative prose anywhere to be seen on the horizon to-day. . . . [It] is made of language as it will come to be used. . . . The interest in the *Portrait* is in the way its aesthetic content is presented" (9–10).

*remarks on the competition:* In the March 1916 issue of the *LR*, MCA announced a contest for "the two best short poems in free verse form" submitted to the magazine. The prize to be awarded would be $25 each to the two winners, the entries to be judged by a panel of three judges (who turned out to be Eunice Tietjens, Helen Hoyt, and William Carlos Williams). It was not until the April 1917 issue, however, that MCA announced the winners with this acerbic comment: ". . . there has never been [a poetry contest] in the history of poetry which could boast so many really bad poems. Personally I think there are not more than four or five with any suggestion of poetry in them: the rest are either involuntarily humorous . . . or pompously anachronistic. . . ." The winners of the contest turned out to be Hilda Doolittle (H.D.) for "Sea Poppies" and Maxwell Bodenheim for "Images of Friendship," their poems being the only ones for which two of the three judges had voted. Printing some of the entries along with the winning poems, MCA commented on the judges' remarks on the entries, saying of one of William Carlos Williams's choices, for example, "I think it a very trite effort" and of two of Helen Hoyt's, "These two poems are pretty awful, I think. Where are the winged words that make poetry something beyond thoughts or ideas of emotions?"

*Lewis' volcano:* Wyndham Lewis's "Cantleman's Spring-Mate," for which the October number of the *LR* was suppressed by the New York Post Office.

**22. TLS–2.**   On stationery embossed: 5, Holland Place Chambers/ Kensington. W. ⟨8⟩ [25 May 1917]

Dear M.C.A.

Subscriber:
   Fred. Etchells, co/ A.I.D.
            44 Bayley Lane, Coventry, England.
                        /// 
I enclose editorial for Aug. (first page large type, others small if necessary.). also small skit to enliven same number. Will send the Yeats poems in a week or so.

Hope the attack on Tagore won't upset you, but some one has got to do it. And all the rest are afraid. Rothenstein who brought Tagore from India comes abjectly to Yeats begging him to stop the flood of inferior stuff. Macmillans apologize but say it pays 'em. etc. etc.

   It may break up my own pleasant relations with Tagore completely, but I must pay that fee if necessary. I was told that he took ⟨very well⟩ my article in the Egoist some years ago (deploring that people made him into a sham messiah instead of treating him as a poet.)
            /// 
Masters I ⟨boomed⟩ reviewed before anyone in England. When I took Sandburgs book to the publisher to whom I had had, I think, Masters recommended (I can not recall whether I did or did not have a finger in getting him to take Masters.) Anyway Laurie who publishes Masters was fed up when I took him Sandburg (I suggested a selection not the whole Sandburg).

            He said "Bringing out another book by Masters. NO good."
            The need of shooting the artist when he has finished is still with us.

DO send me acknowledgements of all mss. when they arrived. It only needs a post card.

            Keep going. And be a comfort to [John] Quinn. ⟨He is about the best thing in America.⟩

                        Yours
                        Ezra Pound
                        25/5/1917

*editorial for August . . . skit:* See Letter 21n.
*the attack on Tagore:* See Letter 21n.
*Rothenstein who brought Tagore . . . :* Sir William Rothenstein (1872–1945)
was an English artist noted especially for his drawings. He was the official
artist of both the British and the Canadian armies during the First World
War. In his memoirs, he had this to say about Tagore's coming to England:

> I happened, in *The Modern Review,* upon a translation of a story signed
> Rabindranath Tagore, which charmed me; I wrote to Jorasanko [the family
> home of the Tagores]—were other such stories to be had? Some time afterwards
> came an exercise book containing translations of poems by Rabindranath, made
> by Ajit Chakravarty, a schoolmaster at Bolpur. The poems, of a highly mystical
> character, struck me as being still more remarkable than the story, though but
> rough translations. Meanwhile I met one of the Kooch Behar family, Promotto
> Loll Sen, a saintly man, and a Brahmo of course. He brought to our house Dr.
> Brajendranath Seal, then on a visit to London, a philosopher with a brilliant
> mind and a child-like character. They both wrote Tagore, urging him to come to
> London; he would meet, they said, at our house and elsewhere, men after his
> heart. Then news came that Rabindranath was on his way. I eagerly awaited his
> visit. At last he arrived, accompanied by two friends, and by his son. As he en-
> tered the room he handed me a note-book in which, since I wished to know more
> of his poetry, he had made some translations during his passage from India. He
> begged that I would accept them. [William Rothenstein, *Men and Memories:
> Recollections of William Rothenstein, 1900–1922,* vol. 2: 262.]

Rothenstein introduced Tagore to his London friends and arranged for the
India Society to publish a private edition of Tagore's *Gitanjali: Song-Offerings,* with an Introduction by W. B. Yeats. (The trade edition of *Gitanjali* was
published by Macmillan in November 1913; at the end of 1913, Tagore re-
ceived the Nobel Prize for Literature.)
*Macmillans apologize:* Macmillan published Tagore's subsequent books.
*article in the Egoist:* EP had reviewed Tagore's *The Gardener* in an article
entitled "Rabindranath Tagore: His Second Book into English" in *The New
Freewoman* (1 November 1913): 187–88.
*Masters I ⟨boomed⟩ reviewed:* In "Webster Ford [the pseudonym of Edgar Lee
Masters]" *The Egoist* (January 1915): 11–15, EP exclaimed, "At last! At last
America has discovered a poet. . . . At last the American West has produced
a poet strong enough to weather the climate, capable of dealing with life directly, without resonant meaningless phrases. Ready to say what he has to say,
and to shut up when he [has] said it. Able to treat Spoon River as Villon
treated Paris of 1460. The emphasis of this treatment consists in looking at
things unaffectedly."
*Laurie who publishes Masters:* The London publisher T. W. Laurie brought out
an edition of *The Spoon River Anthology* (illustrated by Oliver Herford) in
1916.

**23. TLS–1.**   On stationery embossed: 5, Holland Place Chambers/ Kensington. W. ⟨8.⟩ [1 June 1917]

June 1.

1917

Dear M.C.A.

Note following subscribers.

H.T. Tucker Esq. 38 Montpelier St. S.W. 7
Mrs H.T. Tucker                same
Miss G Hyde-Lees              same.
A[lvin]. L[angdorn]. Coburn, 9 Lower Mall, Hammersmith, London W.

///

Also assume that
Rev. Arthur Galton, Edenham, Bourne, Lincs. Eng. subscribes. I have
it by verbal message, but I think it is O.K., at least worth sending Little
Review until further notice.

Am hoping to see the May number before long.

Yours

Ezra Pound

**24. TLS–16.**   [*This letter is written on the 5, Holland Place Chambers/
Kensington. W. embossed stationery. The address has been torn from the
first page, but the subsequent pages are embossed.*] [11 June 1917]

⟨June 11th⟩
‾          Yrs. and "May number" to hand.

Chere M.:

ALL right!
ONLY don't you go wrong about [John] Quinn. Quinn made me mad the
first time I met him. (1910.). I came back on him four years later, and
since then I have spent a good deal of his money. His name does NOT spell
Tight-Wad. The £ 150 is my figure, NOT his.

I am not looking for a soft job, at least not in that way. Quinn
is not a rich man in the American sense of the word. He has what he
makes month by month, and most of it goes to the arts. I know part of
what he does, and I know somewhat of how he does it.

In the present case he is already spending enough on [Wyndham] Lewis. I've lost count but there is no danger of Lewis being in need. At any rate since I first got his drawings to Quinn I have had no need to worry about Lewis' dinners.

Quinn has spent more on other friends and acquaintance[s] of mine than I could have advised.

He is buying [James] Joyce's mss. And any how Joyce is not in need at the moment.

Q. had never heard of [T. S.] Eliot. and Eliot is so far as he is concerned an untried quantity. Eliot has hardly printed anything. "Prufrock" advance copy just came yesterday. And GOD DAMN it Eliot's father is head of the brick trust and he ought to keep T.S.E. instead of leaving him to me, Quinn and his own endeavours. That's an aside. I dare say there is no harm done by these little family disagreements and establishments of independence.

From the editorial point of view Eliot is very uncertain not as to quality but as to getting his mss. in.

Quinn wanted me to take £120 a year for myself in connection with the Egoist a year or so ago.

The point is that if I accept more than I need I at once become a sponger, and I at once lose my integrity. By doing the job for the absolute minimum I remain respectable and when I see something I want I can ax [ask] for it. I mean to say, as things stand I can ask for money when Joyce finishes his next novel, or if Hueffer ever gets his real book finished.

If I began by blowing 5000 dollars and did no more than I shall now do with 750 I should feel a mucker and there would be nothing ahead.

My whole position and the whole backing up of my statement that the artist is "almost" independent goes with doing the thing as nearly as possible without "money".

ALSO I want to deliver the goods. If I see more good stuff than I can buy, it is up to me to complain.

I think also Quinn may know more than you think. He works very hard and I think rather excitedly and his talk after hours may not have the precision a sentence would have if a man had nothing to do but write art criticism, and if he took a day to a paragraph. But he is said to be a rare hand at getting the best drawings out of a pile.

At any rate, take a bit of time before you finally make up your mind. I wish there were one or two more like him.

I dont know whether his talk about art is like all American talk about art, but his act about art is a damn sight different.

That's that.

---

All right let Mrs Turner and Lady Cunard have the gilded label variety. I hope it has gone to them already.

First of month, and regularity of publication, certainly desirable.

It [Walt] Kuhn is providing the paper (this plus yr. remark about no paper bill.) I judge Q[uinn]. is already adding to original "estimate". ??????

Of course I want to go to 64 pages just as soon as it can be managed.

The Lady Gregory play would be a good thing to start the swell on, I was planning to have it (if it is good,) about November. Xmas. would do.

I agree with you solid about the rest of your punches.

The LaForgue [Jules Laforgue] translation is of no importance, BUT a magazine, and each number of it[,] has to have form, just as a poem or a novel, or a book of poems. The Egoist has foozled along and never taken proper rank largely through its stupidity in never recognizing that it was a "paper", first a weekly, then fortnightly, now monthly., all of these varieties must have a form.

i.e. a certain amount of contents, certain variety per issue etc. ⟨in a suitable order.⟩

I needed a poem, a poem not like the current verse in every other monthly, and that translation was the best I could lay hand on at the moment.

I have since done better. It would have been a mistake to do as most new magazines do, i.e. print all their good stuff in the first number and then decline, fade, deliquesce.

The [Iris] Barry and [John] Rodker stuff is not a compromise but a bet. I stake my critical position, or some part of it, on a belief that both of them will do something. I am not risking much, because I have seen a lot of their mss. The Barry has done the draft of a novel, ⟨nearer Joyce in spots than any female established novelist has yet to come.⟩ and it has the chance of being literature. Rodker has convinced me at last, that he "has it in him".

Part, and by no means the smallest part of the glory of the first year and a half of the English Review, is that in that time [Ford Madox] Hueffer printed not only Anatole France, Swinburne, Tho. Hardy, Henry James but also work by all the young men who have since come off. Lewis, [D. H.] Lawrence, Cannon [Cannan], myself etc. this in 1909.

Lawrence never would have been heard from if F.M.H. hadn't routed him out of a board school in Croyden [Croydon].

This sort of thing builds up a certain sort of loyalty about a periodical, which is well worth while.

I dont think the three things of Rodker's and the page of Barry will do us any harm. At any rate I have said I would print 'em.

You can throw 'em out on grounds of my over-running my space, but I should then have to use 'em at some later date, or hem haw, and muddle.

I am glad you dislike 'em. On the other hand I want the full free run of all I.B. and J.R.'s mss. for the next five or ten years. One can only have that by accepting a little copy now and then.

So I am not absolutely mad, in this matter. The magazine is to go on after the first year, and one must have les jeunes. I dont expect to take any more Barry until she finishes her novel, and that probably wont fit.

Rodker is a different proposition. He ought to be up to regulation standard in a few years time.

He will go farther than Richard [Aldington], though I dont expect anyone to believe that statement for some time. He has more invention, more guts. His father did not have a library full of classics, but he will learn. He is in the midst of his tribulations.

### ///

About papa Yeats [John Butler Yeats]. I certainly shouldn't trust him to write an article, and should not think he could write for publication at all. I have however, I believe, made an excellent book ⟨Cuala Press. now out.⟩ by excerpting passages from his letters to W.B.Y., written without any thought of their being printed.

And I think there is more marrow to be got from them. At least I am going to have a try. ⟨His unselected ramble. NO.⟩

### ////

About printing a disclaimer of Barry and Rodker. Certainly do it if you think best. ⟨But⟩ I think it would only call undue attention to them. One glides over the "John Hall" [i.e., EP's Laforgue translation] in May, without much notice. At any rate I'm glad you object. But I think Poggio ["Aux Étuves de Wiesbaden, A.D. 1451"] will carry the one page of I.B. and that the Yeats poems in Aug. and Lewis['s] "Inferior Religions" in Sept, will carry the brief Rodkers. And that in three or four years time I shall be justified for having given them an airing. It is not as if I hadn't seen a lot of their stuff, or followed the sight of the mss. by a personal investigation of the authors.

They are neither of them STUPID, blockheaded as Flint and Lawrence are stupid and blockhead[ed].

Lawrence had less showing above the water line when Hueffer took him up, than Rodker has now. And certainly Hueffer has been justified. Much as Lawrence annoys me, and inferior as he is to Joyce.

I dont know whether it is possible to work with Lawrence. I got some stories of his printed five years ago. Others were "unprintable". I shall try to rake them out when I have time and space. He is better in short stories than in a novel, he has less room for barrocco [blend of *baroque* and *rococo?*] and getting overloaded with ornament.

He will probably want an exorbitant price. Lewis' battery is in action. Joyce is in hospital. Eliot can not be depended on to have stuff in at a given date. The french can not be got at until after the war. [Jean] D̄eBosschère is here, or rather in the country, but he has a contract to illustrate three books for Heineman and that is taking all his time.

HOWEVER I am not stranded for copy. I have four months of Lewis, at least, besides what I have already sent you. Still hope for second "EEl-drop" in time for Aug. though Yeats, will carry that number O.K.

/////

Richard [Aldington] is back from the front, recommended for commission. He and H.D. were out to dinner on Thursday. As they have both been contributing to the L.R. I judge they are part of your section of the magazine, and wont interfere. I think you might get some stuff from them on the grounds that you want the "Hellenists" ⟨I think they will rise to this.⟩ to beat out the "other section", at any rate, stir 'em up.

We want 'em. I cant see that we want any of the rest of the soft-boiled imagists. i.e. apart from Lawrence' harder short stories if I can get at them.

I think a gentle rivalry between Hellenism and E.P.ism might be healthy within the family. (and then, hang it all, I did bring out the first Imagist anthology and even write one or two of the poems. And, worse luck, include[d] Amy [Lowell] despite the protests of the famille Aldington.)

Are there, by the way, any more copies of ⟨1914⟩ "Des Imagistes" on sale by Boni. If so you might put em on sale in your book shop, though the BRUTES have never paid up.

If this little book is out of print. OR even if it is in print, it is probably time for me to make a new arrangement of a contemporary anthology for America. taking the best of it ⟨Des Imagistes⟩, and of the Catholic Anthology, (which I note you have not in your list,) and a few other poems. . I wish you'd let me know, QUIETLY, what you think of an anthology, possibly published by Huebsch or Knopf, (mention it first to Knopf, as he is my publisher) and more or less under the aegis of the L.R. . A SMALL book, in contrast to the voluminous "New Poetry" of our confrères or consoeurs.

I wonder could you sell off a few of my "Provença", pub. Small Maynard, Boston, in the year 1. or perhaps you'd rather not. There is also The Spirit of Romance, Dent and Co. and the "Noh" that Knopf is importing. and "Lustra Etc." which Knopf is about to do.

AND ⟨Frederic⟩ Manning's "Scenes and Portraits" pub. John Murray, 51 Albermarle St. London W.1.

And possibly a few of the second number of Blast to be had from Lane. ???

Joyce's "Dubliners" ⟨(Grant Richards, pub.). or ?Huebsch import.) and his "Chamber Music", (the latter pub. by Mathews.)

F.M. Hueffers Collected Poems. also his Soul of London, Heart of the Country, Duckworth. I think.

And his Ancient Lights or Memoirs of a Yooung [Young] Man. as I think the American edtn. is called.

//// 

I am glad you are up to all necessary clerical work, and that you wont get messed into Washington Sq. the wrong side.

YES the Seven Arts is slop. YES. and the New Republic is dust, with an admixture of dung, also dust dry.

The gold paper label is excellent. Havent yet had time to find printer's errors.

⟨Glad⟩ the editorial suits. Sorry you dont like Jodindra ["Jodindranath Mawhwor's Occupation"], but I must get out of the big stick habit, and begin to put my prose stuff into some sort of possibly permanent form, not merely into saying things which everybody will believe in three years and take as a matter of course in ten.


I.E. articles which can be reduced to "Joyce is a writer, GODDAMN your eyes, Joyce is a writer, I tell you Joyce etc etc. Lewis can paint, Gaudier [Henri Gaudier-Brzeska] knows a stone from a milk-pudding. WIPE your feet !!!!!

For the last five years I have been doing it. And it is a good thing that some one DID do it. Otherwise it wouldn't have been done. etC.

/ / / / / / /

Please send exchange of Little Review to

Holbrook Jackson: Editor.

"To-Day"

10 Adam St. Adelphi. London W.C.2.

/ / / / / / / /

To return: £150 dont measure what Quinn has done and is doing for Joyce, Lewis, and myself. It is what is going into one definite matter.

He is turning cash onto the others and he has put in a lot of time for me, bothers that have saved me bother, and mean more from a man as busy as he is.

Also it is my figure and not his. Eliot is untried, so far as Quinn is concerned,

AND I hope the subscription list will have some effect on your two [you two, i.e., MCA and Jane Heap],

AND after a few more numbers are out, we will be in a much stronger position.

Nearly enough cash on the subs. to date here to pay for increase in format. on one issue,

Dont know whether you have "taken anything".


There is the bother about not being able to import. Q[uinn]. hasn't yet sent the cash. At least it hasn't arrived, you shall have cheque as soon as I know the stuff is in my American bank. There's no use sending it until there is a chance of its being honoured.

/ / / / / /

Keep on with the "punching bag". And make the "vague reasons for dis-like" ⟨into⟩ definite reasons.

/ / /

I think I have said enough re/Barry and Rodker. I dont believe the things will do any real harm, AND I want the future of the two jeunes. I dont think it is precisely a compromise. It may be a mistake. At any rate they have had my word on it, and I've got to go on in error ⟨or out of it.⟩

AND I am glad you dislike it. Let us hope I'll improve. At least I have arranged Rodker's stuff crescendo, the least important first, and the last at least quite readable.

The second thing has a functional place between me and Lewis in Sept. . I come back to the question of form. "Personae", and "Exultations" succeeded because they were books. especially "Personae". When I rearranged "Provenca" for Small Maynard, selecting the best as I thought from both books, I lost the form,. The stuff I ⟨omitted⟩ wasnt as good as what I left in, BUT I had lost something or other. The punch was gone, The result was less convincing.

This is not a plea for bad stuff, OR for compromise. Simply certain elements must be combined in a book, or in a number of a magazine or of a paper. There must be good A.1. stuff, , all the elements ought to be A.1., but at any rate they can not be wholly lacking, and one must indicate them in some way.

Sic: May needed a poem. The lack in May, can not be remedied in June. . Sept. being in the main harsh, acid, satiric needs a certain amount of atmosphere, or "beauty" (whatever that is.).

I dont want muck any more than you do, nor rubbish, but it is a defect, even a defect of ART not to make each number of the magazine an entity; an indication of the necessity of a certain number of elements in one's scheme of things.

1. We are going to be THE only magazine.
2. We can have seven poems by Yeats in June AND in August. (tho the Aug. poems have been hid away for years, because the glorious lady didn't die on schedule[d] time.) BUT we can not have seven poems of Yeats in every number, because they are NOT, neither is there any other W.B. Yeats.
3. Eliot cant write seven poems a month.
   even in Yeats' off months.
4. Nothing can be got from France for some time. At least one cant depend on anything.
5. Common decency, (and cash reasons), but even more common decency demand that I should not throw over Poetry until there are worse rows and disagreements than any that have yet happened.
   Endeavours? NO. Experiments, Yes.

I think the Laforgue may pass as an experiment.

Barry, ⟨this lot⟩ I admit is an endeavour. Peccavi. but print it. I wont do it again.

Rodker is definitely experiment, at least the two things to come. And I am at last convinced that he has the guts to do something, and should definitely be backed, and helped as much as an editor or critic can help a young chap with lots of folly still in his system.

/////

I have at least manouvred [maneuvered] into a position where I shall be able to go through all [Arthur] Waley's translations from the Chinese. I know there is excellent stuff there, BUT if I had to act like a normal editor I should simply lose the man, by the necessity of refusing five mss. running.

Alas, A l a s, A LAS, my own contribution to Sept. will make you curse the day I was born.

Eliot has taken it away to curse and spit upon. All your maledictions await me.

And still it must happen. Once. Once only,  . In the Sept. number.

Under the aegis of Lewis['s] best piece of prose. I'd rather you put in your note of protest then, than that you should jump on the young. Especially at the moment when I am sending them away to grow up.

I wish you'd diagnose Jodindra more definitely, more acidly.

The only criticism I have had is that I ought to stop with "His life was not unduly ruffled".

For the rest the auditors have either chortled with glee or else groaned. Neither of which constitutes a critical formulation.

It is greasy and unpleasant, like most hindoos, but then ..... that is its function.

I wonder what Joyce will make of it. Yeats groaned. The Eliot family went into hysterics, gleefully, Lewis grinned and said there are a number of backgrounds which ought to be so exploited. The Captain quoted the Koran, and our acquaintance was solidified.

///

I think the ⟨May⟩ number LOOKS O.K. the lack of a de luxe dont in the least matter. The gilt [label] is excellent and distinctive.

///

The poor Laforgue, p. 12. should read "Yes, divine, these eyes"

that correction might be noted in June or July. it is rather a bad misprint. (or was it [in] the mss.?)

Do all women (nasty phrase) but do all women loathe Laforgue even in
the original. Pourtant he is a very great artist.

I wonder if the beastly Jodindra goes too fast on paper, and if it is only
good when read with very retarded utterance (as I read it). If that's the
bloody matter.

Still the first ⟨paragraph⟩ in section 3. is, yes, hang it all, IS
an excellent paragraph, and the fourth sentence an excellent sentence.
The beginning of that section, at least, is decently written.

////

Special offer, re/Joyce, back cover, excellent idea.

///

I believe the sentence "The boy was about 12 years of age" is also well
placed. and indeed that the whole ⟨paternal⟩ scene with the boy is not bad.

Oh well, passons. What the thing needs may be
a slowing up of the prose cadence in the opening. That is the devil. If
prose wont read aloud it is bad, and if it will read aloud it is very apt
to be wrong. DAMN[.]

///

I think that answers most of ⟨the points in⟩ your letter.

Certainly dont send more than three numbers to any of the blighters whose
names I sent you. A few are worth three numbers, the rest can subscribe
at once or go to hell. If they subscribe at the end of the three months, it
ought to be counted from May. (though this might peeve 'em.)

Who the devil is "jh" [Jane Heap]? Sherwood Anderson? or what? I
liked his, her, on Joyce in April.

And what about your remark re/ Alice Henderson and the permanent
staff, months ago.

And also who is doing what, if anything, in America.

Why is Gibson on the book store list? Is he any good? (I dont mind, I am
simply curious.) Or is Hewlett, since the early things, the short prose?

Hewlett is a nice chap, and concerned for the comfort of his
friends. Gibson has bored me, bored me. Coram, in person. I mean.

I dont want 'em put off the shop shelf. I only want to "locate"
our points of view.

And is anything to be got from Powys or his friends the Louis Wilkinsons.

Yours

E.

Ezra Pound

11 June 1917

*Quinn made me mad:* EP had met John Quinn in New York on an August afternoon in 1910 when both of them were part of a group (which also included John Butler Yeats and the artist John Sloan) that went out to the amusement park at Coney Island. Why Quinn made EP "mad" at this initial meeting is not apparent. The two had had no further contact until 1915, when Quinn read an article which EP had written for *The New Age* of January 21 in which EP complained about "American collectors buying autograph MSS. of William Morris, faked Rembrandts and faked Van Dykes. . . ." Quinn, suspecting that he was the model for EP's attack, wrote to him, taking exception to the unfair characterization. In his reply to Quinn on 8 March 1915, EP's only reference to their meeting five years earlier is benign enough: "I have still a very clear recollection of Yeats père on an elephant (at Coney Island), smiling like Elijah in the beatific vision, and of you plugging away in the shooting gallery. And a very good day it was" (*Letters,* Paige 52).

*The £150 is my figure:* For an explanation of Quinn's backing of the *LR* see Letters 4n and 7n.

*spending enough on Lewis:* Quinn had bought from the paintings and drawings assembled for the Vorticist Show in New York (1916) a considerable number of Lewis's works. On 19 August 1916, he had spent £300 for twenty-four drawings and water colors and a week later spent £75 for eight additional works. Again, early in 1917, Quinn paid £100 for Lewis's *Kermesse* and *Plan of War* and £61 for a group of drawings (see Reid 254 and 293).

*He is buying Joyce's mss.:* Quinn bought the manuscript of *A Portrait of the Artist as a Young Man,* a purchase that involved a complicated set of negotiations. For a detailed explanation of and the correspondence surrounding these negotiations see Appendix B in *Pound/Joyce* 287–300.

*"Prufrock" advance copy:* Unknown to Eliot, EP had borrowed money to cover the cost of printing the Egoist edition of *Prufrock and Other Observations* (1917). The contents of this edition were subsequently included in Knopf's edition of Eliot's *Poems* (1920).

*Eliot's father . . . brick trust:* Eliot's father, Henry Ware Eliot, was president of the Hydraulic-Press Brick Company of St. Louis. Henry Eliot, contrary to EP's implication, did provide his son with a small (and, apparently, insufficient) allowance until 1919, the year in which the elder Eliot died.

*Joyce finishes his next novel:* i.e., *Ulysses.*

*Hueffer . . . finished:* i.e., *Women and Men.* See Letter 15n.

*If Kuhn is providing the paper . . . "estimate":* B. L. Reid tells of the following episode: "On November 1 [1917] Walt Kuhn telephoned to say that the editors [MCA and Jane Heap] had just been in to see him at the Penguin Club and begged $30 to take their new number to the press; Kuhn had 'practically promised' the money, and so of course it fell to Quinn to send up the $30, by messenger" (289–90). Reid's information comes from an unpublished letter of Quinn's to EP dated 1 November 1917. Given the June date on EP's letter and the November date on Quinn's, we can see that, on more than one occasion, MCA and Jane Heap received additional aid for their magazine from Quinn through Walt Kuhn acting as an intermediary.

*Lady Gregory play:* See Letter 21n.

*The LaForgue translation:* i.e., "Pierrots: Scène courte mais typique (After the 'Pierrots' of Jules LaForgue)," which EP signed "John Hall," in the May 1917 issue of the *LR* (11–12). This poem was later reprinted in *Pavannes and Divisions,* in *Personae: The Collected Shorter Poems of Ezra Pound,* and in *Ezra Pound: Translations.* See Letter 8.

*Barry and Rodker stuff:* See Letters 10n and 17n.

*The Barry . . . a novel:* Perhaps EP is referring to the manuscript of Iris Barry's novel *Splashing into Society* (New York: E. P. Dutton, 1923).

*the glory of . . . the English Review:* See Letter 16n.

*Cannon:* Gilbert Cannan (1884–1955) was an English novelist, dramatist, and critic. Cannan's literary importance rests mainly upon his work as a novelist. His novels include *Peter Homunculus* (1909), *Devious Ways* (1910), *Round the Corner* (1913), *Mendel* (1916), *Time and Eternity* (1919), *Pugs and Peacocks* (1920), and *The House of Prophecy* (1924).

*Lawrence never would . . . in Croyden:* In the summer of 1909, Jessie Chambers, D. H. Lawrence's long-time friend from Eastwood, sent Ford Madox Ford the manuscripts of several of Lawrence's poems and his story "Odour of Chrysanthemums." At the time, Lawrence was teaching at the Davidson Road School, Croydon, South London, and Ford was editing *The English Review.* Ford immediately recognized Lawrence's ability and sent a letter to Jessie Chambers saying he found Lawrence's work interesting. In the November 1909 issue of the *Review,* Ford published six pages of Lawrence's poems, an event which marked Lawrence's debut as a published writer. Ford also introduced Lawrence to a number of his literary friends and convinced Heinemann, the London publisher, to accept Lawrence's *The White Peacock* for publication.

As to the circumstances surrounding Lawrence's leaving the Davidson Road School, Ford's role is not so clear. Lawrence had become seriously ill with pneumonia in the fall of 1911, an illness which forced him into bed until late in December. He then took a leave of absence to convalesce, but he eventually resigned in March 1912. No doubt his introduction to London played a role in his decision to leave Croydon, but his poor health and his general dissatisfaction with teaching must also have influenced his decision.

*an excellent book: Passages from the Letters of John Butler Yeats: Selected by Ezra Pound.*

*Flint:* English poet and translator, Frank Stewart Flint (1885–1960). He was one of the group of London Imagist poets, and EP included five of his poems in *Des Imagistes* (1914).

*I got some stories . . . ago:* The *Smart Set* published the following stories by
D. H. Lawrence: "The Christening" (February 1914), "The Shadow in the
Rose Garden" (March 1914), and "The White Stocking" (October 1914).

*DeBosschère is here . . . all his time:* Jean de Bosschère illustrated the following books for Heinemann: *Beasts and Men: Folk Tales Collected in Flanders
and Illustrated by Jean de Bosschère* (1918); *Christmas Tales of Flanders*
(1917); and *The City Curious: Illustrated by the Author and Retold in
English by F. Tennyson Jesse* (1920).

*first Imagist anthology: Des Imagistes: An Anthology,* ed. Ezra Pound.

*Catholic Anthology: Catholic Anthology: 1914–1915,* ed. Ezra Pound.

*"New Poetry":* The *New Poetry: An Anthology,* ed. Harriet Monroe and Alice
Corbin Henderson (New York: Macmillan, 1917). This 404-page anthology
contained twenty poems by EP.

*"Provença":* Provença: *Poems Selected from Personae, Exultations, and Canzionere of Ezra Pound* (Boston: Small, Maynard and Company, 1910). A second impression of this book was issued by Small, Maynard early in 1917.

*The Spirit of Romance:* Ezra Pound, *The Spirit of Romance: An Attempt to
Define Somewhat the Charm of the Pre-Renaissance Literature of Latin
Europe* (London: J. M. Dent & Sons, 1910).

*"Noh" that Knopf is importing:* In June 1917, Knopf issued *"Noh," or Accomplishment,* the American issue of the London edition (of the same title)
brought out by Macmillan in January 1917.

*"Lustra Etc.":* Lustra *of Ezra Pound with Earlier Poems.*

⟨*Frederic*⟩ *Manning's "Scenes and Portraits":* Frederic Manning, *Scenes and
Portraits* (London: John Murray, 1909).

*second number of Blast:* The second was also the last issue of *BLAST: Review
of the Great English Vortex,* Wyndham Lewis's Vorticist magazine. It was published in London in July 1915 by John Lane.

*Joyce's "Dubliners":* James Joyce's *Dubliners* was first published in London by
Grant Richards (1914). In 1916, Huebsch brought the sheets to New York
and published an American edition which was subsequently reissued in
1917. Joyce's *Chamber Music,* which had been published in London by
Elkin Mathews (1907), was brought out by Huebsch in New York in 1918.

*F. M. Hueffers . . . is called:* The editions to which EP refers are Ford Madox
Ford's *Collected Poems* (London: M. Goschen, 1913; London: M. Secker,
1916); *The Soul of London: A Survey of a Modern City* (London: Duck-
worth, 1911); *The Heart of the Country* (London: Duckworth, 1911); and
*Ancient Lights and Certain New Reflections, Being the Memories of a Young
Man* (London: Chapman & Hall, 1911). *Ancient Lights* was published in
New York under the title *Memories and Impressions, A Study in Atmosphere*
(Harper & Brothers, 1911).

*Seven Arts:* Edited by James Oppenheim, this little magazine was published
monthly in New York from November 1916 through October 1917. See
Letter 20n.

*New Republic:* See Letter 13n.

*when I rearranged "Provença":* For the details on EP's rearrangement of the
contents of *Provença,* see Stock 92–93 and Gallup, *Ezra Pound: A Bibliography* 11–12.

*the glorious lady:* Mabel Beardsley, the artist Aubrey Beardsley's sister. The series of poems to which EP is referring is Yeats's "Upon a Dying Lady," first published in the *LR* and simultaneously in the *New Statesman* in August 1917. The series was subsequently included in *The Wild Swans at Coole, Other Verses and a Play* published by the Cuala Press in November 1917. The poems had actually been written between 1912 and 1914. For obvious reasons, however, Yeats withheld them until after Mabel Beardsley, who had been diagnosed in 1912 as having cancer, had died in 1916.

*Peccavi:* Latin, "I have sinned."

*the two things to come:* "Theatre Muet," published in the August 1917 issue (12–15), and "Incidents in the Life of a Poet," not published until the January 1918 issue (31–35). MCA had already seen Rodker's "Three Nightpieces" (published in July 1917) and, apparently, didn't care much for them.

*Waley's translations:* See Letters 12n and 32n.

*contribution to Sept.:* "L'Homme Moyen Sensuel," published in the September issue (8–16). In a note printed along with this poem, EP explains the following:

> It is through no fault of my own that this diversion was not given to the reader two years ago; but the commercial said it would not add to their transcendent popularity, and the vers-libre fanatics pointed out that I had used a form of terminal consonance no longer permitted, and my admirers (*j'en ai*), ever nobly desirous of erecting me into a sort of national institution, declared the work "unworthy" of my mordant and serious genius. (9)

*The Captain:* Captain Guy Baker (*c.*1874–1918), a close friend of Wyndham Lewis. While recovering from an illness in 1914, Lewis had met Baker—a native of Gloucestershire, a wealthy professional soldier, and a former Indian Army officer—at the London restaurant Tour Eiffel, where each took his meals. Baker subsequently purchased a number of Lewis's early drawings which he left, when he died in the influenza epidemic of 1918, to the Victoria and Albert Museum. Lewis modeled Guy Butcher in *Tarr* after Guy Baker.

*The poor Laforgue . . . a bad misprint:* The *LR* had printed this line: "I thought: Yes, divine, these yes, but what exists/ Behind them?"

*the first paragraph . . . decently written:* The first paragraph of the third section reads (note fourth sentence):

> As to Jodindranath's thoughts and acts after Mohon had left him, I can speak with no definite certainty. I know that my friend was deeply religious; that he modeled his life on the Shatras and somewhat on the Sutra. To the Kama Sutra he had given minute attention. He was firmly convinced that one should not take one's pleasure with a woman who was a lunatic, or leperous [*sic*], or too white, or too black, or who gave forth an unpleasant odor, or who lived an ascetic life, or whose husband was a man given to wrath and possessed of inordinate power. These points were to him a matter of grave religion.

*Special offer, re/Joyce . . . . :* As an incentive for subscribing to the *LR*, MCA, "through the courtesy of Mr. Huebsch," offered to new subscribers or to those who would renew their subscriptions, a package price of $2.50 for both the subscription (normally $1.50) and Joyce's novel *A Portrait of the Artist as a Young Man* (normally $1.50 also).

*the sentence . . . well placed:* This sentence appears in the opening paragraph of the fourth section of "Jodindranath Mawhwor's Occupation":

> Upon the day following, as Jodindranath was retiring for his mid-day repose, his son entered the perfumed apartment. Jodindra closed the book he had been reading. The boy was about twelve years of age. Jodindra began to instruct him, but without indicating what remarks were his own and what derived from ancient authority. He said:—

*I liked . . . Joyce in April:* See Letter 21n.

*your remark re/ Alice Henderson:* Alice Corbin Henderson (1881–1949) was associate editor of *Poetry* (see Letter 36n). Since MCA's letters to EP have not survived, it is not possible to determine what this remark might have been.

*Why is Gibson . . . bored me:* The *LR*'s bookstore offered for sale *Livelihood: Dramatic Reveries* (New York: Macmillan, 1917) by Wilfred Wilson Gibson (1878–1962) and *Thorgils* (New York: Dodd, Mead, 1917; London: Ward, Lock, 1917) by Maurice Henry Hewlett (1861–1923).

*the Louis Wilkinsons:* Louis Umfreville Wilkinson (1881–1966), a staff lecturer at Oxford, Cambridge, and London universities, was a cofounder of the University Lecturers Association in New York. The author of a number of novels, Wilkinson also contributed articles to *The New Age,* the *Forum,* and the *Outlook,* and edited *Letters of John Cowper Powys to Louis Wilkinson, 1935 to 1956* (London: Macdonald, 1958).

At the time of this letter, Wilkinson was married to Frances Gregg (1884–1941), herself a minor poet who contributed poems and short prose to *Poetry, Others, The New Freewoman, The Egoist,* the *Forum,* the *Smart Set,* the *Adelphi,* and other periodicals. She had been the girlhood friend of H.D. and of EP, who often called her "The Egg." Gregg was killed during the bombing of Plymouth, England, in the Second World War.

**25. TLS–2.** On stationery embossed: 5, Holland Place Chambers/ Kensington. W. ⟨8⟩ [12 June 1917]

⟨12–6–17⟩

Dear M.C.A.

Please note subscriber:
Mrs Wallis, 17 Campden Hill Mansions, London W. 8.

////

2.

Irritations:

IF that brute [T. S.] Eliot don't finish and turn in his second installment of his blasted Eeldrop dialogue in time for Aug., ⟨Please⟩ SLAM in this "Theatre Muet" of [John] Rodker's.

It has its merit, and
anyway is the only thing that will fit the number. I've my List of Books
and my short smack. I cant put in anything more of my own. "Noh" play
is too soft to go with Yeats. Lewis story too long. His essay must go in
Sept. as the main feature.

Order of contents for Aug.
1. Yeats seven poems
2. List of Books by E.P.
3. Rodker. the little prose things
   already sent,

3a.                 then the Theatre Muet, put the lot under
one heading as "Sketches by John Rodker".

(OF course If Eliot does finish in time or if I find something
else in the next day or two I will write, and the Theatre Muet can wait
till Sept, as I had intended. I wanted it to be buffer between Lewis' "Inferior Religions" and my own "L'Homme Moyen Sensuel".)

4. Stark Realism, by E.P.

///////

The short Rodker must precede the "Theatre", it mustnt be left out, to
"hang over us".

I have just written to [D. H.] Lawrence, and ⟨to⟩ Lady Gregory. I must
get some stuff in reserve and not be left suspended on Eliot's undependable
volition.

Hang it all the kid's ⟨J.R.⟩ got something in his "Theatre", as he had
in "Fear" in my Catholic Anthology. Perhaps he will show better having
his two things together.

However Eliot ought to have finished his dialogue. He has had reasonable time, ⟨considering it was originally planned for June⟩ and I have kept
off doing a modern dialogue because he was supposed to be doing them.

Ora pro nobis.

yours
Ezra
Ezra Pound
12–6–1917

*brute Eliot don't finish:* The second (and last) installment of Eliot's dialogue,
   "Eeldrop and Appleplex, II: The Passion for Experience," was not published
   until September.
*my List of Books:* See Letter 21n.
*my short smack:* i.e., "Stark Realism." See Letter 21n.

*with Yeats:* with W. B. Yeats's poem sequence "Upon A Dying Lady." See
Letters 17n and 24n.
*His essay:* "Inferior Religions." See Letter 16n.
*The little prose things:* "Three Nightpieces." See Letter 10n.
*Ora pro nobis:* Latin, "Pray for us."

**26. TLS–2.**   On stationery embossed: 5, Holland Place Chambers/ Kensington. W. [16 June 1917]

June 16.
========

Dear M.C.A.

Lady Gregory's play has come. Yeats was right in saying
that it has some of her best writing in it. It is 27 pages of type script, but
that will compress into 18 of print, especially if one prints the
CHARACTER:   Speech, on the same line, fairly close.

We'll be able to contain it in November, with ⟨our⟩ 48 or 64 pages.
AND it ought to do us some good. I will send it along as soon as D.
[Dorothy Shakespear Pound, EP's wife] and one or two people have had
time to look through it.

Please send her the magazine, May and June numbers together,
Lady Gregory, Coole Park, Gort, Co. Galway, Ireland.
Also:
Six months subscription to
Miss Shepeler    266 King's Road, Chelsea,
London S.W. 3.

I think
I did send you notice of subscriber:
Mrs Wallis    17 Campden Hill Mansions, W.8.

Only my copy ⟨of May⟩ and [John] Rodkers have arrived to date.

I suppose the rest are coming in time.

I don't think one should announce Lady G's play before August, as it is

for the November number. Indeed Sept. would be perhaps the better time
to begin the announcement.

I believe May Sinclair's name as subscriber has been sent you twice? . i.e.
She has subscribed through the poetry book shop instead of through me.
I took her ⟨message⟩ that she was going to subscribe to mean that she was
sending me her subscription. She now writes she has ordered the magazine
and back numbers through the P.B.S.

It dont matter, she'll help advertise and a spare copy of May
or June sent her wont do any damage.

avanti

yours

Ezra

Ezra

Pound

16–6–'17

*Lady Gregory's play:* "Hanrahan's Oath." See Letter 21n.
*the poetry book shop:* The Poetry Bookshop (35 Devonshire Street, Theobalds
  Road, London, W.C.) had published the English edition of *Des Imagistes:
  An Anthology* in April 1914.


**27. TLS–3.** On stationery embossed: 5, Holland Place Chambers/ Kensington. W. ⟨8.⟩ [21 June 1917]

⟨June 21st⟩

Dear M.C.A.

Three days ago I committed my first act of editorial cowardice. I
sent [John] Rodker's translation of a [Jules] Laforgue play to another
magazine. I wish I had not done so. But I cant reverse the act until they
have had time to reject it. Besides you would probably have hated the play.
Nevertheless its excellence is born in upon me more strongly as my memory of it matures. IF they reject it, I shall probably send it AT you.

I have also been through a pile of J.B.Yeats' later letters, and doubt if
they are suited to magazine use. THOUGH the book done from the earlier
ones is an excellent book. Both I and the Times reviewer, and "A.E." and
Orage say so, and god knows that is [a] divergent set of opinions.

Mrs Eliot has just been in; says T.S.E. [T. S. Eliot] has done no work
for weeks, that he returns from the bank, falls into a leaden slumber and
remains therein until bedtime. It is extremely annoying that he has to waste
his time earning a living. (However dont despair, something will get itself
done about it.)

[James] Joyce, as before said, is incapacitated.
HOWEVER, there is the Lady Gregory play ["Hanrahan's Oath"] ⟨for
November⟩, and the excellent [Ford Madox] Hueffer [*Women & Men*], to
begin in Dec. or Jan, and keep ON. And there is enough [Wyndham] Lewis
to run till April or May, skipping a month now and then.


Various people seem pleased with the May number, and say they have
"read every word of it".

I dare say [W. B.] Yeats will turn out a few more poems before
the end of the year, and Eliot has several on the way, which even the bank
will not, I presume, utterly stop.

I am going on with the "Imaginary Letters", so as to keep the
series alive till Lewis can take it up again. (I shall write from "Villerant"
to "Mrs Burn".[)] Or rather I have done the first three of my series, and
have a fourth in my head. The first is a condensation of two essays or
editorials, but in the second I have managed better and have the "letter
character" more marked. The matter in the first letter is packed tighter
than it could be in an editorial, however, so there is that much gained.

I am impatient for the arrival of the June number. perhaps
senselessly so.

*////*

HOWEVER, I think things are now water tight. The next expansion
should be to get a set of able "chronicles" like (that is to say unlike) those
at the end of the Mercure de France. (poor old Mercure is pretty well done
for . . . but we should replace it . . . . in time.)


There is no hurry about this, as the continent is not "producing" at the
moment and one doesnt want to compete with war journalism, but that
dept. is the next augmentation to be considered. Possibly it should be held
down to a treatment such as my "List of books" for the Aug. Number.

Have you any opinions about ANY english or con-
tinental authors? Is there any one whom you think it peculiarly desirable
to grab? For one reason or another?

For instance Bridges might conceivably be an advantage to
an English magazine, but I can't conceive his being ANY mortal use in

America. AND I don't want him. And [Rudyard] Kipling has gone to pot . . . . . . besides being too beastly expensive, , but if there is any antik [antique?] figurehead in whom you retain any interest, or about whom you have the least curiosity, DO mention it.

Ultimately I want something from Thomas Hardy. But there is no hurry about it. Anatole France is probably "finished", anyhow he'll probably die before I can get at him. There is no use trying to do anything with Paris until I get actually on the ground with money to spend.

ANYHOW we've got the first year fairly well plotted out; fairly solid, to build on. Lady Gregory shouldn't be announced till Sept. we must keep on springing surprises. It is started O.K. first me, then Yeats, then Lady G. then Hueffer ⟨to come⟩, and then the ⟨as yet⟩ unknown.

And don't worry about John Quinn. He's all there.

Yours E.P.                                        Ezra Pound
                                                  21–6–'17

the book done from the earlier ones: i.e., Passages from the Letters of John
    Butler Yeats: Selected by Ezra Pound.
Times reviewer: A review of Passages appeared in the Times Literary Supple-
    ment of 7 June 1917. In it, the reviewer says that John Butler Yeats "writes
    like one whose business is contemplation and who is utterly content with
    it. . . . You can yield utterly to his thought because of its tranquil delicacy"
    (271).
"A.E.": pseudonym of George William Russell (1867–1935), Irish poet, artist,
    dramatist, and essayist. The production of Russell's play Deirdre in 1902 was
    one of the early moments in the formation of the Irish National Theatre.
    Russell became the editor of The Irish Homestead (Dublin, 1895–1923).
    From 1923 to 1930, he edited The Irish Statesman.
Orage: From 1907 to 1922, Alfred Richard Orage (1873–1934) was the editor
    of The New Age: A Democratic Review of Politics, Religion, and Literature.
    EP became a regular contributor to Orage's journal and through this con-
    nection met many of the other contributors, writers such as T. E. Hulme,
    T. Sturge Moore, Wyndham Lewis, Rupert Brooke, Allen Upward, John
    Middleton Murry, Llewelyn Powys, Katherine Mansfield, and A. E. Randall.
returns from the bank: Eliot worked in the Colonial and Foreign Department
    of Lloyds Bank, first at 17 Cornhill and later at its new location at 20 King
    William Street, London.
Joyce . . . is incapacitated: See Letter 15n.
"Imaginary Letters": See Letter 8n.
Bridges: Robert Bridges (1844–1930), British poet and essayist, who was ap-
    pointed Poet Laureate in 1913.
Anatole France: pseudonym of the French novelist and critic Jacques-Anatole-
    François Thibault (1844–1924), who was awarded the Nobel Prize for
    Literature in 1921.

**28. TLS–4.**   On stationery embossed: 5, Holland Place Chambers/ Kensington. W. [22–23 June 1917]

⟨June 22⟩

Dear M.C.A.

I am afraid my "Homme Moyen Sensuel" will worry you a good deal. But he is about three out of every four of the ⟨male⟩ citizens of New York, and it is time something was done with him. As with various other typical local figures, WHO ARE NOT in the convention of [Edgar Lee] Masters.

Also it is very bad that all the young with anything to them should take exclusively to vers libre. Nobody can write good "vers libre" who hasn't first sweated over regular forms. With Kreymborg (of no importance but as a symptom) and that gang, vers libre as a principle has, and has for a long time become as fixed, stupid and academic as the Century or Scribner "laws of verse".

I dont in the least, at the moment, intend going "back to rhyme". Certainly not as a regular thing. BUT one should use it now and again, if only to prevent a new stupid academicism from replacing an old one.

AND one should set the imitative off on a new trail, if only to protect the real work done in imagism, just as the vers libre has protected the real work of the Yeats period.

Also printed in Sep. just after my long poem serialized (if they keep their promise) in Poetry, June, July, Aug. and with my big American vol. of poems out or just about to appear, the "Homme" will irritate those whom it is our function to irritate, and it wont do us any harm. ⟨Anyhow page 7 justifies the existence of all the rest.⟩

It might be different if it came at a time when I had been or was being "long silent". But the "THREE CANTOS" (more especially the revised version of them in "Lustra and Other Poems", appearing this autumn with Knopf) will balance it, keep it in scale with the rest of my work.

Also satire, discursive satire, as distinct from the brief pithy Catullian satire, is a form and has its place.

Lewis['s] "Inferior Religions" will keep the ⟨Sept.⟩ number firm, and my first Imaginary Letter, plus the first announcement of "A Play by Lady Gregory", will also maintain the balance of ⟨our⟩ tone.

Have I asked you to send the magazine to [George Bernard] Shaw. Please do so.

G.B. Shaw, 10 Adelphi Terrace, Adelphi, London, W.C. 2.
  begin with May number.

---

ALSO DONT send the AUG. number free to anyone whom I have set down merely for sample copies. If it is not too late you might add to the July announcement of "Aug. contents" a statement that people to whom the magazine has been sent at my request, will not receive Aug unless they subscribe.

---

Dont, of course, cut off the small "free list" I have sent. They are all, for one reason or another, worth more than their 7/.

If it is too late to put this in "July", a mimeograph post card, with statement of Aug. contents, and statement that it will be sent on receipt of subscription, might go to the recreants who haven't paid up.

As for "L'Homme", [John] Quinn should see proofs, and delete personal names IF (and only IF) he thinks they would lead to libel actions. Undefendable libel actions. The pestilent Sumner is the only one that seems to [be] at all questionable. . It can if necessary be printed
  "S.....r" or S....... .
Order of contents, Sept.
  1 Lewis "Inferior Religions"
  2 E.P. "L'Homme Moyen .."
    3 Eliot:  ??
    4. E.P., Imaginary Letter. ⟨if there is room.⟩
///
I think Eliot will get through something. ALSO that he can be freed from the servitude of the bank. almost at once.

---

[*The next section of the letter is in EP's handwriting.*]
June 23/.
  Have just been going thru' Lewis again for final corrections. The essay is certainly one of the most profound of our time. It makes Bergson look like a gnat.

=

I don't necessarily mean that I agree with its conclusions, but it is hard on the real. Not doctrinaire ⟨& theoretic.⟩ like Schopenhauer's pessimism. = "rhetoric of the will" etc. in section VII. with its context. gets through the crust of contemporary futility. ⟨= If we never printed anything else it would vindicate our existence.⟩

————————————————————Yours

Ezra

Enclosures
1. Inferior Religions
2. L'Homme Moyen
3.4.5 Imaginary Letters, IV,V,VI.

Ezra Pound

23/6/17

*With Kreymborg . . . and that gang:* Alfred Kreymborg (1883–1966). At the time of this letter, Kreymborg, in collaboration with William Carlos Williams, was editing the journal *Others,* which was published from Grantwood, New Jersey, from 1915 to 1919. Among the contributors to *Others* were Marianne Moore, H.D., Wallace Stevens, Amy Lowell, John Gould Fletcher, and Richard Aldington.

*long poem serialized:* Cantos I-III. See Letters 5n and 21n.

*my big American vol. of poems:* Knopf's edition of *Lustra of Ezra Pound with Earlier Poems* (October 1917).

*page 7 justifies:* page seven of the typescript rather than of the *LR* publication.

*"THREE CANTOS":* Versions differing from the *Poetry* serialization of Cantos I-III were included at the end of Knopf's edition of *Lustra.* Both the *Poetry* and Knopf versions of these Cantos differ markedly from their final form.

*ALSO DONT send the Aug. number . . . unless they subscribe:* The July issue carried the following announcement: "People to whom the May, June and July numbers have been sent at Mr. Pound's request will not receive August unless they subscribe."

*small "free list":* See Letter 13.

*delete personal names IF:* In a critical and jeering tone, "L'Homme Moyen Sensuel" names the following people: "the editor of *The Atlantic,*" Comstock, the president, Henry Van Dyke, [Hamilton] Mabie, Lyman Abbot, George Woodberry, Hiram Maxim, Dr. Parkhurst, "Prolific [Alfred] Noyes," [Richard Watson] Gilder, [Arnold] Bennett, [T. B.] Mosher, [John Saxton] Sumner, and "the editor of *The Century.*"

*The pestilent Sumner:* John Saxton Sumner (1876–1971), a New York attorney who served as associate secretary of the New York Society for Suppression of Vice and as secretary of the Society to Maintain Public Decency. Sumner was a leader in movements and legislation aimed at curbing "demoralizing influences" in publications, on the screen, and on the stage.

*freed from the servitude of the bank:* Eliot did not sever his connection with
  Lloyds Bank until 1925. At a later time, EP attempted to provide Eliot with
  the money necessary to leave his job. See Letter 131n.
*Bergson:* Henri-Louis Bergson (1859–1941), a French philosopher. Bergson's
  ideas had a profound influence on modern thought and literature, especially
  on the works of such novelists as Marcel Proust and Virginia Woolf. EP was
  present at lectures T. E. Hulme gave in 1911 on Bergson's thought and
  doubtless read Hulme's essays on Bergson which appeared in 1911 in *The
  New Age.*
*"rhetoric of the will":* See, for example, Schopenhauer's *The World as Will and
  Idea.*

**29. TLS–1.**   On stationery embossed: 5, Holland Place Chambers/ Kensington. W. ⟨8⟩ [23 June 1917]

⟨June 23⟩

Dear M.C.A.

I sent off a fat wad of mss. for the Sept. number this morning.

Have since burst out into a dialogue, which I believe has some
guttts in it.

//////

Subscriber:

Mrs Haselden, 1 Pelham Place, South Kensington, London S.W.7.
(she says she will get us some more. it is a little difficult, until more copies
are in circulation, still we are under weigh. How is our country "respond-
ing"?

/////

Suggestion for announcement on back cover.

---

IT IS TO THE INTEREST OF EVERY SUBSCRIBER to The Little
Review to get ⟨us⟩ more subscribers AT ONCE, FOR THE SIMPLE
REASON that we have plenty of excellent matter on hand waiting to
be printed. The larger our subscription list the more we can give you
each month.

=====

///// 

Plain simple statement, lacking the air of poverty to which Q. [John Quinn] objects, , should appeal to the common sense of the reader, also to his egoism and cupidity.

yours. E.

Ezra Pound

23–6–'17

**30. TLS–1.**  On stationery embossed: 5, Holland Place Chambers/ Kensington. W. ⟨8⟩ [28 June 1917]

Dear M.C.A.

Note subscribers:

Mrs Marion Ryan, Lyceum Club, 128 Piccadilly, W.1.

Mrs Bayliff, 183 Portsdown Rd. Maida Vale, W. 9.

I think I did report.

Mrs Haselden, 1 Pelham Place. S.W. 7.

All these begin with May number.

I enclose cheque [for] forty dollars on account of subscriptions. Just this hour recd notice from bank that stuff was there.

⟨Hope it will help with printer.⟩

Yours ever,

Ezra

Ezra Pound

28–6–17

*that stuff was there:* The financial arrangement with John Quinn was of such a sort that a subsidy would be sent to EP, who would in turn distribute it among the magazine's contributors.

**31. TLS–3.** [*This letter is written on the 5, Holland Place Chambers/ Kensington. W. embossed stationery. The address has been torn from the first page, but the subsequent pages retain the embossure.*] [29 June 1917]

Dear Margaret:

He is a very nice father, but I don't know which photo he has sent you. One in a boat on the lago di Garda looks as I did five year[s] ago. The group with old [William Scawen] Blunt in it is I think more like me than any other snap shot or professional effigy. The passport photo. is too squarish.

The one in "Lustra" deserves my ex-landlady's comment. She was delighted "the first that had ever done me justice" etc., then as she was getting to the door, diffidently, "eh, eh, I hope you won't be offended, but it is rather like the good man of Nazareth, isn't it?"

The editor of "APOLLO" (the russian affair), was being impressed by a british official, when he came to the photo in Lustra he asked sotto voce "Il est Semite?".

He was forcibly informed to the contrary.

The Gaudier [Henri Gaudier-Brzeska] drawing that is to appear in Knopf's vol. is the "best thing that has been done" of me, but it is more keen than the life,. Etc. and they none of them look alike. Also my hair ⟨nearly⟩ always goes black in a photo which prevents any photo. from "giving away" very much what I look like.

I sent you forty dollars yesterday or the day before, but I'll give Hilda [Doolittle] £5. if she'll take it. She said she had written you something or other, i.e. that she wouldn't take it unless . . . . . this that or the other.

I am glad you like the "Poggio", I think it is perhaps the best of the three things. It has more life than the Rabelais, but the Rabelais has a lot in it that I wanted to get off my chest, and it is much more condensed than it could have been in any other form. Also I think the picture of the old man [i.e., Rabelais] is good.

I hope you'll survive "L'Homme", it is rather rough and tumble, than Olympian, rather jeering than irony, but one needn't play the same string every time. It may penetrate some skulls, and the versification of [Remy] DeGourmont deserves to be printed.

I am sending you Eliot's "Sept." and "Lewis" October as soon as I have time to go through their typescript and see that it is ⟨in⟩ order.

I have revised the long poem "Three Cantos" now running in "Poetry", wait ⟨s.v.p.⟩ till the book comes out, before trying to judge it.

About radicalism and conservatism. etc. etc. qu'est ce que c'est que j'en sais.

Conservatism:: to preserve the best. as a term of abuse to preserve good and bad indiscriminately.

Radicalism:: to get to the root of the matter . . usually to eradicate good and bad indiscriminately.

Besides they are terms filthy from contact with politics.

/ / /

re/ format, I think it is quite good. If the stuff printed is good, the format is quite sufficient. Too arty paper arouses mistrust, people use it who have nothing but paper and a printing press.

   The plain exterior and the coloured label, are <u>right</u>.

Yours

Ezra

Ezra Pound

29/6/'17

*which photo:* The "Blunt photo," the original of which is in the Humanities Research Center of the University of Texas, is reproduced both in Norman and in Stock. The photograph of EP by Alvin Langdon Coburn appears only in the English (Mathews) edition of *Lustra;* the American edition (Knopf) has the Gaudier-Brzeska profile drawing.

*editor of "APOLLO":* Sergei Konstaninovich Makovski (1877–1962) was the editor of the art journal *Apollon,* published in Petrograd from 1909 to 1917.

*I'll give Hilda £5:* H.D. was one of the winners of the *LR*'s *vers libre* contest for her poem "Sea Poppies." The prize was $25. See Letter 21n.

*the "Poggio":* "Aux Étuves de Wiesbaden, A.D. 1451." See Letter 9n.

*the Rabelais:* "An Anachronism at Chinon." See Letter 8n.

*the versification of DeGourmont:* Perhaps EP is referring to the following passage from "L'Homme Moyen Sensuel":

> DeGourmont says that fifty grunts are all that
>   will be prized.
> Of language, by men wholly socialized,
> With signs as many, that shall represent 'em

When thoroughly socialized printers want to
print 'em.

*Eliot's "Sept.":* "Eeldrop and Appleplex, II: The Passion for Experience."
*"Lewis" October:* "Cantleman's Spring-Mate."

**32. TLS–2.** On stationery embossed: 5, Holland Place Chambers/ Kensington. W. [2 July 1917]

Dear Margaret

Here is the [T. S.] Eliot for Sept. . I'll get at [Wyndham] Lewis['s] next copy ⟨(October)⟩ as soon as I can.

Subscriber: (at least I was to have been paid 7/, and hope to be sometime.)
Begin with May number.
Miss S[tella]. Bowen, 2 Pembroke Studios, Pembroke Gdns. W. 8. (the seven shillings has already, i.e. my original 7/ has already been spent feeding her chinese food, but put it down in my debt to the L.R.).

////

News. Have at last got hold of Waley's translations from Po chu I. Some of the poems are magnificent. Nearly all the translations marred by his bungling English and defective rhythm. Actual idiom of his english an improvement on his earlier stuff.

I shall try to buy the best ones, and to get him to remove some of the botched places. (He is stubborn as a jackass, or a scholar.)

They've been accepted for a scholarly magazine here, but it isn't published yet, and may never come out, and in any case its not published in America, and the few bits that are literature will have a very different effect from the whole series.

I dont know that I can get them, but they'll help October, if I do.

If the blighter wont sell, I shall review the scholastic magazine WHEN it appears and quote all the best bits. It will be all the same to our readers, and cost less.

yours annoyed (i.e. because Waley has so much intelligence without having just a bit more. DAMN fool ought to improve on Cathay instead of falling below it.)

Yours

Ezra

Ezra Pound
2–7–'17


*Waley's translations:* Arthur Waley (see Letters 12n and 16n) published "Thirty-eight Poems by Po Chü-i" in the first number of *Bulletin of the School of Oriental Studies* (1917) and "Further Poems by Po Chü-i, and an Extract from His Prose Works . . ." in the second number (1918). The *LR* published eight of the Po Chü-i poems in the October 1917 issue and, as this issue was confiscated by the New York Post Office, reprinted the poems in the December 1917 number along with MCA's comment that they were "too good for anyone to miss" (23). See Letter 43n.

*Cathay:* EP's translations, published by Mathews in 1915 and described on the title page as being "for the most part from the Chinese of Rihaku, from the notes of the late Ernest Fenollosa, and the decipherings of the professors Mori and Ariga."


**33. TLS–1.**   On stationery embossed: 5, Holland Place Chambers/ Kensington. W. ⟨8⟩ [16 July 1917]

Dear M.C.A.

I enclose [Wyndham] Lewis for Oct. and Lady Gregory for Nov.

June number has not yet arrived.

The following subscribers have not received their May numbers. If you have sent them, please send duplicate copies.

Miss A.E. Abbot, 73 Church St. Kensington. W.8.

A.E. Ayliffe, 171 Kensington Hight St. W.8.

Mrs Wallis, 17 Campden Hill Mansions W.8.

////

[Arthur] Waley is revising Chinese translations for Oct. [T. S.] Eliot should have finished revising a poem, and possibly a conversation.

I have done a short modern dialogue for Dec.

Announce, s.v.p. in Sept.

> "HANRAHAN's OATH", a play by Lady Gregory will appear in November.

The Hueffer affair seems to be arranged, re/ terms etc.

Your letter, mentioned in your half sheet note, not yet to hand.

Yours, E.

Ezra Pound

16/7/17

*short modern dialogue:* No such dialogue appears in the December issue.

*Hueffer affair:* the arrangements for the publication in the *LR* of Ford Madox Ford's *Women & Men.*

**34. TLS–7.**  On stationery embossed: 5, Holland Place Chambers/ Kensington. W. ⟨8⟩ [17 July 1917]

JULY 17th, 1917

Dear Margaret:

"June" number arrives. I prefer you and "jh" [Jane Heap] to Amurkn contributors in general. Re/ Bodenheim's gasss [*sic*] at the end. I cant be bothered to answer it ⟨publicly⟩, but in case of future outbreaks, and your answering the same, the following points might be noted. (I think your answer covers the main issue all right, and that it is better than a meticulous confutation, Still. . . . .)

He "happens to know" I omitted a name because of personal dislike.

He is a bloody and louse-eaten liar.

His chance, or "happened upon" knowledge is like the knowledge of the events in the dream which killed the dreamer before awakening.

I think the impossibility of his knowing anything of the sort might be underlined, though I dare say the intelligent will manage to perceive it.

I suppose he refers to his own name being omitted.

??????

/////

As a guide to tender feet, I suggest that my "personal dislike" of individual contemporaries has largely arisen from two causes (also that it has arisen subjectively in the mind or boozum of the disliked and not in my own. ("Je ne hais personne, pas même Fréron".)

⟨A⟩

Cause 1. a. My unwillingness to praise what seems to me unworthy of praise.

1b. my unwillingness, after having discerned a faint gleam of virtue in a young man's work, or even got some of his stuff printed, then to be unable to note signs of progress in later work, or even to be unable to retain interest.

Cause 2. My interest (sudden or gradual) in the work of some other artist or writer.

////

With the exception of one quarrel or elimination, of which Bodenheim has probably never heard and which took place years ago, I think I can trace all my "differences" to the above causes. In the exceptional case I thought I had been damn badly treated. It does not enter the discussion, and I have since, long since received their "regrets" and renewed the acquaintance.

⟨Oh⟩ That one might live to see the expression on the face of a new poet, whom I had just been boosting, upon seeing another still newer poet seated in arm-chair . . . . . . .

eheu fugaces.

///

Bodenheim has been on the grump ever since I was forced to tell him that I could not perceive much originality in his work. Neither is there. He was commendable in the first place because he was trying to take more care of his actual wording than either [Edgar Lee] Masters or [Carl] Sandburg.

In verse having no very marked or seductive cadence, no rhyme, no quantitative measure, the actual language must be fairly near to perfection. The wording bears all the strain.

"jewel-silenced" does not seem to me the perfect word. It is only an attempt at something gorgeous, or luxurious, like the old lady's "Mesopotamia", It is not, qualitatively, Swinburnian, in the bad sense, or Miltonic, in the bad sense. ⟨But.⟩ It is a bluff.

////

Re/ Gilmore. Poppies are dry. They are almost the dryest of flowers. To "thirst" for them shows a muddle.

This is a very meticulous objection. I dont want to make a general fiat or commandment about appetites. All things, save the baptism of infants, are permitted the brethren. You may "thirst after dust" <u>FOR EMPHASIS.</u>

Anything willed and thought ⟨out⟩ clearly <u>and used for an</u> artistic purpose. ⟨is, or rather may be. O.K.⟩

I think Gilmore merely slips, does not, did not see the thing out, feel it out, but just wrote it down.

It doesn't in the least appear to be a violent or contradictory image used with intent.

The preceding three lines are ⟨it seems to me⟩ correct and the best part of his poem.


I prefer you and "jh" to American contributors in the aggregate.


I think there is one slip in the number.


"Help us to make the L.R. a power". ⟨bad wording⟩ nothing but our own blasted contents will do that. ⟨G Henley⟩ was a power, I have heard tell, with the "National Observer", when ⟨its circulation⟩ had shrunk to 80 subscribers.


I dont want to pursue dominion to that extent, but it is a glorious precedent.

⟨I think the "We are a going concern. Get aboard!" is the best line to take. ??? However its your department. I don't want to butt in.⟩

                    ///

As for my "personal dislikes" of poets. CRRRRHist JHEEZUS when I think of the hours of boredom I have put up with from people MERELY because they have in an unguarded and irrecoverable and irresponsible moment committed a good poem, or several, !!!!!!!!!

                    ///

And then there is Amy [Lowell]. Is there any life into which the personal Amy would not bring rays of sunshine?. Is there anyone who would not delight in Amy's companionship.

Alas! and alas only, that the price .i.e. equal sufferage [*sic*] in a republic of poesy; a recognition of artistic equality, should come between us.

Would that I were a composer of music for orchestra and not writer of verses, with a critical tendency . . . . . eheu fugaces.

//// Also the foul Bodenheim distorts my words.

I set my period at three years (definitely and deliberately)[.] Thus H.D.'s early work, [Richard] Aldington's, and William's [William Carlos Williams's] "Postlude" do not come up for comparison.

I don't think any of these people have gone on; have invented much since the first "Des Imagistes" anthology. H.D. has done work as good. She has also (under I suppose the flow-contamination of Amy and [John Gould] Fletcher,) let loose dilutions and repetitions, i.e. some of the long things in the Egoist, so that she has spoiled the BAIA MEN ALLA RHODA. "Few but perfect" position which she might have held on to.

*///*

Anyhow [T. S.] Eliot has ⟨thought⟩ of things I had not thought of, and I'm damd if many of the others have done so. Inventive, creative, or what not. Artists, perfectors, etc. and certainly good poets now and again. AND (damn his eyes) poets whom I said nothing against in my editorial save that they hadn't opened up anything new during the past three years. Which, damn it, they haven't.

All of which things are for you and "jh" and decidedly not for other people, and not to be printed as correspondence over my name.

Though I don't mind the passage marked A. in ink, being used by you as a supposition ⟨or interrogation⟩, in some possible future defence or reply, if you choose to do so, or think it advisable.

Re/ the war, I do think it necessary for art and life and everything that the bosche should be beaten. I have thought so ever since he failed to get to London and Paris during the first six weeks. Had he succeeded, I should have gone peaceably to Leipzig to take my higher degree, and have ended ⟨as⟩ the complete KULTURMENSCH. I don't mean that I wanted him to sack Paris. ⟨or that I desired a Leipzig Termination.⟩

If the german progressive element hadn't always found asylum in other countries, they might have been a preventive. But that country has always pushed out its free, and its lovers of freedom.

Can't go into all this now. Generalities are too vague. The Kaiser is with us. He is present in our American Universities. I wish the peaceful-minded would turn their attention to turning him of [off?] them. It would help as much toward anarchic utopia as getting their faces pushed and going to jail. ⟨I think "jh" treated the thing very well.⟩

However, poor dears, they dont know this, and

there is no reason why they should be expected to know it. There is no help but education. Historical studies beyond their means etc. etc.

At any rate a German victory is not a short cut to the terrestrial paradise.

////

[Wyndham] Lewis and [W. B.] Yeats are excellent. My Rabelais is a bit dull. and sententious.

I sent off Lewis story for Oct. and Lady Gregory's play for November, yesterday.

///

Misprints, the repetition of the second asterisked verses in the Rabelais, which you will have noted.

Also. Lewis surely wrote "only living thing except myself", on the last page of his article. MYSELF not YOURSELF. ????

///

And "the Dial", OH gosh, slosh, tosh, the dial, d, i, a, l, dial. Dial= the stationary part of a clock or other chronometer.

Doublet with "tile", an ancient, demoded headgear.

////

AND the "new republic", dessicated, stodged copy of the dessicated New Statesman. WHY "new", why this passion for "newness" always confined to the title. Put there presumably to keep it out of the way.

Not that one desires newness SO AWFULLY, goodness would suffice.

///

Alleged letter of "tomorrow". i.e. the tomorrow of the last day you scribbled a note, has not come.

basta.    yours    Ezra Pound

*Bodenheim's gasss:* In a letter to the editor printed in the "Reader Critic" department of the June issue (28–29), the American poet, novelist, and dramatist Maxwell Bodenheim (1892–1954) objects to EP's comment in the May number that "the two novels by Joyce and Lewis, and Mr. Eliot's poems, are not only the most important contributions to English literature of the past three years, but are practically the only works of the time in which the creative element is present, which in any way show invention, or progress beyond precedent work" (see 3–6). Bodenheim complains that EP does not document his evaluations and that he is too easily swayed by personal emotions. In fact, Bodenheim maintains, "I happen to know that in an article of his, which appeared in *Poetry,* some time ago [see April 1916, 38–43] he omitted the name of a very good American poet, from the 'American-Team' he was mentioning because he had a personal dislike for that poet." (EP lists Edgar Lee Masters, T. S. Eliot, Robert Frost, H.D., William Carlos Williams, Carl Sandburg, Maxwell Bodenheim, Orrick Johns, and John Gould Fletcher as members of this "American-Team.") Bodenheim also complains of EP's tendency to separate poets "into arbitrary teams of best and worst. Poets are either black or white to him—never grey."

*your answer:* In her response to Bodenheim's accusations, MCA declares that a brain that works aesthetically rather than emotionally has a right to establish "its legitimate autocracy" and that EP seems to her to have such a brain. To those with this kind of mind, she maintains, "things *are* black and white—which means good or bad of their kind." She then questions Bodenheim: "If by grey you mean that a poet is almost good, then the critic will have to call him black, meaning that he is a bad poet. There is no middle ground. If by grey you mean that he is a grey poet doing grey work, then the critic will call him white,—meaning that he is a good poet" (29).

*his own name being omitted:* EP had, in fact, included Bodenheim's name in his list (see above).

*"Je ne hais personne, pas même Fréron":* EP is most likely quoting Voltaire here. As editor of two early French periodicals, *Lettres sur quelques écrits de ce temps* (from 1749) and *Année littéraire* (from 1754), Élie Fréron (1718–76) was a strong and incessant critic of Voltaire, the *philosophes,* and the *Encyclopédie.* The three, Fréron felt, were threats to the Church and the State in France, and Fréron viewed himself as a defender of both. Voltaire responded to these attacks by ridiculing Fréron in such works as *Le Pauvre Diable, La Pucelle,* and *L'Écossaise.* Fréron is mentioned in Chapter 22 of *Candide.*

*exceptional case:* EP may be referring to his quarrel with Amy Lowell, which had begun in 1914 when Lowell contracted with Houghton, Mifflin for the publication of three anthologies to be titled *Some Imagist Poets* (1915, 1916, and 1917). Lowell included the work of Richard Aldington, H.D., John Gould Fletcher, F. S. Flint, D. H. Lawrence, and herself, but omitted that of EP.

*eheu fugaces:* Latin, "Alas, the fleeting years," from Horace *Odes,* II, 14, which begins:

> Eheu fugaces, Postume, Postume,
> labuntur anni nec pietas moram
>     rugis et instanti senectae
>         adferet indomitaeque morti:

*"jewel-silenced":* EP is referring to the final lines of "Gently-Drunk Woman," one of four poems translated from the Chinese of Li Po by Sasaki and Maxwell Bodenheim and published in the June issue of the *LR* ([3]–4). The poem reads:

> A breeze knelt upon the lotus-flowers
> And their odor filled a water-palace.
> I saw a king's daughter

Upon the roof-garden of the water-palace.
She was half-drunk and she danced,
Her curling body killing her strength.
She grimaced languidly.
She smiled and drooped over the railing
Around the white, jewel-silenced floor.

*the old lady's "Mesopotamia":* EP's reference is obscure. It may be a derogatory reference to Rudyard Kipling's poem "Mesopotamia," published on 11 July 1917.

*Poppies are dry:* Louis Gilmore's poem "Improvisation" appears on page 8 of the June issue of the *LR*. The last two stanzas of the poem read:

Your hands are ghosts
That trouble the blue shadows
Of a garden.

Your hands are poppies
For which my lips are hungry
And athirst.

Gilmore was a frequent contributor of poems to the *LR*.

*G Henley:* William Ernest Henley (1849–1903) was the editor of the *National Observer*, the original name of which was *The Scots Observer*, founded in 1888. In 1890 the publication was moved from Edinburgh to London in an effort to broaden its appeal and its audience. Henley, however, resigned from his position in 1894 and the magazine, from then on, steadily declined in quality. During its peak years, the *Observer*'s highest sustained circulation was 200, but, as EP's comment suggests, the number of subscribers was often considerably lower.

*long things in the Egoist:* From November 1915 to July 1917, H.D. had published fourteen poems in *The Egoist*.

*"jh" treated the thing very well:* The June issue included an essay in three parts entitled "Push-Face" (4–7), written by jh (Jane Heap). In the first section, Miss Heap makes the observation that "In the last few years we have had a return to the beginnings of all the Arts. If there ever comes a time in the world when men will give their attention to the life of Art and understand its movements, they will find it alert and inevitable. Life would follow it trustingly if it were not for the intrusions and hindrances of men. The Thing had happened: Life made its protest through Art." The second part offers a description of police and soldiers beating the crowd at an anticonscription rally which was led by anarchists whose principal spokesperson was Emma Goldman. The third section describes an "Alley Festa," staged as a benefit for the Red Cross, at which the onlookers—"children out of the slums" and "fathers holding their babies in their arms"—were "pushed in the face and told to get out, to move on, by policemen and some rough fellows in khaki—because . . . this was a fete for humanity." Everyone, Heap contends, plays the game of "push-face," and the article ends with this observation: "When you're little children you play it and call it push-face; nations call it government; the 'people' are playing it now in Russia and call it revolution."

*Misprints:* In the *LR* publication of "Anachronism at Chinon," this sentence appears twice during the course of one of Rabelais' speeches: "Where s......, s.... and p..... on jews conspire, and editorial maggots .... about, we gather .... smeared bread, or drive a snout still deeper in the swim-brown of the mire."

In Wyndham Lewis's "Imaginary Letter," the passage in which the misprint appears reads as follows: "I feel you, in my absence, becoming enmeshed in environing respectability and its amiable notions. I feel that this letter may require another fervour to drive home, or excuse, its own = A *coup de poing* is the best method of enforcing an idea (or a shell) = the mouth is similarly a more satisfactory aperture than the ear for introducing a philosophy into another body. Yorke is the embodyment of my philosophy. I love Yorke in exactly the way that I love a character in Molière or Turgenev. Yorke is the only *living thing except yourself,* that I know or find alive to the same extent" (26).

*"the Dial":* At the time of this letter, the American journal *The Dial*—which was owned by Martyn Johnson, who had bought it in 1916 from Francis F. Browne—was based in Chicago and was being edited by George Bernard Donlin. Its contributing editors included Conrad Aiken, Randolph Bourne, Padraic Colum, Van Wyck Brooks, and John Macy. For a history of this period of *The Dial*, see Nicholas Joost's *Years of Transition: The Dial, 1912–1920*.

## 35. TLS–2.   [1 August 1917]

Dear M.C.A.

[Ford Madox] Hueffer's mss. has come in, and it is as good as I remembered it to be.

I plan to begin ⟨it⟩ in Jan., skip Feb, as the two first chapters would be rather spoiled by dividing 'em, go on into March, April, etc.

With Lady Gregory's play ["Hanrahan's Oath"] in Nov., Longish story by [Wyndham] Lewis in Dec. and Hueffer beginning in Jan. I think we might seriously consider raising the price to .25 cents (one shilling), and $2.50 or $3. dollars a year for new subscribers, i.e. for people who subscribe after Jan. 1. 1918. or who let present subscriptions lapse.

I have never known a paper to lose by raising its price.

I am getting into touch with [Thomas] Hardy's agent, or rather my agent has done work for Hardy, and I am consulting him. ⟨Have seen him & he is writing today[.] H. got £25 for his last poem!!!⟩
         ////
Arthur Symons has submitted a one act play, unasked. I have

declined to pay for it. It might be worth squeezing in if he wants to give it [to] us.

How is he regarded in America? The playlet is coherent. Doesn't speak to me particularly. Should like it if our format were larger. I mean simply the thing is not bad, dont think it would harm us. But it dont particularly "belong", or to have any particular significance.

It is definitely good enough to use IF his name would bring us 50 or 100 subscribers.

*/////*

Note new subscriber.

The ⟨dont omit this useless word in the address[.] I want 7/ next year too⟩ Lady Tredegar    45 Grosvenor Sq. London W. 1.

Begin her with May. Note that she has sent only 6/3. I suppose this little ⟨yellow-orange⟩ paper slip originates in N.Y. As long as they are asked for 1.50 dollars they'll send /6/3 and not ⟨7⟩ shillings. One can't ask for the extra nine pence.

NOTE.    Dont send any more sample copies to
        The Hon. Evan Morgan. and THE Lady T. is his mama and that sample copy has done its job and winged its subscription.

One or two other people say they are subscribing, but I want their MONEY first. (Base commercial instinct)

Hope the enclosed note announcing Hueffer isn't too long for October number.

Hope to send [T. S.] Eliot's stuff and [Arthur] Waley's chinese stuff shortly. Eliot has gone to the sea coast for a week and that may get him through something.

Just time to get this to post.

> yours ever    Ezra
>             Ezra Pound
>             1/8/'17

*Hueffer's mss.:* Ford Madox Hueffer's (Ford's) series of essays *Women & Men* ran in six installments in 1918. In the first essay, Ford states his purpose: "I have been trying to get at what, if any, is the essential difference between man and woman in the life that to-day we lead in Western Europe" [*LR* (January):21]. What complicates the matter, he observes, is the fact "that no sooner does either man or woman approach this theme of the difference between the sexes than straightway all reason deserts him. . . . [T]he never-failing rule with man as well as with woman is to revenge in his public utterances his private wrongs against a sex" [*LR* (January): 29]. The essays were subsequently published, in an edition limited to three hundred copies, under the title *Women & Men* (Paris: Three Mountains Press, 1923).

*Longish story by Lewis:* Wyndham Lewis's "A Soldier of Humour" was published in two parts in the *LR,* the first in December 1917 (32–46) and the second in January 1918 (35–51). Lewis later rewrote this story, changing the name of the narrator from Mr. Arthur Pine to Ker-Orr, and included it, along with other stories narrated by Ker-Orr, in *The Wild Body.*

*Arthur Symons:* (1865–1945), British poet and critic. The "playlet" to which EP refers is "Barbara Roscorla's Child," published in the *LR* in the October 1917 issue (25–36).

## 36. TLS–5.   [3 August 1917]

Dear Margaret

Yours of July 17 to hand. Re/ trials and insurrections. I am very glad America is in [the War] AT LAST, and think we should have been in long ago. BUT I prefer volunteer armies. I honestly think the bosche is to be beaten, must be beaten FIRST, and that the effective order of action is to get him beaten and then start on the lesser tyrannies.

I think the german insurrectionist is always kicked out of Germany and then starts to insurrect his asylum of protection. However . . . . . . . . lets keep to literature.

I have just mailed [Arthur] Symons' play to the 14th St. address. I hope you[r] mail will be duly forwarded.

My agent has written to [Thomas] Hardy offering £10 for a poem. That's all I can swing at the moment.

[George Bernard] Shaw is not of my party and he has always sniffed a bit at the arts and gone with the Sidney Webbs, and ⟨held⟩ the belief you can save people from the outside by "social action".

I therefore must approach him with money in my hands.

I think the [Ford Madox] Hueffer stuff more valuable than anything Shaw could have given us,, though it is of less worth as advertis[e]ment.

I'd rather announce Hardy first, if there is anything of his to be had.

I have sent Hilda [Doolittle] her £5. The enclosed receipt is not legal, because it hasn't a stamp on it. Still it indicates to you that cash has been delivered.

*///*

I'm glad you like my "Letters", and dont mind "L'Homme [Moyen Sensuel]". [Wyndham] Lewis' "[Inferior] Religions" is a fine job.

[T. S.] Eliot's second "Eeldrop and Appleplex" you will have rec'd in time for Sept.

⟨The rest of⟩ October is still to be sent.

Hueffer's stuff is quiet, but its all there. Lady Gregory [i.e., "Hanrahan's Oath"] has been sent.

re/ the [John] Rodker "LaForgue" play. I don't think we could afford to use it UNTIL we are better established. I will send you a copy of it some-time when I am less rushed.

*////*

Re/ White cats and ebony eroticism. Perhaps "The Soil" might be left its corner of eroticism. ??? ⟨489 Fifth Ave.⟩

Merely as an editorial convenience or convention.

---

All eroticism is "in bad" here. There have been so many attempts to revive the ⟨nine⟩neties. A rag called the "Gipsy" and another called "Form". And then "Vanity Fair" has "fish".

I know this is not what you mean, but there are these shoals to be kept clear of.

I suppose my "Dance Figure" in "Lustra" is eroticism ???? Perhaps after all, at this date and for our decade its place is life and not art.

Or shall I write a child's guide to adventure?

I am fed up on the Edward Carpenter tone. Hueffer wipes Weiniger [*sic*] off the earth.

DeGourmont [Remy de Gourmont] has written "Physique de l'Amour" and "Chevaux de Diomedes". One mustn't have anything intellectually lower than that achievement.

*////*

Glad you've seen [John] Quinn in action. He is all right[.]

*/////*

Glad Mrs Gardner is also in action.

/ / /

Difference of having Rodker in July and [Iris] Barry in Aug. is not vital or fatal.

I think "Alice Corbin" has done two poems, and certainly her criticism has been the best American criticism in Poetry. [John Cowper] Powys ⟨I⟩ can not feel as reliable intellectually. [Theodore] Dreiser I really know nothing about. I protested about the suppression of his book "on principle". God know[s] I can't see any genius busting out in the U.S.A. at the present moment.

The erotic here is only deliquescent [Aubrey] Beardsley, and that's NO good.

Mrs Jordan is an imbecile, BUT she coughed 1.50 (at least you imply that she subscribed, and I HOPE she paid.)

My other american acquaintoi are mostly paupers or "that which it is unfitting to write", perhaps the term louse implies a sufficient degree of parasitism.

HOWEVER let us keep the flag flying for a while, after we have really done something, really printed a sequence of numbers we may be able to club in some more supporters.

Rebecca West is a journalist, a clever journalist, but not "of us". She belongs to [H. G.] Wells and that lot. Hueffer got her into the first BLAST, but she is a journalist, and a journalist from the heart.

[D. H.] Lawrence has pewked in the English Review.

Still I'd print really good stuff by either of them, or by anyone. There is a forgiveness of sins, even in literature.

La Baronne de Brimont or Vail de Lencour could either of them do your white cats and ebony, but LaBaronne hasn't an ounce of brains, only perfect finish ⟨literary & personal⟩, and poor Vail has no energy. Still I will ask her.

/ / /

Rebecca would, I think, be always on the side of the majority.

DO not confuse La Baronne de Brimont, with La Comtesse de Bremont. They are NOT the same person. I dare say no one in N.Y. has ever hear[d] of either. ⟨no reason why anyone should.⟩ The one with the i lives in Paris, the other one is a London impossibility[.]

Lewis has sent in three more letters. I haven't had time to look at them.

Must get on to proofs. etc.
⟨Salutations to jh.⟩

Yours

Ezra

Ezra Pound

3/8/'17

*the Sidney Webbs:* Sidney Webb, First Baron Passfield (1859–1947), and Mrs. Beatrice Potter Webb (1858–1943), English economists. Socialists and deeply involved with the labor movement in England, the Webbs were principal founders of the Fabian Society in 1884.

*announce Hardy first:* Nothing of Thomas Hardy's appeared in the *LR*.

*"the Soil":* Five issues of *The Soil: A Magazine of Art* were published in New York beginning in December 1916 and running until July 1917.

*"Gipsy":* Two numbers of *Gypsy* were published in London, one in May 1915 and the other in May 1916.

*"Form": Form: A Monthly Magazine Containing Poetry, Sketches, Essays of Literary and Critical Interest* was also a short-lived London journal, publishing only two numbers (April 1916 and April 1917). The journal was briefly revived in 1921, publishing three numbers from October 1921 to January 1922.

*"Vanity Fair" has "fish":* The well-known magazine *Vanity Fair* (New York) featured a monthly series of black-and-white cartoonlike drawings, with captions, in its "All Seriousness Aside" department. The drawings were signed "Fish."

*"Dance Figure" in "Lustra":* EP may be referring to such lines as the following from his poem "Dance Figure":

> Thine arms are as a young sapling under the bark;
> Thy face as a river with lights.

> White as an almond are thy shoulders;
> As new almonds stripped from the husk.

*Edward Carpenter:* (1844–1929), English poet, essayist, and social reformer. An admirer of the poetry of Walt Whitman, Carpenter traveled to the United States in 1884, where he met the poet and became a devotee of his poetry and thought.

*Weiniger:* The second essay of Hueffer's series *Women & Men* is devoted primarily to a critique of a book written by a German physician named Dr. Otto Weininger (1880–1903) on the subject of men's superiority to women. Weininger's "study" *Geshlecht und Charakter; eine prinzipielle Untersuchung* (1903) was translated into English and published by Heinemann in London and Putnam's in New York in 1906 under the title *Sex and Character*.

*Mrs Gardner:* Isabella Stewart Gardner (1840–1924), American art collector and social leader. The wife of John Lowell Gardner of Boston, she was an enthusiastic patron of the arts. When her husband died in 1898, she devoted more of her time and money to the support of the arts, eventually opening Fenway Court in 1903, where she entertained writers, musicians, artists, and visiting celebrities. Her will established Fenway Court as a public museum.

*"Alice Corbin":* Alice Corbin Henderson (1881–1949), American poet, critic, and editor. From 1912 to 1916, she was an associate editor of *Poetry.* In 1916, she moved to New Mexico, the folklore of which she incorporated in a number of poems.

*I protested about the suppression . . . . :* EP had sent to *The Egoist* a letter of protest he received from a group of American writers concerning the suppression in the United States of Dreiser's *The "Genius."* The letter was published in the October 1916 issue.

In a follow-up letter to *The Egoist,* EP lists the names of the sixty members of the Council and Executive Committee of the Authors' League of America, marking those who had signed the Dreiser protest. Only seventeen had signed. [See *The Egoist* (Oct. 1916): 159; (Feb. 1917): 30].

*Mrs Jordan:* Perhaps EP is referring to Viola Scott Baxter Jordan. Prior to her marriage, EP had met her in 1905 at the end of his undergraduate days at Hamilton College. When he returned to his parents' home and was doing graduate work at the University of Pennsylvania, he carried on a correspondence with Miss Baxter. EP's letters to her are now in the Collection of American Literature, Beinecke Rare Book and Manuscript Library at Yale University.

*Rebecca West:* Dame Rebecca West (1892–1983), English novelist, critic, and essayist. Miss West began her career as a journalist, joining the staff of *The Freewoman* in 1911. In 1912, she became the political writer on *The Clarion.* Interested in feminist issues and women's suffrage, she was a frequent contributor to such newspapers and periodicals as *The Star, The Daily News,* and *The New Statesman.*

West's story "Indissoluble Marriage" was published in the first issue of *BLAST: Review of the Great English Vortex* (20 June 1914): 98–117.

*Lawrence has pewked:* D. H. Lawrence's essay "The Reality of Peace" was published in two installments in *The English Review* (May 1917, 415–422; June 1917, 516–523). In the first section, Lawrence argues for a conversion to a new way of life through the abandonment of will, that is, through the giving of ourselves to the "current" or the "stream" of the "great systole diastole of the universe." In the second section, he speaks of the necessity of man's understanding both the "angels" and the "devils" within his soul, both (to use Lawrence's metaphors) the water-lily on the still pond and the snake within the festering marsh.

*Vail de Lencour:* Brigit (Ethel Elizabeth Morrison-Scott) Patmore (1882–1965), the wife of John Deighton Patmore. Prior to the War, Brigit Patmore traveled in the circle of writers who gathered at South Lodge, Violet Hunt's home in London—writers such as Ford Madox Ford, H.D., Richard Aldington, and EP.

In her published memoirs *My Friends When Young,* Brigit Patmore accounts for the name "Vail de Lencour": "As Violet Hunt told me, Ezra was fascinated by Provence and the time of the troubadours, the singing poets, and he gave me the name 'Vail de Lencour'. Later, he dedicated to me under this name one of his first books, *Lustra*" (60). The dedication of *Lustra* reads, "V. L. *Cui dono lepidum novum libellum*."

**37. TLS-3.** On stationery embossed: 5, Holland Place Chambers/ Kensington. W. [3 August 1917]

Dear M.C.A.

The gods thrust this play ["Barbara Roscorla's Child"] of [Arthur] Symons upon us with no little vigour. As you can see by Mathews' card, Symons would rather have it in us and not get paid than to have me send it elsewhere and get paid. Which we may take as a compliment.

The circumstances as follows: Card from Mathews asking me if I will print a play of Symons in "next number".

Card from me saying "next number already in the press, full up till Jan., cant accept mss. till I've seen it." Afterthought that Oct. is possible. card to that effect

Mss. arrives.

I go to see Mathews, say I wont pay for mss. THAT I will recommend "Drama" to pay for it, but cant promise a date. That Century, Harpers, etc. probably would pay. That I cant promise Oct. will ask you to try and get it into that month if Symons prefers us to others.

Enclosed card for Mathews.

////

This I state in order that you may not think I am merely raking up everybody with a reputation indiscriminately. [Thomas] Hardy is another story he has never flagged or caved in.

//

Symons didn't cave in either, he simply went off his head. He has recovered. This play was done before the break-down. It cant do us any harm. It must even have a certain cash value as he still appears in well-paid places. ANYHOW under these circumstances one simply cant refuse to print a coherent piece of work with an excellent main idea from the author of "I am the torch she saith", and "Spiritual Adventures".

It will annoy a few of the older men here who belonged to the definitely "other" party in the 90's and who[m] I have not yet asked in. It will also console some who will have been distressed by "L'Homme Moyen Sensuel".

–––––––––––––

Yesterday I got proof ⟨of an article of mine⟩ in which "fecundity" had been editorially changed to "fruitfulness", SO perhaps the Century wouldn't take "Barbara Roscora [Roscorla]". As a thing done when it is dated, the play is, I suppose, remarkable and daring. AT LEAST no one else has used the plot of a lady suiciding first rather than die in production.

I wont have the [Arthur] Waley chinese mss. crowded out. I think the best thing to do will be to print all my ⟨own⟩ stuff in small type. And to print the stage directions in Symons in very small type. That will keep the number inside its covers.

        And if we are going to raise the price in Jan. it will have been wise to get a good deal of actual matter into Oct, Nov, Dec. EVEN if you have to use newspaper paper.

Symons at least agrees with us in that his playlet isnt a concession to the public. And I am not conceding to the public, but rather to Symons in passing it, despite the fact that it "isn't exactly what I mean". It's not what I mean at all.

        A few months ago we'd have thought ourselves lucky to get it, perhaps.

I think the Symons better go between "Cantleman" [Wyndham Lewis's "Cantleman's Spring-Mate"] and my "Imaginary Letter".

Order of my stuff being

> Note on [Ford Madox] Hueffer (small print)
> Poem by Eliot (IF he gets it in[.]
>         It's writ, but he
>         is still revising)
> Chinese by Po Chu I, by Waley
>         Cantleman by Lewis
>         Symons
>         E.P. Imag. Let. (small print).

////
ETC.

Some one must have heard of our existence, or Symons wouldn't be wanting admission.

The Hueffer stuff is very important. I sent off a note on it and notice of a new subscriber about two days ago.

yours ever

Ezra

Ezra Pound

3–8–'17

*Mathews:* London publisher Elkin Mathews, who published EP's first books.

*"Drama":* The Drama, a magazine published, at first quarterly and later monthly, in Chicago from 1911 to 1931. In 1917, the time of this letter, the magazine was edited by Theodore Ballou Hinckley, who served as its editor from February 1913 to January 1931. In their *The Little Magazine: A History and a Bibliography,* Hoffman, Allen, and Ulrich point out that "From 1916 to 1919, the magazine has the character of a little magazine of the theater. Printed during those years are Ezra Pound's essay on 'Mr. James Joyce and the Modern Stage' [February 1916: 122–32] and a translation of a play by Remy de Gourmont" (379). EP's "The Classical Stage of Japan: Ernest Fenollosa's Work on the Japanese 'Noh' " was published in the May 1915 issue (199–247).

*Century:* Century, A Popular Quarterly, published from November 1870 to May 1930, was known variously as *Scribner's Monthly, Century Illustrated Magazine* (1881–1925), and *Century Monthly Magazine* (1925–29).

*Symons . . . simply went off his head:* See Letter 35n.

*"I am the torch she saith":* part of the first line of Arthur Symons's poem "Modern Beauty," first published in *Images of Good and Evil* (1899) and later reprinted in *Poems by Arthur Symons,* Vol. II (London: Heinemann, 1909): 150.

The first stanza of the poem reads:

I am the torch, she saith, and what to me
If the moth die of me? I am the flame
Of Beauty, and I burn that all may see
Beauty, and I have neither joy nor shame,
But live with that clear life of perfect fire
Which is to men the death of their desire.

*"Spiritual Adventures":* Symons's *Spiritual Adventures* (1905) is a series of seven sketches of Londoners told by a narrator who has come to London and has become enchanted by the sights.

*Poem by Eliot:* No further poems by T. S. Eliot appeared in the *LR* until the four that were published in the September 1918 issue: "Sweeney Among the Nightingales," "Whispers of Immortality," "Dans le Restaurant," and "Mr. Eliot's Sunday Morning Service."

**38. TLS–2.**   On stationery embossed: 5, Holland Place Chambers/ Kensington. W. [6 August 1917]

Dear Margaret:

I have just had a fit of energy, probably misdirected. Anyhow I have written to Owen Hatteras, and to a friend of Agnes Repplier's. The latter female is probably by now completely THE journalist.

Hatteras has passion and may have some "inedits," I don't know, its a gamble. I haven't pledged anything to either of them. Old Hatteras probably has and had more to him than [Maxwell] Bodenheim.

Same with Jepson here. I think possibly some of the early intention may remain even after years of popular writing.

I am by no means sure. Contributions from "practical" "professional" writers like Replier [*sic*] and Hatteras, might be of no small use. PROVIDED they were the right sort of contributions.

Edith Wharton once wrote some prose. I wonder if she could be got at. Does Mrs Gardiner know her?

At any rate, free subs. to the review, beginning with May might be sent to all three of these "elders". They have all had moments in which they arose above the baboon level of their "fellow authors".

On the other hand they have all so perfectly fitted into the existing scheme of things-publishable that I doubt if they will care to help the L.R.

I think I shall ask May Sinclair to do 500 words on [T. S.] Eliot.

I dont suppose the names of female English novelists in general, would be any use to us. ???

Ethel Mayne, the last of the Yellow Book staff has been enquiring whether she was modern enough. Violet Hunt would like etc.

People who sell serials to the Century, would probably only damage their own prices and do us no good if we had them in. ????

M.S. [May Sinclair] once had a name in America, but I suppose that's a thing of yester-decade. ???

I shall end by buying an author's year book.

Mosher once published Fredk. Wedmore as a rarity. I dare say the old boy is past all pen pushing. I [It?] would annoy Mosher if we printed F. W., but I dont know that it's worth it.

My main drift is that there are a few people who have not definitely come out on the side of Belial. Can they be of any use to us ?????

            a bientot    E

Ezra Pound                     6–8–1917

*Owen Hatteras:* the pseudonym of H. L. Mencken (1880–1956) and George Jean Nathan (1882–1958). At the time of this letter, Mencken and Nathan were co-editing *The Smart Set*. Evidently, EP did not know that "Owen Hatteras" was a pen name the two editors were using, or he simply was accepting "Owen Hatteras" as a literary entity.

*Agnes Repplier:* A native of Philadelphia, a city where she lived most of her life, Agnes Repplier (1858–1950) was the author of numerous volumes of essays, two biographies (*Life of Père Marquette*, 1929; *Mère Marie: of the Ursulines*, 1931), and the compiler of *A Book of Famous Verse*.

*Jepson:* Edgar Alfred Jepson (1863–1938), English novelist and, for a time, editor of *Vanity Fair*. He wrote a number of novels, mostly romantic adventures.

*Mrs Gardiner: Isabella Stewart Gardner.* See Letter 36n.

*May Sinclair:* English novelist and essayist, May Sinclair (1865?–1946) focused on an exploration of the subconscious, a focus which proved to be an important early contribution to the development of the stream-of-consciousness technique. Her article on Eliot entitled "Prufrock: And Other Observations" was published in the December 1917 issue of the *LR* (8–14). See Letter 47n.

*Ethel Mayne:* Ethel Coburn Mayne (1870?–1941), English novelist, short-story writer, literary historian, and translator. Miss Mayne's first published story appeared in John Lane's *Yellow Book* in 1895 under the pseudonym Francis E. Huntley, but she published her first collection of stories *The Clearer Vision* (1898) under her own name.

*Yellow Book:* an English quarterly published from 1894 to 1897. Among its contributors were Aubrey Beardsley, Max Beerbohm, Henry James, Edmund Gosse, and Walter Sickert.

*Mosher:* Thomas Bird Mosher, American publisher. Mosher, a Welshman who had settled in Portland, Maine, specialized in publishing reprints. EP had tried unsuccessfully to get Mosher to bring out the collection of poems which was eventually published in *A Lume Spento*.

*Fredk. Wedmore:* Frederick Wedmore (1844–1921), English journalist, novelist, and art critic. Among his works published as books are *A Snapt Gold Ring* (1871), *Two Girls* (1874), *Studies in English Art* (1876), *Pastorals of France* (1877), *Four Masters of Etching* (1883), and a novel, *The Collapse of the Penitent* (1900).

**39. TLS–1.**   On stationery embossed: 5, Holland Place Chambers/ Kensington. W. [7 August 1917]

Dear Margaret:

All I can say is that the enclosed is SOME copy. You'll have to use your judgement about when to use the Soldier of Humour. i.e. to get it all into Dec. or to continue it into Jan.

The [Ford Madox] Hueffer must start in Jan. anyhow.

I think you'll have to put at least the second part of the [Wyndham] Lewis in small print. either in Dec. or Jan.

ANYhow its corking stuff and ought to sell the magazine.

*//*

I shall put only my "third" letter, the short one, into Nov. with Lady Gregory.

A brief note on Degourmont [Remy de Gourmont], printing his last letter to me, in Dec.

The long first chapter of Hueffer into Jan.

Omit Hueffer from feb. so as to get in other stuff. Take him up again heavily in March and April, and divide the 4th. chapter in May and June.

I think we left the amateur touch now all right enough.

I shall send the [Arthur] Waley in a few days, for Oct. but want to get this off today.

Yours E

7/8/1917                          Ezra Pound

**40. TLS–6.**   On stationery embossed: 5, Holland Place Chambers/ Kensington. W. [10 August 1917. *Incomplete item: pages one and two of this letter have been lost.*]

I might have set Lady Gregory's play for Oct. and crammed the rest of the stuff in by Sept. BUT I expected [T. S.] Eliot's prose and left a space for it, (i.e., in my plan).

We may as well take [James] Joyce's name off the announcement list. Heaven knows when he'll get anything done.

[John] Rodker is too good not to be printed now and again. One must keep a chap like that "of us". He will do something.

[Maxwell] Bodenheim?? . May be. Morgan is ⟨perhaps⟩ the best of the three "native" poets. in July.

I am tired of people saying "my thoughts are" this that and the other. "My mind is" that and the other.

"My mind to me a kingdom is". "Mon âme est une [un] paysage choisi". "Mon âme est une infante en robe de parade."

All these have been good. But a little art might be expended in finding a variant on that particular phrasing.

[Louis] Gilmore is better in July than in June, however. His "II" has a germ of thought. I think it is prose however. One should have a little more action in one's rhythm if one is going to print as "vers" however "libre".

BUT one must not wholly smother or exclude all unfinished writers.

I mean these remarks as criticism not as objection to his existence or inclusion.

Morgan might have another show sometime. His "spectric" business is however a little late. People intending to be "schools" should have "done it first".

Or rather they should ⟨base⟩ their school on something having to do with their art, not on a vague aesthetic theory. His manifesto advanced no proposition affecting his own medium. i.e. words, rhythm, etc. only some twaddle about ultra-violets. jejune. There is no difference between his free-verse and any other free verse.

After all Imagisme had three definite propositions about writing, and also a few "dont's". ⟨And it differed from the neo-Celtic-twilightists etc. who preceded. Morgan is only another Imagist imitator with a different preface from Amy's [Lowell].⟩

I dont know that there is anything to him.

Is old Kerfoot of "Life" any use. I suppose not. The Smart Set has probably drained off any spirits there were in J. McClure.

May Sinclair is going to ⟨do⟩ 500 words in praise of "Prufrock". That may silence a few dissenting wails. <u>Dont announce it.</u> Let me know if her name is any use for anything else.

ANYHOW its all right. We <u>are</u> under weigh.

Note: when people send in saying "discontinue" subscription. One might leave them with the uncertainty as to whether their letter appears. It would cost them 15 cents to find out. and keep their curiosity awake.
///
Bookshop. ⟨suggestions:⟩
Padraic Colum "Wild Earth" (at least whatever U.S.A. editions contain "The Drover" and "Woman shapely as a swan".)

Arnold Dolmetsch "The Interpretation of the Music of the 17th and 18th centuries".
H. W. Gray and Co. New York.

What else ??? Knopf sends me a notice of "Crimes of Charity" by Bercovici.
⟨Also. J. M. Synge. = so classic now that one had almost forgotten to put him down.⟩
Is it any good?
Knopf ought to advertise in the L.R.
so ought Huebsch.
////
Question for Pukekis: Are the majority of the readers of the L.R. "vulgus"?
We had hoped the few choice spirits were gathered. Perhaps they have only migrated to this side of the ocean.
////
On the whole the Fourth Vol. is going to be a good Vol. Let us hope that the Fifth Vol. will be better. . It is a great comfort to have ones editor with one.
////
As policy, what about "jh" [Jane Heap] signing her name? On the New Age all contributions signed with initials are supposed to be the editor. Wouldn't it have more effect if two people were writing, than if, as per, 1st. correspondent. they were <u>supposed</u> to be the same person. ???

She writes quite well enough to have a name of her own. IF on the ⟨other⟩ hand . . . she dont want to use it. . . . . Or if she has other careers that the use of her name here would interfere with etc. . . . I shut up.

*////*

?? Can you get in touch with Charles Demuth. I see he is exhibiting in the Independent Artists. N.Y. I think he'll subscribe if he has the price. And that he might help.

I will try to get Bill [William Carlos] Williams' brother to submit a BLAST on American architecture. He once had some sense. Heaven know[s] . . . now. . . . ??

Still I do know both these men personally, and they have heard of civilization. Edgar ⟨Wms.⟩ had the fellowship to Rome and I knocked about with him in Italy. Demuth I last saw in Paris.

*////*

AT ANY RATE ever[y] number has <u>something</u> worth reading in it. Can any other magazine say as much?

Yours

Ezra

Ezra Pound

10–8–1917

⟨Since we're printing Symons one might leave that scoundrel Mosher's selection of him in the book shop. Its a good selection. and well worth $.50 cents.⟩

*Morgan:* Emanuel Morgan, pseudonym of Witter Bynner (1881–1968), American poet. Under this name, Bynner and Arthur Davison Ficke, who used the pseudonym Anne Knish, published in 1916 a book of poems entitled *Spectra,* the work supposedly of new Imagist poets. The book was a hoax but was, apparently, clever enough to be taken seriously by a number of critics. (In this letter, for example, EP seems unaware of the joke.) The poem in the July 1917 issue of the *LR* to which EP refers is Emanuel Morgan's "Spectrum: Opus 96."

*"my thoughts are":* The first of Louis Gilmore's "Improvisations," three of which were published in the July 1917 issue, reads:

My thoughts are fish

That dwell in twilight

Of green waters:

They are silver fish
That dart here and there
Streaking the still water
Of a pond.

My thoughts are birds
That have hung their nests
Near the sun:

They are yellow birds
That stretch on stretched wings
Over a sea untroubled
By a sail.

My thoughts are beasts
That crouch and wait
In a black forest.

My thoughts are apes
That clamber through the tree-tops
Toward the moon.

*his "II":* The second of Gilmore's "Improvisations" reads:

In winter
People intensify
Their individuality
In houses.

In spring
By the side of lakes
Beneath trees
People walk
Vaguely sentimental.

In summer
Lying on the warm earth
They hear the grass grow;
Or they become impersonal
In a contemplation
Of stars.

In autumn
People dispel
The characteristic
Melancholy of the season
With a cup of tea.

*a vague aesthetic theory:* Writing under their pseudonyms in the June 1916 issue of *The Forum,* Bynner and Ficke explain the two propositions of the Spectrist School of poetry. The first is that the "subject of every Spectric poem has the function of a prism, upon which falls the white light of universal and immeasurable possible experience; and this flood of colorless and infinite light, passing through the particular limitations of the concrete episode before us, is broken up, refracted and diffused into a variety of many-colored rays. . . . [T]he theme of the poem is to be regarded as a prism upon which the colorless white light of experience falls and is broken into glowing, beautiful, and intelligible hues." The second proposition relates to the functioning of the mind of the poet. His mind "must recombine by . . . [an] act of the intelligence the parted rays, in order that it may grasp the unity, the white light, the Platonic Idea . . ." of the object of poetic speculation.

*Imagisme had three . . . a few "dont's":* In "Imagisme," an article drafted by EP, rewritten by F. S. Flint, and published in the March 1913 issue of *Poetry* (198–200), the three well-known "rules" of Imagism were prescribed. In a following article in the same issue (200–06), EP specified a few "Don't's" for the Imagist writer.

*Kerfoot of "Life":* John Barrett Kerfoot (1865–1927), American editor. From 1900 to 1918, Kerfoot was literary editor of *Life*. He published three books: *Broadway* (1911), *How to Read* (1916), and *American Pewter* (1923).

*500 words in praise of "Prufrock":* See Letter 47n.

*Bookshop. ⟨suggestions:⟩:* EP recommends three books for inclusion in the *LR* Bookshop offerings: Padraic Colum, *The Wild Earth* (New York: H. Holt, 1916); Arnold Dolmetsch, *The Interpretation of the Music of the XVIIth and XVIIIth Century Revealed by Contemporary Evidence* (London: Novello; New York: H. W. Gray, 1915); and Konrad Bercovici, *Crimes of Charity* (New York: Knopf, 1917).

*Question for Pukekis:* In a letter to the "Reader Critic" department of the *LR*, Louis Puteklis of Cambridge, Massachusetts, complains of the recent decline in the quality of the magazine: "It seems to me that the last few numbers of *The Little Review* have been below your earlier standard—almost below zero. What sympathy can the majority of readers feel for the foreign editor, Ezra Pound, with his contemptuous invective against the 'vulgus'?" (28).

*Charles Demuth:* An American painter, Demuth (1883–1935) was a friend of Alfred Stieglitz and a member of the Gallery 291 group.

*Bill Williams' brother:* Edgar Williams, William Carlos Williams's younger brother, had studied architecture at the Massachusetts Institute of Technology and was awarded in 1909 the Prix de Rome to study architecture for three years at the American Academy in Rome.

*Mosher's selection of him:* EP may be referring either to Symons' *Lyrics* (Mosher, 1903) or to his *Silhouettes* (Mosher, 1909).

**41. TLS–1.** On stationery embossed: 5, Holland Place Chambers/ Kensington. W. [11 August 1917]

Dear Margaret:

I should not send any more numbers of the L.R. to Mrs Jordan. Her papa was more or less off his nut. She is quite capable of writing to Comstock's committee (whatever its present name is) or of making trouble in some utterly idiotic way.

Dont return her money, for heaven's sake. It will take her some time to find out what I have done about her letter to me. And dont send the review.

///////

Have I asked you about Robert Gilbert Welsh. some time poet some time dramatic critic. He is a decent chap, loose somewhere in New York. Williams may know where is is. Or Quinn May.

I think I have written about Charlotte Teller, now Mrs Gilbert Hirsch. She ought to be of some use if one can find her.

AND for heavens sake send, May, June, July, to

Miss K.R. Heyman, The Judson, 53 Washington Sq. New York.

The things one forgets, in the scrabble to eat three meals, and get something done.

Yours

E

Ezra Pound

11–8–'17

*Mrs Jordan:* Probably, Viola Baxter (Mrs. Virgil Jordan). See Letter 36n.

*Robert Gilbert Welsh:* (1869–1924), a minor American poet whose verse was published in a variety of periodicals. After Welsh's death, a friend of his, Charles Hanson Towne, collected these poems and published them under the title *Azrael and Other Poems* (New York, London: D. Appleton, 1925) "as a lasting memorial to a man whose work surely deserves to live."

*Miss K.R. Heyman:* pianist, Katherine Ruth Heyman. For a short time in 1908, EP "managed" Miss Heyman's musical career. See Stock (48–50).

**42. TLS–2.**   On stationery embossed: 5, Holland Place Chambers/ Kensington. W. ⟨8⟩ [17 August 1917]

Dear M.C.A.

Please dont send any more extra copies of L.R. to G. Hyde-Lees.

also please send
G. Hyde-Lees,

H.T. Tucker
and Mrs H.T. Tucker, all to 38 Montpelier St. ⟨S.W. 7.⟩ and not to address to which they have hitherto been sent.
Miss Shepeler, 266 Kings Rd. Chelsea S.W. 3. complains about non-
  receipt of magazine. (sub. to begin may, and run six months.)

*///*

Eliot is coming in tomorrow. I hope with a poem.

Am writing to [Arthur] Waley to hurry copy for Oct.

Whereafter my mind will be at rest. . I enclose an autograph signed E.J.
(I know its a J. though a stranger mightn't. hence the typed statement.)

I leave it to your discretion. It shows feeling.

One lady has written ⟨(from U.S.A.)⟩ to say the review is "bad for her
milk". The official reply is:
  Madame, what you need is lactol not literature.

However the note was personal, and one can't print such replies. Perhaps
M. Villerant [EP's persona for his "Imaginary Letters"] may refer to it
in due time..

The rest of [Wyndham] Lewis letters of W.B. Burn have come. I shall
start them in Jan. . probably skip Feb. as I have a longer thing of his
"called" a play. which I want to get out.
  etc.

Yours

E.

Ezra Pound
17/8/17

*"called" a play:* Wyndham Lewis's play "The Ideal Giant" was published in the
  May 1918 issue of the *LR* (1–18).

**43. TLS–3.** On stationery embossed: 5, Holland Place Chambers/ Kensington. W. [20 August 1917]

⟨Agenda marked in pencil⟩

Dear Margaret:

You are a great comfort. And your letter of Aug. 1. contains several jems of Americitis. "Invention rather than interpretation" IS as you observe in your margin "too" too excellent.

And poor dear Amy [Lowell]. It is only a month ago that I heard someone manifestly NOT an enemy refer to the "Hippopoetess" (A native amurkn joke, I should say.).

I think, despite the difficulty of knowing what one will think in a year's time, I think, credo che credessi, etc, that dear Amy's talents and temperament will always be political rather than literary or artistic.

As for her enemies, [Wyndham] Lewis and [James] Joyce have never heard of her, and [T. S.] Eliot is certainly not stirred by a personal spleen.

He did once say "the Lowells are woolens" (at least I think it was to that industry he ascribed their source.).

Her brother Percy was a fine chap. and she is delightful.

ONLY she wanted me to sell out lock stock and barrel, and I said it didn't interest me, and she asked again, etc., and I said it didn't interest me.

And still she would have it, so I named a price. i.e. I said I would contribute to a democratized anthology IF she would institute a yearly prize for poetry to be adjudged by [William Butler] Yeats, [Ford Madox] Hueffer, and myself. (I even went so far as to name a committee including herself. I can't remember whether it was She, I and Yeats, or she, I and Hueffer ⟨(or all four)⟩. BUT that touched the sacred springs of wrath.)

I think she was a bloody fool, for we could have bust the British academic committee (called the British Academy) to smithereens, and she could have been somebody over here (which she wanted to be) rather than being driven back to Hylo Kennels.

I considered the sacrifice of my artistic dignity would have ⟨been⟩ compensated for by the good one could have done in encouraging the right kind of thing in poetry or in prose.

However this is internal history and you and jh [Jane Heap] must bury it in your boozums.

I do not really see that I could have been expected to sell out without receiving some sort of return.

"Je ne hais personne, pas meme Freron."

These matters are too minute to be recorded. But still you may as well know what "has gone before".

////

I have written for 3 copies of [James Joyce's] "Chamber Music" to be sent to you from [publisher, Elkin] Mathews, 20 "Prufrock" from the Egoist. and will try to get at the other books soon. I dont remember who publishes some of 'em.

//

I dont think Eliot or anyone noticed the Hippopotamus not being in the dead centre of the page.

I never shall be able to get details of caps. etc. dead right, but I am not distressed when the printer follow[s] my errors. All early books are full of em, and they have done no real harm to literature YET.

However I will try to improve.

/////

I had more to say and answer but immediate matters plus interruptions make it necessary for me to "git on".

////

That brute [Arthur] Waley has muddled, and sent the marked copy of his mss. to the country etc. etc. etc. etc. damn.

Anyhow he turns up at the last minute, the LAST LAST etc. with two of the poems I asked for and one that I didn't. AND as he has nobly declined payment and left the cash for me to buy something else, I cant curse and swear at him.

⟨1.⟩ DO get the "Harper" and the "Way to Hang Chow" into October.

If you dont like the third poem, leave it out and say that the copy arrived too late to go in, no space. etc.

⟨2⟩ Note subscriber:

The Honble. Mrs Nicholson, 182 Ebury St. London.

S.W.1.

This beautiful and distinguished person has also sent a poem. Which I enclose, and which you will please return to her direct with a polite rejection. The poem does not deserve any politeness, ⟨it is perhaps the worst ever written by mortal hand⟩ but . . . . . . . etc. . . . . I wrote her that decision in these matters rested with the N.Y. office. That was the most delicate circumlocution I could devise. I want some more subscriptions from her strata. ergo suaviter.

Say to her that we are "full up, and cant afford to ask her to wait so long for publication" or any dam lie.

/ / /

⟨3⟩ Last night White recited his lines, and they were amusing. I should probably have refused "did opine" had I seen it on paper, but I was intent on the cadence, which is "interpretative", i.e. the over light syllables and the thuds.

So please put it just after Lady Gregory's play ["Hanrahan's Oath"] in Nov. . it wont take up much room, and will pave the way to my brief prose article ["Imaginary Letters, VI"]. ⟨It will amuse him to be with Lady G. & I promised it.⟩

It has, at least, "certitude", and a magnificent swell and squelch corresponding to the emotion of the subject.

That's all I can think of at the moment. Waley is going to bring some more chinese stuff, BUT I dont think we can hold up October number any more. I think I was perfectly clear and it is only his muddle that we haven't ten good chinese poems instead of two and a tolerable third.

However.

　　　　yours ever. Ezra.

Enclosures.

　　　1. Waley, for Oct.
　　　2. White, for Nov.
　　　3. poem to be returned to Mrs N.　Ezra Pound
　　　　　　　　　　　　　　　　　　　　　20/8/17

---

*poor dear Amy:* For further insight into EP's quarrel with Amy Lowell, see Letter 34n and Stock (163–65).

*Hylo Kennels:* Hylowe Kennels was the name Amy Lowell gave to the kennels she kept for her Old English Sheepdogs at her home Sevenels.

*"Je ne hais personne, pas meme Freron":* See Letter 34n.

*the Hippopotamus:* T. S. Eliot's poem "The Hippopotamus" had been published in the July 1917 issue of the *LR*.

*Do get the "Harper":* Eight of Arthur Waley's translations of the poems of Po
Chü-i were printed in the October 1917 issue, among them "The Harper of
Chao" and "On the Way to Hangchow: Anchored on the River at Night."
When the New York Post Office confiscated the October issue, MCA had
these poems reprinted in the December 1917 number (23–27).

*White recited his lines:* The poem by J. R. White to which EP refers is entitled
"The Soul's Awakening." It was published in the November 1917 issue (39):

> I am drunk as drunk
> And in the ebb of the last wave of wine
> I did opine that I had sunk.
>
> I am drunk as drunk
> But on the crest of this last wave of drink
> I really think I can not sink
> So I will rest.

No other poems by J. R. White appear in the *LR.*

**44. TLS–2.** On stationery embossed: 5, Holland Place Chambers/ Kensington. W. [23 August 1917]

Dear Margaret:

I keep forgetting to write it. But I think we can irritate by hoist-
ing the flag:
The L.R. The magazine that is read by those who write the others.

/////

You have probably noticed that you have still got the old address on the
back of the July number.

And do for heaven's sake put in the Egoist ad.
They have printed our[s] regularly and we haven't had theirs for all the
May, June, July period.

////

What do you think of a combined subscription. England or america, both
papers for say 2.50. ten shillings.

Our subscribers to get the Egoist for one dollar extra, Their subscribers
to get us for 1.00 extra.

New subscribers to pay 2.50, of which the home country magazine gets, 1.15, and the foreign 1.35.

I think we should get more out of it than they would.
Especially as they have the English sub. list.

If or when we raise our price, the combined price would of course go up.

Yours<br>Ezra

23/8/'17

Ezra Pound

**45. TLS–1.**   On stationery embossed: 5, Holland Place Chambers/ Kensington. W. ⟨8⟩ [23 August 1917]

23/8/17

Dear Margaret:

Here at last are the rest (or at least part) of the group of [Arthur] Waley's translations.

I hope, against much chance, that they are in time for October. I rather want to "establish" his existence with a fairly large group "all to once".

I should like these IN, and the weak third one of the lot I sent Monday, left out.

However, do what you can. If these are too late, get them in when you conveniently can. I feel we must get more into each number than we have yet done.

///

Have just seen Miss Weaver. She approves of combined subscription rate for Egoist and Little Rev. but we didn't decide on definite price. She says omission of Egoist adv. from L.R. is her fault, as she told you to wait for new version. So that's all right.

Printing manager who promised to set up second edition of Joyce's "Portrait" unexpurgated has been called up, and the substitute refused. So that fight is all a recommencer.

Magnificent letter re/L.R. and Christianity has been sent to a friend. Am trying to get permission to publish it. And more stuff from its author.

Yours<br>E.

Ezra Pound

⟨Do try to<br>get these<br>into October⟩

*Waley's translations:* See Letter 43n.

*Miss Weaver:* Harriet Shaw Weaver, editor of *The Egoist.* See Letter 4n.

*that fight is all a recommencer:* During the serial publication of Joyce's *A Portrait of the Artist as a Young Man* in *The Egoist,* Harriet Shaw Weaver's printer had deleted material which might be judged obscene and thus open him to prosecution. When Joyce tried to get *A Portrait* published in book form, there were also problems. Four London publishers—Grant Richards, Martin Secker, Duckworth, and T. Werner Laurie—rejected the manuscript, and when Miss Weaver attempted to bring out the book through the Egoist Press, a succession of seven printers, fearful that litigation would follow, refused to set the type. Eventually, B. W. Huebsch in New York agreed to publish the novel. (See Ellmann 400–06.)

*Magnificent letter re/ L.R. and Christianity:* See Letter 46n.

**46. TLS–6.**   On stationery embossed: 5, Holland Place Chambers/ Kensington. W. [13 September 1917]

⟨For God's sake
  be careful about        13 Sept.
      the accents        1917
          & the spelling of [Remy] De Gourmont's
                              french.⟩

Dear Margaret:

Note subscriber:
        Miss Bertra A. Jones, Brookeside, Bournemouth, Eng.
(I have sent May to Aug., so begin her Sept. and complete year.)
                */////*

I enclose the DeGourmont letter and some comment. This is to go in Dec. with Lewis story. (And, I hope, May Sinclair's critique of Eliot. Very brief, but will add sting to slap on Quarterly to have a brief bo[u]quet from the former generation.) I think she'll get it done in time.

///

I have just heard from Davray and Valette, so our French number is assured. I will quote their letters. I think we should give up the Feb. number to french poets. Valette gives his permission, and he publishes most of them. Dont announce this number, let it come as a bomb. We have enough announcements. Let us vary it, by an unexpectedness. I wanted to make the number a simple anthology, Valette says the authors are scattered all over Europe, and that it will take forever to get permission to do this, though he is willing to forward the letters etc. etc.; Davray says the simplest thing is for me to "entrelarder" a few lines of criticism. So I shall do that; I can be all the more vigorous and free, simply because the critical function is imposed by circumstance.

We must do the thing in Feb. in case the Egoist wants to begin Joyce's novel [*Ulysses*] in March, for I have promised to publish it simultaneously with them.

ANYHOW keep the little French anthology quiet until it is launched. Especially on account of dear Amy [Lowell]. I think I can get about as much in one number as there is in her volume. (6 Fr. poets).

I have a fine letter for Jan. ⟨(from our deist)⟩ which I will send on shortly.

Oh YES. head this letter of Remy's simply.
        A LETTER FROM REMY DE GOURMONT
and put it so on the cover (list of contents.) let DeG. name come with the Authors of other things. or perhaps better, put the whole in caps. (but dont put it as "A Letter from R.G."        by E.P.)

////

Egoist ad. of "The magazine that is read
        by those who write the others"
looks good to me. Our list of contributors is getting shaped up.

/////

Next question: WOT abaht AWT? Pyintin' I mean. I wish the mysterious "jh" [Jane Heap] would let loose to me on the subject.

I suppose "The Soil" is adequately financed. Still it has got pixtures.

Now, what is the best work being done in America? IS any of it worth looking at?

Would "JH" run an art section? Would the galleries that run the better artists pay for the necessary plates, or are they all too rotten, or is there any just man among them with whom one could make alliance.

"The Soil" is obviously cracked. It is also obviously run to some extent in the interest of Coady's gallery. There are some brains in the concern.

On the Mercure [*Mercure de France*] each man is responsible for his own "Chronique". If we "got in" an art critic, or art editor, we could say he or she was independent, and that we weren't responsible. "jh" is of course the first person to consider. At least she is, if she besides being a painter is still interested in painting. "OR has she giv' it up" in favour of social what do you call it?

I'm not being insulting. I only want to know IF she will or wants or wont art-edit. Art-editing dont of necessity mean writing gasssss about pictures, it can confine itself to selecting one or more pictures to be re-produced each month.

HAS she seen [John] Quinn's collection. Can she stand [Wyndham] Lewis? Would somebody pay for four plates a month? On say such terms as: we will reproduce 8 of Q's Lewis', and four X's, 2 of Y's, etc. from your gallery or your exhibits. Chosen by us.

I assume that Mr Quinn would let us reproduce almost any of his modern purchases. He has plenty of stuff to keep us going for several years.

Art-editing shouldn't limit itself to vorticism. That is one reason why an independent critic is better than one nominally under the general editors.

Are [Walt] Kuhn and [Arthur] Davies any good, or are they only the best (or modernest) in America. An editor ought to be able to see more than one school. At present ALL America[n] and English art papers stop JUST SHORT OF the real. (Like the Century in literature).

There is a chance to do what the "Soirees de Paris" was doing before the war. (Only we have real literature as well.) They will start up again, I suppose, after the war, but that's no reason why we shouldn't start first.

[André] Derain had something to him. I dont mean that all the Soirees illustrations of him were master pieces.

The sort of basis I mean is "Picasso not Piccabia [Francis Picabia]", "[Wyndham] Lewis not [C. R. W.] Nevinson", [George] Innes rather than the later [Augustus] John, Classical remains from the Gauguin-Van Gogh period, if necessary.

The illustrations in "The Soil" for July are interesting. They are quite good enough. They form a report.

[Charles] Demuth had some brains once. I think he would help with this sort of thing. Only: What about "jh", and what about Davies, and Kuhn, etc. I want information.

                /// 

As a basis of discussion, take the Soil illustrations of the Independent (their July number).

Whitney (rubbish); Signac (presumably colour and unjudgeable from reprod. probably bad). Rivera, decorative, not badly decorative, but certainly nothing more than decorative, ///// Halpert, after Derain; Forbes, ?? after Casteluccio; Gleizes, clean, but derivative note the Picasso spanish town in the background. not unpleasing; Vlaminck, more Derain, and not improved, Hale, Mucha very very much delayed; Demuth, individual, very sincere, and I think good (unless it is derived from something I have not seen. But no, I think there is a personal intensity in his Dancer.); Brenner, rot, bloody rot of the bloodiest; Derain, bad example,: Hartley, unadulterated rubbish,; Brancusi, sperm untempered with the faintest touch of intelligence; Maris [Marin], probably painted in the clear blue, impossible to tell anything from reprod.; Walkowitz, something to it; Weber. NO; Metzinger, rubbish; Stella, worth looking at (at least interesting in reprod, possibly better so than in original ???, cant tell). Delaun[a]y, not much, and very old game; Gris, on a par with the usual humorous tiles in a saloon. . Photo of shops, interesting. Renoir's Jongleuses are excellent. So also the African head on the cover. ///

Our question is: Is there anyone with who[m] we can make an alliance, say an alliance for a year or so. We want all the available energy poured into our vortex.

You people have got to arrange this, if it is to be arranged, I cant do anything about it here. For one thing I am too much allied with Lewis and Brzeska [Henri Gaudier-Brzeska] to form any new connections; for another it is a job for your end of the concern. Everyone here has got their "organ".

An exhibit of the best American stuff (with interlarding of foreign stuff in American collections) would be of interest here as well as at home.

So far as material is concerned, an illustrated catalogue of Quinn's collection (as I imagine it) ought to provide matter enough. One couldn't do that openly or definitely, as it would publish his connection with the magazine, and that he dont want done. I think he is right in believing that we have more force by reason of our resources being shrouded in mystery. Apart from his not wanting to be plagued by people wanting to "get in".

Ezra Pound

*DeGourmont letter:* EP had written Remy de Gourmont to request assistance in founding "a magazine which should establish some sort of communication between New York, London and Paris." In his response, de Gourmont promised to do what he could to aid the venture, but warned that he was not in good health. His letter to EP ended with the following advice: "Le but du *Mercure* [*de France*] a été de permettre à ceux qui en valent la peine d'écrire franchement ce qu'il[s] pense[nt], —seul plaisir d'un écrivain. Cela doit aussi être le vôtre" [*LR* (December 1917): 5–6].

*May Sinclair's critique of Eliot:* See Letter 47n.

*just heard from Davray and Valette:* Henry D. Davray and Alfred Vallette of the *Mercure de France.* EP had written Davray, who was then living in London, to ask whether the *Mercure* would grant the necessary permission to publish, in an issue of the *LR,* the work of the French writers associated with the magazine. EP's original intention was to print selected works of the French poets as a small anthology. But Vallette, whom Davray quotes in his letter to EP, points out that, while one has "le droit de citation" when writing a study of a literary movement, to reproduce the texts "sans critique, avec de simples chapeaux ou notes, ou seulement quelques explications pour l'intelligence des textes, il lui faut l'autorisation ou [des auteurs] des propriétaires des textes." Since, as Vallette notes, the *Mercure* poets were spread throughout Europe (Cros in Germany, Arcos in Switzerland, Elskamp in Holland), Davray suggests to EP that "le plus simple serait d'entrelarder . . . les citations avec quelques commentaires" [*LR* (February 1918): 3–4].

*I think I can get . . . in her volume:* Amy Lowell's *Six French Poets: Studies in Contemporary Literature* comes to 488 pages. The six poets included in the study are Émile Verhaeren, Albert Samain, Remy de Gourmont, Henri de Régnier, Francis Jammes, and Paul Fort.

*fine letter for Jan.* ⟨(*from our deist*)⟩: The January issue of the *LR* prints a letter which EP explains has been sent to a friend from "a vicar highly efficient and deeply respected by his parishioners." The letter, entitled "Thoughts from a Country Vicarage," maintains that the "errors" of Christianity ("a doctrine of death") "took a very large part in wrecking civilization, fifteen centuries ago; and, so far as they were able to prevail they made a hell of Europe for over a thousand years. The same principles would hand us over again to the same barbarians, if they were as influential now as they were in the fifth century, which fortunately they are not; but they are still mischievous and prevalent enough, so I hope Pound and his allies will go for them with their sharpest weapons, though I think only clubs and stones are effective against the density of theologians. . . ." EP's commentary on the letter claims, "We are not out to support or destroy any religion. We stand simply for the free right of expression" [*LR* (January 1918): 52–53].

*"The Soil":* Five numbers of *The Soil: A Magazine of Art* were published in New York from December 1916 through July 1917. The art editor was R. J. Coady and the literary editor, Enrique Cross.

*Coady's gallery:* The Coady Gallery was located at 489 Fifth Avenue in New York. An ad for the gallery in *The Soil* made this promise: "The Art Value and the Market Value of each Work Permanently Guaranteed."

*"Soirees de Paris":* Les Soirées de Paris published twenty-seven numbers from February 1912 through August 1914. The journal was edited by Guillaume Apollinaire.

*The illustrations in "The Soil":* R. J. Coady's "The Indeps," a review of an exhibition of the Society of Independent Artists in the July 1917 issue (202–10) included reproductions or photos of works by Mrs. Harry Payne Whitney, Paul Signac, Diego M. Rivera, Samuel Halpert, L. S. Forbes, Albert Gleizes, Maurice de Vlaminck, Gardner Hale, Charles Demuth, Michael Brenner, André Derain, Marsden Hartley, Constantin Brancusi, John Marin, A. Walkowitz, Pablo Picasso, Max Weber, Jean Metzinger, Joseph Stella, Robert Delaunay, Juan Gris. A reproduction of Renoir's "Jongleuses," along with other reproductions of his paintings, was included in an article by Ambrose Vollard, entitled "How I Came to Know Renoir," in the same issue of the magazine (189–93).

**47. TLS–1.** On stationery embossed: 5, Holland Place Chambers/ Kensington. W. ⟨8⟩ [21 September 1917]

Dear Margaret:

I think May [Sinclair] has done the Eliot job very nobly. It is an excellent BLAST. It is a wee bit longer than I expected, but it is firm. I hope you can get it into Dec.

Note change of address.

Miss Saunders, now, 4 Percy St. W.1.

New subscriber from Paris, but I'm not sure of the street, and have written for a clearer caligraphic statement of address. I thought it was rue Flerus [Fleurus?], and sent May to Aug. there, then looked at note, and felt uncertain.

*/////*
    Perhaps you'd better send.
Miss J. Dismorr, in my care until further notice.
at any rate the sub. is paid.
        *///////*
I enclose also a brief note of wants. for insertion if you see fit.

You can scrunch M.S.'s article into small space by printing quotations from Prufrock [in] very small type. Smaller than the quoted verse in my Rabelais.

> yours ever
> Ezra Pound
> 21-9-17

*Eliot job:* May Sinclair's article on T. S. Eliot's *Prufrock and Other Observations* was published in the December 1917 issue (8–14). In it, Miss Sinclair says of Eliot that he "does not see anything between him and reality, and he makes straight for the reality he sees; he cuts all his corners and his curves; and this directness of method is startling and upsetting to comfortable, respectable people accustomed to going superfluously in and out of corners and carefully round curves. . . . [Eliot] knows what he is after. Reality, stripped naked of all rhetoric, of all ornament, of all confusing and obscuring association, is what he is after."

**48. TLS–6.** On stationery embossed: 5, Holland Place Chambers/ Kensington. W. ⟨8⟩ [27 September 1917]

⟨Sept. 27.
1917⟩

Dear Margaret:

        September here. You do fetch some beauties in the correspondence column.

    The "Old Reader" is "sure" the "reel" type of American cad. (The word that really applies is not one I can write even to you.). He has never supported the paper. (vide lovely euphuism "never been a real subscriber"). Too god damn stingy to fork up. Parasite to the bone, getting his students by reason of reputation for having watched you bathing in the great (expansive Harriet-Monroe-wide) Pacific. He now groans.

I remember, as I have writ you, the chap who having come into a comfortable fortune wrote me for free copies of my early books, at a time I couldn't be sure of next weeks dinner.

Presbyterian horse-dealers, they love the naive and spontaneous because it is an easier mark for their sponging.

/////

Good old [Rabindranath] Tagore. He'd be invaluable if he hadn't got mixed up with the soapy-mouthed religiose element.

///

As for H.L.C. (? half-louse contingent). They've as "jh" [Jane Heap] says, got the whole reeking desert from constipated Maine to the sage-bush of Nevady, and not one decent writer in the whole dasted zoo . . . . . . . . really.!!!!

Moral cowardice, and the terror of competition have never been carried further, not even in the society of British native musicians, and the British concert ballad singer is a pretty tough nut.

If this keeps on we will have to disinfect ourselves and transfer the main office to Paris (faith or no faith in jejune America)[.]

/////

I enclose 20 dollars, advance on subscriptions I haven't yet taken but expect to. I have caught up with the $40 sent and the $25 paid to H.D.

Have I sent you the order for one copy

DUBLINERS?

I cant remember. One cant get it here, and a subscriber wants it. So please send it (to me) and charge to the account. (There is only one copy ordered, so IF [I] have ordered it and it is sent, don't bother to send a second.)

Subscriber:

Lieut. Brenan, The Closes, Edgeworth,
Cirencester, Glos. England.

⟨Begin Aug
I have sent May
June July.⟩

The Poetry Book Shop has written for single copies of June. I dont think it is worth bothering about @ 7 d.

I have quoted them these prices.

May 1/6, June 2/ shillings, July 1/6

so dont sell 'em cheaper if the P.B.S. writes to you.

Our bound vol will be worth, or at least should be worth something. I dont think it is worth humoring misers, and the review is so cheap at 7/ a year that those who merely want the Yeats poems ought to fork out.

Besides people will want back numbers a lot more if they think the price is going up.

Is Miss Bertha Fiske a friend of yours, I have had a good letter from her. (Los Angeles)

///

Damn [T. S.] Eliot. He hasn't finished that poem yet. BUT GAWD'A'MITY it is a comfort to get someone who dont bring in the stuff half baked. I wish to heaven there was as little rubbish in what I have printed as there is in what he has.

My "Homme [Moyen Sensuel]" is unsatisfactory, but not so bad as I thought.

Perhaps it will set off some others. I think that sort of thing wants doing. "Old Subscriber" would make a fine subject.

With verse as free as Sanborn's I don't think there is any excuse for such hackneyed rhymes, or words like "bade". I think the general faults ⟨in his poem⟩ are those which Dante labels "muliebria". Would Sanborn read the De Volgari Eloquio [Dante's *De Vulgari Eloquentia*] if someone told him of its existence?

Of course you can use hackneyed rhymes IF you do it in the right way, . It is perfectly permissable and is good art to use hackneyed things IF you reinvigorate them[.]

Eeldrop II, seems to me better on the page than it did in typescript, but then I rushed it off to you almost before I had read it.

I still dont see how I could have got the few decent stabs in "L'Homme" into anything much shorter, one has to string 'em together somehow. ACH '!!!

I wonder even now if it [is] loose-knit enough to reach the store-post-office mentality.

You might correct the line
Upon a tale, to combat other tracts
in a copy for Knopf. You've got "facts" as it now stands. ⟨p. 11. & O clap hands ye moralists p. 15⟩ It is not serious, and one needn't put an errata

slip into the L.R. But Knopf is to decide whether the poem goes into my prose miscellany, and he may as well have a correct text.

The damn French number is going to be about as much work as a book.

///

Confound propaganda. . Still I hope a few phrases in L'Homme will stick in a few heads and convert 'em.

////

Gargoyles '!! Whoop !!!

///

I suppose J. is J.Q. [John Quinn], I am glad he is taking an interest.

///

[James] Joyce's wife writes that the operation on his eye has been I suppose successful, at least he is getting well, and there have been no after effects. [Wyndham] Lewis is not in a safe place, worse luck, and damn the bosche, and the people who keep him there. It is not as if the country were crawling with artists, or could afford to dispense with him.

////

"Phosphorous surf and other delightful sins", really that chap is too tew delightful. 'E 'ad a vision, a wishion. Like the prophets of old. He 'ad all the gamut of lov pashions, save the impulse to buy the laidy a plate of ice-cream.

////

Lewis repeating Remy [de Gourmont] is another prize bit of guff. "Inferior Religions" ought to smack that in the eye.

///

"Rite heer in yer owne country".

reminds me of Rummel. He lectured me most sternly in 1910. he was going back to America, american artists ought to go back etc.

Met him in America. six weeks had finished him. he fled to the sanctuary of my parental home, he fled back to Europe four months before I did. I at least waited until the country had brought on a jaundice. (physical, hospital case jaundice).

gross earnings during eight months, exactly 70 dollars, precise fare from Phila. to Paris, second class.

And DAMMMMN well spent.

Of course I'm coming back to have a look round, and place a wreath on the tomb of freedom one of these days, (besides I want to see dear old New York, the sole last oasis.).

L'Homme is "familiar subject" all right enough. We do occasionally seem to anticipate the onslaught. Lewis in July rounded up a whole lot of 'em.

/ / /

What do you make of Eunice Tietjens chinese impressions. They seem to me pleasant but lacking in impact. Possibly worth a half page review. Her previous stuff, at least all I have seen, seemed that of an utter fool.

I think it is important to keep at least an American (native) department. Old Hatteras, or Agnes Repplier, or Edith Wharton might easily turn the edge of this "native" attack . ?????

Though their alliance, i.e. that of the last two, may be as impracticable as it would be if you suggested my getting Gosse and the British Academy to declare for us. Still I dont think it is quite the same. Agnes has fought most frightfully for a long time. (uncreative, but not giving in) and Edith can or could write good prose.

I think you might do an article on her work, if you dont too much loathe it. Or if it hasn't gone off too much since I last saw anything by her.

⟨basta

This is getting too long.⟩

Yours ever E.

Ezra Pound

*"Old Reader":* The Old Reader's letter begins with the admission, "I have never been a real subscriber. The only copy of *The Little Review* I ever bought was the memorable March issue with Galsworthy's letter in it." He continues: "Of late I have thought a good deal about the magazine. I have been camping near the ocean, and have spent some time in your various haunts of last summer where the various natives still gossip about the *Little Review* crowd. Plunging at night into the phosphorous surf and other delightful sins, mingled with communion with some *Little Review* worshippers, has disturbed my academic calm and provoked my reveries. One night I was awakened and perceived an apparition moving from the roaring sea toward my gigantic fire. I heard a voice, a wail: 'Help! Margaret Anderson is murdering me!' Was it the spirit of *The Little Review?"* The letter ends on a bitter note: "An Ezraized *Little Review* is gargoylitic, monstrously so. . . . [I]t is Ezra who sprawls all over *The Little Review* and bedecks it with gargoyles" [*LR* (September 1917): 31–32].

*Good old Tagore:* In her reply to a letter written by "H.L.C." (see following note), Jane Heap complains of America's provincial attitude toward art as exemplified in customs and tariff restrictions on the importation of art and books. To illustrate her point, she refers to two experiences Tagore had when he visited the U.S. During his first visit, he wrote to his London publisher to send more copies of his books to present as gifts. When he discovered the large tariff he would have to pay and the red tape involved, he abandoned the idea. On his second visit, he tried to bring with him a small collection of Indian water colors so that Americans could see Indian art firsthand. At Seattle, however, the authorities required him to deposit forty thousand dollars and, according to Miss Heap, to "swear all kinds of oaths" [*LR* (September 1917): 34].

*H.L.C.:* H.L.C. of Chicago writes, "I wish you didn't have such a craze for foreigners and self-exiled Americans. I think you have missed your chance right here in your own country. . . . I am tired of these floods of Russian, French, Scandanavian [*sic*], Irish and Hindoo stuff that have swept the country" [*LR* (September 1917): 33–34].

*verse as free as Sanborn's:* Robert Alden Sanborn's poem "The Children of Judas" was included in the September 1917 issue (22–30).

*my prose miscellany:* i.e., *Pavannes and Divisions,* which included "L'Homme Moyen Sensuel."

*the operation on his eye:* See Letter 15n.

*reminds me of Rummel:* American pianist Walter Morse Rummel. In March 1910, while on a trip to Italy, EP stopped in Paris and spent several days with Rummel, who was then living there. EP's visit to America took place between June 1910 and February 1911.

*Eunice Tietjens chinese impressions:* Chicago poet Eunice Tietjens (1884–1944) had published *Profiles from China: Sketches in Verse of People and Things in the Interior* (Chicago: R. F. Seymour, 1917), free-verse sketches of the country in which she had lived for two years.

*Gosse:* Sir Edmund Gosse (1849–1928), a prominent British essayist and biographer. The British Academy was incorporated in 1902.

*article on her work:* MCA evidently declined EP's suggestion as no article on Wharton appeared in the *LR*.

**49. TLS–2.**   On stationery embossed: 5, Holland Place Chambers/ Kensington. W. [8 October 1917]

> Oct. 8th. 1917
> ⟨You and J.Q. [John Quinn] seem to be "understanding" each other rather more⟩

Dear Margaret

Packet of Septembers arrives.

The enclosed card has a moral ::: "If the blighters wont subscribe, MAKE 'em pay". The P.B.S. [Poetry Book Shop] has cashed in 7/6 for five numbers, and the "public" will have paid 9/ for the same.

Now that we have published something, and that the bound vols. will be worth something OBVIOUSLY, it is foolish to sell back numbers for 6 d. . Possibly the bound vol May to May, ought to be announced as 2.50 dollars, fairly soon.

///

Have I by the way sent you the name of Subscriber.
Miss M[ary]. Butts, 1 Glenilla Studios, Glenilla Rd. N.W. 3.

IF not, put her down. I have just sent her Sept. Sub runs. May to May. She has had earlier nos. from me.

///

Dont send any more extra copies to Tucker or Hyde-Lees.

s.v.p.

/////

I hope to send off French number this week. I have put a lot of work into it.

I hope it will be possible to set it up on arrival, AND let me have a proof. With so much furring langwudg it will want some correcting.

Of course you might correct it, BUT the french authors wont like it if they are misprinted, AND if possible I should like a proof.

I think the number should be a "special number price 25 cents", with the announcement that price will go to 50 cents as soon as March number appears.

///

Write when you've the time.

AND please acknowledge french no. mss. on arrival. I have a carbon, but its on bad paper, and needs a lot of accent marks etc. and I dont want the fag of putting in order UNless the first mss. gets itself sunk.

///

Oh Yes.
Arthur Symons address is
       Island Cottage, Wittersham, Kent. .
I will send him copies from May to Oct. and two extra Octobers. You might also send him three more copies Oct. (as he is not getting paid for his play), and continue him on free list for rest of the year.
       now to work.

yours ever, saluti to "jh" [Jane Heap].
Ezra           Ezra Pound
               8/10/'17

**50. TLS–3.**   On stationery embossed: 5, Holland Place Chambers/ Kensington. W. [9,10,11 October 1917]

⟨Oct. 9 & 10 & 11⟩

Dear Margaret:

    I figure at two pages of my typescript to one of the L.R., this will go inside 48 pages. That will raise the printer's bill, BUTT you must consider that the number will be a definite property, Like a book and there should be a steady demand for it. . It should be sold first at 25 cents. then at 50 and probably at 75[.] It has more in it than Amy's $2.50 ⟨volume⟩, and there is no other French anthology in English to compete with it. VanBever and Leataud costs $1.25, (probably more in America)[.]

  Harold Monroe's [Monro's] magazine printed a treble number for Flint's study of french stuff in 1912, and it sold over all other nobers [numbers], I'm not sure there wasn't a reprint, and it made the years volume.

  So a slight rise in printing costs is probably not bad as business.

  OF course IF there aint ⟨simply aint⟩ the cash. It could be printed as Feb. and March combined number. BUT I DON'T think this would help in the long run. Anyhow IF my old Spanish mss. sells for anything like a decent sum, there'll be something toward the extra printing.

  Do your damdest anyhow. (Useless exhortation, I know you'll do that in any case, even if I go off my head.)

    As I said in last week's letter. I want the thing sent to the printer at once, so that I can have a proof in time to correct and return to you.

  STILL, at the worst, I have marked the accents almighty big, and you and father (who is not a bad proof reader) could probably see that my mss was followed.

It is rather important that there be no mistakes, or at least no howling mistakes.

  I have had several people run through the typescript, BUT you never can trust anyone to do this sort of thing really perfectly.

  Dieu te benisse.

I have had a lucky day, and found a copy of Gavin Douglas, really better luck than one might have expected. Let us hope it is good augury for the article and the number.

I plan to use this "study" as the backbone of a larger book of "French Studies" but that wont be ready for a year and a half ANYHOW so it wont overcrowd the L.R. sale of the number. But, I hope, act as a buttress, when reviewed.

[T. S.] Eliot has just been through the thing (Oct. 9th. 10.45 p.m.) and thinks I've got the gutts of the animal.

saluti to "jh" [Jane Heap],

yours Ezra

⟨vide p.s.⟩

Ezra Pound

⟨P.S. we will have to devote at least one adv. page of Feb to French publishers. I will send it in a few days (or enclose it). "Mercure" [*Mercure de France*] in particular with list of books, of poets quoted in essay.

This can go  inside ⟨back⟩ cover if there is no other place. or even on back of back cover.⟩

Yours

E.

*It has more in it:* EP's study discusses and quotes from the work of the following poets: Jules Laforgue, Tristan Corbière, Arthur Rimbaud, Remy de Gourmont, Henri de Régnier, Émile Verhaeren, Francis Vielé-Griffin, Stuart Merrill, Laurent Tailhade, Francis Jammes, Jean Moréas, André Spire, Charles Vildrac, and Jules Romains.

*Amy's $2.50 ⟨volume⟩:* See Letter 46n.

*VanBever and Leataud:* Adolphe van Bever and Paul Léautaud's *Poètes d'aujourd'hui, 1880–1900: morceaux choisis accompagnés de notices biographiques et d'un essai de bibliographie* (Paris: Mercure de France, 1900). By 1917, this volume had undergone several revisions and was in its twenty-eighth edition. At least fifty-three editions were eventually published.

*Harold Monroe's magazine:* From January through December of 1912, Harold Monro edited a London monthly entitled *The Poetry Review*. F. S. Flint's study "Contemporary French Poetry" was published in the August 1912 issue and ran fifty-nine pages.

*my old Spanish mss.:* EP was attempting to sell some autograph manuscripts he owned of King Ferdinand and Queen Isabella of Spain, dated 1492. In late August 1917, he had instructed John Quinn to retrieve the manuscripts from his father's safe and sell them. If they brought more than a thousand dollars, he told Quinn, half the money would be put into the *LR*.

*a copy of Gavin Douglas:* EP is probably referring to the following collection of the works of Gavin Douglas (1474?–1522): *The Poetical Works of Gavin*

*Douglas, Bishop of Dunkeld, with Memoir, Notes, and Glossary*, ed. John Small (Edinburgh: W. Paterson, 1874).

*a larger book of "French Studies":* EP included "A Study of French Poets"—expanded with "Unanimisme," "De Bosschère's Study of Elskamp," and "Albert Mockel and 'La Wallonie' "—in *Instigations*.

**51. TLS–2.** On stationery embossed: 5, Holland Place Chambers/ Kensington. W. ⟨8⟩ [14 October 1917]

⟨14/10/'17⟩

Dear M.C.A.

Subscribers:
S[acheverell]. Sitwell, 22 Mulberry Walk, Chelsea, S.W.
Mrs Greenlaw, 13 Linden Gdns. Notting Hill Gate, W. 2.
(numbers May to Sept. supplied, so start em with Oct. and stop with next May.)

I think I sent you notice of
Lieut. Brenan. The Closes, Edgeworth, Cirencester, Glos.
    (May to Aug. supplied).
        ////
I have only two June left. So you might send a few more if convenient . .

Let me know if early nos. show signs of running low. When they do I will stop starting all subs. with May no.
        ////
[William Butler] Yeats say[s] for success we ought to print more book reviews and criticism. There may be something in it. He has a practical streak. I am trying to get the right person for monthly note on France. We might begin fairly soon devoting two sides of a page to American books, Eng. books. Fr. books of the month. (or not necessarily OF the month, but books worth while that have appeared reasonably recently.) My "List of Books" and "French number" of course anticipate W.B.Y's remarks, but still, a regular monthly habit is different from a spasmodic gulp. It would be best for you and "jh" [Jane Heap] to do the American reviewing. But if you are too busy. . . . . ? . Oh hell, if you are too busy Gawd knows who can be got to do it.
    Alice Corbin [Henderson] is the only person who ever showed a grain of intelligence (not infallible), and she's Harriet's [Monroe] I presume.
    There ought to be at least these three 2 pp. articles, (the List of

books sort of thing) every month. between the "creation" and the reader critic., or at the back end of the number.

Also we ought to have £10,000 a year. etc. . . . .

yours      E

Ezra Pound

*My "List of Books":* See *LR* (August 1917): 6–11.
*"French number":* i.e., "A Study in French Poets," *LR* (February 1918): [3]–61.

**52. TLS–2.**   On stationery embossed: 5, Holland Place Chambers/ Kensington. W. ⟨8⟩ [5 November 1917]

⟨5–11–17⟩

Dear M.C.A.

I am still awaiting twenty letters and the Oct. number.

In the mean time re / Minaret. a new topic. I don't know whether this paper still exists. I have not seen any copy later than Nov. 1916. But that number is right in spirit.

It strikes me that we might incorporate to mutual advantage.

I mean if you note the format of the "Mercure" [*Mercure de France*] you will find the rubrics or little chronicles at the end. Lettres Portugaise[s], Lettres d'Hollande, Lettres Allemande[s], etc.

These chronicles are, I believe, independent, and under the control of the men whose name appears on the cover.

Not to copy the Mercure too closely, I think we might have Washington, Boston, even Chicago, as separate rubrics in the L.R., and as good men would want to be independent, they might, if discoverable, have control of their sections. (You have not curtailed me, and I dont suppose you want to curtail anyone else.)

The editor of the Minaret is, or was, Herbert Bruncken, associated with him Richard C DeWolf,[.]

I wonder would they pool resources, and perhaps even keep their Title as a heading, 7 or 8 pages a month, printed in the L.R., headed "The Minaret" Washington.

Their subscribers to go onto our list, or the "combined list".

I should think Bruncken and de Wolf could be trusted to edit themselves or each other.

We must build up a stronger party of intelligence in America. I think a union of small papers of the right spirit is as likely a way as another. One must avoid papers like the N[ew]. Republic and the Seven Arts, the difference between heavy stupidity and light silliness.

The Minaret looks to me a possible paper to combine with. One can only join one from each city or section of the country.

If you dont want to write to Bruncken, I will do so, or you can forward this to him. I think the advantages of a free union are obvious. His, Bruncken's address is, or was, 1724 Kilbourne Place, Washington.

> Yours
> Ezra Pound
> 5–11–17

*Minaret:* Edited by Herbert Bruncken, *The Minaret* was published monthly in Washington, D.C., from November 1915 to October 1926, suspending publication, however, from July 1917 to April 1923. In an editorial in the first issue, Bruncken announced the magazine's goal: "We are not Cubists, Futurists, or Imagists. We do not pretend to stand for the past or future, but for the present. We have a single aim, and that is to produce a magazine that we hope will appeal to those who are fond of good literature. In a word, we are interested in the literature of our own country, but we believe that by publishing in this magazine, in the future, translations of the modern French and German poets, we are enriching our own literature."

**53. TLS–6.** On stationery embossed: 5, Holland Place Chambers/ Kensington. W. [5 November 1917]

Dear Margaret

You wrote a while ago that you wanted "to absorb everything". Here are a few absorbent suggestions. Tear 'em up if you, being on the ground, see reasons against 'em not visible at this distance.:

1. Pause and read enclosed (a), note re The Minaret. written so that you can forward it to [Herbert] Bruncken without bothering to copy it. IF it looks good to you.

@ 2. Assuming you have read note to Bruncken.

I think we might absorb several small papers. Giving to none more than 8 pages.

Making sure that they contribute enough to cover cost of ⟨printing the⟩ eight page[s] allowed them.

Also making it clear that each rubricist is responsible for the stuff in his rubric AND that the central editors assume no responsibility for opinions or quality in rubric. Rubricist is given the "rope".

If he makes an ass of himself, connections can be severed.

NEXT.

A chap with the awful name of Glen Levin Swiggett, once edited a paper called the "Pathfinder" address Sewanee, Tenn. IS he by any chance good enough to represent the "South", or the Middle S.W. in the "L.R."?

Would he slide in ? His paper used to be 20 small pages. Eight of our size should hold it.

NEXT.

Could Amy [Lowell] be trusted to be the Boston rubric. She would have to find the cash for the printer (and that she would not like.).

I have had a brief line from her in reply to my opening demarche. I have also written again to her lest she should get the eronious [sic] idea that I had apologized for ANYTHING she had ever done. Passons.

The point of a rubric is that we get support ⟨or should get it⟩ without assuming responsibility.

We get possibly a wider subscription list without conceding an inch of our OWN position re/ what is fit to read.

/////

Anyhow, there's the suggestion.

I think J.Q. [John Quinn] is more pleased with us. He will be able to get us more subsidy than we should ever get for ourselves IF he once gets it imbedded in his head that we are worth tackling his friends for.

Nail a copy of the "Mercure" [Mercure de France] to your wall, and keep your eye on its magnitude. (remember its quondam quality, and make allowances for effect of war on France if you happen [to] get a current number.)

Joyce seems pretty sure his novel [Ulysses] will be ready ⟨to begin in⟩ our March number.

Details.

Free subs. beginning May.

Arthur Symons, Island Cottage, Wittersham, Kent. Eng.

///

Mercure de France, 26 rue de Condé, Paris,
          ///
Theodore Stanton, co/ the Mercure de France
          ////
Free, beginning with Sept. to
H.D.Davray, 8 St Martin's Place, London W.C.2.

Send me more copies of all issues up to date. I am at about the end of my supply. If we can only hang on a bit longer results will begin to arrive.

⟨Poetry's page is smaller than ours. We must go to 64. (their number of pages) as soon as possible.⟩

                    yours ever
⟨vide P.S.⟩                    E.                    Ezra Pound
                                                     5–11–17

P.S. To hammer out the whole thing again:

> IT IS RIDICULOUS that the English speaking world can't turn out a magazine as good as the "Mercure". Even as good as the "Mercure" was at its best when all its contributors were in their best vigour.
>
> The "Mercure" represents the opinion not of one man but of a committee, or rather of a selected lot.

(Some of them block heads, but still the most intelligent available.)
          ////

> WE CERTAINLY MUST NOT give up an inch of our central position or let in any paper or group that would over balance the present core of the magazine.
>           //
> I think the very small magazines with decent intentions may be of some use. Or some few of them may be found that would be of use.
>
> I think the form of approach would be better comprising pp. 1 and part of 2, as inked, above. Then the query "Will you take on a rubric of the L.R. as Gustav Kahn, Appollinaire, etc. do on the Mercure. Independent inside your rubric.
>
> "Will your paper consent to Amalgamate, on these terms, by so doing you will get a wider public, and chance of higher returns in every way?"

Bruncken and Swiggett are the only possibilities I can see at the moment ⟨from here.⟩ With a possible Amy TO BE CONSIDERED. Always remembering that she will be in a constant "fronde" to push us out and run the whole paper. And that both you, jh [Jane Heap], and I will have to keep a constant eye on her.

She could help.   BUTTT . . . . . . . . . ! ! ! ! ! ! ! ! ! !

I dont think [Alfred] Kreymborg would do. We must have people who can do criticism. NOT fools who think they can write. We ⟨have⟩ practically got ⟨NOW⟩ enough creative stuff to carry us, the next problem is the coating, the axle grease, the stuff which is [would] make us appear "not too wholly foreign and exotic".

I don't want to sleep until we can steam-roller over the Century in a magazine using just as much paper.

Above all we mustn't make mistakes. We can afford quite well Not to absorb anything. It is simply a question whether certain small periodicals are not our natural aliment.

They must be tactfully swallowed. I can, of course, always be called upon to testify "that Miss Anderson has assigned to me the London rubric and that I have had no cause to regret accepting it, that I have in fact been most happy, etc. I recommend you, Mr Plughoff, to do likewise and thank your gods the chance is allowed you."

⟨We are a going concern people will be increasingly anxious to get in with us.⟩

Half baked people are no use to us. Only men who have run a small periodical fairly decently for a year at least could be trusted, or men of decent intelligence and conscious of the rotundity of the planet.

Amy has heard of Paris, and she would be able to pay the printer, And she would advertise us like HELL. It is her talent. Only for GOD's sake be careful if you enter into any relations with her save those of an editor to an INCIDENTAL contributor.

I think you were very wise to refuse any thought of combining with "Others", none of that gang have the necessary knowledge of the proportion of things.

(I hope [William Carlos] Williams will send you something fit to print, and that his brother will send you some good copy on American architecture, but heaven alone knows what they will send.).

I think Alice Henderson might do "Chicago". (In fact "Poetry" itself would do excellently well as an absorbed rubric . . . . HUSH, HESH YO! NOISE, CHILE. Harriet [Monroe] would commit murder if she overheard us.).

　　　　Now I'm going to stop, and see what can be done with L'Alliance Francaise, An american society which ought to make us its official mouthpiece. IF it isn't defunct.

yours

E

*re The Minaret:* See Letter 52n.

*Glen Levin Swiggett:* Swiggett (1867–1961), an American educator and publicist, was a professor of languages in a number of American universities. In 1906 he founded *The Pathfinder* (Sewanee, Tennessee), a monthly devoted to literature and art. Swiggett edited the magazine until its demise in December 1911.

*Gustav Kahn:* French Symbolist poet Gustave Kahn (1859–1936) was one of the early practitioners of *vers libre,* about which he also wrote numerous articles.

*"Others":* See Letter 3n.

*his brother:* See Letter 40n. No articles by Edgar Williams appeared in the *LR.*

**54. TLS–7.**   Incomplete item. The first page and half of the second are missing. [probable date: 6 November 1917]

///

I think the enclosed of J. R.'s [John Rodker's] is fairly amusing. Do what you like with it.

////

I sent you yesterday's boiling of ideas re/ the magazine.

///

I see you have the Modern Gallery ad. Their list of names is good. Are our illustrations from J. Q.'s [John Quinn's] collection or from them.

　　　　If I didn't say so before, I will say now, that the Mod. Gallery ought to pay for half a dozen reproductions a month, simply cost of blocks and printing. It would add to us, and advertise their painters. Probably better for both of us, NOT to say "Work of Picasso, now at Mod. gallery". Or perhaps have five illustrations not saying where originals are, and then one (somewhere third or fourth in the lot) "at Mod. gal."

////

I can't greatly regret the demise of the "Seven Arts", But you are quite right to deplore its having died of strangulation.

Are there any fragments (authors I mean) worth picking from its wreckage ?????
                    Je m'en doute.
IF Frost had the makings, or the beginnings of the makings of a man in him, he would have seen to it that the Seven Arts had printed something of mine, however small.

This is not a grouch, it is simply a statement. I don't much mind having been shut out, and now they are dead and buried, BUT after my reception of Frost here, AND the fuss I had to get Harriet [Monroe] to print him, or rather to start printing him; AND the fact that I hammered at him the fact that his North of Boston series was the next thing for him to do.

He had the thing in mind, I dont want any credit for a jot more than I did, which was simply to hustle to get the first of those idyls into print, and to emphasize the fact that "That was his job".

But how the devil after that and the detail it implies UNLESS HE DEFINITELY THINKS MY WORK ROTTEN, (which he has never had the frankness to say). IF he thinks my work rotten, then its all right, but if he don't think my stuff worthless, I'm damd if I see how he could have been on the advisory board of a paper without trying to get its taboo off me.

However, that's an aside. I dont imagine he will contribute to the L.R. without being paid. Was there anybody else on the Seven A. who can write. ?

Masters has gone damn well futt in the Oct. "Poetry".

I dont know [*crossout:* Untermeyer] ⟨Oppenheim⟩ save in the 7 A. BUTTT we might make a star hit by offering him a rubric in the L.R.

An assylum [*sic*] in time of stress (NOT for politics, that is not our affair.).

Magnanimity to a fallen (so far as I am concerned) inimical party.

(I have just written Untermeyer for Oppenheim, I suppose they are different ????? ) )

Of course I DONT believe in any of 'em. A man with any mental alertness COULDN't have run such a dull paper. AND with such a subsidy.

On the whole I am for not bothering with them, but you are in N.Y. and are in a better position to judge.

What does J.Q. think of the various members of the ex-staff ???? I know he thought the whole paper bad.

*

It might, of course, be possible to offer the ex-editor in chief a temporary rubric. Just that, a ⟨shelter⟩ in time of storm. (Not political.) Simply a statement. Mr. O. is an american literateur [*sic*] of some standing deprived for the present of his roof-tree. We disagree with him (IF you do disagree) but we give him a corner of the settle, until he is ready to get out and get on.

[Robert] Frost's work had something to it. I haven't seen any since North of Boston. It always was a bit dull, but still real, certainly he never got as bad as Masters in Oct. Poetry.

DAMMN how I do run on. Dont bother to answer all this. ONLY, as we can't talk (and talk would get through ⟨the matter⟩ a dozen ten page letters in an evening) I may as well slap down anything that comes into my head.

////

Minor detail. Address of London Office, omitted from current number.

///

SUBSCRIBER

Lytton Strachey, Esq. 6 Belsize Park Gdns.

                 Hampstead, London N.W. 3.

(May, July, Aug. Sept. supplied.) Please send him June and
     continue from Oct.

DO you realize that this is of the very camp of the "Spectator" clan.

It is what it would be if Carson's family took to subscribing to Sinn Fein publications.

BAIA MEN ALLA RHODA, freely "Few, but bulls-eyes"[.]

////

Returning to the Oppenheim, Untermeyer, contingent. Do for God's sake make sure they aren't German subsidized. Vierick was of course definitely in German pay. I ⟨believe⟩ they had nothing directly to do with him. Still there is a point beyond which literary courtesy can not go. And we have too much at stake to take on suspects.


REMEMBER that the Kaiser was giving prizes for "art" in California before the war, long before it. And this not for any artistic reason. Remember that he practically barred French art, Manet and that lot from Berlin. And that he was ⟨I believe⟩ a constant damn nuissance in Germany with his interference in artistic affairs.

I know you dont see the serpent in the same scales that I do. BUt, but, but, . . . .

*////*

The possible error in your slash at Mrs Rankine, lies in chance she may have subsidized a magazine for the arts; and that she would then have had the right to object to its being turned into a political organ.

(I don't in the least know that such was the case. I dare say you have more data than you have printed.) Consider how jolly much quicker the Kaiser would have withdrawn a subsidy, if the least tendency to freedom had shown itself.

(Bugbear ??? )

My whole position is that we want all the freedom we can get, and I see Habsburg and Hohenzollern as the two most powerful enemies to freedom; even more powerful than the prohibitionist. Austria in history !!! utter repression.

*///*

I was talking to a conscientious objector, Whitham, who has been jailed and let out to do clerical work. At the end he said to me "Of course, I admit that in Germany I should have [been] shot long ago.".

Only England has allowed conscientious objection. And most of the fuss that has been made has been made by objectors who werent particularly conscientious. The few c.o's that I know seem to object more to being herded with other c.o's, than anything else that has befallen them. Perhaps I exaggerate this a little.

Still when one thinks how long England retained the voluntary system, . . . England alone . . . .

How she has persisted in keeping up freedoms that amount almost to criminal negligence in time of war.

Oh well, enough of this. Let us get on with our own affairs.

I shall treat German poetry in due course.

yours  E.        Ezra Pound

*the Modern Gallery ad:* The October 1917 issue of the *LR* contained an advertisement for the Modern Gallery, 500 Fifth Avenue, which listed the names of the following artists: Daumier, Cézanne, Toulouse-Lautrec, Van Gogh, Picasso, Brancusi, Picabia, Derain, Vlaminck, Rivera, and Braque. The advertisement also announced Mexican Pre-Conquest art and African Negro sculpture.

*the demise of the "Seven Arts":* In an editorial in its last issue (October 1917), the editor of *The Seven Arts* James Oppenheim explained the magazine's difficulties:

[The War] carried with it a menace to what we believed to be the promise of American life. We found then that we could not ignore it: that everything THE SEVEN ARTS stood for was bound up with this new national action. We were forced, for the time being, to include it in the work and expression of the magazine.

As a result, the idea of combining financial backing with full editorial freedom has broken down, the subsidy has been withdrawn. Perhaps this was to be expected. It is proof of the overmastering national obsession of the war. They who could agree to disagree on so many things, have here an irreconcilable and dividing difference. And such is the awakening tribal consciousness in the madness of war, that no longer is there that generous allowance for free expression, for diversity of opinion (672a–c).

*If Frost had the makings:* Robert Frost was on the advisory board of *The Seven Arts.* The fact that EP's work never appeared in the magazine, even though Frost held the position he did, must have seemed to EP the height of ingratitude, for EP had exerted considerable effort in promoting Frost's early work.

*Masters has gone damn well futt . . . :* EP is referring to Edgar Lee Masters' poem "Canticle of the Race," which was published in *Poetry* (October 1917): 1–5.

*Oppenheim:* James Oppenheim (1882–1932), American writer of plays, stories, novels, and verse. Oppenheim's work often expressed radical social ideas and his pacifist's views led to the withdrawal of funds from *The Seven Arts.* See above note.

*Untermeyer:* New York poet and editor Louis Untermeyer (1885–1977).

*very camp of the "Spectator" clan:* The Strachey family had close ties to the *Spectator,* a London weekly. St. Loe Strachey was the journal's editor from 1898 to 1925, and Lytton Strachey contributed, from 1904 to 1914, more than ninety reviews to its pages.

*Carson's family:* EP's reference is to the family of Edward Henry Carson (1854–1935), an Irishman and a vehement opponent of Home Rule for Ireland.

*Vierick:* George Sylvester Viereck (1884–1962), a German-born American poet, novelist, journalist, and political writer. During the First World War, Viereck was strongly criticized for expressing pro-German views in his magazine *The Fatherland* (later renamed *The American Monthly*). Viereck was a friend of Wilhelm II and kept close ties with him following his abdication, collaborating with him on many articles published under the ex-Kaiser's name. During the Second World War, Viereck was imprisoned for failing to register as a foreign agent. His correspondence with Wilhelm II has been purchased by Harvard University.

*your slash at Mrs Rankine:* Mrs. Rankine had furnished the subsidy for *The Seven Arts,* a subsidy she withdrew because of the pacifist stance of the magazine. (See above note.) MCA took Mrs. Rankine to task in the October 1917 issue of the *LR.*

**55. TLS–2.** On stationery embossed: 5, Holland Place Chambers/ Kensington. W. [6 November 1917]

Dear M.

I trust Mr Abel Sander[s]'s little attempt may find a place in the correspondence col.

It is time something was done about [Vachel] Lindsay's manner. It really is tew bloomin easy.

S.O.S's little vignette had better not go into the same month.

*////*

If I have left out any of Lindsay, please let me know, I've got the religion and the "whistled, gristle" pseudo rhyme, etc. and the touch of [W. B.] Yeats, and such ingredients as I have noticed.

*////*

We must have a real cow-boy ballad sometime.

I've only got as far as
  "Then out spoke Bishop Talbot
      of Wy o ming,
  "I'm a man of peace, my brethren,
      But that greaser's got to swing." "

???? what price a leetle real Chippewa folk lore,

      Bone arrow,
      bow of beaver wood,
      my squaw is a corker
      my cork is a squa[w]ker,
                  minne-hoo-loo
            Laughing water.
Lone on the lost trail the brave of the Chippewas
Searches for the moose tracks
In Northern Wisconsin.
      Death to narrow feet from the bad lands.

This wont do, but something may come in time.

                  Yours
                    E.
                  Ezra Pound
                  6/11/17

*Mr Abel Sander[s]'s little attempt:* "Abel Sanders" was a pseudonym used by EP. The "little attempt," a poem entitled "Mr. Lindsay," parodied the style of Vachel Lindsay. At the end of the poem, "Abel Sanders" wrote, "Time consumed in composition 4 minutes 31 seconds." The first two stanzas of the fifty-eight line poem are representative:

> Whoop golly-ip Zopp, bop BIP! !
> I'm Mr. Lindsay with the new sheep-dip,
> I'm a loud-voiced yeller, I'm a prancing preacher,
> Gawd's in his heaven. I'm the *real* High Reacher.
> When Moses to the Red Sea came
> He yelled to Jehovah and the answer was the same:
> "I will lead you onward, in a pillar of flame".
>
> Oh, the little red fox whistled,
> Tho' my heart was like gristle,
> The little red fox whistled and smoothed his reddish breeches,
> There's a wide wind blowing in the Illinois beeches.

The parody was published in the "Reader Critic" of the January 1918 issue of the *LR* (54–55).

*S.O.S.'s little vignette:* i.e., "The Quintuple Effulgence or the Unapproachable Splendour," signed S.O.S. Donald Gallup attributes authorship of this "vignette" to EP (see *Ezra Pound*, C318b). Contrary to EP's instructions, MCA included it with the Lindsay parody in the January 1918 "Reader Critic" (56). The short piece pokes fun at John Masefield and others:

> At a feast of honour to Masefield
> The following people sat for their photograph:
> Mr. Lawrence Housman
> Mr. Witter Bynner,
> Mr. Cale Young Rice,
> Mr. Edwin Markham,
> Mr. Louis Untermeyer
> Miss Amy Lowell
> Mr. J.D. Something or other,
> Mr. Masefield,
> Mr. Noyes.

**56. TLS–3.** On stationery embossed: 5, Holland Place Chambers/ Kensington. W. ⟨8⟩ [11 November 1917]

Dear Margaret:

Subscriptions (paid.) begin May. number.
Flight Commander B.C.Windeler, to be sent
       co Windeler & Co. 20 Basinghall St. E.C.
    and marked "please forward"

(I have sent all but June and Sept. (i.e. May to Oct. minus those nos., so please send them. to him)

Lady Leslie, 46 Gt. Cumberland Place. W. 1.

Shane Leslie, "Cedars", Port Washington, Long Island. U.S.A.

Sir Thomas Beecham, "The Albany" W.1.

(I asked you to send him free copies. I dont know how many you sent. you'd better send him all since Aug. he has paid up 10/ so call it sub. to end of second year (i.e. Apr. 1919.))

The following will probably subscribe at any rate start sending them the magazine.

Duchess of Rutland. 16 Arlington St. S. W.

Duchess of Marlborough 38 b. Curzon St. W. 1.

(I have sent her May to Oct. so begin with Nov.)

E. Marsh Esq. co/ Poetry Book Shop, Devonshire St. W.C.

Lady Howard De Walden, Seaford House, Belgrave Sq. ⟨W.1.⟩

Rt Hon. Mrs. Montagu ⟨24⟩ Queen Anne's Gate. ⟨S.⟩ W. 1

Mrs John Astor, 18 Grosvenor Sq. W.1.

Rt. Hon Augustin Birrel, ⟨70⟩ Elm Park Rd. S.W. ⟨3.⟩

/////

The important thing is in my cable (which goes tomorrow a.m. that being Monday). "Print December immediately send ninety copies immediately important"

Pound.

It is to put on the book stall at the big bazaar for Soldiers benefit, early in Dec. I dont know quite what the date is. At any rate it will go to the right people. And also as the charity will make a bonus, the postal authorities shouldn't mind the ninety copies. I should by that time have some extra copies of early nos. as asked for. in earlier letters, in case more or [are] wanted. IF by any miracle there are any more demanded, the names of subscribers can be put down, and copies sent later.

I believe it [is a] wounded soldier benefit (so "JH." [Jane Heap] may pacify her antimilitarist mind).

I would cable you to send 'em to Lady Cunard, but the name and address would cost me eight shillings [and] might not be clear in the cable, and it is just as good to send 'em to me.

Now that there is something to show I think we can introduce ourselves more openly.

IF the Dec. dont get here in time, I shall use back numbers, BUT I have NONE on hand now, and don't know when more will arrive.

I hope you ⟨will⟩ have a gorgeous colour [for the magazine's wrapper] for Dec. but trust all that to you and luck. I think my cable is adequate. AND I think the Lewis, De Gourmont, plus the Eliot boom by M[ay].S[inclair]. are the right number to have current. at an important moment. Nov. is too retrospective. London has heard of Lady Gregory before. (some time before.)

I shall try to print an announcement and blank of review, and have it put in all books on the book stall if that is agreeable to the ruling powers, who are at the moment quite amiable.

### ///

P.S. One M. Michelson of Chicago has sent me some poems, which I criticized firmly and returned. he has emended, and sent 'em back. I have again told him to reamend, and then to submit to you, as he was in your dept. not in mine. He seems more intent on getting something done, than do some others. One or two looked good enough to print. (oh, perhaps . . I'm not very sure but one must devote an occasional half page to possibilities.)

Yours

Ezra

P.S. IF this reaches you before you have sent the Dec., send half of them to Lady Cunard, 2 Upper Brook St. W. 1., and the other half to me.

From now on you might send her six copies each month, I think she can be relied on to distribute them to advantage.

Ezra Pound
11/11/17

*Lady Cunard:* Prominent London hostess, Lady Maud Alice Burke Cunard (1872–1948), the American wife of Sir Bache Cunard and mother of Nancy Cunard.

*the Lewis, De Gourmont, plus the Eliot boom by M.S.:* i.e., Wyndham Lewis's "A Soldier of Humour," a letter from Remy de Gourmont, and May Sinclair's review of T. S. Eliot's "Prufrock and Other Observations."

*Lady Gregory:* i.e., Lady Gregory's "Hanrahan's Oath," published in the November 1917 issue. See Letter 21n.

*M. Michelson:* Two poems by Max Michelson, "A Woman Tramp" and "Dans l'eau," were published in the June 1918 issue of the *LR* (38).

**57. TLS–3.** On stationery embossed: 5, Holland Place Chambers/ Kensington. W. [12 November 1917]

Dear Margaret

Forgot to say yesterday that the Flight Com. wanted also "The Portrait of Artist"

to Flight Commander B.C. Windeler

co Windeler and Co. 20 Basinghall St. E.C.

marked "please forward."

////

Also, until I find out where the possible boom here is going, I think you may as well go slow on the alliances suggested in my letter of last week. I dont know that either the "Minaret" or Amy [Lowell] will carry to this side of the water.

Lady C. says "DONT make it bigger. DONT make it any bigger, or I wont have time to read it."

C'est une egoisme. But still it is also a point of view and a preference. Beecham, who is not by any means an imbecile, says there isn't and wont be enough French to be chronicled more often than once in three months.

ON the other hand "the public" likes a lot of paper for its money.

One has to think of it both ways.

I'm not sure but 64 pages would be enough. 64 exclusive of reproductions of pictures and sculpture.

Possibly reproductions, eight or 16 pages every third number, would be enough.

I think I could get a shilling [a] copy, three dollars a year, for the magazine at that size. HERE.

????? The reader in Omaha???

????? the proportionate possible number of readers here, to number in Omaha????

/////

Fundamental (though irrelevant consideration), the smaller the paper, the lower the printer's bill.

///

The smaller, the higher it will be possible to keep the quality. (Certainly we mustn't get too big. Poetry is swelled so that . . . . ! ! ! !)

///

This looks like damn vacillation from my letter re/ swallowing small papers, sent last week. However ! ! ! ! The one thing that prevents, utterly prevents a paper from moving on or up is a set block of the WRONG thing, (like Dora [Marsden] in the Egoist).

///

All that it comes to is that IF I can now get the right sort of support here, we wont need to bother with Alliances in the U.S.A. with other papers or persons.

////

I think the [Ford Madox] Hueffer stuff [*Women & Men*] ought to start another group of subscribers here, also.

At any rate I am going to print some stationery and some sub. blanks.

AND there is the Dec. bazaar, re which I have just telegraphed you to print and send Dec. immediately.

It will be excellent luck if it gets here in time. It happens to be just the right number for the purpose. [Wyndham] Lewis story. Remy [de Gourmont]'s letter, and M[ay].S[inclair]. on Eliot.

Especially as Lewis has been on leave and been seen in the glory of his trappings.

/////

At any rate we ought to be in a position to start importing when the war stops, whenever that is to be.

//// I dont make the quotations on p.1. with open mouth accepting them as gospel, but put them down as they came, that being the briefest way to indicate two points of view that I had not much considered.

The amount of print in Oct. would make nearly 64 pp. if it were printed a little more openly. D.[Pound's wife, Dorothy] finds the number about the right size, she had felt it a bit too short before.

⟨more when I think of it⟩

yours

E.

Ezra Pound

12–11–17

---

*"Minaret":* See Letter 52n.
*Lady C.:* Lady Cunard. See Letter 56n.
*Beecham:* London conductor, Sir Thomas Beecham (1879–1961). In August 1916, EP had translated the libretto of Massenet's *Cinderella* for the Thomas Beecham Opera Company, of which Lady Cunard was a principal patron. For his efforts, EP was given free seats at the opera.

**58. TLS–1.** On stationery embossed: 5, Holland Place Chambers/ Kensington. W. [15 November 1917]

Dear Margaret:

Subscribers
Horace ⟨Priestley⟩, Ashburton, 125 Kings Ave. Clapham Park

London. S.W.

Lady Randolph Churchill, 8 Westbourne St. Hyde Park. W.2.
begin ⟨both⟩ with May. I have sent no copies to Priestley as I have no spare ones.

I have sent Lady R.C. May and Oct. but dont count 'em send her the lot. It wont do any harm for her to have duplicates.

Yours

E.P.

⟨Miss B. Jones
Brookside
Bournemouth
complains of non. arrival of the L.R.⟩

Ezra Pound

15–11–17

**59. TLS–9.** On stationery embossed: 5, Holland Place Chambers/ Kensington. W. [17 November 1917]

⟨Sat

    17 Nov⟩

Dear Margaret:

           I have just rec'd ⟨this a.m.⟩ Amy's book on "Tendencies in Am. Poetry," and Mencken's "Book of Prefaces". I think Amy has a vaterersatz, as they call in it [it in] the later Freudian books. Or perhaps an Ezra-ersatz. The book from hurried reading, or rather mere skimming, (as I have done 3000 words today besides glancing at it) The book is a great lark from the ironic point of view. I believe it is better written than the 6 French Poets, which I could not read. Any of it!

           This is between ourselves.

                      What I am now writing about is the last essay in Mencken's book. "Puritanism as a Literary Force," which is all of the book I have read, or perhaps can read. He is so weak when he gets onto something really good (vide ⟨as for example⟩ H. James).

           I knocked off the enclosed at once. IT is NOT good enough to print. AND moreover I think from the point of view of the magazine, editorial policy etc. the LESS I impinge on American matters the better, AND certainly for all our goods, and mine in particular the less I think myself dowered with a mission to EDUCATE untutored America, the BETTER.

           If I had ANY sense whatever I should confine myself exclusively to writing for the ten or a dozen intelligent people I know, or have heard of.

I do however think the Mencken book (or at least the final chapter) deserves a note in the L.R.

           I think it ought to be done on the ground and not from over here.

           (He makes one awful slip, which should not be noted. i.e. he refers to Crowley's article in the English Review . . . which would queer his effect at once over here.). However skip that footnote, as most American readers will ⟨not notice it⟩ do anyhow.

I am sending you my typescript, so that you or "jh" [Jane Heap] can have ⟨before you⟩ the points I thought of, to consider. Just that, to consider, to incorporate if any are worth it, and to chuck when uninteresting and to ignore completely if you like.

I think there are people (as Graham Phillips was), as Mencken, Hatteras etc. now are, Who are unsatisfactory, and who yet ought to be dealt with. Who aren't with us, but who yet are in agreement with us on some points and who may (???) be some use in clearing away underbrush.

DONT for gods sake print my note on Mencken, or even pp. [paraphrase] from it. It is simply a substitute for talking over M's book in the editorial office.

The book itself may irritate both of you to the point of not wanting to notice it. M. may have done all that is necessary re/ Comstockianism, and may not need a puff. etc. At any rate the note will come better from you or "jh", AND the less I appear in the magazine unnecessarily the better.

Also it is bad economy not to keep me to the things that no one else can do better.

Re/ M. you will also know better, how much it is worth while flying direct at the Comstock clutch, how much it is more advisable to stimulate the reading of Mencken without any direct reference to his attack on the suppressors.

Amy's statement of the comparative glories of Fletcher and Rimbaud is deelightful.

⟨Whew! here's a funny one[.] Menken [*sic*] p. 152 talks about French imagistes[.] This is extremely interesting as I made the word = on a Hulme basis — and carefully made a name that was not & never had been used in France. I made one specifically to distinguish "us" from any of the French groups catalogued by Flint in the P.R. =

Of course it may be his way of ⟨sneering at⟩ calling Imagism ⟨as⟩, neo-symbolism but it looks like a break.

---

I suppose (—i.e. after another 20 minutes of Mencken.)—⟨it is the⟩ same old American trouble. Mencken just doesn't quite know. = not an ounce of original discrimination in all his book.

= = Still useful as statement of facts up to a point.

?? useful in U.S.A. & not interesting here. ⟨same⟩ as news re/. the hesperian continent.⟩

Yours
E Pound

On "A BOOK OF PREFACES" (%%)

America has "at last produced" a critic, or rather a native American critic
has at last succe[e]ded in extracating [*sic*] his mind from his surrounding to
such [a] degree as to be able to envisage the said surroundings. This does not
mean that we have coughed up a new aesthete who will remurmur ⟨(anno
domini 1918)⟩ in rather more veiled and semidiaphanous tones, the same
velleities which Arthur Symons uttered in 1891.

H.L.Mencken has read his Mark Twain. It is a great blessing that at last
someone with fibre tough enough to read Mark Twain, and intelligence
enough to perceive the part which is not simple "Hee-Haw" has at last diagnosed Mark Twain's trouble. Pages 203–5 of Mr Mencken's book show
him to [*crossout:* a critic born, and a critic of no mean profundity]. (By
that I do not mean that one is expected to agree with all that Mr Mencken
says in all other places. A critic may have a flair or flash of deep insight at
one point, without having the four-hour touch, without being a standard
scale or electrometre warranted to read right in all circumstances, save when
intoxicated or out of order.) ⟨? or perhaps this is all Dr. Kellner.⟩

(%%) A Book of Prefaces by H.L.Mencken, pub. A.A.Knopf 220
W. 42 nd. St. New York. 1.50 net.

The point, the present point is that in these pages mentioned Mr Mencken
(or Dr Kellner to whom he refers) has given a correct diagnosis. He has
put his finger on the plague spot. My own detestation of Twain has stayed
vague for a number of years, there were too many more important things
to attend to, I could not be bothered to clarify this patch of vagueness. A
detestation of a man's tonality does not necessitate a blindness to his abili-
ties. And when a man's rightnesses have been so lied against as Twain's
were in America[,] one ⟨could well conceal⟩, or [at] least I have been well
content to conceal a private and unimportant detestation. One could not
express a dislike of any man, for instance, whose ⟨posthumous publica-
tions⟩ have been so lied about and distorted as Twain's final pessimistic
expressions.

Put this aside as footnote that has crept into my text. The next
point is that Mencken is in some circles considered a purely frivolous person. . . . . because he edits or half edits a frivolous magazine. In a half
baked country one has to use what tools one can lay hold of. I would call
one fact to the attention of the cognoscenti, namely that the Smart Set is the
only magazine in america that has ever reduced a circulation from 70,000

to 20,000 in a quixotic attempt to break the parrochial [*sic*] taboo and give America free literature.

I have it on my personal knowledge that Willard Huntington Wright came to London about five years ago determined to buy up the best stuff he could find. I do not in the least mean to imply that Mr Wright and I would see eye to eye in questions of excellence. I may reserve my opinion that literature is not a commodity, that literature emphatically does not lie on a cou[n]ter where it can be snatched up at once by a straw-hatted young man in a hurry.

An editor pleased with "Ozymandias", or with the Fifth Act of the "Cenci" might have rushed up to Shelley, for example, and found nothing in that worthy's desk but "The Sensitive Plant" (than which no [*crossout:* American] poet ⟨of any reputation, ever⟩ penned anything less desirable.) Moreover the better the author the greater his detestation of magazines and the less likely he is to believe in, or take the slightest interest in the success of, any magazine for which he has not some very personal security in his own private knowledge of the editors and the ⟨business⟩ management.

Let us remember that Graham Phillips had been shot by a fanatic, that various living writers were under contract elsewhere, and that the Smart Set did publish some of the first stories of Joyce, and some of the ⟨short stories of D.H.⟩ Lawrence. Also that Wright resigned reasonably soon after he found that he was not free in his selection.

These huge mechanisms have to be kept going, if they are to remain huge mechanisms, in that condition they can be of very little service to literature, until there is, what is almost unthinkable, a "really large" public intensely interested in literature.

The point I wish to emphasize in this note, in part replying to people who object to my asking and repeating the pertinent question re/ Whistler and Henry James and their protracted foreign residence; is that New York has a critic dealing with native affairs. I dare say he will be shot before long. Graham Phillips dealt with native affairs, in a style as crude as the types he depicted. he was painful to read, but he was working in honesty, he was shot by a fanatic (not a New Englander) I dont know that he had been taken very seriously. Dreiser is taken seriously because the violent opposition to him has been longer, it has not been settled at the point of a ⟨maniac's⟩ pistol.

In all this the American hatred of liberty, their peculiar loathing of ⟨all forms of⟩ intellectual freedom, is striking and apparent. The last study in Mencken's book is full of fruitful suggestion; one animadverts to Franklin and Jefferson, and remembers how carefull[y] they are screened in school histories; how few Americans looking back upon the glory of America's founder have the slightest notion of Franklins ideas upon God, or of Jeffersons ideas upon dalliance. ⟨This might be quoted as from a personal letter from me, if you chose, or simply perhaps better, quoted anonymously.⟩ (Still they [are] represented in the standard school histories as men of great brilliance and acumen.) Washington's intelligence is, I believe, left unmentioned[,]

[*The final section of EP's article is lost. What follows is the ending of the article as it appeared in the* LR.] as are his personal law-suits regarding certain acerage [*sic*].

On page 218 Mr. Mencken falls heavily, treats W. D. Howells and Henry James together, and shows a total inability to get any further with Henry James than the mentioning of a limitation which Henry James had himself better defined. I venture to suggest, very simply, that Mr. Mencken has read very little of the author, and that he is so intent on his main theme (wherein he is right in the main) that he has rather warped his idea of James to his own particular purpose and treated one superficial aspect rather than James in toto. If this error is not an oversight on Mr. Mencken's part, it allies him to the philistines he inveighs against, and shows him bit by the very bacillus that he is out to exterminate, — adding perhaps by this very misfortune to the cogency of his warning.

With the excision of this one excessive page, the essay can be recommended as a necessary text book in all high-schools, wherein there is now current too little plain-written history.

We should be grateful to Mr. Mencken for the actual names of the "dozen men", page 294. His history at this point is important enough to be worth a little documentation.

Mencken in this part of his book, at least, is guarded and careful in his statements. Whether he can preserve this gravity of tone sufficiently to be really effective, whether he is indeed what his adversaries would call "the chosen instrument of the Lord's vengeance upon them", I do not know; but his book is at least enough to convince one that whatever America's part in world war, and whatever its results to her, she is faced at home with a no less serious war for internal freedom, and for the arteries and capillaries of freedom, the mail-routes and presses.

It is a sinister and significant fact that even a campaign for the freedom of art becomes in American [*sic*] a "campaign", a sort of super-religious crusade; so does the actual genius of the country, the actual volk-geist, enforce its forms upon contemporary expression.

(As ever in prose, compare for example the wholly mediaeval and limited Dante of the prose works, modeled by and conforming with his time, with the lasting Dante who flashes out of the emotional passages in the poetry . . . . passages which form only a part of his terza rima).

*Amy's book:* i.e., Amy Lowell, *Tendencies in Modern American Poetry.* The book contains discussions of the work of Edwin Arlington Robinson, Robert Frost, Edgar Lee Masters, Carl Sandburg, H. D., and John Gould Fletcher.

*Mencken's "Book of Prefaces":* i.e., Henry Lewis Mencken, *A Book of Prefaces.* Mencken's book includes four essays: "Joseph Conrad," "Theodore Dreiser," "James Huneker," and "Puritanism as a Literary Force."

*6 French Poets:* See Letter 46n.

*vide ⟨as for example⟩ H. James:* Mencken's comments on Henry James, whom he treats in conjunction with William Dean Howells, are as follows:

> As for Howells and James, both quickly showed that timorousness and reticence are the distinguishing marks of the Puritan, even in his most intellectual incarnations. The American scene that they depicted with such meticulous care was chiefly peopled with marionettes. They shrunk, characteristically, from those larger, harsher clashes of will and purpose which one finds in all truly first-rate literature. In particular, they shrunk from any interpretation of life which grounded itself upon an acknowledgement of its inexorable and inexplicable tragedy. In the vast combat of instincts and aspirations about them they saw only a feeble jousting of comedians, unserious and insignificant. Of the great questions that had agitated the minds of men in Howells' time one gets no more than a faint and far-away echo in his novels. His investigations, one may say, are carried on *in vacuo;* his discoveries are not expressed in terms of passion, but in terms of giggles. (Third edition, 218)

*Crowley's article:* Aleister Crowley, "Art in America," *English Review* 15 (November 1913): 578–95. "Aleister Crowley" was the pseudonym of Edward Alexander Crowley (1875–1947), a British writer notorious as a practitioner of black magic and a devotee of the occult, subjects about which he wrote a number of books.

*incorporate if any are worth it:* MCA printed, with only a few alterations and under the pseudonym of Raoul Root, EP's comments on Mencken's essay [*LR* (January 1918): 10–12]. She also included Jane Heap's comments on the book ("Mr. Mencken, Philistine") and her own ("Mr. Mencken's Truism").

*Graham Phillips:* David Graham Phillips (1867–1911), American journalist and novelist. Phillips' fiction and essays, often muckraking in tone and intention, revealed his deep concern with social problems and with political corruption. His career was sadly cut short when he was murdered by a lunatic.

*Hatteras:* Owen Hatteras. See Letter 38n.

*Comstockianism:* A large part of Mencken's essay deals with the negative effects on literature of the Comstock Postal Act of 1873 and the operations of the New York Society for the Suppression of Vice.

*Amy's statement of the comparative glories . . . :* After having compared Rimbaud's poem "Voyelles" with John Gould Fletcher's "The Vowels" (to the latter's advantage, incidentally), Lowell makes the following declaration: "Mr. Fletcher is a more original poet than Arthur Rimbaud, and has a finer ear" (295).

*Mencken . . . talks about French imagistes:* Mencken's "slip" occurs in this context:

> As for Poe and Whitman, the native recognition of their genius was so greatly conditioned by a characteristic horror of their immorality that it would be absurd to say that their own country understood them. Both were better and more quickly apprehended in France, and it was in France, not in America, that each founded a school. What they had to teach we have since got back at second hand—that tale of mystery, which was Poe's contribution, through Gaborian and Boisgobey; and *vers libre,* which was Whitman's, through the French *imagistes.* (152)

*I made the word:* See Letter 4n.

*on a Hulme basis:* Thomas Ernest Hulme (1883–1917), British poet and philosopher, had advocated the "hard dry image" in poetry, and his thought had a direct influence on the development of what EP called "Imagism."

*catalogued by Flint in the P.R.:* See Letter 50n.

*which Arthur Symons uttered in 1891:* EP is perhaps referring to Arthur Symons' *The Symbolist Movement in Literature* (1899) and is mistaken about the date.

*Dr. Kellner:* Mencken quotes frequently from Leon Kellner's *American Literature,* tr. by Julia Franklin (New York: Doubleday, Page, 1915).

*Willard Huntington Wright:* (1888–1939), American editor and novelist. Wright, whom EP had met in London in 1913, edited *The Smart Set* from 1913 to 1914. He is popularly known for his creation of the master-sleuth Philo Vance. Wright's mysteries were published under the pseudonym of S. S. Van Dine.

*the Smart Set did publish . . . :* *The Smart Set* had published two stories from Joyce's *Dubliners,* "The Boarding House" and "A Little Cloud" in its May 1915 issue (93–97; 129–36). Three of D. H. Lawrence's stories were also published in the magazine: "The Christening" (February 1914), "The Shadow in the Rose Garden" (March 1914), and "The White Stocking" (October 1914).

**60. TLS–4.** On stationery with top and left corner of first page cut off. [22 November 1917]

Dear Margaret:

I am having this stationery done for use here. The omission of London address on October number has been a bit of a bother. I haven't put N.Y. address on this stationery because it might cause confusion; people keep asking "where do I send etc. . . ."

I have just written J.Q. [John Quinn] that I have a guarantor for £10 a year for three years.

It happens to be May Sinclair, and is very sporting of her. She will also give us three or four short articles each year without payment. I think we had better keep this to ourselves, for the present at any rate.

It will enable me to pay Joyce the proper £50 for the American rights on his novel. Which is a comfort.

Subscribers: begin with May.

Mrs O. Valentine Nossiter, 19 Oxford Rd. Putney, S.W. 15.
H. Beecham Esq. 6 Barclay House, Hay Hill, W. 1.
L. Beardmore Esq. 19 South St. S.W. 7.
Mrs John Astor (I asked you to send her the magazine in letter before
    last.)
             18 Grosvenor Sq. W. 1.
              ////

If the Dec. no. dont get here in time for the book stall, I shall use these letter heads as receipts, and mail the Dec. nos. to people as soon as they arrive.

                  //

This sheet [of the *LR* office stationery] is a proof, and the only spare one, correct copies are being printed today.

Do take a few minutes off and let me have answers to the following string of questions

1. I want to supply L.R. complete from May, to all subscribers, BUT I must know how many copies you have left, ⟨of each month to date.⟩ so as to know when to stop, and when to put up the price.

2. How are U.S.A. subs. coming in?.

3. Is it too flaming a nuisance to send me notice that my notification of sub. is rec'd and copies sent. You might perhaps send when you write the single name of LAST sub recd. from me, and to whom L.R. has started. DONT if it is too much bother.

4. How many subscribers at say 12/ or £1/ would you need to pay for

printing a de luxe edition on really fine paper, for those who preferred it? People who subscribe from an opera box dont care about the difference of a few shillings, and some of them are fussy over these details, or at least think the ⟨material⟩ paper ought to be splendid (whatever the contents)

///// 

While I think any cash I can raise ought to be spent on contents and improvement and embellishment of same, especially when we consider that Paris will have to be paid [for the "French number"] . . . . . STILL I wish you'd let me know how things stand re/ the printer. I enclose 20 dollars. I think I have recvd cash about up to what I have sent you. This advance 20 however appears warranted by prospects.

/// 

IF London and particularly Mayfair, is going to take up the magazine, we must be more careful than ever NOT to have in too much Amy [Lowell], and suburbs.

My suggestion re/ cooperation with smaller American magazines was probably untimely. Done in the dark quart d'heure before sunrise.

The reader critic is O.K., let us hope the complete imbeciles will keep on.

/// 

I have just sent D.[Dorothy Pound] out to borrow back all available copies of back numbers so that I can have something to send people who subscribe, or who are considering doing so.

//// 

Ernest Boyd wants the file of the L.R. from the beginning of Vol I. can you send it [to] me, or is it scattered from Chicago to S. Francisco?

He brought prize tale of the "Atlantic", which I enclose on sep. sheet. for reader critic.

Also note from [John] Rodker showing proper respect.

Also small cheque as mentioned.

    yours ever
⟨vide                Ezra
  P.S.⟩              Ezra Pound
                    22–11–17

Re/ Amy, I dont want to hedge too much. I dont think we need bar her from the magazine, but she cant quite write for the mondaine London clientele. At least I cant see Lady Randolph Churchill ⟨or May Sinclair⟩ (for example) reading her with any spirit of reverence. These people can take it just as strong as [Wyndham] Lewis can pitch.

Your own tone suits 'em O.K. (Not that you'd care a damn if it didn't, but you may as well know it.)

You and "jh" [Jane Heap] are to my present vision the only American, as yet unexported, ⟨real⟩ assets to the contributing list.

yours

E.

*for the book stall:* See Letter 56.
*Ernest Boyd:* See Letter 21n.

**61. TLS–1.** On stationery headed: THE LITTLE REVIEW/ London Office:—5, HOLLAND PLACE CHAMBERS, W.8.

[30 November 1917]

Dear Margaret:

Continue subscription to
Miss Shepeler, 266 Kings Rd. Chelsea. SW.3
(she sends in half yearly, but you can go on continuing her sub. without any danger of its stopping. ALSO PLEASE SEND HER "MAY" 1917)
Subscriber: Curtis Brown ⟨Esq.⟩
6 Henrietta St. Covent Gdn. W.C. 2.
(begin this either May or Nov. as you like, depending on how early issues are holding out.) I think we should sell off all but 150 or 200 sets, which could be kept for binding and advance in value. Could be stored with H.L.Pound [Homer Loomis Pound, EP's father], if you have not room.

Have had no letter from you for ages. Nov. no. not here yet. HAVE you got my french mss. ??????? and the Hueffer [*Women & Men*]?

yours ever
Ezra
Ezra Pound
30 Nov. 1917

**62. TLS–2.**   On stationery embossed: 5, Holland Place Chambers/ Kensington. W. [5 December 1917]

5 th Dec.

Dear Margaret:

Single copy of Nov. just here. Delighted with reproductions. Excellent editing to have started them in same no. with Lady G's play [Lady Gregory's "Hanrahan's Oath"]. Which without them would have looked too much as if we were sinking into the past.

I am convinced (vide Smart Set, and other popular papers) of the value of having a number of SHORT things in each no. One must have the long, and it is NOT a question of giving way to commonness, BUT a paper with a number of short things certainly does seem more alive to the person picking it up. ⟨Not a matter of morals, merely of practicality.⟩

The FIRST impression of Nov. is that it is dull apart from the drawings. This is simply because one reads the short things before getting out of bed, and does not take a shot at the play.

Oct. seemed much more alive. (as indeed, it was.) This is simply a constation [EP's misspelling of the French word *constatation*?] re/ first impressions. The Gregory play ought to do us good. AND I am, as stated[,] delighted with the drawings.

We certainly should print reproductions at least once in three months, if not every other month, better have 'em in every number IF we can stand the tax.

The Lewis and Gaudier look curiously neat and elegant among the other things. Almost too much so.

My one suggestion is that for reproduction in such small blocks, one might do well to take ⟨the⟩ smaller drawings. ⟨They would lose less.⟩

OR if one is taking anything as large as The Starry Sky, one should I think add a note s[t]ating. "The Starry Sky, about one tenth original diameter.". I suppose it is really ⟨nearer⟩ one seventh, in this particular case.

One should not publish the exact measurements of original drawings, because they are too useful to forgers, as someone or other communicated to me after bitter experience.

This is just a jab. I've got to run. More anon.

> yours
>                          E.
> Ezra Pound


*Delighted with reproductions:* Pages 17–32 of the November 1917 *LR* contained
   reproductions of the following pieces of art: drawings by Max Weber, Marie
   Laurencin, Henri Gaudier-Brzeska, André Segonzac, and Jules Pascin; a carv-
   ing by Walt Kuhn; an engraving by Arthur B. Davies; and a painting, "The
   Starry Sky," by Wyndham Lewis.


**63. TLS–2.**   On stationery embossed: 5, Holland Place Chambers/ Kensington. W. ⟨8⟩ [7 December 1917]

Dec. 7/

Dear Margaret:

>               I enclose yesterday's bag, 10 dollars, 6 subs. as follows:
Mrs H.G. Wells, 52 St. James's Court, Buckingham Gate. S.W. 1. (as M.S.
>          [May Sinclair] remarks. "She has some sense of decency even
>          if he (H.G.) hasn't". Mrs W. has also sent on assurances
>          of H. G's admiration of [James] Joyce. H. G's review having
>          been a valuable piece of imbecility.)
Miss Aphra Wilson, 116 Fellows Rd., London N.W.3.
Miss Netta Syret, 84 Hamilton Terrace. N.W. 8.
Wm. T. Horton. Studio 2. '
>               63 Cartwright Gdns. W.C.1.
Miss Hannay, Coombe Edge, Oak Hill Way, Hampstead. N.W.3.
Miss T. Bosanquet 38 Cheyne Walk. S.W. 3.
>          (I have given her my file copies and have NO Sept. left.
>          She was Henry James['s] secretary. Learned typing and
>          stenography with object of getting that particular job. She
>          should be of use when we come to doing our Henry James
>          number. Also a possible avenue to Mrs Wharton.) ⟨ergo
>          begin her with Nov. & send me a file May-Oct.⟩
All these subs. to begin with May. number.

The illustrations are distinctly the right note. I begin to think we are really going to make a go of it.

We should try to "reproduce" at least every other other month, I think.

[Elkin] Mathews is going to put up a sample number, and try to get a few subs. I am offering him commission of ⅓.

Joyce writes that the first division of his novel [*Ulysses*] is at the typists. Enough for three numbers. So it looks as if we should be able to start him in March, O.K.

I doubt if there will be enough [Ford Madox] Hueffer [i.e., *Women & Men*] to run until June 1919. (If there aint, we can do like the astrologers and say it was a misprint for 1918.). First payment, which I shall make as soon as second half year's cash arrives from J.Q. [John Quinn] may lubricate F.M.H.

Write when you get the time.

yours<br>E.

Ezra Pound
7/12/1917

*H.G's review:* H. G. Wells's review of Joyce's *A Portrait of the Artist as a Young Man* was published in the *Nation* (London) 20(24 February 1917): 710, 712; and was reprinted in *The New Republic* (10 March 1917): 158–60. In it, Wells remarks that "Mr. Joyce has a cloacal obsession. He would bring back into the general picture of life aspects which modern drainage and modern decorum have taken out of ordinary intercourse and conversation. Coarse, unfamiliar words are scattered about the book unpleasantly, and it may seem to many, needlessly." But Wells goes on to praise the novel, saying that "it is by far the most living and convincing picture that exists of an Irish Catholic upbringing" and that the "interest of the book depends entirely upon its quintessential and unfailing reality." Of Stephen Dedalus, he says that one "believes in [him] as one believes in few characters in fiction." Wells does, however, use the review as an occasion to comment on the tension between England and Ireland and to remind the reader that "these bright-green young people across the Channel [like Stephen Dedalus] are something quite different from the liberal English in training and tradition, and absolutely set against helping them. No single book has ever shown how different they are, as completely as this memorable novel."

*T. Bosanquet:* Theodora Bosanquet was educated at London University and for a time edited *The Journal of the Society for Psychical Research.* Having been secretary to Henry James, she used her inside knowledge to write *Henry James at Work* (London: Hogarth Press, 1924).

**64. TLS–1.** On stationery headed: THE LITTLE REVIEW/ London Office:—5, HOLLAND PLACE CHAMBERS, W.8.

[14 December 1917]

Dear Margaret:

The use of official stationery for official business is pure swank. AT the present price of paper !!!

English edition of Cantleman now on the market.

[William Butler] Yeats says suppression of October number is great luck, and ought to be the making of the magazine.

[James] Joyce, as I think I wrote, says his mss. [*Ulysses*] is at the typists. So it should be in time for March.

Reproduction[s] cause excellent comment. Habit of printing reproductions should help a lot.

Dec. number not here yet. Do send some more Sept. and all back nos.

Subscribers: from May.

Miss W.G. Rinder 14 Westgate Terrace. Redcliffe Sq. S.W.10

(have supplied June number, to keep her pacified.)

L/ Cpl H.Hinco b 3124 R.A.M.C.

attd. Left Half

43 rd. Siege Battery. R.G.A.

Salonika Force

British Army.

better mark this via England. I have sent him Nov. number.

yours

Ezra Pound

14/12/17

⟨merry Xmas.⟩

*Cantleman:* Wyndham Lewis's "Cantleman's Spring-Mate" was published in *The Ideal Giant* (1917), an edition privately printed "for the London Office of the Little Review" and limited to a small number of copies (perhaps fifty, perhaps a few more, according to Omar Pound and Philip Grover's *Wyndham Lewis: A Descriptive Bibliography*).

**65. TLS–1.**   On stationery embossed: 5, Holland Place Chambers/ Kensington. W. [27 December 1917]

⟨27/12/1917⟩

Dear Margaret

I enclose Lewis "Ideal Giant", to be used when we need a brace. It is from the private edition here. It would be a good start off for first no. next vol. i.e. May.

You may be surprised at my sending Keary. but I think it wise. I think we shoul[d] publish a serious essay on some literary subject, not current or topical, each month. (size, permitting.). ⟨Keary⟩ makes as good a start as any we'd be likely to get. He has a circle of admirers here. (God knows who or what. I dont know his work.) ⟨At least he had never sold out to the mob.⟩ He has just died and there may be some sort of boom. He also serves as Lady Gregory does, to reach the elder strata. Also I have got the essay for nothing, though The Contemporary Rev. had accepted it, and was to have paid. The essay is perfectly respectable, and impeccable. Perhaps the three intelligent Am. college profs. will be encouraged to rally, by the display of it.

I should put it and my "List of books" in April. Essays on Keary are to appear here in Feb and March.

No news and no Dec. nos. yet.

yours   E              ⟨enc. also a
                        squib for
                        correspondence col.
Ezra Pound              if worth it.⟩

---

*Lewis "Ideal Giant":* Wyndham Lewis's playlet "The Ideal Giant" was published in the May 1918 issue, the first number of the fifth volume of the *LR*.
*Keary:* Charles Francis Keary (1848–1917), British novelist, poet, and writer on historical subjects. Educated at Marlborough and Trinity College, Cambridge, Keary worked in the Department of Coins at the British Museum and wrote as an avocation. His novels include *The Two Lancrofts* (1893), *Herbert Vanlennart* (1895), *The Journalist* (1898), *A Mariage de Convenance* (1899), *High Policy* (1902), *Bloomsbury* (1905), and *The Mount* (1909). Keary also wrote several histories, *The Vikings in Western Civilization* (1890) and *Norway and the Norwegians* (1893); two books of poetry; and a philosophical treatise entitled *The Pursuit of Reason* (1910). *The Wanderer* (1888), published under the name of H. Ogram Matuce, records the musings of a supposed retired man of letters; Keary enthusiasts often identify this as the

best of his work. From the wider public, however, his work has received little critical or popular attention, and, as later letters indicate, MCA was not favorably disposed to publishing the Keary article (on Elizabethan drama) EP had sent her. Nothing of Keary's was to appear in the *LR*.

*The Contemporary Rev.:* The London journal *The Contemporary Review* had begun publishing in 1866, its primary interest being articles about philosophical and theological issues. It did, however, publish essays relating to literary topics.

**66. TLS–6.** On stationery embossed: 5, Holland Placc Chambers/ Kensington. W. ⟨8⟩ [30 December 1917]

Dear Margaret:

For God's sake do something to cheer [John] Quinn. He is the best and most effective friend I have in America. He writes very much depressed by L.R. case. Furious over the paragraphs on p. 39. which are my bloody fault, and which I have writ to him to say so, and over J.H. [Jane Heap] acceptance of the 2.50 at the Post Office, after he had cautioned you.

For God's sake either do something "businesslike" . . . . God knows what. If you had "business sense" you'd never have taken up with me, and you wouldn't care a damn about literature. etc. etc. And I dont in the least know what it [arrow drawn to *"business sense"*] is.

The other star play would be to get Mrs ⟨Wharton.⟩ That might fetch him. It would be decidedly more in our line, than showing business acumen. I don't know how its to be done. If she were over here I would have a go at her. I dare say she's too old.

Anyhow send her a copy of the L.R. with my note on H. ⟨James⟩, and the pat of butter.

*///*

The other thing is not to let J.H. cheek Quinn too much. I think he likes you both. But still I think it would be better if YOU saw him, than that she should. If they meet, whatever she may think of his artistic judgement, do let her remember that some of the best living artists think a great deal of it. NOT merely because he buys their stuff.

I take ⟨as example⟩ [Wyndham] Lewis['s] phrase about Quinn, running through a pile of [Augustus] John drawings with great speed, and at a glance "getting all the good one's.".

Set that against whatever she thinks is overenthusiasm on his part for a few of his friends. See whether in his admiration for [Arthur] Davi[e]s and [Walt] Kuhn, Q. does not really know their best work for [from] their next best.

Don't insist on his toning down his enthusiasms to a given foot rule.

Old Yeats (J.B.) describes Q., in a letter as, the "kindest, most generous, most ira[s]cible" of men. I have never known anyone worth a damn who wasn't ira[s]cible.

///

The serious thing is that he has been so bored with the "case", that while four months ago he was considering getting more guarantors for the second year of the subsidy. He now says the thing can't ever be really self-supporting, and that he can't ask guarantors on the present business management.

It is very easy to snap ones fingers, and say to hell with guarantors. ma che . . . . .

It would be much better to have them[.]

I am doing all I can to make the contents so bloody good that we will simply "have" to go on.

Quinn says a number of nice things about both of you, and admires your courage and nerve and energy. That's perfectly good ground. This is not a grouch but a prayer. Do try to remember how really busy he is, and the state of nerves man (me for a sample) gets into when he has to get 25 hours into a 24 hour day.

I don't believe anybody else will do half or a tenth as much for us, or give us so many chances to make good after a slip.

ANYHOW we aren't dead yet.

How much of Oct. can you reprint. ??

Reprint not as "October", but simply as part of later nos. Villerant's letter might be worth it ????

I don't care, whether it is used or not. Perhaps it would be better to let the stuff lie. Certainly it ought not to interfere with the new stuff, of which there is perhaps more than we can print.

///

I dare say it would be imprudent to use the [John] Rodker thing. Everything else looks safe enough to me, until we get to [James] Joyce [i.e., *Ulysses*]. Whom we have got to print. Suppression or no suppression.

One might save by printing only 300 copies. sending them as a test and then doing the full 3000.

Etc. I will have something to say about circulation of classics. as soon as I have time to take breath.

yours ever

Ezra

P.S.  Re/ business management. Do you want to business-manage? It is inconceivable to me that any sane person should want to business manage anything. I don't know quite what it means. All I know is that I am bloody thankful that I have nothing to do with it.

If the review is a good enough property by May 1918, would you be willing (ecstatic or whatever the term is) to go on editing it WITH a business management attached ??? IF anybody is fool enough to put business sense to such a purpose.

I can't see any man of necessary ability who would touch the thing. BUT . . . . . . . some people have a mania for being business men under all circumstances, just as I have for spending a month on an unlucrative troubadour.

Were I the editor and publisher I should go to sleep in joy on any business-managing bosom that presented itself. I doubt if even Quinn could find us ⟨a⟩ business manager. But if he did, could you use one? Could you work with, or around one?

This is my suggestion, not his.

If it meant the difference of a large lump of guarantors it ought to be worth trying. (or suggesting. not at the wrong moment.)

Business manager to have NOTHING to do with contents, save where it was case of utterly unexpected fuss, as over Abel Sanders. Joyce to be printed at all costs, always.

I am going to try to swing, besides the [Ford Madox] Hueffer [i.e., *Women & Men*] and Joyce, a full number (about the size of the Feb. french,) on Remy DeGourmont. A complete little book on him. (by me) and a full James number, by me, Eliot, Miss Bosanquet (who had article on ⟨H.J.⟩ in June "Fortnightly Rev.".) She learned typing in order to be his stenographer, and was with him nine years, until his death. Has also done some short stories and collaborated in a novel. Not one of "the promoted typist type" to which I have occasionally referred.

Q. seems well influenced by my prospect of Feb. french number.

Don't quite know who else can come into James no. May Sinclair will probably do something too. Mrs Wharton would be the catch. She is the only person he really talked to,. i.e. about his stuff.

Q. also says you are careless about proof correcting. This is quite true.

No one is more aware than I am that it is utterly impossible to detect the errors of a printer when glaring in fury at one's proof-sheets; nor to tell what the hell a printer will do on receiving a sheet of proofs with all errors clearly corrected.

No work of mine is without numerous misprints. STILL . . . . . .

I hope to God I get proofs of Feb. in time to go through it. If you can't get 'em here, for the love of the Angels do get someone to look at 'em. Get Bill [William Carlos] Williams, get the Mayor of Manhattan, get the janitor, get Mr [Woodrow] Wilson. Get the late J. L. Sullivan.

Softly the evening air

Ezra Pound
30/12/17

*to cheer Quinn:* John Quinn had represented MCA and the *LR* in the case involving the suppression of the October 1917 issue by the New York Post Office authorities. The case was heard by Judge Augustus N. Hand, who eventually ruled against the complainants.

*paragraphs on p. 39:* Under the pseudonym of Abel Sanders, EP had written a letter to the October 1917 "Reader Critic," passing on a supposed translation of a document which had been taken from a German soldier captured near Ypres, France. The "document" outlined a plan devised by the "Committee for the Increase of Population" whereby able-bodied German men were to "interest themselves in the happiness of the married women and maidens [who had been, due to the war, deprived of their men] by doubling or even trebling the number of births." The men so-instructed were to perform their duties "for the sake of the Fatherland."

*over J.H. acceptance of the 2.50:* In a letter he wrote to EP dated 16 October 1920 (now at Northwestern University), Quinn claimed that MCA and Jane Heap had seriously damaged his case while it was still pending by applying the money the Post Office had been paid for the October issue to the mailing costs of a subsequent number.

*do something "businesslike":* Quinn often expressed irritation at the lack of "business sense" he perceived in MCA and Jane Heap's handling of the *LR*'s affairs.

*How much of the October can you reprint?:* Only Arthur Waley's translations of the poems of Po Chü-i and EP's "Editorial on Solicitous Doubt" were reprinted, both in the December 1917 issue (23–27 and 53–55, respectively). Villerant's letter—i.e., EP's "Imaginary Letter, V"—was not reprinted.

*circulation of classics:* See Letter 67n.

*May 1918:* i.e., the first issue of the fifth volume.

*a full number . . . on Remy DeGourmont:* The combined February–March 1919 issue devoted thirty-four pages to discussions of the work of Remy de Gourmont, including articles by EP ("De Gourmont: A Distinction"), Frederic Manning ("M. De Gourmont and the Problem of Beauty"), T. T. Clayton ("'Le Latin Mystique'"), John Rodker ("De Gourmont—Yank"), and Richard Aldington ("Remy de Gourmont, After the Interim").

*a full James number:* The August 1918 issue was devoted to Henry James. Articles by A. R. Orage, John Rodker, and Ethel Coburn Mayne—as well as those by EP, Eliot and Theodora Bosanquet—were included.

*Miss Bosanquet . . . in June "Fortnightly Rev.":* Theodora Bosanquet's article "Henry James" appeared in the *Fortnightly Review* (June 1917). The article was reprinted in the *Living Age* (11 August 1917), and, under the title "Henry James as Literary Artist," in *The Bookman* (New York), 45 (August 1917). In her article, Miss Bosanquet describes, among other things, how she obtained her position as James's secretary.


**67. TLS–2.** On stationery embossed: 5, Holland Place Chambers/ Kensington. W. [17 January 1918]


⟨17/1/1918⟩

Dear Margaret:

      I am comforted by the arrival of [Jean] De Bosschere's and [John] Rodker's copies of Dec. No others have come yet. I have sent one to the editor of the Quarterly. and am keeping the other.

      Am much cheered by its appearance.

The one mistake is not to have printed. Section 211 of the U.S. Criminal code.

It is the most outrageous and incredible document I have ever read. You have it with the papers of the case, so please fill in the gap in my accompanying article. We must print that and the pp. [paragraph] about the classics from [Judge] Hand's decision. EVERY MONTH. just have it set up permanently and put in "regular".

It is a labour of patriotism wherefrom we must not shrink.

I have been in bed with hell's own cold. So I shant type any more than absolutely necessary.

Another chunk of Joyce [i.e., *Ulysses*] has come so you can print all the lot I have sent in one no.

It might be well to leave gaps, at the questionable points. well marked. Saying "until literature is permitted in America" we can not print Mr. J.'s next sentence. Mr. J. is the author of "the Portrait" etc. recognized as literature ⟨but he⟩ lacks the sanction of "age".

He refers here to tribal custom of the Hebrews, often mentioned in Leviticus.

He refers here to certain current statements of the New Testament. He refers here to natural facts, doubtless familiar to the reader.

This might help more than anything else to enlighten our public.

"We do not consider these gaps in the least necessary, but we can not afford to be suppressed. We are doing our best for the freedom of literature in America. We trust the "Dictionnaire Philosophique" is increasing in circulation; but ⟨not⟩ so rapidly as to get itself into trouble."

If this don't make a few fools bust their spleens and die of it, we will at least have done our part for their salvation.

A few unexpurgated copies might also be struck, but not sent through the post. Or they could be printed NOT bound into the review at all.

                    yours
                    Ezra Pound

                              ⟨I enclose also
                              May Sinclair
                              on D Richardson.⟩

*the editor of the Quarterly:* i.e., Sir George Walter Prothero (1848–1922), the editor of the *Quarterly Review.*

*The one mistake . . . :* In the *LR*'s December 1917 issue, MCA briefly explained the fact that the October number had been suppressed and that the case had been lost in court. She then took issue with the manner in which Lewis's "Cantleman's Spring-Mate" had been read, arguing that any story must be approached as "a piece of prose," which meant read "for the spirit contained in the rhythm"—the only way of getting at the story's context. Since the quality of prose is dependent upon "mysterious laws" of rhythm (she provided several examples to illustrate her point), it is by rhythm alone that prose can be judged. It is rhythm which separates "what is good from what is bad. 'Good' and 'bad' in literature have no other connotation than this."

In her article, MCA quoted a substantial portion of the written opinion of Judge Augustus N. Hand. (See "Judicial Opinion: (Our Suppressed October Issue)," 46–49.)

*Section 211 of the U.S. Criminal code:* EP's *LR* article on the suppressed October issue ("The Classics 'Escape,' " March 1918: 32–34) did include the text of this "outrageous and incredible document":

> Every obscene, lewd, or lascivious, and every filthy book, pamphlet, picture, letter, writing, print, or other publication of an indecent character and every article or thing designed, adapted or intended for preventing conception or producing abortion, or for any indecent or immoral use; and every article, instrument, substance, drug, medicine, or thing which is advertised or described in a manner calculated to lead another to use or apply it for preventing conception or producing abortion, or for any indecent or immoral purpose; and every written or printed card, letter, circular, book, pamphlet, advertisement, or notice of any kind giving information directly or indirectly, where, or how, or from whom, or by what means any of the hereinbefore-mentioned matters, articles, or things may be obtained or made, or where or by whom any act or operation of any kind for the procuring or producing of abortion will be done or produced, whether sealed or unsealed; and every letter, packet, or package, or other mail matter containing any filthy, vile, or indecent thing, device, or substance; and every paper, writing, advertisement, or representation that any article, instrument, substance, drug, medicine, or thing may, or can be, used or applied for preventing conception or producing abortion, or for any indecent or immoral purpose; and every description calculated to induce or incite a person to so use or apply any such article, instrument, substance, drug, medicine, or thing, is hereby declared to be non-mailable matter and shall not be conveyed in the mails or delivered from any post-office or by any letter carrier. Whoever shall knowingly deposit, or cause to be deposited for mailing or delivery, anything declared by this section to be non-mailable, or shall knowingly take, or cause the same to be taken, from the mails for the purpose of circulating or disposing thereof, or of aiding in the circulation or disposition thereof, shall be fined not more than five thousand dollars, or imprisoned not more than five years, or both.

*the pp. about the classics:* In his written opinion of the case, Judge Hand made the following observation: "I have little doubt that numerous really great writings would come under the ban if tests that are frequently current were applied, and these approved publications doubtless at times escape only because they come within the term 'classics,' which means for the purpose of application of the statute, that they are ordinarily immune from interference, because they have the sanction of age and fame and usually appeal to a comparatively limited number of readers." He conceded, however, that it would be "very easy by a narrow and prudish construction of the Statute to suppress literature of permanent merit."

In his article on the suppression (see preceding note), EP jumps on Hand's comment that the classics "appeal to a comparatively limited number of readers." EP invites the "gentle reader [to] picture to himself the state of America IF the classics were widely read; IF these books which in the beginning lifted mankind from savagery, and which from a.d. 1400 onward have gradually redeemed us from the darkness of mediavalism [*sic*], should be read by the millions who now consume Mr. Hearst and the *Lady's* [*sic*] *Home Journal* ! ! ! ! ! !" He also points out that, under Hand's reasoning, "no living man is to contribute or attempt to contribute to the classics" and that as the U.S. statute is being applied, one individual (the Postmaster General), "without any examination of his literary qualifications," is the final judge of the merits of any piece of literature. "No more damning indictment of American civilization," EP concludes, "has been written than that contained in Judge Hand's 'opinion'. The classics 'escape'. They are 'immune' 'ordinarily'."

Despite EP's instruction to print Hand's comment every month, MCA did not do so.

*so you can print all the lot:* Joyce's *Ulysses* began its run in the *LR* in the March 1918 issue (3–22). It was printed without "gaps, at the questionable points."

*"Dictionnaire Philosophique":* Voltaire's *Dictionnaire philosophique portatif* (1764) was a collection of short articles which were, for the most part, attacks on religious dogma. Immediately after its publication, it was ordered to be burnt at Geneva and, in 1765, it was condemned both by the *parlement* and by Rome. In the Kehl edition (part of the collected works of Voltaire published from 1784 to 1790), under the title *Dictionnaire philosophique,* the work contains additional material as well as the *Lettres philosophiques,* which originally had no connection with it.

**68. TLS–2.** On stationery embossed: 5, Holland Place Chambers/ Kensington. W. ⟨8⟩ [23 January 1918]

⟨May Sinclair
on D Richardson
   is to go into
   April number.
      Egoist is
         printing
            it here.⟩

Dear M.C.A.

    Subscriber: Miss E.K. Grainger.   Pioneer Club
        9 Park Place.   St. James's. S.W.
(I have sent her 2 copies.) Begin her Dec. and run 10 months.
                    ///
[James] Joyce sends on following corrections.
Episode 1.  p. 4.  par. 9.  read Cranly's not Crauley's
      1.     10.     8. after I $\overline{\text{am, m'am}}$, Buck.  etc.
           read.  "Look at that now," she said "We're always tired
           etc.
    1, 13, 7.  for "We're always tired." read
             "I'm always tired"
        ///
All the first lot of Joyce can go in March. I strongly recommend the omissions AND the comments thereon used in my last.

I enclose the Joyce for April. AND another imaginary letter. TO be used AFTER the three remaining Lewis letters have appeared. If they went into Jan. all well and good.

If they are being held for Lewis' corrections. This one of mine must wait until they have come out.

        yours E.

Only 2. copies Dec. recd to date.
    Jan. 23. 1918                  Ezra Pound
                                vide
                                  P.S.= =

*May Sinclair on D Richardson:* i.e., "The Novels of Dorothy Richardson"
(April 1918: 3–11).

*another imaginary . . . all well and good:* Actually, only two of Lewis's "Imaginary Letters" remained to be published—the first of these in the March 1918
issue (23–30) and the second in the April 1918 issue (50–54). EP's "Imaginary Letter" was published in the May 1917 number (52–55).

*vide P.S.:* The postscript has been lost.

**69. TLS–3.**   On stationery embossed: 5, Holland Place Chambers/ Kensington. W. [25 January 1918]

Dear Margaret:

Right you are. Re/ [John] Quinn, remember: Tis he who
hath bought the pictures; tis he who both getteth me an american publisher and smacketh the same with rods; tis he who sendeth me the SPONDOS OLIGOS, which is by interpretation the small tribute of spondooliks
wherewith I do pay my contributors, WHEREFORE is my heart softened
toward the said J. Q., and he in mine eyes can commit nothing heinous.

Can you, on the other hand see [H. L.] Mencken, he writes
hoping the suppression wont drive you out of business; and if he chose to
wail in his back pages re/ Cantleman, it might do some good. After all he
still has a circulation. AND his eyes discerned me years since.

Re/ Amy [Lowell]. I DON'T want her. But if she can be
made to liquidate, to excoriate, to cash in, on a magazine, ESPECIALLY
in a section over which I have no control, and for which I am not responsible. THEN would I be right glad to see her milked of her money,
mashed into moonshine, at mercy of monitors. ⟨Especially as appearance
in U.S. section does NOT commit me to any approval of her work.⟩

Of course IF (which is unlikely) she ever wanted to
return to the true church, and live like an honest woman. Something might
be arranged. BUT. . . . . . . .

Is she yet weary of Braithwaite, and the mulattoism, mental and physical.

Do, or perhaps DO NOT, regard the prospectus of Contemporary Verse. Of all the crapule that a reputed millionaire was ever
responsible for . . . . . . I hope it COSTS Stork something.

                    ////

At any rate do try to swing Mencken. (And also remember that

I CAN'T possibly know from this side which of my damn suggestions are any good. Probably ANY suggestion I make re/ American policy is bad. However I may as well send 'em. You can reject 'em with perfect ease.)

[Lady] Gregory and [Arthur] Symons are good names to have on the list of contribs. They needn't reappear.

You'll have got Lewis "Ideal Giant" by now. And will have my note on suppression sometime.

Etc. I do have to stop and earn my board now and again. Malhe[u]reusement. However Joyce for April, and a letter from Villerant go by this post, via chief censor.

Don't worry about my initials on Longfellow paragraph. No harm done.

French proofs not here yet. I shall trust to the cultured and intelligent frenchman. and PRAY to Apollo.

Have done a little "Cantico del Sole.", but want to see if I can't first finish a little note on suppression in the vein of L'Homme Moyen [Sensuel], to appear first.

Don't believe [Ford Madox] Hueffer will ever be able to do the continuation of his series. Have some excellent stuff from a new man, ⟨conteur.,⟩ but it must wait till I can revise it somewhat.

Am going out for a session with the new diseuse. May have a note on that art before long.

Dont worry about writing, only I do want eclaircissements now and again.

I still think Q. is too good to waste; despite your difficulties. (Which I can comprehend)

yours<br>
Ezra Pound<br>
25–1–18

*Braithwaite:* Black American poet, author, and editor, William Stanley Braithwaite (1878–1962), best known for his anthologies, which included an annual

*Anthology of Magazine Verse and Year Book of American Poetry* (1913 ff.). As poetry editor of the *Boston Transcript,* Braithwaite had favorably reviewed Amy Lowell's *Sword Blades and Poppy Seed* on 28 November 1914. Furthermore, he had responded, at her request, to an attack on Imagism written by Conrad Aiken and published on 22 May 1915 in *The New Republic* under the title "The Place of Imagism." (*The New Republic* carried Braithwaite's response in its 12 June 1915 issue.) A year later in May 1916, with the financial backing of Lowell, Braithwaite founded *The Poetry Review of America* (Cambridge, Massachusetts), a monthly he edited until its demise following the February 1917 issue.

*Contemporary Verse:* From 1917 through 1925, Charles Wharton Stork edited the poetry journal *Contemporary Verse* (Philadelphia), a monthly which had begun publication in 1916 and which continued through 1929. The editorial policy favored traditional verse forms ("there is no point in the use of *vers libre,* unless it is illuminated by a great idea, as in the case of Whitman"), but the journal eventually opened its pages to some practitioners of free verse.

*initials on Longfellow paragraph:* The December 1917 "Reader Critic" carried EP's comments on the event of Longfellow's birthplace becoming a national monument: "The house wherein this eminently moral and eminently proper and eminently 'suitable for the school-child' luminary mewled and peuked [*sic*], is to be taken on as a national shrine, by the 'International Longfellow Society', and the mortgage on it removed. . . . It is in fact an eloquent tribute to the popular lust after some place where they can leave orange peel, and feel they have 'shown reverence', without troubling their cerebra with such detail as standards of literature" (55–56).

*"Cantico del Sole.":* EP's short poem "Cantico del Sole" (signed Ezra I.Y.H.X.) followed his article "The Classics 'Escape' " in the March 1918 issue.

*the new diseuse* . . . *:* Raymonde Collignon. EP's note appeared in the March 1918 "Reader Critic": "There is a new *diseuse* loose on London. She will go to France after the war, and heaven knows when she will get to America, but she will sometime. She is singing folk-song without the vegetarian and simple-life elements. She is the first singer to work on Walter Rummel's reconstructions of XIIth. century Provençal music. . . . She is really a consummate artist" (60). On 27 April 1918 at the Aeolian Hall in London, Collignon performed some of the troubadour songs Walter Rummel and EP had put together in 1911 and 1912.


**70. TLS–1.**   On stationery embossed: 5, Holland Place Chambers/ Kensington. W. ⟨8⟩ [29 January 1918]

Dear Margaret

[Alfred] Knopf has besought me for a paragraph on "Tarr" for his announcement. I have just done [it], and think it so good, that you'd better rush it into the L.R., along with announcement of Knopf's pending publication. ⟨Or rather⟩ Find out when he is to issue the book, and print it in the L.R. six or seven weeks before hand.

//////

TARR

"Tarr" is the most vigorous and volcanic English novel of our time. Lewis is that rarest of phenomena, an Englishman who has achieved the triumph of being also an European. He is the only English writer who can be compared with Dostoievsky, and he is more rapid than Dostoievsky, his mind travels with greater celerity, with more unexpectedness, but he loses none of Dostoievsky's effect of mass and of weight.

Tarr is a man of genius surrounded by the heavy stupidities of the half cultured latin quarter, the book delineates his explosions in this oleaginous milieu; as well as the debacle of the unintelligent emotion-dominated Kreisler. They are the two titanic characters in contemporary English fiction. [H. G.] Wells' clerks, Bennet's [Arnold Bennett's] "cards" and even Conrad's russian villains do not "bulk up" against them.

Only in James Joyce's Stephen Daedalus [Dedalus] does one find an equal intensity, and Joyce is, by comparison, cold and meticulous, where Lewis is, if uncouth, at any rate brimming with energy, the man with a leaping mind.

⟨signed Ezra Pound.⟩

Yours E.P.

Ezra Pound.

*Find out when he is to issue the book . . . :* Knopf published Wyndham Lewis's *Tarr* on 25 June 1918. EP's review appeared in the March 1918 issue of the *LR* (35).

**71. TLS–2.** On stationery embossed: 5, Holland Place Chambers/ Kensington. W. [2 February 1918]

Dear Margaret:

What the ensanguined lllllllllllllllllllllllll is the matter with this BLOODYgoddamndamnblastedbastardbitchbornsonofaputridseahorse of foetid and stinkerous printer ????????????

Is his serbo-croatian optic utterly impervious to the twelfth letter of the alphabet ?????

JHEEZUSMARIAYJOSE ! ! ! ! Madre de dios y de dios del perro. Sacrobosco di Satanas.

OF COURSE IF IF IF bloodywell IF this blasted numero appears with anything like one twohundredandfiftieth part of these errors we are DONE, and I shall never be able to cross the channel or look a French ecrivain [écrivain] in the face. . . .

I enclose mss. for galley 2. omitted line.

You have my only text of the Corbiere [Tristan Corbière] "Sainte-Anne" so I can only put question marks on it. And pray that you will correct it.

Lewis is in a stew over the multiple mistakes in his Soldier of Humour ????
     Lord be gracious unto Moses.
     IN THE DAY OF THY WRATH
IF the mistakes in this french number aren't corrected before it is sent out we will have to put an errata slip into the next number. BUT that is a great nuisance and wont in the least wipe off the disgrace.

However I have your "swear" on the top on galley 1. and may as well repose on it for the present, and not go off into hysterias.

           yours E.
⟨But
confound it
the matter is
    ≡
   serious.⟩
          Ezra Pound
2/2/1918


72. TLS–1. On stationery embossed: 5, Holland Place Chambers/ Kensington. W. [10 February 1918]

Dear Margaret:

      Here's this. The beginning of the extract from J.R. [John Rodker] is not perhaps very exciting, but it has to be there to lead on to the rest.

Slap it in when you get ready. I've rather lost count of when what is to go in, also it is impossible for me to tell how much the enlarged format will eat up per month. I think I can get on the copy in time. This chunk hardly counts as a contribution by me.

I have the Windeler story, and would have sent it in this letter, but typist is busy. I think he may be an asset.

Can you drop me a line to say whether you have, with the receipt of this enough mss. actually rec'd to fill both April and May. The Ideal Giant is a good big chunk. ??? will it end in May or lap over into June?

It is (as I think I wrote) to start the new vol. with a heave.

Ah yes. I had almost forgotten my little Cantico. I enclose that also. Print it after the regular monthly extract from the judge's speech.

Et Dominus tecum

yours E                                                          Ezra Pound
                                                                 10/2/18

*the extract from J.R.:* It is difficult to say which of John Rodker's selections EP is referring to here. Following the publication of Rodker's "Incidents in the Life of a Poet" in the January 1918 issue, the next Rodker selection to appear was his contribution to the August 1918 Henry James issue, "The Notes on Novelists" (53–56).

*the Windeler story:* i.e., B. Cyril Windeler's "Elimus," published in the April 1918 issue (12–26). This story was later reprinted in an edition published by the Three Mountains Press (Paris) in 1923. For this edition, Dorothy Shakespear Pound provided twelve designs.

*will it end in May . . . :* Wyndham Lewis's "The Ideal Giant" appeared in its entirety in the May issue.

*my little Cantico:* See Letter 69n.

**73. TLS–7.** On stationery embossed: 5, Holland Place Chambers/ Kensington. W. [20 February 1918]

Dear Margaret, Perla di Neve, etc.

I still think you under-appreciate mon cher ami J.Q. [John Quinn].

Perla di Neve, he as the rest of us has his characteristics. Also you put me in the hell of a hole by this fuss over a wholly innocuous article on the Elizabethan Stage, to print it is but the decent lifting of one's hat as the funeral passes; [Charles Francis] Keary will trouble no one again. Also as it was handed me by a friend, a most old and intimate of the late Henry ⟨James⟩ on whom we hope to devote some space, and as the one person who seems capable of helping much with the H.J. number is also a fruit of my entering that house, and as we want Mrs Wharton (who wont care a curse for ten Kearys, but who might be susceptible, at least more susceptible to approach via personally known channels). etc. etc. God damn it. What do I get for this job anyhow.

Do give me credit occasionally for at least a reason for my acts. Even if it isn't the sole and surviving reason left on the planet; and even if I occasionally do not hit a bullseye. ⟨I dont ask you to like the bloody article or even to read it. ==I ought to have marked it "not to be read by the editress"⟩

And do for god's sake realize that, having graciously wasted a week explaining that I would accept Keary, but could not pay for him; I can not waste another saying that we wont print him. I have only a certain amount of energy and that I have A. to get my poetry written; B. pay my rent etc. C. assist in the promulgation of the L.R. (letters to be placed in any order you like.).

Also that I have just drawn my Nov. allowance on L.R. as during period when further funds were uncertain I tried to live on my earnings wholly apart from L.R. £5/ per month; this during preparation of Feb. number, and during my work on my Arnaut Daniel.

ETC. I can not waste more time and energy than it would take to do two articles, in negotiating with Keary's relatives etc. and acquaintance. The thing is perfectly innocuous. I never said it had the punch of my helter-skelter notes on Eliz. Classicists.

For God's sake print it, and thank god I have been content to have my avalanchingly scholastic Arnaut privately printed instead of sending it to 24 W. 16th. St.

///// 

Use Windeler's story in March IF by any ⟨chance⟩ it arrives in time. If you still find a hole in that number. New prose author. ??? WOT the bloody hell do you expect. I mean there's enough in that story, let alone the egregious [James] Joyce to carry ten Kearys.

And, serieusement, we have got occasionally to print essays. There appears to be nothing in America between Professors and [Alfred] Kreymborgs and [Maxwell] Bodenheims. Platonic hemiandroi. Anemia of guts on one side and anaemia of education on the other.

Some of the best material in America has lain a long time unused because the few human professors (il y en a) have not known what to do with it. There has been nothing open to them but philological disquisition in technical reviews. Rennert's extremely vivid Life of Lope is unknown. Schelling once wrote essays that had they been done here would have gained him a definite position (at least that is my memory of them.)

The few people who have enough knowledge [to] ⟨form a basis⟩ for critical comparison in literature are mostly cooped in colleges.

There has got to be a fusion of this element into the element of ignorant exuberance in America before ⟨its⟩ writing will get any better.

I don't want MORE Keary, but Keary is a perfectly good decoy duck, and he had the inestimable advantage from my point of view of being physically dead.

etc. etc.

I have writ [Hart] Crane a line. Don't publish him.

By all means send back the "List of Books" if you dont like it. I haven't seen Harriet's assassination of my Swinburne, but if she has seriously deranged it, I will send you full text. IF I have a copy.

I have occasionally been puzzled before; seemed to miss things in "Poetry" prose section, but as I never have a duplicate copy, and as it is so damd hard to remember whether one wrote a thing in one article or another, and as she keeps things so long, and as IT is extremely hard to remember what one wrote, as distinct from what one said on a particular evening or what one thought and did not say, I have never caught her out.

////

The New Age gives us a full page this week (Feb. 21.), entire, or rather, a very considerable distortion of my position, but I am too exhausted to reply. [A. R.] Orage does the essential in quoting the judge's speech.

///

I should be very glad if you can manage to consider the printing of Keary as a saving of my energy, rather than as a tribute to a past generation.

I have got to be allowed

some margin of mistakes, even, (as this is not,) of mistakes having no ul-
terior and possible compensations.

As yet ⟨since May last year⟩ America has coughed up no "creative" stuff,
i.e. no poetry or fiction to the L.R., apart from Jh. [Jane Heap] on females
with faces with noses level with ears which wasnt fiction. But apart from
the editorial, the U.S. has given nothing to contents of L.R. save that treacle about Judas which affected me much more violently than Keary seems
to have affected you.

Even so I think you were "right" to print it, on the principle that one must
accept something now and again, if one is not utterly to choke off all in-
flow of mss. (a very damn dangerous principle, ⟨but pragmatic⟩)

And, as you say, I am ageing rapidly. Byron is described as very old, or
at least grey and showing age at 36. I have but a few years left me. I can
not be expected to keep up sufficient interest in the state of public imbecility to go [on] being "astringent" (as J.Q. calls it) perpetually.

I am at the moment interested in Henry Lawes, who knew "how to do
it", and the Collignon is doing some of the XII century provencal music
[Walter] Rummel and I dug up in Paris six years ago. And Dolmetsch
plans to herd a lot of "great pianists" into my kitchen (they not to know
what den they are entering) in order that they may hear Bach properly
played on the clavichord. Don't mention this. As it may not come off, only
such was his intention when he left ⟨here⟩ last Friday. (Incidentally he
mentioned the two I have been damning in my musical criticism.) I wonder at what point a discussion of music would lead you and me into mutual assassination ?????????? Gawd only knows.

   Joyce, by the way, approves of the clavichord. And he has also sung in
opera. [Wyndham] Lewis, I think, regards the instrument as a strange un-
accountable sort of mouse-trap; the char-woman (after four months services) spoke of it the other day as "the little black table" (observation the
leading characteristic of the "lower orders").

Chere amie, I am, for the time being, bored to death with being any kind
of an editor. I desire to go on with my long poem; and like the Duke of
Chang, I desire to hear the music of a lost dynasty. (have managed to
hear it, in fact,.) And I desire also to resurrect the art of the lyric, I mean
words to be sung, for Yeats's only wail and submit to keening and chaunt-

ing (with a u) and Swinburne's only rhapsodistify. And with a few excep-
tions (a few̄ in Browning) there is scarcely anything since the time of
Waller and Campion. AND a mere imitation of them wont do. And Rummel's modern settings are made to whistle.

For instance in ⟨the case of⟩ my "The Return" he has done the meaning of the poem in his music, but the singer's notes should sound quite as
well, or rather better on the violin, and the words were never intended to
be sung.

Also I have not been to Italy since 1913. I have not baked in the sun, nor
swum in my blue sulphur lago, and you are probably right in saying that
I show signs of decay. Five english winters uninterrupted. I shall grow
blubber like a walrus.

[Ford Madox] Hueffer is dead, absolutely dead with army. [T. S.] Eliot is
dead with his bank. Lewis wanders about interrupting, and he thinks he is
hunting for a studio (only he isnt) in which to paint his picture for the
Canadian govt.

And the effects of the vernal ingress can not be expected to op-
erate for some weeks.

I shall follow the example of St. Augustine, and take a bath (in
hot water).

buona sera

yours   E

Ezra Pound

20–2–1918

*Perla di Neve:* Italian: "Pearl of Snow."
*article on the Elizabethan stage:* See Letter 65n.
*H.J. number:* i.e., the August 1918 issue.
*my Arnaut Daniel:* At this time, EP was again translating the poems of the
   Troubadour poet Arnaut Daniel. "Homage à la langue d'or [i.e. d'Oc. "Alba";
   I–V]" was published in the May 1918 issue of the *LR* and "Glamour and
   Indigo: A Canzon from the Provençal of 'En Ar. Dan'el" was printed in the
   November 1918 issue.
*on Eliz. Classicists:* Five essays entitled "Elizabethan Classicists" were published
   in *The New Age* (September 1917–January 1918) and were reprinted as
   "Notes on Elizabethan Classicists" in *Pavannes and Divisions.*
*avalanchingly scholastic Arnaut:* EP included the following note with his
   "Glamour and Indigo" in the November 1918 *LR* (5):

> I had not intended to print this translation or any other of the complete set of
> Daniel's canzos apart from their Provençal originals, in a separate booklet. But

as the full Mss., an affair scholastic rather than artistic, yet of interest to serious students of the craft, appears to be spurlos verschwindet, along with the Clark's [Clerk's] Press, of Cleveland Ohio (fate not unique with Mss. sent to America) I make sure of this much of the work before leaving my papers for an indefinite period. I find my spare copies of the remaining translations rather too over-scored to be much use to anyone but myself, but could probably duplicate the printer's copy with time.

*Windeler's story:* See Letter 72n.

*Rennert's . . . life of Lope:* Hugo Albert Rennert's *The Life of Lope de Vega* (1904). See Letter 65n.

*Schelling:* Felix Emanuel Schelling. See Letter 65n.

*send back the "List of Books":* EP's "List of Books" in the March 1918 *LR* had this to say about Charles Francis Keary: "C. F. Keary is recently dead. He had written divers novels greatly admired in certain circles and a volume of pagan poems entitled 'Religious Hours', printed with black borders like a book of devotions. He was a contributor to the more solid english quarterlies and reviews. The poems are in the tradition of english poetry as it was before Keats and Shelley, they are consistent within themselves, and it is extremely difficult to appraise such work in a hurry. One must sink into the given period. It is not my period, nor even one of my periods, and I have not yet found the right critic to do the job for me. I hope to give some adequate notice of the novels after I have arranged suitable complete numbers in appreciation of Henry James and Remy de Gourmont, in each case a lengthy matter . . ." (56).

*Harriet's assassination of my Swinburne:* i.e., Harriet Monroe's publication of EP's "Swinburne versus Biographers," in *Poetry* (March 1918): 322–29, a review of Edmund Gosse's *The Life of Algernon Charles Swinburne*. This article does not appear in the *LR*. See Letter 83.

*distortion of my position:* regarding the unfavorable disposition of the case of the suppression of the October 1917 *LR*.

*judge's speech:* See Letter 66n.

*on females with faces . . . :* EP's reference is to Jane Heap's "Push-Face" in the June 1917 issue (4–7). See Letter 34n.

*treacle about Judas:* Robert Alden Sanborn's poem "The Children of Judas" (September 1917): 22–30.

*Henry Lawes:* (1596–1662), English composer, a friend of John Milton, Edmund Waller, and Robert Herrick.

*the Collignon . . . :* See Letter 69n.

*Dolmetsch:* Arnold Dolmetsch (1858–1940) restored and re-created early musical instruments. At the time of their wedding, Dolmetsch had given the Pounds a clavichord which became one of EP's prized possessions.

*in my musical criticism:* Under the pseudonym William Atheling, EP wrote music criticism for *The New Age*.

*my long poem:* i.e., *The Cantos*.

*Waller and Campion:* English poets, Edmund Waller (1606–87) and Thomas Campion (d. 1619).

*Rummel's modern settings:* i.e., "Three Songs of Ezra Pound for a Voice with

Instrumental Accompaniment by Walter Morse Rummel," first published in 1911 by Augener Ltd. (London). The three songs included were "Madrigale," "Au bal masque," and "Aria," the first and third of these reprinted from *Canzoni* (1911); "Au bal masque" was printed here for the first time. In 1913, Augener brought out a musical setting of EP's "The Return," also for voice and instrumental accompaniment, done by Walter Rummel (see Gallup, *Pound*, E4a–b).

*his picture for the Canadian govt.:* Wyndham Lewis was working for the Canadian War Memorials department of the Canadian Army, an organization which had been started in October 1917 by Lord Beaverbrook to honor Canada's part in the War. During 1918 and 1919, Lewis worked on completing two large war paintings: *A Canadian Gun Pit* (National Gallery, Ottawa) and *A Battery Shelled* (Imperial War Museum, London).

**74. TLS–1.** On stationery embossed: 5, Holland Place Chambers/ Kensington. W. [21 February 1918]

Dear M.

Joyce has run wode, as per enclosed p.c. However, I suppose we may as well let him have his own way.

This installment is magnificent in spots, and mostly incomprehensible. Ma che.

Brief note on The Dial, perhaps not worth inclusion.

21/2/1918   E

Ezra Pound

*Brief note on the Dial:* See Letter 75.

**75. TLS–1.** On stationery embossed: 5, Holland Place Chambers/ Kensington. W. [22 February 1918?]

## CARO   MIO

The following is extracted from a publisher's letter. The letter deals with the announcement of Mr Pound's Lustra. After stating where announcements of its publication had appeared the publisher continues:

"I also had it included in the copy I gave The Dial for a quarter page a couple of weeks ago, but quite improperly they failed to show me proofs, and as the copy ran over they themselves took the liberty of deleting LUSTRA from that advertisement."

Liber arbitrio: Deal [Dear] old Dial doing it quietly. There is also the Macmillan Co. of New York.

*LUSTRA:* EP's *Lustra* was published by Knopf in New York in October 1917. *There is also the Macmillan Co.:* John Quinn had attempted, unsuccessfully, to get Macmillan in New York to publish *Lustra*.

**76. TLS–4.** On stationery embossed: 5, Holland Place Chambers/ Kensington. W. [22 February 1918]

22 Feb. 1918

Dear Margaret:

Jan. number arrived. Feeling better. Number looks business-like, and "about to continue". Damn, damn, DAMN I must pull myself together and DO something.

I wish to Christ you would take an anaesthetic and print this cursed thing of [Charles] Kearys; thereby saving me time to breathe and get something written.

Rodker that you cursed me for, has ornamented the issue.

Bill Wms. is the most bloody inarticulate animal that ever gargled. BUT its better than Amy's bloody ten cent repetitive gramophone, perfectly articulate (i.e. in the verbal section.).

Whereas the bleating genius of the HOME product. Hecht might write good DeMaupassant if he didn't try to crack jokes and ring bells; and if he would only realize that he DONT need to exaggerate to be interesting.

You will by now know that there is enough Joyce [i.e., *Ulysses*] to use the full installment in March, not stringing it over three issues. That will have helped with the gap you were bewailing.

Your appeal for more copy was too late to help March in any case.

Slap in Windeler [i.e., "Elimus"] as soon as you like. Will try to pry something out of the valetudinarian [T. S.] Eliot.

SANGRE DI SAN PIETRO ' ! ! WHY ' ' ' do you recall that better to be forgotten libellule of Wilkinson's ????? Raoul Root INDEED. KHRRIST. Am I a pet pug to have blue ribbons curled in my tail?

It dont matter. BUTTTT. (Incidentally [Richard] Aldington ought to stave in the author's posterior if he ever reencounters him.) I dont think it makes it any better that I am very leniently dealt with. However, it is of no importance.

IF Lewis after all this time dont get his corrected copies of those letters handed in ! ! ! ! ! !

Cut the passage about Lloyd George, and any too flagrant sentences, and proceed.

*///*

Bless my soul, if here isn't that little cat Jessie Dissmor [*sic*] turned up again with a poem. (And one which doesnt detract.). Sly devil dodging my venomed gaze.

*///*

And: re Mr Cline: Dont the bloody fool know that Lustrum means a brothel?

*///*

Re the Quintuple. It should read "Mrs J.D. Something or Other"

(Josephenine Dodge Daskomm Bascom Cumflascum)

Despite your wail. Lewis description of the three American rescuers in the second half "Sol. Humour." is excellent, Digit of the Moon. etc. Oh very good. I got him to rewrite some of it, but wot the hell can a man do in his present circumstances. It is, as he recognizes, a question of doing his stories some how or other, or not doing them at all.

He will, if he dont get killed, revise later. before book publication.

IT IS I PERCEIVE up to me to contribute something to our pages.

Are you sending exchange copies of L.R. to "New Age"

38 Cursitor St. E.C. 4.

Please do.

I dont think there is any chance of there being any more Hueffer mss. [i.e., *Women & Men*] than what you have already rec'd.

Must fish up some KELTIK glamour.

The white cats and ebony pianos lady has faded. Nothing to be hoped for from her.

IF Lewis gets his new copy of "Letters" in. I dont see why you shouldn't publish his three, and my final farewell to Lydia, all in the same number. The thing has been hung up long enough.

Villerants further correspondence will be addressed for the present to his cousin, a highly cultured female. Villerants last letter to Lydia, ought to precede the note of Jules Romains. Confound Lewis anyhow.

WINDELER can very well go into April. Better go into April in fact, if you havent used him in March.

IDEAL Giant to go in May. That will give me breathing space.

Dash it the James and DeGourmont numbers are six months work each. AND I do not want to sink wholly into criticism to the utter stoppage of creation. ETc.

Put ALL Ideal Giant in May. And I will get ready for a brand new REFLUGE in the June Number.

E.

Ezra Pound

*Rodker that you cursed me for:* John Rodker's "Incidents in the Life of a Poet" (January 1918): 31–35.
*Bill Wms. is the most bloody . . . :* EP is referring to William Carlos Williams' "Improvisations" (January 1918): 3–9.
*Hecht might write . . . :* In the January 1918 "Reader Critic," MCA had reprinted Ben Hecht's comments on EP which had originally appeared in the *Chicago Daily News:*

> In Ezra, thus, I have belatedly discovered a creature given over heart and soul to the art of writing. I have discovered in him, belatedly, of course, a decadent after my own fancy, a thin little voluptuary of phrase, but a voluptuary none the less. I would he had more sonority to his rainbows (I refer, gentlemen, to the rainbow used by Demetrius as an oboe summoning together the gods for conference). I would that he, Ezra, were a bit more luscious in his piquancies, more

lyric in his outlinings. But given moonlight one should be reconciled to the absence of the moon.

There is in Pound, as he stands published to-day, a gift of irony and color which, wan though it be, is to be treasured like a full goat-skin in the desert. He alone, of the few bards with whose work I am acquainted, preserves an exquisite balance in the current of his own emotions. Of material things he is never serious, of passions he treats with a sharp tongue held in his cheek. Of ideas, thoughts, meditations, he is drolly cynical, even when they are the product of his own enfevered fancy. And of color, wherever he finds it, he is properly rapturous. Nothing is too small to receive the salaam of an adjective. Nothing too unimportant to receive the touch of his illuminating phrases.

*that better to be forgotten libellule of Wilkinson's:* EP's reference here is obscure. "Raoul Root" is the pseudonym MCA created for EP's article on Mencken. See Letter 59.

*Jessie Dismorr:* British painter and poet Jessica Dismorr (1885–1939) in 1914 signed the Vorticist manifesto in *BLAST*. She also exhibited at the Vorticist exhibition at the Dore Galleries in London and contributed to the second issue of *BLAST*. Dismorr's contribution to the January 1918 issue was a poem entitled "The Convalescent in the South" (15–16).

*re Mr Cline:* A letter written by Leonard Cline of Detroit was included in the January "Reader Critic." In part, it reads:

> It is a tremendous shock to be hurtled into the company of devil-begotten Ezra Pound, put up between yellow boards by Alfred A. Knopf, under the nomenclature of "Lustra." This word "lustra" means two things, either expiatory sacrifices or morasses. Ezra Pound is too absolutely degraded to offer sacrifices, much less expiatory ones; therefore we must be content to consider the book a collection of morasses, quicksands.
>
> Bogs the poems certainly are. There is an enormous charm about some of them, and one is in jeopardy of being lured to tread out upon them, and only when the hungry mud sucks a shoe off and one gets a stocking slimy, realize one's delusion. They have the appearance of poetry; the lines are split up; and now and again there is a really delightful metaphor, to give the devil his due. This it is which has induced people out upon them, and has given Ezra's corrupting influence a wide scope. As a rule these poems are not poems; beauty is never flippant. . . .

*Re the Quintuple:* i.e., "The Quintuple Effulgence or The Unapproachable Splendour" (56). See Letter 55n.

*Lewis description:* In the second part of Wyndham Lewis's story "The Soldier of Humour," Blauenfeld, one of the three Americans who "rescues" the narrator, had a copy of the *Digit of the Moon* in his coat pocket. "So had Morton in his. The book had been recommended to them by an American girl in a Paris studio. They had very seriously and gratefully made a note of it, after several weeks had procured it and were now reading it assiduously [*sic*]." We are also told that "Morton possessed a little seraglio of ladies that his undecided and catholic fancy had made him indul[g]e in. They all had great sexual charm, tactfully displayed. He had his favorite photograph, of course. It was the least tactful, merely, I am afraid" (47–48).

*the white cats and ebony pianos lady:* EP is probably referring to "Vail de Lencour" (Brigit Patmore). See Letter 36n.

*the note of Jules Romains:* EP's "Unanimism" (April 1918): 26–32.
*WINDELER:* B. Cyril Windeler's story "Elimus" was published in the April 1918 issue (12–26).
*IDEAL Giant:* Wyndham Lewis's play "The Ideal Giant" was published in the May 1918 issue (1–18).

**77. TLS–2.**   On stationery embossed: 5, Holland Place Chambers/ Kensington. W. [22 February 1918]

FEB. 22. Third Letter.

Dear Margaret:

I have spent this whole bloody day writing letters. bar. interruption for tea to discuss music with La Belle Collignon. (here, and very short interruption). And the seven minutes devoted to three brief squibs. "The Criterion" etc.

It is damnd silly for me to exhaust meself at this sort of thing when most of it could have been done by an auxiliary from two lines of notes.

It so happens that I have the chance of getting a good typist or secretary for £2/ per week.

Could you, in the face of the new subsidy (1600 dols. raised acc. last report that reached me.) (WHICH same I will not touch, as it is for N.Y. office. well deserved.).

But with that air of "being a going concern", plus the apparent boost I am getting from Eliot's (Knopf's) brochure. Strike somewhere for enough to raise me to £2/ per week.

I am now drawing £5 per month. (Transcendent genius etc.). It means £40, or to be exact £44/ ⟨per year.⟩ to lift that to the wages of a typist.

IF I had ⟨the⟩ said secretary I could give a lot more energy to "composition".

Anyhow I'm an ass to spend so much time and energy on purely clerical work, and simple letters.

If you can raise the £44/ per annum, I can use the present L.R. £60/.

I could under that arrangement afford to give ⟨unpaid⟩ much more time to L.R. than I have been giving. ⟨@ the current £5)⟩

It is perfectly sane economy, ALL round. Not unadulterate avarice.

I could just as well have spent today doing, or at least preparing an "Etuves de Wiesbaden" as in hacking at this machine.

AND the proper doing of the James and DeGourmont numbers, needs TIME.

Someone, emphatically NOT [John] Quinn, who is doing ENOUGH, might be sandbagged.

"Softly the evening air" as you put it.

yours      E
Ezra Pound

*La Belle Collignon:* See Letter 69n.

*"The Criterion":* Two squibs entitled "The Criterion" were published in the *LR*, the first in the April 1918 issue (11) and the second in the May 1918 issue (62):

I.
"Art", said the chimpanzee, "which *I* have to *study* before *I* can understand it, is lacking somewhere." "Upon this principal [*sic*]", said the chimpanzee, "we must reject Mr. Browning's *Sordello.*"
II.
"Art", said the aged Mr. William Dean Howells, speaking for Mabie, Wood-bury, Van Dyke and Co., and the whole of their *papier mache* [*sic*] and never to be sufficiently ridiculed and wholly contemptible generation of male American matrons, "Art which upsets me, Art which the mind of the artist has moved more rapidly than my mind habitually moved, Art uttered by persons who see a bit more than I do, who feel more deeply than I do, cannot be sufficiently re-gretted. Give me C. Wharton Stork, I am never disturbed by his magazine."

*Eliot's (Knopf's) brochure:* T. S. Eliot had written *Ezra Pound: His Metric and Poetry,* a pamphlet (31 pages) which was published anonymously in January 1918 by Alfred A. Knopf in connection with the publication of EP's *Lustra* (1917).

**78. ALS–3.**   On stationery embossed: 5, Holland Place Chambers/ Kensington. W. [25 February 1918]

25–2–'18
Dear M.

I think you may as well have Lewis "Letters" set up. and make any emendations in the "proof".

Use Windeler [i.e., "Elimus"] & my "Romains" [i.e., "Unanimisme"] in March if you need to.

Cut the reference to "Keary" out of list of books if that is all that pains you in it.———

Drop me a line on proposed list of contents for March, Apr. May = as soon as you can. I've rather lost count of where what comes.

———

The only requisites are that Windeler's story & Lewis "Ideal Giant" shall not be in the same number.

My imaginary letter must n't precede Lewis three. but they can all go in one number.—mine following his three— if there is need. Dont reserve things for "future" use. I lost time on the first five numbers, through that sort of caution. The big chunks of Joyce [i.e., *Ulysses*] & Hueffer [i.e., *Women & Men*] will fill space=

Perhaps less Hueffer can be used per. number— as there is only what you have rec'd already.

Shall probably do DeGourmont number before the James as I presumably will have to do most of the DeG. myself=

———

Saluti to jh [Jane Heap].

yours
E.
Ezra Pound

*My imaginary letter . . . :* Contrary to what EP indicates here, only two "Imaginary Letters" written by Wyndham Lewis remained to be published, the first in March 1918 (23–30) and the second in April 1918 (50–54). EP's "Imaginary Letter (W. Villerant to the ex-Mrs. Burn)" was published in the May 1918 issue (52–55).
*DeGourmont number:* See Letter 66n.

**79. TLS–1.**   On stationery embossed: 5, Holland Place Chambers/ Kensington. W. [25 February 1918]

⟨25/2/18⟩

Dear M.

> Here AT LAST is Lewis revise.

It is simply that the long political allusion which formed nearly all of page "31" MUST absolutely come out.

The letter is to run on as in enclosed mss.

> "The thing that

is not. . . . etc. . .lands.

> So my opinion of this precious revolution."

etc.

So that's that.

> Everything between "lands" and "So my opinion" is to come

OUT.

> /////

Subscriber ( @ 12/)

Miss Ethel C. Mayne, 11 Holland Rd. W. 14.

> Sub begins Jan. but I have supplied Jan. and will supply Feb. so

run her from March to Dec. inclusive. (She wrote for the Yellow Book, and The Savoy.)

> ////

I have not accepted the enclosed versicles of Miss Barry's. Take 'em or throw 'em out, one or all as you see fit. I have no convictions about 'em. "Romance" is probably the best, but it is not worth risking suppression for it.

I should certainly not print it unless Q. [John Quinn] thinks it safe. it is not worth it.

> E.
>
> Ezra Pound

---

*Lewis revise:* Wyndham Lewis's revision of his "Imaginary Letter, VIII" for the
   March 1918 issue (23–30).
*She wrote for the Yellow Book . . . :* See Letter 38n.

*versicles of Miss Barry's:* Besides those poems which had already been published
in the August 1917 issue (17–19), only two additional poems by Iris Barry
were ever published in the *LR:* "Nishi Hongwanji" (July 1918: 19) and
"After Hafiz" (October 1918: 13).

**80. TLS–2.**   On stationery embossed: 5, Holland Place Chambers/ Kensington. W. [27 February 1918]

Dear M.

As I said in my last, Since "Jodindranath", we have neglected
the great and fertile land of India. I enclose a bit of undreamt of splendour. Also we have GOT the right person to do our notes on that part of
the orient. Perfect tone due to french education. Put the dear Sentam
Edoyarder in April or May, if there's room.

People have trusted too much to Rabi [Rabindranath Ta-
gore] and Rudyard [Kipling], we have here different type of Indian mind.
Would to God I could forward also the ILLUSTRATIONs of the two
books, that however is out of the question, as they belong to the College
of Oriental Studies.

If you are using it in May, announce it in April, simply as "Saptam
Edoyarder Svargabohan".

////

You will have got my note saying that in Lewis "Imag. let." page 32, everything from the top of the page beginning "A tyrant says . ." to the
bottom "myself once more, unforgettably", must come out.

Also my poems, should arrive with or before this, sent em off last night.

Have also asked Q. [John Quinn] to get the Fenollosa essay on Chinese
character back from the Monist. With our printing bill guaranteed, I feel
we must now make the big heave, and really get on a permanent footing.

                    yours
                      E.
                 Ezra Pound
                 27/2/'18

"*Jodindranath*": EP's "Jodindranath Mawhwor's Occupation." See Letter 8n.

*the right person to do our notes:* Iseult Gonne, the daughter of the Irish revolutionary Maud Gonne. Miss Gonne was, at the time, working as a librarian at the School of Oriental Languages in London (Levenson 316).

*the dear Sentam Edoyarder:* An essay entitled "Saptam Edoyarder Svargobohan" by Iseult Gonne was published in the July 1918 issue (31–34). The article is a discussion and summary of a poem ("perhaps the last great epic of our times") by the Bengali poet Tarini Prasad Jyotishi. The poem had originally been published in Bengali, along with an abbreviated prose translation in English, in Calcutta in 1911. Shortly after its publication, a more powerful verse translation into English by an anonymous Bengali poet appeared under the title "The Ascension of Edward VII to Heaven." Gonne's article focuses on the merits of this translation and quotes substantial portions of the poem to demonstrate its brilliance.

*the Monist: The Monist: A Quarterly Magazine Devoted to the Philosophy of Science* was published in Chicago from October 1890 to July 1936. See Letter 84.

EP's "The Chinese Written Character as a Medium for Poetry, by Ernest Fenollosa and Ezra Pound" was published in the *LR* in four installments: (September 1919): 62–64; (October 1919): 57–64; (November 1919): 55–60; and (December 1919): 68–72.

**81. TLS–2.**   On stationery embossed: 5, Holland Place Chambers/ Kensington. W. [28 February 1918]

⟨Feb 28⟩

Dear M.C.A.

The New Age, as I said, has given us a full page, their double col. meaning about 1200 words, it is a bit grumpy, but that is the tone of R.H.C. and he knows his public.

I think the enclosed will encourage him to go on quoting and observing us. Do you send the L.R. to the New Age? If not please do so.

New Age, 38 Cursitor St. E.C.4.

*///*

Re/ Old Mencken. You will make due allowance for my calling him a critic, perhaps more of American conditions, than of books, re/ which last I think I said in my letter "M. just dont know".

You and "jh" [Jane Heap] have covered it. It is not worth Mr. R. Root's writing a letter to the editor to adjust.

/////

The New Age as a 6d. weekly, does not compete with us, a 1/monthly, and might help a lot in introducing the L.R. here after the war.

One cant agree with the N.A.  . The whole centre of it is social and political, and the political mind is bound to fall out with the artist and with literature, tolerating them only up to a point, and as "addenda".

Another point in the N.A's improvement, which I do not mention, can not graciously mention in print. One of the chief members of the staff has finally got rid of a mistress who can only be defined as a bitch, and who wrote voluminously in the paper and interfered with all the decent authors, and generally vulgarized the paper. She has, thank heaven, gone to the continent, and been replaced here (I hope permanently). There was in the earlier order of things, a constant editorial mania to prove the first female wrote literature (which unfortunately she did not.).

The paper now prints an occasional readable article.

---

⟨Sorry to be so damn tiresome over old [Charles] Keary.

==

on ne peut pas porter partout le cadavre de son père. == Still one may provide one funeral without committing oneself perpetually to the trade of embalmer & undertaker.⟩

28–2–'18                    yours E.

Ezra Pound

*R. H. C.:* A. R. Orage (1873–1934), editor of *The New Age.*
*Mr. R. Root's:* Raoul Root, a pseudonym of EP. See Letter 59n.
*a mistress . . . :* EP is perhaps referring to "Beatrice Hastings" (Emily Alice Haigh), who had been Orage's mistress for six years between 1907 and 1914 and who had published "voluminously" in *The New Age* under various pseudonyms—she used thirteen of them ("Beatrice Tina," "D. Triformis," and "Roberta Field," for example). Orage's affair with Beatrice Hastings had, in fact, ended much earlier than EP's comment would seem to suggest, as Hastings had moved to Paris in April 1914. From Paris, however, she regularly contributed articles to *The New Age,* writing on Parisian life, the effects of the war on Paris, and a variety of other topics. By 1918, the number of her contributions to the journal had dwindled to three (all of which were published early in the year), and her very last article, a notice of Cocteau's *Le Boeuf sur le Toit,* appeared 11 March 1920.

The extent to which Beatrice Hastings exercised control over *The New Age* during a certain part of its existence is a matter of debate. In a pamphlet she published following Orage's death in 1934, Hastings claimed to have been a "sub-editor . . . who for all but a few months of those six years [1907 to 1914], had entire charge of, and responsibility for, the literary direction of the paper." She also maintained that it was she who had decided to print Katherine Mansfield's first stories and who had fought to get EP a place in the paper. John Carswell's estimate of her contribution and influence seems reasonable:

> Her claims to have had an important influence on what was printed in the *New Age* cannot be altogether dismissed. Her claims to her own voluminous contributions are valid and there is considerable evidence that Orage himself recognised her in her hey-day as a great deal more than a contributor. Orage's devoted secretary, Miss Marks, who had no cause to like Beatrice, is recorded as saying that "Orage considered Katherine Mansfield's writing as precious, B.H. did not agree with this, but could not alter O's verdict. This and many other affairs ended her association with the *New Age.*" But looking back she could see that as a journalist in her own right she had made no impact. The style of alias and ambuscade in which she delighted and no doubt encouraged had robbed her of a public personality. (Carswell 224–25)

**82. TLS–1.**   On stationery embossed: 5, Holland Place Chambers/Kensington. W. [? January–February 1918]

Dear M.C.A.

As to [H. L.] Mencken's letter. You know Hecht and Bodenheim. I am not very keen on "aphorisms" in anybody's manner. However I think it important to get locus standi with "professionals" as far as possible, i.e. as far as one can go without compromise. Both Mencken and Owen Hatteras write approvingly of the L.R. One cant quote their letters as they are private, but approval by "established magazine writers" can be mentioned; as a disciplinary measure to the refractory, AND to encourage investors.

Hatteras writes "You are doing excellent work with the L.R." and that he wont forget us, if several plans he has in mind "come to fruition."

I take more stock in him than in the men Mencken mentions. However, all good will should be turned to account. He is bringing out a 50 page book, probably out by the time this reaches you. You might see if it is any good, and "notice" it, if it is. His address is co/ the Smart Set for the rest of the year. He says he will be in N.Y. for the rest of the year.

I dont scorn the S.Set crowd, for I remember that Wright did his best with the magazine. It reduced the circulation from 70,000 to 20,000. Then they had to quit. No other American magazine of our time has made as gallant an effort. Not that Wright's ideas are mine, but he was going the limit, as he saw it, and he was accepting stuff on its literary value as he understood it, and damning the public's eyes.

These people might help with news-stand companies, general circulation, and possibly (though doubtfully) investors. (Investors subject, I should say to Mr Quinn's investigation of them, their characters, and their motives.) AND yours. I think the present condition of the L.R. warrants one calling it a property. Whether anyone would invest in 49% of the stock, is another matter, and whether that kind of arrangement is more fuss than it is worth, and whether pure hearted donation isn't rather to be recommended. I dare say we'd better let stock comparing alone.

yours<br>E.

*Hecht:* American novelist, short-story writer, and playwright Ben Hecht (1894–1964). Born in New York and raised in Wisconsin, Hecht became associated with the literary group that flourished in Chicago in the years just after the First World War. He gained some degree of notoriety when he carried on a well-publicized literary feud with his friend Maxwell Bodenheim (see below), with whom he also wrote a number of plays, the first of which was *The Master Poisoner* (1918).

*Bodenheim:* American poet, novelist, and playwright Maxwell Bodenheim (1892–1954). Bodenheim was born in Mississippi, but eventually moved to Chicago and then to New York, where he published his first volume of poetry *Minna and Myself* (1918), a collection of poems in which he employed many of the techniques of the Imagists.

*Both Mencken and Owen Hatteras:* "Owen Arthur James Hatteras" was the pseudonym used by H. L. Mencken and George Jean Nathan, co-editors of *The Smart Set*. See Letter 38n.

*a fifty page book: Pistols for Two* by Owen Hatteras (New York: Knopf, 1917). The book was forty-two pages long.

*Wright:* Willard Huntington Wright. See Letter 59n.

**83. TLS–2.** On stationery embossed: 5, Holland Place Chambers/ Kensington. W. [about the end of February 1918]

Dear Margaret:

Do get ALL my poems into "April" in one lump. (If its not too late, if so get 'em ALL into May.) They'll have more effect all together. (Also Poetry is in a softer mood. DONT delay.).

Harriet [Monroe] has only cut six lines from my Swinburne, but I'll send 'em to you soon, when I've a spare moment.

I have done about 5000 words on H. James. Orage promises a note of about 1500. I shall reprint my note on "The Middle Years", and another I must do for the "Future" by Sat. a.m.

They ("The Future") offer me a monthly page, and Gerfalk who has taken it on is adviser to a Copenhagen firm, (Ibsens publishers) and more or less the key to Scandanavia and north europe. So we are getting internationalized. (Keep this quiet, wait till I can chalk up a few results. G. had turned out his coeditor and se[n]t for me at once.)

The New Age is cutting down to 16, possibly to 12 pages, and I (via my aliases,) am the only regular to be kept on.

This is all very mild, but it keeps open the "lines"[.] I have written to Mrs Wharton, a letter worthy of Cincinnatus, or Cicero. God knows if it will have any result.

May Sinclair will do something on H.J. but cant be sure of having it ready on time, as she is in the middle of a novel. We can announce her, though, and if it isn't ready we can put in a foot-note M.S's ar[t]icle late, will appear in  .  .  .  .  . , ⟨Shall drag something from Eliot⟩

Macmillan are lending me the big collected edition to finish up my job on.

///

Have had a talk with Morales, and will do a Spanish number soon after the James. Not so much poetry as the French, as it is less important, also will have to print both Spanish and a translation, as one can not insist on everyone's knowing Spanish. Don't announce Spanish number. Certainly dont announce it YET. Must keep on "jolting 'em."

///

NOTE. Send 10 copies of L.R. I mean ten subscriptions. ⟨instead of one.⟩
to Flight Commander B.C. Windeler,
    co/ Windeler and Co. 20 Basinghall St. E.C.2.


I enclose the equivalent. Though I suppose you are "rolling" in it. W. is a
model young man. This is the first result of his leave from the Eastern
Mediterranean. He wants to put his back into it "after the war".

        Yours      E.        Ezra Pound


*ALL my poems into "April":* The poems were published in the May 1918 issue
    (19–31). Those included were "Homage a la langue d'or [misprint for
    "d'oc"]" (comprised of "Alba," "Compleynt of a Gentleman . . . ," "Avril,"
    "Descant on a Theme by Clercamon [Cerclamon]," "Vergier," and "Can-
    zon") and "Moeurs contemporaines" (comprised of "Mr. Styrax," "Clara,"
    "Soirée," "Sketch 48b.11," "Nodier raconte," "Stele," "I Vecchii," "Ritratto,"
    and "Quis multa gracilis?").
*my Swinburne:* See Letter 73n.
*Orage promises a note:* "Henry James and the Ghostly" by A. R. Orage was
    included in the Henry James number [*LR* (August 1918): 41–43)].
*I shall reprint my note . . . :* EP's "The Middle Years" in the Henry James
    number (39–41) was reprinted from *The Egoist* (January 1918). His "The
    Notes to 'The Ivory Tower' " (62–64) is recast from a review he wrote for
    *Future* (April 1918) entitled "Henry James as Expositor."
*"The Future":* Future, the official organ of the English Language Union, was
    published in London from November 1916 through September 1919. The
    magazine was founded by Charles Granville, who invited EP to contribute
    articles and reviews. The first of EP's pieces to appear was an article en-
    titled "The Rev. G. Crabbe, LL.B." published in the February 1917 issue
    (110–11). EP continued to contribute not only reviews and articles to *Future*,
    but also poetry. For example, in the February, March, and April issues of
    1918, he published the first three cantos (considerably reduced, however,
    from their first publication in *Poetry*).
*Copenhagen firm:* EP is probably referring to the publishing house of Gyldendal,
    Ibsen's publisher in Copenhagen.
*The New Age is cutting down . . . :* In *Lives and Letters,* John Carswell re-
    ports that "in 1918 newsprint rationing was imposed. In 1914 [*The New Age*]
    had offered thirty-two pages for sixpence. By 1917 it was offering twenty, and
    in 1918 a mere sixteen" (144).
*via my aliases:* EP was writing music criticism under the pseudonym William
    Atheling and art criticism under the pseudonym B. H. Dias for *The New Age.*
*May Sinclair will do something on H. J.:* Apparently May Sinclair did not com-
    plete this article, as it did not appear in the *LR.*
*Morales:* Spanish poet Tomás Morales (1885–1921). A native of Las Palmas,
    the Canary Islands, Morales had studied medicine in Cadiz and in Madrid,
    returning to his island to practice in 1911. Much as William Carlos Williams

had, he maintained the practice of medicine while he wrote poetry, the best of which lyrically evoked the sea which surrounded his home. His volumes of poetry include *Poemas de la Gloria, del Amor y del Mar* (1908) and the two volumes entitled *Las Rosas de Hércules* (the second volume published before the first in 1919; the first published posthumously in 1922).

**84. TLS–1.**   On stationery embossed: 5, Holland Place Chambers/ Kensington. W. [8 March 1918]

Dear M.

> Subscribers:
> Agatha Blunt. 16 Ely Place, Dublin, Ireland

Send Sept.    . I have sent Nov. to Jan. inclusive. (She has sent in 7/ technically too late, but I dare say we can afford to continue her for 6 months, starting with Feb., at any rate start her with Feb.)

> Thomas Cassels, 129 Coronation Rd. Bedminster
> > Bristol Eng.
> > (12/)

Sub. to begin May. 1917. I have applied all but Sept and Oct.

begin him therefore with Feb. and run to May (inclusive, as we cant send Oct.)

> Rev. A. Pannell, Bulmer ⟨Vicarage⟩, Sudbury, Suffolk, Eng.

start March and run to next Jan. inclusive.

> (I will supply him with Feb. from my lot.)
> > */// /*

Mrs Wharton's address recd.

> > E.
> > 8–3–18
> > Ezra Pound

**85. TLS–1.**   On stationery headed: THE LITTLE REVIEW/ London Office:—5, HOLLAND PLACE CHAMBERS, W.8. [27 March 1918]

> Dear Margaret:

> > March here, thirty copies.
> GOSH!! Solid dynamite, all except Symons stale orange. (Bad

habit, that I am responsible for. I began ⟨him⟩ it, damn my hall-
yards)

I suppose we are suppressed by now. If however we and the nation survive, Both of us on the one same sole and exiguous continent. The next thing to do IS DEFINITELY to see about that
big Fenollosa essay on the Chinese Written Character. It is extremely important. I sent it to Carus, of the Monist, it was
accepted last Feb. or some such time. They have long since
exceeded their time limit. We are now big enough (64 pp.) to
carry it. [John] Quinn is trying to get it back for me.

IF Carus wont give it up, I think it would be worth while to cable me, simply "Send Fenollosa" and I will have a new copy made from
the mss. (Which will be rather a job, but still . . . . . )

I have done about 5000 words of the Henry James number. I
have a long Laforgue affair which I will get into shape for July, and run
the Henry in Aug. or Sept. and then proceed to the [Remy] De Gourmont.
IF we survive.

That at any rate will give the ⟨thing⟩ some mass and weight for the year.

> yours
> Ezra

> Ezra Pound                    27/3/18

*Symons stale orange:* Arthur Symons' "Bertha," *LR* (March 1918): 51–53.
*big Fenollosa essay* . . . *:* See Letter 80n.
*Carus:* Paul Carus (1852–1919), a German-born philosopher, had emigrated
  to the U.S. in 1883 and had settled in Chicago, where he became the editor
  of a weekly (later a monthly) called *Open Court,* a magazine founded in
  1887 by a zinc manufacturer named Hegeler. Carus also edited *The Monist*
  and supervised the operations of the Open Court Publishing Company.
*a long Laforgue affair:* "Our Tetrarchal Précieuse (A Divagation from Jules
  Laforgue)" by "Thayer Exton" (a pseudonym of EP) was published in the
  July 1918 issue ([3]–12). EP later included this "Divagation" in his *Instigations.*

**86. TLS–2.** On stationery headed: THE LITTLE REVIEW/ London Office:—5, HOLLAND PLACE CHAMBERS, W.8. [10 April 1918]

Dear Margaret:

Subscribers:
Mrs. Fowler, 26 Gilbert St. W.1. (all back numbers save Sept. and Oct. supplied.) Please send Sept. and start her with April. continue till further notice, she will ultimately pay up her second year as she has the first.

Mrs. J.A. Selby-Bigge 5 Phene St. S.W. 3.

begin April. run to next March. I have sent her this March.

I enclose some translations from Rimbaud. H.R. has done all the prose poems. And ought to be encouraged to go on working. This lot will do for July. Jourdain has written to Carus again, so I hope you'll get the Fenollosa essay before long.

Max Michelson wanted to do a series of articles on contemporary poetry, for the Egoist. i.e. he proposed it to me for the Egoist. I think it might do better for us. He at least criticizes a poem as if it were a work of art. It's a beginning, and he doesn't exude and exuber like M.B. [Maxwell Bodenheim] address 3214 Crystal St. Chicago.

We must have some American contributions. ???? Mina Loy ?? (On re-reading I find parts of her better than Marianne Moore, though perhaps she sinks further and worser in others.)
Is the American male extinct?
I think we ought to have two poems each from M. Moore, Loy, Michelson. (perhaps a larger group of Michelson, sometime. ??????) It is your dept.

Mrs [Edith] Wharton is ill, also occupied with war work. That's that. Orage has promised an essay for the number. He practically never will write for any paper but his own [i.e., *The New Age*], so this is in the nature of a compliment.

Neither my fantasia from Laforgue, nor three playlets of my own, nor my last imaginary letter seem good enough to send you.

If you get the Me-Fenollosa it will nearly fill July, and I am trying to get the James ready by Aug.

I will try to get the DeGourmont for Oct. or Nov. though it will rather crowd me.

If there isnt 64 pages on hand, we had better print 48, (on thicker paper), or reproduce works of art. One 48 page number either just before the James, or between the James and the DeGourmont would pass. (perhaps).

I think Michelson can be trusted to do his essays carefully.

yours

Ezra

Ezra Pound

10/4/'18

*translations from Rimbaud:* The July 1918 issue of the *LR* (20–24) contained English translations, done by Helen Rootham, of six prose poems of Arthur Rimbaud (1854–1891). The works—translated as "Vagabonds," "Toilers," "Devotion," "Soir Historique," "Promontory," and "The Stage"—were selected from Rimbaud's *Les Illuminations,* most of which had been written while he was living in England in 1874.

*H.R. has done all the prose poems:* Helen Rootham's translations were first published, with an introductory essay by Edith Sitwell, in London by Faber and Faber in 1932 under the title *Prose Poems from the Illuminations of Arthur Rimbaud.* New Directions (Norfolk, Connecticut) published the translations under the same title in 1943.

*Jourdain:* The English literary agent P. E. B. Jourdain, working for Paul Carus of *The Monist* (see Letter 80n), had solicited from EP the essay "The Chinese Written Character as a Medium for Poetry," which EP had edited and annotated from the notes of Ernest Fenollosa. The essay was never published by Carus and EP was, understandably, exasperated with Carus's negligence in returning the manuscript. The manuscript was, however, eventually recovered, and the essay appeared in four installments in the *LR* (see bibliography).

*a series of articles on contemporary poetry:* The series did not appear in the *LR.*

*Mina Loy:* Born in London and trained as an artist in Munich and Paris, Mina Loy (1882–1966) had settled in New York, where she associated with writers whose work was being published in Alfred Kreymborg's magazine *Others.* Parts I and II of Loy's *Anglo-Mongrels and the Rose* was published in the *LR* (Spring 1923: 10–18 and Autumn-Winter 1923–24: 41–51). Previously, her poem "Lions' Jaws" and two prose selections, "John Rodker's Frog" and "Psycho-Democracy: A Movement to Focus Human Reason on the Conscious Direction of Evolution," had been published in the *LR*, the poem and the first essay in the September–December 1920 issue (39–43 and 56–57) and the second essay in the Autumn 1921 issue (14–19).

*Marianne Moore:* American poet (1887–1972). Moore was the editor of *The Dial* from 1925 through 1929. The only poem of hers to appear in the *LR* was "You Say You Said," which was published in the second "American Number" (December 1918: 21).

*a larger group of Michelson:* Only two poems of the Chicago poet Max Michelson were ever published in the *LR:* "A Woman Tramp" and "Dans l'eau," both in the June 1918 number (38).

*Orage has promised:* A. R. Orage's contribution to the "Henry James Number" was entitled "Henry James, and the Ghostly" (August 1918: 41–43).

*my fantasia from Laforgue:* i.e., EP's "Our Tetrarchal Précieuse (A Divagation from Jules Laforgue)," published in the July 1918 *LR* ([3]–12) and signed with the pseudonym "Thayer Exton."

**87. TLS–2.**   On stationery headed: THE LITTLE REVIEW/ London Office:—5, HOLLAND PLACE CHAMBERS, W.8. [14 April 1918]

Dear Margaret:

I have recollected my ashes and redone all the Laforgue thing [i.e., "Our Tetrarchal Précieuse (A Divagation from Jules Laforgue)"]. Cutting 35 pages of french to these 16 pages enclosed[.]

It has its points, and will at any rate serve to stir up the rural population.

At ⟨least⟩ it is not like the contributions to our current contemporaries.

Use it for July IF that swine [Paul] Carus doesn't forward the chinese essay [i.e., "The Chinese Written Character as a Medium for Poetry"] in time.

If he does forward it, save Our Tetrarchal Precieuse for Sept.

(counting Aug. the H. James.)

The squib labeled "The recurrence" is for the correspondence column. of the month in which the Tetrarchal stunt appears.

///

I think the verses signed "Crelos" are worth putting in. They are well written, i.e. in decent english, and the speculation whether the official ⟨food dept.⟩ is thinking of the blocks of margarine or only of official language is new. It is not a large glass, but it is not a borrowed one.

£ £

The Laforgue has two points: one, that it indicates a state of sophistication which the denizen of Oshkosh might be well reminded of.

(two) I think the rhythm is fairly decent. [*crossout:* At least I find I can't change a syllable or a sound value anywhere, (anywhere I have thought of) without upsetting everything in the vicinity.]

On the other hand it is too nearly verse for anything save so fantastic an affair as it is.

The best thing from the original is the reality of the people, maintained in the midst of the general larking.

A good deal of the fun ⟨of the original⟩ is in the parodying of Flaubert and the general tying knots of blue ribbon in the tail of "Salammbo" and "Herodias". I have cut a little of this as it certainly would miss fire with an audience unfamiliar with Flaubert.

⟨I can conceive nothing more than a literal ⟨i.e. word for word⟩ rendering of the original but I may have gone too far in the opposite direction however.⟩

yours

E

Ezra Pound

14/4/1918

*The squib labeled "The recurrence":* "The Recurrence" was included in the July 1918 issue (58):

"AINT no sech animal" said Silas on first beholding an elephant.
In our day the literary hecker [heckler?] thinks he has finally dismissed a thing when he has called it a "gargoyle".

*the verses signed "Crelos":* MCA did not print these verses, entitled "Whitehall" and signed "Crelos," until the June 1919 issue (31–33). The passage to which EP refers is as follows:

Men pass through the room
To spend hours of daylight
Discussing the price of margarine

And the equivalent weights of meat.
I look at each man's face,
I look at each man's eyes,
They fill me with a passion
Of unappeased curiosity.
Some day I shall take courage,
I shall get drunk and say to each man:
"What do you see behind those eyes?
Are you forever picturing
Slabs of yellow grease that weigh twenty-eight pounds?"

But I am afraid,
Afraid of knowing for certain
That they do not see blocks of margarine,
Or carved joints of butcher's meat,
Nothing but departmental English
Printed in black letters on buff paper.

*"Salammbo" and "Herodias"*: two works by Gustave Flaubert (1821–1880).
*Salammbô* (1862), a novel, was set in ancient Carthage; and "Hérodias," one
of Flaubert's *Trois Contes* (1877), was set in the Biblical past in Judea and
in Rome. In each, Flaubert was meticulous in rendering the historical background.

**88. TLS–1.**   On stationery embossed: 5, Holland Place Chambers/ Kensington. W. [23 April 1918]

⟨23/4/'18⟩

Dear Margaret:

Subscriber. Hugh Walpole, 2 Ryder St. St James, S.W. 1. (begins March.)
    have sent him march and will send him an April, (as I presume
        he is fussy.) so begin him with May, and continue to next
    Feb.
        DONT under any circumstances send him more copies. i.e. a
    March 1919 until he has renewed. It has taken him four months to
    get round to sending in his cash.

renewal.
    T. Cassels, 129 Coronation Rd. Bristol. England.
(he complains he hasnt yet rec'd a copy of Sept. 1917. I dare say there
    hasn't been time for it to reach him.)
His subs run from May to May.
          *///*
Following squib will do for correspondence.

"Are you Christians?" asked the West Ham magistrate of a coloured sea-
man charged with having assaulted another man. "No," he replied, "we
quiet men.".

J.D.T.

//////

I enclose next batch of Joyce [i.e., *Ulysses*].

Let me hear how things are, effect of "March" etc. when you have breathing space.

yours
Ezra

Ezra Pound

**89. TLS–2.**   On stationery embossed: 5, Holland Place Chambers/ Kensington. W. [30 April 1918]

Dear Margaret:

Here is an harangue to the plebiscite. I think it is so worded
as to give you some sort of leverage.

I have been pouring out journalism to pay the rent, I am smothered in the Henry James. (It ought to take two years, but it must be in
your hands in time for August.). . . But I get no poetries written. I simply cant run the triple ring circus forever.

If the L.R. were, is, can be (whatever mood of the verb you
like) founded (not to say anchored, run aground, stuck, sandburged and
sandbanked like "Poetry") with a yearly stipend of £ 400 to its ever glorious foreign protrusion. (Let me speak of the truly desirable . . . let me
not bow to plausible solutions . . .)

In any case we'll have had two years damn good fun, and it will
have been almightily worth doing. And the plebiscite has got its chance of
deciding whether it will pay for our piping. Not being able to import here
has been a nuisance, but there it is, and no likelihood of its altering very
soon.

"April" hasn't arrived yet, but I write the enclosed as if it had. I hope the
Fenollosa essay ["The Chinese Written Character as a Medium for Poetry"] has turned up [;] it will enrich our soil.

So far we have lived up to our boasts, we have gone to 64 pages, gone to 25 cents, gone to [Ford Madox] Hueffer [*Women & Men*] (what there is of him.) etc. It is quite certain we wont get anything till we say clearly that we want it. Ergo the enclosed.

⟨regards to "jh" [Jane Heap]⟩

yours

E.

Ezra Pound
30/4/1918

*harangue to the plebiscite:* EP's "harangue" was published in the July 1918 *LR* (54–56) under the title "Cooperation (A Note on the Volume Completed)." It is of interest not only for its summation of the accomplishments of the *LR* during EP's first year as Foreign Editor but also for the tone of weariness which is clear throughout:

I see no reason for diffidence regarding the fourth volume of the *Little Review,* and the first volume of the present effort.

We have published some of Mr. Yeats' best poems, poems as obviously destined for perpetuity as are those in his "Wind Among the Reeds"; we have begun publishing Hueffer and Joyce; if we have not published "Tarr" it is only because "Tarr" is already in process, and we have published whatever else of Wyndham Lewis's work has been ready. We have published the small bulk of Mr. Eliot's poetry that has been written during the current year. And we have brought out a French number which may serve as a paradigm for the rest of America's periodicals.

The response has been oligarchic. The plain man in his gum overshoes, with his touching belief in W. J. Bryan, Eddie Bok, etc., is not with us. There are apparently a few dozen people who want, with vigour, a magazine which can be read by men of some education and of some mental alertness; there are a few hundred more people who want this thing with less vigour; or who have at their disposal fewer "resources."

My net value to the concern appears to be about $2350; of which over $2000 does not "accrue" to the protagonist. It might be argued with some subtlety that I make the limited public an annual present of that sum, for the privilege of giving them what they do not want, and for, let us say, forcing upon them a certain amount of literature, and a certain amount of enlightened criticism.

This donation I have willingly made, and will as willingly repeat, *but* I can not be expected to keep it up for an indefinite period.

"Et les vers cerchent [cherchent?] le repos".

I have done my French number, I find it necessary to do most of the Henry James number myself; I will willingly do a Remy de Gourmont number, and even a Spanish number if the available material proves worth the trouble, but I can not indefinitely do the work that is performed on the *Mercure* by a whole staff of rubricists. (A condensation of this sort of hundred-eyed labour is no saving of energy for the condenser).

Creation is a very slow process. It is possible, by doing a certain amount of well-paid but unimportant work, for me to buy leisure sufficient for whatever creative processes are possible to me. It is not possible for me to add to that dual existence a third function. Leaving polysyllables, either the editing of the foreign section of the *Little Review* has got to pay my board and rent, etc., and leave me sufficient leisure for my own compositions, or I have got to spend my half time on something more lucrative.

It is bad economy for me to spend a morning typing up stray copies of the *Little Review* for posting, or in answering queries as to why last month's number hasn't arrived. This function could be carried on by a deputy, almost by an infant.

It is not that I desire to "get" such a lot of it ( £.s.d) as that I decline to have my own work (such as it is) smothered by executive functions. And unless said functions can relieve me of the necessity of writing ephemeral stuff for other papers I shall be compelled to "relinquish them."

Or, still more baldly, I can not write six sorts of journalism four days a week, edit the *Little Review* three days a week, and continue my career as an author.

There are plenty of voices ready with the quite obvious reply that: nobody wants me to continue my hideous career as either author, editor, or journalist. I can, in imagination, hear the poluploisbious twitter of rural requests for my silence and extinction. This rumble is however exaggerated, there are several score, perhaps even several hundred (certainly not a full thousand, but perhaps several hundred) people who would rather I wrote a few good poems than a great fatras of newspaper or periodical comment, and these few score or few hundred are (with my own feelings included) the only people for whom I care three fourths of a tinker's curse.

(Add to the verse, perhaps, a little prose, perhaps imaginative, which I might regard as literature, not merely disputation, didacticism, higher instruction, post-graduate learning, acting as battistrada for new artists and writers, etc.)

So that, roughly speaking, either the *Little Review* will have to provide me with the necessities of life and a reasonable amount of leisure, by May 1st. 1919, or I shall have to apply my energies elsewhere.

**90. TLS–2.** On stationery embossed: 5, Holland Place Chambers/ Kensington. W. [? May 1918]

Dear Margaret

I dare say I needn't have been in a panic. Copy seems to be coming in.

I shall probably have to have two James numbers. Aug. for me, and Oct. for the rest of the essays. ⟨with Sept. in between for variety.⟩

IF we survive. J.R. [John Rodker] is I think going to justify his existence. At any rate he is all "les jeunes" that there are. The rest of us verging into demi-aînés.

For you[r] comfort, I have just heard the L.R. described approvingly as "the only thing of its kind in Europe". (Je ne crois pas that that has ever been said of the Century or of Poetry . . . passons.)

I think I sent notice of H. Walpole. subscription
           2. Ryder St. S.W. 1.
RENEWALS. T. Cassels. (129 Coronation Rd. Bedminster.
                              Bristol Eng. [)]
           Miss E. A. Abbott. 73 Church St. W.8.
           A. E. Ayliffe 171 Kensington Hight St. W.8.
           Miss M. Thomson.
                  CHANGE address to/
           9 Great Pultney St. W.1.
Subscriptions to begin March.
           Miss Berry, 2 Sesame Court. Chelsea. S.W. 3.
           Chas. Ginner. at 16 Fitzroy St. W.1.
                  (am sending him a "March", so begin him April and run to next Feb.)

I think most everyone will renew, any how go on sending L.R. to all my subs. save the following, some of whom haven't paid up for last year, and some of whom I am out of touch with, and unlikely to GET the coming year's cash out of. It is their own fault if they dont send in renewals early enough to prevent delay.

STOP. Miss Booth. 37 Stanhope Terrace.
           R. Wilenski. 10 Grays Inn Sq.

           A. L. Coburn (not paid yet)
           Duchess of Marlborough.
           L. Beardmore.

Am worried by non-arrival of April. Hope nothing has happened to it.

⟨Should like J.R.s. note on "Books" in July. & the sketches as soon as you like. separate or together.⟩

                  yours E.
              Ezra Pound

*J.R.s note on "Books"* . . . : John Rodker's "Books" was published in the September 1918 issue (47–50) and the sketches entitled "Incidents in the Life of a Poet" in the June 1918 issue (31–35).

**91. TLS–4.**  On stationery headed: THE LITTLE REVIEW/ London Office:—5, HOLLAND PLACE CHAMBERS, W. 8. [? May 1918]

Dear Margaret:

I enclose another lost sheep. It has taken me months to recover it, all samee [*sic*] Fenollosa.

It is not wildly exciting, and it is not news, but it is a small scrap of Voltaire's Dictionaire Philosophique, which considering its date might serve to show how far far far etc., how long long long etc. it takes for a light to travel across the darkness of Anglo-American literature.

I know it is too long, BUT it simply wont cut, and p. 17. with the passage about Sarah is almost worth waiting for.

also p. 3. "It seems probable that god was not attempting to educate the jews in philosophy or cosmogeny".

etc. etc. The damn thing has bits, and they wont come out of the whole mass of it.

Fraser has of course done the whole job monumentally, BUT good god how slowly, in how many volumes, No reader of the Golden Bough is likely to relapse into bigotry, but it takes such a constitution to read it.

A reminder that "There once was a man called Voltaire" can do no harm. The measure in which he is unread, can I think be found by printing the fragment as "translated from an eighteenth century author" and seeing how many people place it.

At any rate you can keep it on hand, and use it in the L.R. if there is space. It will at least be more respectable than Amy [Lowell], or some of our "enlightened" contemporaries.

Dont put a name to it, just print it as "translated from".

Poetry has just come with a very asinine note on the Feb number.

Bad poetry being alike everywhere it is natural that Rimbaud should differ more from Longfellow and Vaughn Moody, and Hen Van Dyke, & that Byron from Musset (both romantic and careless writers of same degree of relative goodness and bandeness [*sic*], (should be about even[;] Byron rather more snap. a good satirist if a loose writer.)) but again the "canton of Arabia" and its affairs is of no great matter.

///

Of course if you or "jh" [Jane Heap] see your way to condensing this Voltaire, do for god's sake condense. I must get on with that bloody H. James stuff. Volt. neednt all go in one number. (needn't go in at all for that matter, but you can split it. perhaps to advantage if the pages come that way.). There are still plenty of readers to whom it will be quite fresh enough. and not among those who consider themselves illiterates.

On the whole (damn it all) I think we may as well print it. It will clear away a lot of snags for the DeGourmont number [i.e., February-March 1919]. (It should be got thru with before that number). I am looking forward to the Remy, where I shall have, I think, several larks.

The Dictionaire Philosophique, is a fairly good rock, it is not the start of the whole thing, but it has more finesse than Bayle, and is better written, though Bayle has the acid and vinegar it is often roughly sarcastic, where Volt. is mild and ironic. Bayle's dict. was burned publicly all over the place. Between 'em I suppose the[y] wiped off the slime of the counter reformation, so far as it is wiped off, which isn't saying very much.

Still one oughtn't to let the Y.M.C.A. historians conceal their existence so fully. One never hears either name in an American university. One is given Chas. Dickens.

It is all such a bloody waste of time, the Am. education, all so padded, and cushioned, and unhistoric (with all historic pretense.)

Its all very well to say Volt. has been dead for a long time, but look at this from a College catalogue that came a few weeks ago:

"The coll. while under no denominational control, is distinctly Christian and regards divine worship as a regular part of the life of its students. It avows its historic debt both to the Xtn. faith and to" etc. "devout recognition of God, revealed in His word, as elemental and indispensable. in the development of true manhood."

Great hogs . ! ! ! what a world we live in.

It is not the individual instance that matters, it is simply a symptom of the buncomb in all american (and english "ways of thinking") the desperate insistence on NOT recognizing any fact as fact, the absolute insistence on continuing to "avow" all sorts of spoof, mental, moral, religious, ethic, etc. etc. political, economic, etc.

The inquisition was last set up in 1814, but . . . but . . . but . . . American collegiate thought is back somewhere before that.

Landor's "Imaginary Conversations" are not "entrusted" to the American undergraduate student of literature.   .   (it would be quite safe, as many of them are dull, and the student would probably not persevere to the fine ones,). Indeed Landor has only been accessible to the general public quite recently, in the Dent. edition. Such is the force of gum-shoe opinion. The public has had Colvin's selections.

IF the college would give its "Bible study" in such a way as to include comment. (Dictionaire Philosophique etc. ah. . . ah. . . , but no.)
⟨—orang[e] peel or Longfellows tomb.⟩

> yours ever E.P.
> Ezra Pound

*another lost sheep:* This article appeared under the title "Genesis, or, The First Book of the Bible: ('Subject to Authority')" in the November 1918 issue (50–64). It was left unsigned and carried the footnote, "translated from an eighteenth-century author."

*Voltaire's Dictionaire Philosophique:* Voltaire's *Dictionnaire philosophique portatif* (1764). See Letter 67n.

*Fraser:* EP's reference is to Sir James Frazer's twelve-volume *The Golden Bough* (1890–1915).

*Poetry has just come . . . . :* The note on the *LR*'s February 1918 French number appeared in the April 1918 issue of *Poetry* (54–55) under the title "Our Contemporaries: A Modern French Anthology" and was signed by S.W. It runs, in part, as follows:

> The Little Review, with Ezra Pound as its spokesman, has come to the conclusion that America can no longer conduct its intellectual affairs on a monolingual basis. It proposes to print criticism of current French literature as well as English, and for a starter devotes its February number to an anthology of modern—that is, post-Gautier—French poetry.
> It isn't often that one can get such an anthology at the price of a magazine, nor for that matter at any price, since the anthology fever has not hit the French publishers quite as it has the American. And Mr. Pound's selection is a little more than an anthology. In compiling it, he found that the poets and heirs who would have to be consulted for permission to reprint, were so scattered by the war that he would save time by embedding the anthology in an article. The result is a running commentary, now facetious, now important, always contra-

dictory; as if to give the reader a number of opinions to choose from, but not allowing him to leave any poem without one.

The poems themselves make a substantial enough showing to tempt the reader into generalizations on the difference between modern poets here and in France. . . . In general it seems as if poetry in French and English, in spite of the gradual rapprochement of the three nations since Napoleon, were never farther apart than now. With Byron and Alfred de Musset they were still within shouting distance, and so too, though by direct importation, with Swinburne and Gautier. But here are poems which would never tempt the translator. However, as Mr. Pound says, he has intentionally chosen the things that would sound freshest to us, omitting the Parnassians for instance, of whom he says we have plenty ourselves, leaving Gautier, Baudelaire, Mallarmé, Verlaine, Samain, Heredia, to be read in volumes. He includes Laforgue, Corbière, Rimbaud, de Gourmont, de Régnier, Verhaeren, Tailhade, Jammes, Moréas, Spire, Vildrac, Romains—a characteristically random list. For though he has read other poets and would like very much their friendship the next time he goes to Paris, he insists that there are bad poets in French as well as in English.

*Vaughn Moody:* American playwright and poet William Vaughn Moody (1869–1910). Moody's works were collected and published in two volumes as *Poems and Plays* in 1912. Collections of his letters have also been published (1913 and 1935).

*Hen Van Dyke:* American writer Henry Van Dyke (1852–1933). Van Dyke's writing—popular but of little critical interest—included essays on outdoor life and moral issues, short stories and romances, travel sketches, and poetry.

*Musset:* French Romantic poet, novelist, and dramatist Alfred de Musset (1810–1857). Musset's early poetry, particularly *Contes d'Espagne et d'Italie* (1830) and *Rolla* (1833), reveals the influence of Byron.

*Bayle:* EP's reference is, most likely, to the *Dictionnaire historique et critique* of French lexicographer, philosopher, and critic Pierre Bayle (1647–1706). The *Dictionnaire* was first published in 1697, enlarged in 1702, and supplemented in 1704–06 by *Réponses aux questions d'un provincial*. The articles deal with biographical, philosophical, and theological subjects, expressing for the most part orthodox viewpoints. In the footnotes to the articles, however, Bayle raises a number of questions and expresses criticisms which challenge orthodoxy. Later, his *Dictionnaire* provided a rich source for the French *philosophes*.

*Landor's "Imaginary Conversations":* the principal prose work, published 1824–27, of English writer and poet Walter Savage Landor (1775–1864). Dent's edition of *Imaginary Conversations* ("with Bibliographical and Explanatory Notes by Charles G. Crump") was published in 1891.

*Colvin's selections:* Sir Sidney Colvin (1845–1927), Slade Professor of Fine Arts at Cambridge (1873–85) and keeper of prints and drawings at the British Museum (1884–1912), had published in 1881 a biography of Walter Savage Landor as part of the English Men of Letters series.

**92. TLS–3.**   On stationery embossed: 5, Holland Place Chambers/ Kensington. W. [23 May 1918]

Dear Margaret:

I have this a.m. delivered five articles to my employer (fruit of a weeks effort), also during past seven days have delivered type-scribble, amounting to 39½ pages typescript, to typist, for H.J. number; also attended various concerts in my Rhad[a]manthic capacity.

What the hell is expected of me as a correspondent.

"April" here thank God, this a.m. also years L.R. gone to binders to be monumentalized.

⟨quote in R. Cr. if you like⟩

Hecht is an asset. Hard reading and a bit heavy, but the man who can write "Philosophy etc. . . .profound etc elimination of adjectives from life". etc. Night, gt. adj. of dark. and other sentences in his stuff; has the root of the matter in him. He is trying to come to grips. Also, when he gets out of his head the idea that he must suit S. Set public. and recalls the fact that Maupassant does not exaggerate, he CAN write ⟨contes⟩ i.e. can, (future tense) ⟨will be able to.⟩

He is the sound stuff, that with right pages open to him can develop. He ought to grow into us permanently.

(I haven't been inclined to say this of most other chance U.S. contribs.)

Three letters from France in last two days. Mockel, biographer of Verhaeren, reminded of his youth, "when symbolist movement was starting" "no comp. with pub. taste. etc."

Stanton saying he will give us or me (his sentence a little ambiguous) as much space as is permitted individual topic in his Mercure rubric.

Romains "admirable verities" owe me "expression saissante" (re French number.) etc.

Glad to be in communication. (Don't know whether he means personally with me, or officially with L.R.)

Have written him to take on the French end of ⟨us⟩ as soon as he likes. Hope for best.

Have French reply to the blubbering drivveling asininity of Poetry's note

⟨under weigh⟩ on Feb. number. 7 mis-statements of fact on less than 2 pages.

Easier to retain J.Q's [John Quinn's] subsidy and make his crowd "annual" than to get equal sum elsewhere ?????

ANYHOW we've got to do so damn much in the next 12 months that we CANT BE LET STOP in 1919.

If Romains does bring in all the best french stuff it ought to help.

Yeats writes that he has another bunch of lyrics about ready for us.

Am in state of complete physical exhaustion, and will probably collapse into chronic and total aphasia.

Didn't expect to get to end of this letter, or topics included.

/// /

Renewal.      S. Sitwell.    new address
                   5 Swan Walk. Chelsea. S.W. 3.

/// 

Don't know French importation regulations. Those of French who read english might see what we are at quicker than AM. or Eng. ⟨readers⟩

At any rate last three letters seem to be aware of it, more so than some local luminaries.

Dont want to quote their letters. Hope for something more lengthy, at any rate dont want to contravene any punctillio about printing private communications; dont quite know what the bloomin' politesse requires.

H.J. number gathering. Windeler a find.

⟨M.S. [May Sinclair] as 1st. it['s] an excellent camoufl[a]ge.⟩

ever

E

Ezra Pound 23/5/18

*to my employer:* A. R. Orage, editor of *The New Age.*
*Rhad[a]manthic capacity:* Under the pseudonym "William Atheling," EP wrote music reviews for *The New Age.*

*Hecht is an asset . . . . :* EP's comments on Ben Hecht's "Fragments," which
had appeared in the April 1918 *LR* (45–49), were published in the "Reader
Critic" of June 1918 (55).
*Mockel, biographer of Verhaeren:* Belgian Symbolist poet and critic, Albert
Mockel (1866–1945). His biography of fellow Belgian Symbolist poet Émile
Verhaeren (1855–1916) was published by La Renaissance du Livre.
*Stanton:* American journalist and writer Theodore Stanton (1851–1925) was, for
a time, a correspondent for the *Tribune* in Berlin. Later, he became the editor
of the Department of American Literature for the *Mercure de France.*
*asininity of Poetry's note:* See Letter 91n. EP's "French reply," entitled "Note
upon Fashions in Criticism" and signed J. H. Le Monier, appeared in the
October 1918 issue of the *LR* (24–25). Although this article has not been
noted in Donald Gallup's bibliography of Pound, based on the comment in
this letter, it no doubt should be attributed to him. The article as printed
below is as it appeared in the *LR;* the mistakes in spelling, omissions of accent
marks, etc., are EP's:

> Après une visite de plusieurs mois en Amérique où j'avais accepté un poste
> de professeur dans une des universites du Centre-Ouest, et après avoir assisté à
> nombre de conférences dans les réunions des differents "Discussion Circles"; je
> remarquai chez l'Americain cultivé un curieux enthousiasme superficiel à recueillir
> des informations sur la chose du moment, en même temps qu'une également
> curieuse et fondamentale répugnance à comprehende aucune nouveauté ayant
> trait à autre chose.
> Je suis donc peut-être mieux à même de juger que la plupart des autres
> Francais des difficultés qui ont du assillir la "Little Review" en présentant à son
> public le numéro français. L'accueil qui fut fait à ce numéro par d'autres revues,
> soit-disant modernes, fut, il me semble, inutilement grossier. "Poetry", magazine
> qui s'intitule fièrement "La plus vivante expression de cet art" (poèsie), me
> parait dans un article "Our Contemporaries" superlativement inexacte.
> "The anthology fever has not hit the French publishers quite as it has the
> American." "La fieire des anthologies n'a frappé les éditeurs français tout à fait
> aussi rudement que les Americans.
> Je ne sais trop s'ils en sont frappés *tout-a-fait* aussi rudement que les Ameri-
> cains, mais à coup sur, il y a un nombre respectable d'anthologies en France.
> 2. Monsieur S. W. [the author of the article in *Poetry*] dit que le commen-
> taire de Monsieur P. est toujours contradictoire. Ce commentaire contredit peut-
> être en effet le goût courant de l'Université de l'Illinois, ou de Chitauqua, et très
> certainement le gout de Monsieur S. W., mais il ne se contredit lui-même en
> aucune maniere; il est, en fait, parfaitement cohérent.
> 3. Monsieur S. W. nous announce que Byron et Alfred de Musset furent à
> portée de boix, à "Shouting distance" l'un de l'autre. "Shouting distance" est
> plaisant! Leur période fut sans doute plus impétueuse qu la nôtre; ils furent
> tous deux de vagues romanistes se souciant peu de la technique de leurs vers.
> Il n'y a pourtant dans Musset rien qui ressemble à Don Juan.
> 4. Swinburne a eu beau admirer Gautier: seul un lecteur sans discernement
> parlera de proche parenté entre l'oeuvre de ces deux hommes.
> 5. Monsieur S.W. dit que Monsieur P. choisit des poêmes qui n'auraient jamais
> tenté le traducteur. Traducteur dans ce cas, signifie évidemment Monsieur S. W.
> 6. Il déclare que le choix des poètes fait par Monsieur P. est une liste dressée
> au hazard. La fausseté de ce jugement peut être dèmontrée par quiconque voudra

bien se donner la peine d'observer que Monsieur P. fournit toujours des raisons spécifiques pour traiter chacun des poètes qu'il inclut.

7. Voici d'ailleurs qui peut servir comme échantillon de l'inexactitude secondaire caractéristique des mauvais journalistes qui pullulent également en France, en Angelterre et en Amérique. Il cite Monsieur P. et lui fait dire: Nous *avons* (We *have*) beaucoup de parnassiens". Si Monsieur P. avait dit cela, il aurait, ce me semble, fait erreur, si je puis m'en rappoter à la poèsie contemporaine d'Amérique que j'ai lue. Mais voici textuellement ce que Monsieur P. a dit: "L'Amérique *a eu* (*Has had*) suffisemment de parnassiens, peut être de second ordre, mais pourtant suffisemment."

Monsieur S. W. conclut en faisant remarquer que Monsieur P. insiste sur un point, à savoir: qu'il y a des mauvais poètes en Francais aussi bien qu'en Anglais. Monsieur P. constate légèrement. Faut-il insister?

*Yeats writes that he has another bunch of lyrics:* The *LR* published Yeats's "In Memory of Robert Gregory" in its September 1918 issue ([1]–5) and in the October 1918 issue ([1]–5) seven short lyrics: "To a Young Girl," "A Song," "Solomon to Sheba," "The Living Beauty," "Under the Round Tower," "Tom O'Roughley," and "A Prayer on Going into My House."

**93. TLS–3.**   On stationery embossed: 5, Holland Place Chambers/ Kensington. W. ⟨8 London Eng.⟩ [24 May 1918]

Dear Margaret:

Here is most of the Aug. [Henry James] number, perhaps all 64 pages will hold.

The essential part, nucleus is [Ethel Coburn] Mayne, me, and [A. R.] Orage, get that in anyhow.

Omit Joyce [i.e., *Ulysses*] for that month. The two other mss. on James should follow.

Please keep the order of mss. I have indicated. Print "In Explanation" and "Brief Note" in small type if necessary or convenient, or print "In Exp" in small if that seems advisable.

⟨Eliot's In Memory & my "Middle Years" from Egoist enclosed.⟩

Four T.S.E. poems in hand, one or two questions I want to ask T. before sending them. Also attack on some sorts of Am. poetry by old Jepson. Harriet [Monroe] ordered it, but didn't find it flattering enough. Have had him cut it down a bit. Will go well with Eliot's poems. Hope for some [Wyndham] Lewis, and some [B. C.] Windeler for Sept.

My Laforgue thing would fit Sept. IF it hasn't gone in before, in-going dependent on arrival or non-arrival of the Fenollosa. etc. leave it to you.

yours

E.

24/5/18                    Ezra Pound

Enclosures
==
1 Contents
2. H.J. by Mayne
5 articles including "Shake Down"
A.R. Orage by E.P.
Eliot on HJ.
[John] Rodker

Ethel Mayne happens to do us about as well as Mrs Wharton would have. It was only after seven weeks that I got her mobilized, and then by a chance remark (not the one she quotes about bulls, that was someone else.)

Roughly, I should say: "Get as much of stuff now on hand, out of the way by July number." Though I dare say you will have sent that number to press by the time you get this.

With James DONE I feel less anxiety about filling late numbers. Also have got my other "Chores" well in hand.

yours

E

Ezra Pound

*two other mss. on James:* Only EP's "The Notes for 'The Ivory Tower' " was published in the September number (50–53). The other Henry James articles were published in the August issue. For a listing of these see Letter 66n.

*Four T.S.E. poems:* i.e., T. S. Eliot's "Sweeney among the Nightingales," "Whispers of Immortality," "Dans le restaurant," and "Mr. Eliot's Sunday Morning Service"—all of which were published in the September 1918 issue (10–14).

*attack on some sorts of Am. poetry by old Jepson . . . :* The British critic and novelist Edgar Jepson had published in the May 1918 issue of the *English Review* an article on the poetry of the "Western School," that is, on the poets of America's Midwest. His comments were focused on the poems of Vachel Lindsay, Edgar Lee Masters, and Robert Frost that had been published by

*Poetry,* paying particular attention to those that had been awarded *Poetry*'s annual prize. Jepson explained the circumstances of his article in this way:

> I wrote to [Harriet Monroe] at the end of 1917 to ask her if she would like an appreciation of recent United States poetry. She wrote that she would, sent me twenty-eight numbers of her magazine, ranging over three years, and in those numbers marked the typically United States poems. . . . I read those marked poems and taking three of them to which *Poetry* had awarded a prize in each of those three years, as typical of the typical, I dealt chiefly with them. I said, as politely as my outraged aesthetic sensibilities would allow, that they were punk; I quoted enough of them to demonstrate that they were punk; and punk they are. [*LR* (February–March 1919): 62]

In his article Jepson was, however, admiring of the work of T. S. Eliot and quoted passages from a number of Eliot's poems and the whole of his "La Figlia che Piange" "to demonstrate that [Eliot] is the greatest master of emotion, intensity, and the beautiful music of words the United States has produced since Poe" (63).

EP's decision to publish in the September *LR* a condensation of Jepson's article is, in one sense, a curious one: he was still nominally functioning as *Poetry*'s editor, and he must have known how the article would touch a sensitive nerve in Harriet Monroe. In another sense, however, the decision is also characteristic of EP and consistent with his *modus operandi,* reflecting as it does his ongoing warfare against what he perceived to be American parochialism and intolerance—even suppression—of views which go against the grain.

*My Laforgue thing:* i.e., "Our Tetrarchal Précieuse (A Divagation from Jules Laforgue)."

*the Fenollosa:* See Letter 80n and Letter 84.


**94. TLS–1.** On stationery embossed: 5, Holland Place Chambers/ Kensington. W. [30 May 1918]

Dear Margaret:

Here is Miss Bosanquet's article. A good piece of work, and an integral part of the Aug. number. Please change title in index to fit that which she has put at the head of it. ⟨All the revisions were dictated to her by H.J. [Henry James]⟩

Make Aug.: Mayne, Me, Orage, and this. and the other articles IF there is room, keeping order as supplied in index.

Enclose also a snarl from [Edgar] Jepson for Sept. with note in explanation. Haven't an exalted opinion of it, but there are plenty of reasons for printing it, as you will see. Pages 6 and 7. do say something, something that needs saying. ⟨(T.S.E's poems to be in same number.)⟩

Hope to send off Eliot's second "H. James" and his new verses tomorrow.

Joyce again down with eye trouble. so its just as well we dont want him in Aug.

////

Renewal.

Rev. Cavendish Moxon. new address

3 St. Georges Sq. S.W. 1.

Subscription.

Mrs. S. Hart-Davis

Norton Priory, Near Chichester

Sussex.

begin June. I have sent Apr.

and will send May.

yours

Ezra Pound

30/5/1918

*Miss Bosanquet's article:* For a listing of contributions to the Henry James number, see Letter 66n.

*snarl from Jepson:* See Letter 93n.

**94a. TLS–1.** On stationery embossed: 5, Holland Place Chambers/ Kensington. W. [approximate date, May 1918]

Dear Margaret:

This preface to "Germinie" ought to be at the beginning of every school text book on literature.

Please print it at once. I suppose that means "July"[.] It is the answer to all that may be said against Joyce, as well as being the kindergarten course in literature for our "numerous and devoted" . . . . (readers ?)

yours

Ezra

Ezra Pound.

*preface to "Germinie"*: i.e., the preface to *Germinie Lacerteux,* a novel by Edmond and Jules de Goncourt published in 1864. The preface was printed in its entirety in the July 1918 issue of the *LR* (56–57), along with EP's introductory remarks: "I am tired of rewriting the arguments for the realist novel; besides there is nothing to add. The Brothers de Goncourt said the thing once and for all. . . . The programme in the preface . . . states the case and whole case for realism; one can not improve the statement."

**95. TLS–?**    On stationery headed: THE LITTLE REVIEW/ London Office:—5, HOLLAND PLACE CHAMBERS, W.8. [*Incomplete item*] [4 June 1918]

⟨4 June 1918⟩

    Dear Margaret:

>         You may announce that: JULES ROMAINS, indicated in our February number as the most important of the younger French writers, is about to join the staff of The Little Review.

He writes that I seem to have understood his french etc.

        "Je vous remercie de m'ouvrir si largement votre revue. Je ne demande mieux que d'etre votre "French Editor", comme vous me le proposez. Mais j'aimerais que vous me disiez en quoi au juste consisterait cette fonction, et de quoi j'aurais à m'occuper."

    Don't print that. I have told him it would consist in getting £2 a month, in sending in from 5 to 10 pages of the best stuff he can find. In sending us an opening manifesto saying why he has joined us; and that he can hope for better things in proportion as the scheme works.

    I also told him to keep a third of whatever he can manage to rake in on subscriptions. I think that is fair and probably to our ultimate advantage

    DO print on the title page.

> English subscription 12/ per year
> Abonnement fr. 15. par annee

I have also asked him for a permanent address for a French office. When we get that we'll put him down as

    [*page(s) missing*]

I feel ten years younger now that the weight of the James is off my back. Can only hope it will settle on, and help to sink, some of the old heavy U.S. magazines.

The French anthology, H.J. [Henry James], the Fenollosa, when recovered, and the Remy [de Gourmont] number which I shall begin after a month's recreation, should give the year four CHUNKS, four hunks of momentum, to maintain the active motion of Joyce, Lewis, and now thank god some more T.S.E. [T. S. Eliot]

I think I wrote that Yeats also says he has another bundle of lyrics. Also news from France.

My hopes "respire". Even the tone of my letters to you may take on a little of its earlier vivacity.

If you want to know what I've been through go look at the collected edition of H.J. in any book-shop, and remember that it dont contain by any means all of him.

Subscriber, to begin with June, and run to Dec.
> Mrs Hart Davis, Norton Priory, near Chichester, Sussex. (asked for
> > a year and sent 7/6)

~~Stop S. Bowen's subscription till she pays up.~~

stop Etchells.
> R. Wilemski [Wilenski], E.W. Sutton. A.L. Coburn (I think I said before)
> E. Marsh, when due. Dont know when he began.

yours

Ezra Pound

*an opening manifesto:* Although Jules Romains was listed as the French editor of the *LR* from the September 1918 issue onwards, he contributed nothing to its pages.

*some more T.S.E.:* See Letter 93n.

*Yeats also says he has another bundle of lyrics:* See Letter 92n.

*the collected edition of H.J.:* The Macmillan edition of *The Novels of Henry James,* published in 1908, included twenty-four volumes.

**96. ALS–2.**   On stationery headed: THE LITTLE REVIEW/ London Office:—5, HOLLAND PLACE CHAMBERS, W.8. [6 June 1918]

>       For the
>       love of Christ
>       get a proof

reader==

>       [B. Cyril] Windeler was off his head last month—
>       Youve bitched three of my poems.
>       We'll lose Romains first smack if
>       SOMETHING
>       can't be done.

>                      E.

Ezra Pound

*Windeler was off his head:* regarding the misprints in his story "Elimus" in the
    April 1918 number (12–26).
*Youve bitched three of my poems:* See Letter 97.

**97. TLS–3.**   On stationery embossed: 5, Holland Place Chambers/ Kensington. W. [6 June 1918]

Dear Margaret:

       Briefer holograph ⟨sent⟩ this a.m. contains what I <u>really</u>
think.

Idea of American number excellent. Time we had something wholly exotic.

What we never will get is an English number. There aint any. [Wyndham]
Lewis is a collection of races. And [Ford Madox] Hueffer's papa was a
Hun. [B. Cyril] Windeler looks more english than anything that has ever
been known. perhaps he should be counted. Celts abound. No, we will
never have an English number.

And Now. Chere Amie:

       For Gawd's sake be reasonable for FIVE minutes. By
the perfectly simple device of paying five dollars per issue to some utterly

stupid, but efficient and professional proof-reader, these horrors can be averted, without injury to your inner nature.

There is no reason what [that] anyone's intelligence should be brought to bear on the matter. or why the lofty soul should be damblastedlybothered with proofs.

Do for God's sake get someone to look through the Henry James proofs.

⟨In the⟩ May number:                                              ⟨6–6–1918⟩
Page 21, second strophe should end:
            With frost and hail at night
            Suffers despite
            'Till the sun come, and the green leaf on the bough.

Page 29.      STELE should read:
            After years of continence
                  he hurled himself into a sea of six women;
            Now quenched as the brand of Meleagar
                  he lies by the poluphloisbious sea-coast
            παρὰ θῖνα πολυφλοισβοίο θαλάσσης
            Siste Viator
If printer has no greek type, print the greek line in caps sic:
PARA THINA POLUPHLOISBOIO THALASSES

Page 30. end of the first paragraph:
            And that was an anagram for Vittorio
            Emanuele Re D' Italia

Two lines below the line
            "And that other, balancing on the edge of a gondola"
should be printed only once.

⟨Damn it all
      if one dont                                    Langue D'OC
         quote Homer,                             not Langue D'Or
            where does                           but that dont matter.
            the fun disappear
                  to.⟩

*American number:* Two "American Numbers" of the *LR* were published: June 1918 and December 1918.

*Hueffer's papa was a Hun:* Ford Madox Hueffer (Ford) was the son of Francis Hueffer (Franz Carl Christoph Johannes Hüffer), a native of Münster who had emigrated to England in 1869, four years before Ford Madox Ford was born.

*second strophe should end:* In the *LR* the last line reads, " 'Till I have my hand 'neath her cloak."

*STELE should read:* The *LR* prints these lines:

> After years of continence
> > he hurled himself into a sea of six women,
> Now quenched as the brand of Meleagar
> > sea-coast
> SISTE VIATOR

*end of the first paragraph:* This section reads as follows in the *LR:*

> And he said he used to cheer Verdi
> In Rome, after the opera,
> And the guards couldn't stop them
> And that was an anagram for Vittorio
>
> And that other, balancing on the edge of a gondola . . . . .
> Emanuele *Re D' I*talia,
>
> And the guards couldn't stop them.

*Langue D'OC not Langue D'Or:* The *LR* had the title "Homage a la langue d'or." *Langue d'oc,* the Provençal language, was spoken in the south of France.

**98. TLS–1.**   On stationery embossed: 5, Holland Place Chambers/ Kensington. W. [10 June 1918]

⟨10–6–
1918⟩

Dear Margaret:

Here are Eliot's cameos. for Sept.

Clutton Brock has gone off the free list and now pays.
Note renewal. Mrs Shakespear. 12 Brunswick Gdns. ⟨W.8.⟩

The Brock matter amuses me. He is a large filler of the Times Lit. Sup. He, [Lytton] Strachey, Hugh Walpole, and Ethel Mayne, are all payers, and a decided collection of points giving way before the advance of light. We will ultimately have Henley's "eighty". And the fact of our second device "read by [those] who write" is becoming demonstrable.

2.

No, no, IT IS N̲ O̲ good this printing-sloppiness. What is the use of having stuff that has m̲o̲re care per square inch than the current novelists use per square mile, IF the bloody printer is to reduce it to guff.

A misprint that makes sense is the worst. A mis-spelling or a word spelled "wrod" dont matter, but to make hash of whole paragraphs is TROPPO ! ! ! !

3.

Yeats again writes that there is a lot of stuff ready, and about to be sent in.

⟨T.S.E. & I have both enjoyed the enclosed. for R. Crit ["Reader Critic"]⟩

yours E.

Ezra Pound

*Eliot's cameos:* See Letter 93n.
*Clutton Brock:* English journalist, critic, and essayist Arthur Clutton-Brock (1868–1924).
*Henley's "eighty":* See Letter 34n.
*our second device:* The *LR* advertised itself as "The magazine read by those who write the others."
*the enclosed. for the R. Crit:* The following letter appeared under the title "From the Clergy" in the July 1918 "Reader Critic" (60–61):

> For practical me to assume the role of critic of the work of T. S. Eliot after reading the hearty endorsement, is presumpt[u]ous indeed. But since you have asked me to report the impression made upon me as I read,—just a word. In reading the review I was impressed with the power of the reviewer rather than of the reviewed.
> The chair car being filled on my journey home, I was given temporary place in the drawing room, alone. There I read aloud and thus reading caught the cadence of the verse without the stilted monotony of the more regular verse. But that was many, many times rudely jarred by the language of the commonplace—yes, even the crude—and the metaphors impossible.
> I presume the effort is to present the real—but there always is to me a realism into which poetry should not enter—the poet has always given me the soul of things and used externals but to suggest the finer things which lie within. Of course Mr. Eliot by his abrupt boldness does give a true presentation but I would rather that he who handles prose found that his mission rather than the poet with his sensibilities keyed to the spiritual values.
> This is an age of revolt, I know—in government, socialism and anarchy—in art, the cubist—in society, the libertine—the extreme of the pendulum; but when applied to poetry it seems like the mailed fist of kultur rather than the tapering fingers of culture.

Who would think that I should have attempted an expression of thought which I seem so unable to suggest. I know Mrs. T. will say that one who has not yet traced the first faint glimmerings of the cubist's art cannot comprehend the work that you have presented to me, but when you have read the book which I am returning by mail under separate cover, it would be of keen interest to me to know how you are impressed.

**99. TLS–1.** On stationery embossed: 5, Holland Place Chambers/ Kensington. W. [18 June 1918]

Dear Margaret:

Thomas [Eliot] is leisurely but he does get home on the jaw. I hope this article is in time for the James number, but if it isn't, please announce it for Sept. and it can go in with T.S.E.'s poems.

Another note from Yeats to say his poems are coming.

Subscriber (⟨notice⟩ sent you I think)
    Capt. R.M. Muir, R.A.M.C. co J. Nathan and Co.
                88 Gracechurch St. E.C. 3.

Renewals.
        E.R. Brown. (change address to)
            2 Fitzroy St. W. 1.
Bertra A. Jones (same address)
            Brookside, Bournemouth
                *////*
DO let me know if the Chinese mss. has arrived.

                Yours E.
⟨18/6/1916 [1918].⟩
            Ezra Pound

*I hope this article:* i.e., "The Hawthorne Aspect," published in the August 1918 issue.
*the Chinese mss.:* See Letters 80n, 85, and 85n.

**100. TLS–2.**   On stationery embossed: 5, Holland Place Chambers/ Kensington. W. [19 June 1918]

⟨19–6–1918⟩

Dear Margaret:

Renewals:

> H.T. Tucker Esq. 27 Royal Crescent. W. 11.
> > (that's a new address.)
>
> Mrs. H. T. Tucker.
> > 27 Royal Crescent ⟨W. 11⟩
>
> Mrs. W.B. Yeats. no change of address
> L/Cpl H. Hicnhco [Hinco, see Letter 64] 63142 R.A.M.C.
> > attached 43 d. Siege Battery RG.A.
> > Salonika Force
> > In the Field
> > > Salonika, ⟨very enthusiastic⟩

New Subs.

> Senior Juanito Sempu
> > Zuricherstrasse 160
> > > Houss, Zurich
> > > > Switzerland.
>
> ⟨Walter H. Walsh. 9 Catherine St., Waterford
> > Ireland⟩

also 1/2 sub. beginning feb. (Mrs Hutchinson.) wont bother you with that, will send it from here.

/////

I notified you, I think,
renewals. Bertra A. Jones, no change of addr.
> E.R. Brown, now, 2 Fitzroy St. W. 1.


Thanks for writing to Lady Tredegar. ⟨good wishes from her for L.R.⟩

///

We are out £5 on those subs. for Windeler. I misunderstood him and he me. I said we couldn't import L.R. for sale he thought it would help if ten copies could be sent to him. He piously brings them to me on arrival.

As he is giving me his stuff free, and as I may get a little out of him for French contributors, AND as he thought he was helping when he asked to have the copies sent him, I cant insist on the view that he did subscribe for ten copies.

Fine lot of Yeats poems on hand. You can announce seven poems by W.B.Y. for Oct. . I must take 'em to typist and have duplicate[s] made for him before sending them to you.

There are two longer poems but I don't know whether they are for us. Will get one of them anyhow.

He is leaning more in our direction. Has at last found something in [Wyndham] Lewis.

??? Always fertile (I) in suggesting labours for others. What about ads. ??? There are those who would be more convinced of the practicality of the L.R. IF we carried more ads.

I enclose one of my own. It wont be paid for, but if it had any effect, I might get a regular ad. out of [publisher, Elkin] Mathews.

It is a damn bore to print ads. when one wants ALL ones paper for contents.

I wonder if we will swing the turn of next May. Present indications are against present guarantors or up-spotters going on with the subsidy. However we'll have some run in the interim.

New subscrip. price is certainly an advantage, it takes fewer of them to make a ten dollar bill.

yours

E

Ezra Pound

*Lady Tredegar:* Lady Katherine Agnes Blanche Carnegie, daughter of the ninth Earl of Southesk and mother of Evan Frederic Morgan, the founder of the Tredegar Memorial Lecture Royal Society of Literature.

*those subs. for Windeler:* EP had asked MCA to send B. Cyril Windeler ten subscriptions to the *LR*. See Letter 83.

*seven poems by W.B.Y.:* See Letter 92n.

*Will get one of them anyhow:* See Letter 102n.

*New subscrip. price:* Prior to February 1918, subscription rates were fifteen cents a copy and $1.50 per year. With the February 1918 issue, the rates were raised to twenty-five cents a copy and $2.50 per year.

**101. TLS–1.**   On stationery embossed: 5, Holland Place Chambers/ Kensington. W. [26 June 1918]

Dear Margaret:

Here are the seven Yeats poems for Oct. The Round Tower is good.

Gent. whose note is on the reverse displays N.Y. bank acc. I enclose his economy of 2/. He is a perfidious greek.

Costa Varda. 31 Eastcheap E.C. 3.

Have I sent subs. as follows:

Capt. Desmond Coke. Claymore School, Northwood Park

Winchester. Eng.

begin May.

Shepeler. renewed for 1/2 year.

another half year sub. beg. May. I will send the remaining three.

Herbert Read. renewal. (he is on American list direct sub. before.)

⟨complains of not receiving May no.⟩

Brynholme, Roundhay. Leeds.

STOP.

S. Bowen. Pembroke Studio

L. Beardmore

Yours ever.

Ezra

⟨26–6–1918⟩          Ezra Pound

*whose note is on the reverse:* The note reads:

31 East Cheap
E. C. 3
25th June 1918

Dear Sir,

Many thanks for the Dec. & March copies of the "Little Review" duly received.

I believe subscriptions can be made through you. If so I enclose you a cheque on New York for $2.50, which I trust you will find correct.

In case you wish me to send you back the two copies, kindly let me know.

Yours faithfully
Conanvarda

**102. TLS–1.**   On stationery headed: THE LITTLE REVIEW/ London Office:—5, HOLLAND PLACE CHAMBERS, W.8. [4 July 1918]

⟨4–July 1918⟩

Dear Margaret:

That animal Yeats has now got another poem (about four pages long) which he wants printed before the lyrics. I shall waste this morning getting it typed. Damn it.

Please hold, if possible, space in Sept. for it. I dont want to waste the lyrics by putting them with the Eliot poems. Nor waste the effect of Yeats by having both the lyrics and the longer poem in the same issue. NOR do I want to hold over the lyrics for Nov. Might want that No. for [Remy] DeGourmont. etc. etc.

yours
E.
Ezra Pound

⟨June no.
not yet
here.⟩

*Yeats has now got another poem:* i.e., "In Memory of Robert Gregory," a tribute to Lady Gregory's son, who was killed on 23 January 1918 when his plane was shot down as he was returning from a flight over enemy lines in northern Italy. The poem was published in the September 1918 issue (1–4).

**103. TLS–1.**   On stationery embossed: 5, Holland Place Chambers/ Kensington. W. [5 July 1918]

Dear Margaret:

As I wrote yesterday. Yeats has a bee in his cap about wanting this Gregory poem printed as soon as possible. before the lyrics.
ERGO. Get it, and the little trailer into Sept. if possible.
If you cant do that, use these two in Oct. with a foot-note, stating clearly that the "Seven Lyrics by Mr Yeats, announced for this month, will appear without fail in November number."

///
Shall do my article on "La Wallonie" before the [Remy] DeGourmont. I
have asked you ??? to send the L.R. to Albert Mockel, 109 Avenue de Paris
          La Malmaison,
                    Rueil, (S. et. O.)
                    France.
Brief note in this months Mercure [*Mercure de France*], not important.

          yours E
                    Ezra Pound
                    ⟨5/7/1918⟩

*this Gregory poem:* Yeats' "In Memory of Robert Gregory." See Letter 102n.
*my article on "La Wallonie":* i.e., "Albert Mockel and 'La Wallonie,' " published
     in the October 1918 issue (51–64). *La Wallonie,* a journal published by
     Belgian poet and critic Albert Mockel from 1885 to 1892, became the organ
     of the Symbolist movement in Belgium. Published from Liège, the journal
     printed the first works of many French as well as Belgian Symbolist writers.

**104. TLS–2.**   On stationery embossed: 5, Holland Place Chambers/ Kensington. W. [7 July 1918]

7th. July.

Dear Margaret:
          June not here yet. The enclosed scrap is hardly worth print-
ing. Having done it, I send it to be used or not as you see fit.
          Looking over schedule of next six months. I don't think the
Fenollosa mss. ought to come too near the heavy artillery H. James.
          James is Aug., Sept. has Eliot, and should have all the pos-
sible snap. Probably my Tetrarchal Precieuse, [(]unless she is July.), and
Edouardi Svargebohan, unless he is in July.
          ///
Oct. I am specially preparing. "La Wallonie" number. quotes from ten
Wallonie poets in french, note on DeBosschères [Jean de Bosschère's] "Els-
kamp", I hope a poem and possibly a couple of De Bosschère drawings.
          The Yeats lyrics to lead off.
Both "La Wallonie" by E.P.
     Seven Lyrics by W.B.Y
                    to appear, s.v.p. on cover.
          ///

That being so, should hold over Fenollosa for Dec. alternating heavy artillery with rapid fire numbers.

THUS if the Fenollosa mss. hasn't been rescued by Sept. 1. will you write on that date. (((Mais! non! NOT a letter ⟨Je n'en espere.⟩) A simple line to the effect that Fenollosa mss. is not in hand.

I will in that case have the damn pencil scribble recopied. and get it you by Nov. 1st. or thereabouts.

Then I'll hope to finish the big DeGourmont essay for Feb. making Feb the anniversary French month. That will give the VI th. vol. rather more form than vol. V. has.

yours

E.

Ezra Pound

⟨7–7–1918⟩

*Probably my Tetrarchal Precieuse:* Both EP's "Our Tetrarchal Précieuse (A Divagation from Jules Laforgue)" and Iseult Gonne's "Saptam Edoyarder Svargobohan" were published in the July 1918 issue.

*ten Wallonie poets:* EP quotes the following poems in his article: Stéphane Mallarmé's "Sonnet" and "The Whirlwind" [misnamed in the *LR;* the poem is "Billet à Whistler"]; Stuart Merrill's "Ballet"; Edmond Hanton's "Le Bon Grain"; Achille Delaroche's "Sonnets Symphoniques"; Albert Saint-Paul's "Petales de Nacre"; Jules Bois's "Pour la Démone" and "Pour la Démone, V"; Georges Rodenbach's "Paysages Souffrants, II"; Francis Vielé-Griffin's "Hélène"; Albert Mockel's "A Clair Matin"; and Mockel's death notice on Jules Laforgue, which itself quoted Laforgue's "Le Crapaud" and passages from *Les Complaintes.*

*big DeGourmont essay:* EP's "De Gourmont: A Distinction," published in the combined February–March issue of 1919 (1–18).

**105. TLS–2.**   On stationery embossed: 5, Holland Place Chambers/ Kensington. W. [9 July 1918]

Dear M.

June number rather hard reading. Haven't got to the end of it yet. Or rather, read the end before I could penetrate ⟨all⟩ the contents.

I think it was right to have it.

Have wasted the morning typing these enclosed reactions ⟨for Sept. if possible?⟩ Suppose I am fool to do it. However, here they are. Please keep the notes together. The two squibs "Audience" ⟨Reader Critic⟩ should be separate as "The criterion"'s [*sic*] were.

///

Am getting on with Wallonie number. ⟨OCTOBER⟩. This list of contents will take about 16 of the pages. Perhaps twenty or 25.

Seven poems by W.B.Y. [Yeats)   (lyrics must go in Oct. if the Gregory poem didn't get into Sept. it must wait till Nov.)

La WALLONIE. by E.P.

    1. DeBosschere's study of Elskamp.

    2. Albert Mockel and La Wallonie ⟨2 pages⟩

            Mallarme

            Hanton

            Rodenbach

            V Griffin

            Merril                           ⟨about a page

            Bois                                each⟩

            A. Delaroche

            Raynaud

            Albert Saint-Paul

            Mockel

            Mockel on Laforgue

Poem or two by DeBosschere,

    with, I hope, a couple of his drawings.

Rest of the number ad. lib.

                  ⟨enclose De B's note⟩

Have two brief poems of my own, which might make a page with the two Chinese translations I sent you ⟨a⟩ year or more ago. If you still have the mss.

MUST STOP writing so much prose. Will do the DeGourmont heave. And THEN pray god I may quit concern with criticism for a time. Time I quit fussing about other men's work and attended to my own.

                yours

                  E.

[*Crossout:* 8th]

9th July.

Ezra Pound

*these enclosed reactions:* EP's reactions to the June 1918 issue, the first "American Number," were published in the "Reader Critic" of September 1918 (62–64). About the Stanislaw Szukalski drawings reproduced in the issue, EP writes, "Interest in the drawings leaks perceptively in half an hour, and completely disappears at the end of forty-five minutes. . . . They are not original work. This is not an utter condemnation. All good artists pass through a borrowing and copying phase." He goes on to say that Mark Turbyfill, whose poems "Shapes" and "She Goes to Pisa" had been included in the number, "has perhaps the cell-nucleus of something about which a book of poems might form itself." In response to Israel Solon's essay "The Writer and His Job"—in which Solon denies "Ezra Pound's insistence on literacy" ("I do not say that writers should know the classics; I do not ask that all stories should be literature")—EP clarifies his own position: "I have merely said that young men hoping to leave permanent works were rather stupid not to enlighten themselves." The article ends with EP's observation that there are "some good sentences in William Carlos Williams's 'Prose About Love'" and his quotation of Henri Barbusse's poem "La Lettre" from *Pleureuses* (1895).

*The two squibs "Audience":* The first of these was published in the October 1918 "Reader Critic" (64):

> "Art should conceal art", said the parrot.
> "Art is ennobling", said the parrot.
> "Art is the ultimate combustion of the social-consciousness of the proletariat into the fine flower of penultimate culture; it is the expression of the soul-wave into the infinite of the understandable je ne sais quoi", said the parrot.
> *Damn the parrot!*
> Damn the parrot, although there is a faint dilutation of verity in each of these three remarks.

The second "Audience" squib appeared in the November 1918 "Reader Critic" (44):

> "The use of articulate speech by human beings is inconsiderate", said the pig. "They should consider our capacity for comprehension. We can neither express ourselves in this fashion, nor can we comprehend the utterance of these humans."
> "O que le monde soit porcine!"

This squib was dedicated to E. Hamilton of Chicago, who had complained in the "Reader Critic" of June 1918 of the "audacity of publishing Pound's study of French poets," calling the issue "ridiculous besides being inconsiderate of non-French-speaking readers." EP's first "Audience" squib was no doubt also inspired by E. Hamilton's comments in this same letter:

> Mary Garden and Art seem to have become a fetish with you. Art! Art! Art! Why all the babbling about Art? Give us more Art and less talk about it! The perfection of art is to conceal art.

*Poem or two by DeBosschere . . . :* The October 1918 *LR* (14–22) carried four of Jean de Bosschère's poems: "Dear!," "Momie," "Silence," and "Le Chien domestique." The poems were accompanied by reproductions of four of de Bosschère's drawings.

*two brief poems . . . with the two Chinese translations:* The November 1918

issue ([1]–6) published nine of EP's poems, including two "translations":
"Cantus Planus"; "Chanson Arabe"; "Dawn on the Mountain" (trans. from
Omakitsu); "Wine" (trans. from Rihaku); a three-poem sequence: "Rose
White, Yellow, Silver," "Saltus," and "Concava Vallis"; "Glamour and In-
digo"; and "Upon the Harps of Judea."

**106. TLS–1.**   On stationery embossed: 5, Holland Place Chambers/ Kensington. W. [10 July 1918]

Dear Margaret:

   WHAT have I done that I should receive 100 yea five score
[Max] Michelsons for my breakfast. Eheu fugaces, Postumé! Postumé!
POPPOI! POPPOI.!!
   It is bloody awful. Out of forty reams or so I have culled
these microscopical antennae-twitches. I think at least the first three are
probably worth printing, the scoundrel seems intent on his work. I can
vouch for ⟨his⟩ more than semetic [Semitic] perseverance AT ANY RATE.
Vide my waste basket for long dreary weeks.
  Deal with him as thou list.

P.S. I enclose some further ⟨minuscule⟩ revisions by Yeats. Use the enclosed
mss for printer, for as many poems as they cover. (Note especially
  "LOADSTONE" not L<u>andstone</u> mountain in line 11 of "A Prayer on
going["] etc.)
Order of lyrics, as in mss. sent you before.

     yours
     E.
  Ezra Pound
   10–7–1918

*Eheu fugaces . . . :* See Letter 34n.
*Deal with him as thou list:* MCA published none of these poems.

**107. TLS–1.**   On stationery headed: THE LITTLE REVIEW/ London
Office:—5, HOLLAND PLACE CHAMBERS, W.8. [19 July 1918]

⟨19–7–'18⟩

Dear Margaret:

Here are the four DeBosschère drawings to go
with his poems in Oct. number. LINE blocks will do them, no
wild expense for half tones. (as you doubtless know.) Line
blocks @ I suppose two dollars each??

Note renewals.:
S. Bowen, 2 Pembroke Studios, Pembroke
Gdnsm W.8.
Mrs Patmore, Baylis House, Slough. Bucks.
Eng.
*/ / /*
Keep the Deb. [de Bosschère] drawings. Haven't seen him since he sent
them in. Should probably be sold for his benefit if the printers dont spoil
them. .

Can they be printed on pages facing the poems?. That is the way
his books are done.

Enclosed to be used when space permit[s]. Sent off one squib this a.m.
Bulk of Oct. two days ago.

yours
E.
Ezra Pound

*four DeBosschère drawings to go* . . . . *:* See Letter 105n.

**108. ALS–1.**   On stationery embossed: 5, Holland Place Chambers/ Kensington. W. [19 July 1918]

Dear M.

You are a fairly bad correspondent yourself——but please insert
the enclosed in the L.R. as soon as possible

———

unless the Chinese mss. has come in.
═══════

yours

E

Ezra Pound

19–7–'18

*the enclosed:* See Letter 109.

**109. TLS–3.**　On stationery embossed: 5, Holland Place Chambers/ Kensington. W. [19? July 1918]

WANTED, AND BADLY: A Lynch-law for manuscript thieves.

A reward of $10 will be given to any one providing me with adequate means of recovering a manuscript entitled "The Chinese Written Character, by Ernest Fenollosa, edited and annotated by E.P.".

This mss. was extracted from me by P.E.B. Jourdain english agent or correspondent for Dr. Paul Carus, editor of the "Monist" and of the "Open Court". It was received by said Carus.

I have private hopes that he is now dead or hung, but at any rate he does not answer letters, and having failed to print said mss. in reasonable time, neither forwards it at request of his agent, nor responds to letters either from New York or this side of the Atlantic.

Other bipeds have at different times stolen my mss. and other possessions; have sequestered mss. for periods of over a year. ⟨(Four years is about the maximum.)⟩

Carus is said to live in La Salle, Ill. Action on the part of his townfolk would be appreciated.

Something called the Open Court Pub. Co. is or was situated at 122 South Michigan Ave. Chicago. I don't know whether it is an appendix to Carus.

Local action would be appreciated.

My private feeling is that perpetrators of these petty thefts should be made a sort of caput lupinum; not in the full sense that they need, or may, be killed on sight by any good citizen, but that any honest member of the public should be at liberty at all times and in all places to administer a sound and vigorous coup-de-pied to the buttocks of branded sequestrators and detainers as well as ⟨to⟩ out and out thieves of mss.

I don't quote [quite] know how long a man can keep a mss. entrusted to him, in defiance of demands for its return, before such holding ranks as theft. Delay beyond a certain time is dirt-meanness, perhaps not within scope of the courts but still an offense which the righteous might punish by at least vocal contempt.

I should welcome correspondence from La Salle containing information about Dr. Carus. We may even inspire a biography or some record of his life, origin and activities.

///

I should also welcome vendettas upon some people named Wheatley who stole my furniture in the holy state of Indiana; ⟨also⟩ upon the son of an American Ambassador named Wilson (no relation of Pres. Wilson.) who stole my text of the Poema del Cid; ⟨also⟩ upon an ex-New York publisher named Marshall (spurlous verschwindet) disappeared with mss. of a long book.

Also has anyone any news of the Rev. C.C. Bubb, of the Clerks Press, 2077 East 36th. St. Cleveland Ohio.? . He should have rec'd a mss. from me ⟨to be privately printed⟩ but I have had no response from him since a few days before said mss. should have reached him. He is a charming ⟨correspondent⟩ and this contretemps may be due merely to letters going astray, or to sudden death or other unavoidable accident. ⟨This last is a mere matter of weeks. The other affairs are of over year-long duration.⟩

Ezra Pound

Dr. Paul Carus . . . "Monist" . . . "Open Court": See Letter 85.
people named Wheatley: In a letter to his father dated 18 June [1908] and now at the Beinecke Library at Yale University, EP wrote the following:

> Also with one Brother Wheatly [sic], Brick House, next Big 4, station, Crawfordsville. Give greeting in the name of peace & suggest that $25. now 3 months due on furniture should be sent. the agreement was that they pay at end of 3 months — march, april, may, make it now overdue.

Subsequent letters give no indication that the money was ever received.
son of an American Ambassador . . . who stole . . . the Poema del Cid: The

facts behind this episode must be conjectured. EP may be referring to one of the three sons of Henry Lane Wilson (1857–1932). Wilson was a native of Crawfordsville, Indiana; a graduate of Wabash College; and was, at the time EP was teaching at Wabash, the U.S. minister to Belgium (1905–1909). Perhaps, while at Wabash College, EP had run into one of Wilson's sons who may have been a student. The *Poema del Cid,* written anonymously about 1140, is the best surviving example of the medieval epic in Spanish.

*ex-New York publisher named Marshall:* See Letter 5n.

*Rev. C. C. Bubb, of the Clerks Press . . . . :* The manuscript to which EP refers is his study of Arnaut Daniel. See Letter 73n.

**110. TLS–2.**   On stationery embossed: 5, Holland Place Chambers/ Kensington. W. [23 July 1918]

⟨23/7/1918⟩

Dear M.

I enclose the two other [Jean] DeBosschère poems, to be the third and fourth of his group with illustrations in OCT.

Also some copy of my own to aliment the pages when needed or convenient.

Chien domestique is O.K.

Note renewals. (Mrs Montgomery paying up 4/6 to make 12/ instead of 7/)

Curtis Brown renew. vide slip

Hutchinson, pays up remaining 6/

making 1 year.

Did I send this, or did I intend to send them June and July nos.

Any how. start 'em in Aug. I will attend to other numbers. They began with Feb. and expire therein.

Sic. Mrs Hutchinson. Eleanor House

West Wittering, Chichester. Eng.

Patmore renewed.

Subscriber. (plus 13/ for back numbers. and extra Febs.)

(which I have delivered.)

C.H. Marsh Roberts. (began Feb. have sent back numbers)

1 Artillery Buildings. S.W. 1.

You might send him a May 1917, if you have it. I have supplied complete file save for that number.

AM OUT of Feb. 1918.

Bookseller in Charing X. Rd. has put some extra back numbers on sale.

Saw Monro (Harold) last night. More befuddled than ever[.]

OH yes. I enclose note from the simple Sweed. She'll certainly need editing, hope she'll send in something decent.

One must collect and treasure tendencies to enlightenment. It is possible that some damn Sweed may have written something. At any rate we ought to show that we are willing to receive news of foreign products.

AND there is no use in letting it be supposed that Stork (of all the dundering mops) has a monopoly.

⟨?Tanto cosé⟩

E.

Ezra Pound.

*two other DeBosschère poems:* See Letter 105n.

*Saw Monro (Harold) last night:* Harold Monro (1879–1932) founded the *Poetry Review* in 1912 and was its editor for that year. During his time as editor, Monro published the writings of Ezra Pound, F. S. Flint, and others. In 1913 in London, Monro opened the Poetry Bookshop, which became a gathering place for those interested in the discussion and reading of poetry. In July 1919, Monro founded the *(Monthly) Chapbook;* he served as its editor until it ceased publication in 1925. A collection of Monro's own verse was published posthumously in 1933.

*the simple Sweed:* probably Svea Bernhard, who is mentioned in Letter 111. Nothing of Bernhard's was ever published in the *LR,* nor is there evidence of her having brought any Scandinavian literature to the magazine.

*Stork:* See Letter 69n.

**111. TLS–4.** On stationery embossed: 5, Holland Place Chambers/ Kensington. W. [20 August 1918]

⟨20 Aug. 1918⟩

Dear Margaret:

Your as usual voluminous correspondence has not arrived. Note renewals.

Edward Wadsworth (or Mrs.) 1 a. Gloucester Walk.
Capt. Baker.

new sub.
Mrs. E. Mc Cormick (begin with first chap. Ulysses)
Hotel Bauer au Lac. Zurich, Switzerland.
////
Suggest for heading to Reader Critic, following motto.

"Le public! le public! combien faut-il de sots pour faire un public?"
            Chamfort.
//////
Also enclose correspond. re/ my carefully-considered-by-daylight-working-nachtigal.

       The greek means ["]to spit profusely,["] I should prefer it in greek type if the printer has it, omitting the english putidzo.

The Bengali has come up very well.
Thank GOD the Chinese essay has come in.

It is very important, AND it gives me leisure to do the DeGourmont properly.

I have asked for three short essays on Russian literature . . . from a chap named Bechhofer whom I dont much trust . . . BUT he does know Russian, and has been over, and is not of the gang that swallow Stephen Graham, and does not fall for Slobagob and Co.

       It is no recommendation that Rasputin authorized him to do his biography, save in so far as it shows that B. had some sort [of] initiative, at least enough to get at Rasputin. However an adventurous temperament does NOT necessarily mean critical discrimination. STILL the stuff wont be everybodys opinion, and I dont think it will be the blithering wish-wash of untempered admiration, which sozzles through general press.

       ///
I wrote to Svea Bernhard somewhere in the wilds to send in some notes on Scandinavian literature. Given time we might get a staff of competent international critiques, one must begin with what is available.

OH God, if [Ben] Hecht would only come over here long enough to learn how to write. Mostly, in his case, what to scratch out after he has written a rough draft ! ! ! !

There is something to him, and also to Sherwood ⟨A.⟩ [Anderson].

My Laforgue [i.e., "Our Tetrarchal Précieuse . . ."] shows lamentable marks of haste, BUT madre di dios, something had to be turned in.

There are decent bits in it, and it can be worked up in time for my next prose book.

Is anyone reviewing "Lustra" or "Pavannes"?

Alice Groff has been writing to the Egoist for years, dont know anything else about her, but from the energy she displays in writing TO papers, I should think she might be willing to work for one, without wanting to be paid. Dont know that she knows anything about poetry, but she might do a careful review of "Pavannes", and might I think be persuaded to do a monthly col. of book reviews. Would probably keep an eye out for books worth reviewing.

One ought to concentrate these scraps of enthusiasm.

What about the Carr. female.?
Brief reviews, make a circulation. On the Poetry Review (old P.R. not the present one.) we used to meet weekly and kill off the fools, results in the way of two to four line notices used to enliven the P.R. considerably.

Is Babette Deutsch, who reviewed me in Reedy's Mirror, any use?

There OUGHT to be plenty of people in America capable of doing monthly rubrics.
          Also if the rubrics were done in the U.SA. it might stop this clamour for "more American contributions". ⟨Or⟩ at least go toward evening the balance with the exotic.
                    *///*
Why doesn't Mr Stuhlmann publish a literary review of his own. True his name is german and of an untranslatable obscenity, but still the censors might pass it.

                    yours
                    E

*correspond. re/ my carefully-considered-by-daylight-working nachtigal:* EP's reference is to the nightingale in "Alba," published in the May 1918 issue.

EP is reacting to the comments in the "Reader Critic" of July 1918 (63) in which a Louis Puteklis of Cambridge, Massachusetts, writes to complain that the *LR* is "full of 'rotten stuff,' " and that it is "flourishing only decadent blunderings under the magical wand of the grand dervish, Mr. Ezra Pound":

> Many times [Pound] pictures as facts aberrations of his fancy, as when he rhapsodizes over a nightingale. To beautify his rhyme he thinks he must mention the sweetest of all songsters. But in so doing he over-compliments the little bird when he states:
> "When the nightingale to his mate
> Sings day-long and night late."
> If Ezra Pound had ever with his own ears heard a nightingale, he would have to admit that the bird sings to his mate only at night during the short mating period. Whether he mistook an English sparrow for a nightingale I know not; the fact remains that the poet does not know when the nightingale sings.

For EP's reply, see Letter 112.

*The greek means to spit profusely:* See ending of Letter 112.

*The Bengali:* i.e., Iseult Gonne's "Saptam Edoyarder Svargobohan."

*the Chinese essay:* See Letter 109.

*chap named Bechhofer:* Carl Eric Bechhofer-Roberts (1894–1949), whom EP had met through A. R. Orage of *The New Age.* He had served with the British military mission in Russia before becoming a foreign correspondent for *The Times* and other English, continental, and American newspapers. Although Bechhofer-Roberts wrote several books about Russia, he did not publish a biography of Rasputin.

*Stephen Graham:* (1884–1975), English writer and authority on Russian literature and history. Among his works on Russia are the following: *A Vagabond in the Caucasus* (1910); *Undiscovered Russia* (1911); *A Tramp's Sketches* (1912); *With the Russian Pilgrims to Jerusalem* (1913); *With Poor Immigrants to America* (1914); *Through Russian Central Asia* (1916); and *Russia in 1916* (1917).

*Svea Bernhard:* See Letter 110n.

*my next prose book:* i.e., *Instigations* (1920).

*Alice Groff:* a Philadelphian who was an avid reader of the *LR* and a correspondent of the "Reader Critic." Her letter in the May 1918 number reads:

> Up to now the *Little Review* has been a delightful youth, gifted, daring, insolent, swash-buckling, with flashes of divine discernment and discrimination. With the March number it comes to its majority, superbly full-statured, speaking with social authority upon all that pertains to life. May its further growth and development be the fulfillment of this glorious promise of maturity. (64)

Aside from her enthusiastic letters, however, Alice Groff did no other work for the *LR*.

*the Carr. female:* Daphne Carr of Pittsburgh, another enthusiast of the *LR*, writes in the May 1918 "Reader Critic":

> I want to thank you so much for sticking out in these beastly times with your *Little Review*. Other prints yap and bellow and throw mud. The *Little Review* stays as serene and beautiful as a chatelaine of Azay—a singing chatelaine with a

strangely sweet lute. How grateful I am for "Ulysses"! I call you blessed, even as the rest of the country will some fifty years hence. (64)

*old P.R. not the present one:* that is, the *Poetry Review* of 1912, the year in which Harold Monro was its editor. Beginning with the second volume, the monthly was edited by Stephen Phillips and came almost entirely under the control of the British Poetry Society. Phillips retained the editorship through the end of 1915; at the time of this letter, the *Poetry Review* was being edited by Galloway Kyle.

*Babette Deutsch:* (1895–1982), American poet, novelist, and critic. Miss Deutsch's article on EP appeared on 21 December 1917 in *Reedy's Mirror* (860–61) and has been reprinted as Number 52 in Homberger (131–136).

*Mr Stuhlmann:* Frank Stuhlmann of Vernon, New York, wrote a letter to the July 1918 "Reader Critic" in which he maintained, among other things, that the "much bepraised Joyce's 'Ulysses' is punk, Lewis' 'Imaginary Letters' are punkier and Ezra Pound is punkiest. You may transpose the names and the values will fit just as well" (64). In German, *stuhl* can mean *excrement.*

**112. TLS–2.**   On stationery embossed: 5, Holland Place Chambers/ Kensington. W. [? August 1918]

O excellent Editress:

I knew some jackass would bite on that nightingale[.]

The comments of young Greek gentleman from Brookline are what one would expect from a district where there are no nightingales and where people believe all that they read in text books.

Mr Patmos is at liberty to translate

Quan le ressinhols escria
ab sa par la nueg e-l dia,

in any way he likes.

I have never heard the nightingale in America; if nightingales inhabit the purlieus of Boston I do not doubt that their mating season is duly and eugenicly restricted! I will not deny the brevity of its duration; I will not deny that the Boston nightingale takes the rattle of the morning (sterilized) milk-can for his curfew and that he lapses into silence incontinent.

To hear a bird sing at night is of course irrefutable evidence that the bird does not sing in the daytime. This is typical logic as dished up by Mr Pratkins.

I have heard the nightingale very early in the evening; certainly well before dusk.

Richard de Brebez⟨ieu's⟩ apparently ridiculous remark on the elephant

"que quan chai, no-s pot levar"
⟨has⟩ recently been confirmed by a zoo keeper, also, for the instruction of future ornithologists, the lark does sing as it soars. I have seen and heard it by the field full, at Allegre.

The person at ⟨my⟩ elbow declares that the nightingale sings in the daytime. Mr Pratkins should reprove the nightingale for not living down to its name; he should apply to the Neapolitan nightingale his blood brother and semblable. Even if he does derive his name and lineage from putidzo ⟨(πυζτιΣω)⟩

, the greek gentleman should not confuse the nightingale with cuckoo.

yours<br>Ezra Pound

*young Greek gentleman from Brookline:* i.e., Louis Puteklis from Cambridge, Massachusetts (see Letter 111n). Note that EP refers to him variously as "Mr. Patmos" and "Mr. Pratkins."

*Richard de Brebezieu:* Troubadour poet, active around 1170 to 1200 and known variously as Richart de Berbezill, Rigaut de Berbezilh (or Barbezieux). The line EP quotes comes from the following Canso, the French translation being provided by France Igly (82–83):

Canso
Atressi com l'olifanz
Que, quan chai, no-s pot levar
Tro que l'autre, ab lor cridar
De lor voz lo levon sus,
Et eu segrai aquel us,
Quar mos mesfaitz m'es tan greus e pesanz
Que si la cortz del Poi e:l rics bobanz
E l'adreitz prez dels leials amadors
No-m relevon, jamais non serai sors;
Que denhesson per mi clamar merce
Lai on prejars ni razos no:m val re.

Chanson
De même que l'éléphant
Qui choit, ne peut se lever,
à moins qu'autres, à grands cris,
De leur voix ne le relevent,
Las, je suis semblable à lui,

Car mon méfait est si grand et pesant
Que, si la cour du Puy et nobles gens
Et les grands mérites des loyaux amants
Ne me relèvent, onc ne m'en sortirai.
Qu'ils daignent donc pour moi clamer merci
Là où prières ni raison ne valent.

*The person at ⟨my⟩ elbow:* probably Dorothy Pound, EP's wife.
*putidzo:* See Letter 111n.

**113. TLS–2.** On stationery embossed: 5, Holland Place Chambers/ Kensington. W. [3 September 1918]

Dear Margaret:

Note the following (first of which I have perhaps sent before)
Sub.

     Mrs E. McCormick, Hotel Bauer au Lac. Zurich Switzerland.
Renew.

       M. Ryan, Lyceum Club, Piccadilly.

       F.T. Brenan
Sub.

     Mrs. Jay E. Gordon Ede, Wayside Inn, Bishops Court
                       Chancery Lane, W.C.2.

(sold back numbers 12/.[)]

     Start Gordon Ede with Sept. I will supply Aug.

     Sub. began with July (delivered)

Please send me some more Feb. Fr. Anthology.

     also a few copies of May 1917. (Have had to borrow back one, to make up text for Eliot's book.)

I enclose two poems from Spire. Neither bad nor super excellent, but we are lucky to get started. We have got to print what new french we can get for a beginning in order to start them sending in stuff.

Should use them to Nov. Hope to have something from [Jules] Romains in time to keep the appearance of having some french ever[y] month after Oct.

Thank God the Chinese essay has come in. (i.e. to you.)

Hear my Arnaut Daniel mss. has disappeared, or has not been rec'd by
Bubb. One would think the bloody fool would have got round to saying so
before, as the thing was shipped on Jan. 23.

yours

E.

Ezra Pound

3–9–18

*two poems from Spire:* French poet André Spire's "Saint-Moritz" and "Bla-
mont," both of which were published in the November 1918 issue (13–15).
*Chinese essay:* See Letter 109.
*Arnaut Daniel mss.:* See Letters 109 and 73n.

**114. TLS–1.**    *Incomplete item.* [? September–October 1918]

Complaints of non arrival from
Jane Moncur 51 Maple St. W.1.
                (I sent four numbers.[)]
                no July or Aug. Recd. , half your renewal beginning Sept. no.
Also
                H. Wellington, co. J. Moncur, 51 Maple St.
sub to begin with March this year.

Seems some chance of my getting Gourmont ready by Feb.
⟨Have had to
fold margins to get
into envelope—
but you will judge how          yours E
to place cuts on page.          Ezra Pound
without indication⟩

**115. ALS–1.**   On stationery headed: THE LITTLE REVIEW/ London Office:—5, HOLLAND PLACE CHAMBERS, W.8. [? September–October 1918]

> Dear M.C.A.
>
> Note subs as per enclosed slips.
> > G. H. Bonner.
> > E. Wadsworth.
>
> Also Capt. Guy Baker has paid second year. Enclose poems for Nov. or later. also Critique by J[ohn].R[odker]. === He is worth keeping on. He really does get toward the feel of a thing.
>
> > I wish I could use his Ch. L. Phillipe paper—but the time is not yet ripe.
>
> > yours E.
> > Ezra Pound

⟨P.S. I mean that J.R. has the makings of a good critic. a sensitive critic[.] he has sense enough to differ with me in a sensible way.⟩

*Enclose poems for Nov.:* The November 1918 *LR* carried nine poems by EP: "Cantus Planus," "Chanson Arabe," "Dawn on the Mountain," "Wine," "Rose White, Yellow, Silver," "Saltus," "Concava Vallis," "Glamour and Indigo," and "Upon the Harps of Judea" ([1]–6).

*critique by J[ohn]. R[odker].:* Rodker's "List of Books," in which he first discusses briefly the poetry of Mina Loy and Marianne Moore that had been published in the *"Others" Anthology,* comments on Aldous Huxley's *Jonah* ("some of the most finished poems provided in this country during the war"), William Carlos Williams's *Al Que Quiere!* ("the most important book which has come from among the Imagists"), an anthology *Poems of Today,* Mary Richardson's *Wilderness Love Songs,* and Ford Madox Hueffer's *On Heaven.* The critique was published in the November 1918 issue (31–33).

*his Ch. L. Phillipe paper:* Rodker's essay on French novelist Charles-Louis Philippe (1874–1909) was eventually published under the title "A Barbarian" in the December 1919 issue of the *LR* (40–42), some months after Rodker himself had assumed the foreign editorship of the magazine. The novels of Charles-Louis Philippe include *Bubu de Montparnasse* (1902), *Le Père Perdrix* (1903), *Marie Donadieu* (1904), *Croquignole* (1906), and the unfinished *Charles Blanchard* (1913).

**116. TLS–1.**   On stationery headed: THE LITTLE REVIEW/ London
Office:—5, HOLLAND PLACE CHAMBERS, W.8. [4 November 1918]

⟨4th Nov.⟩

Dear M.C.A.

Subscriber:

> Aldous Huxley. The Old Christopher
> Eton College,
> Windsor

Reader Critic:

> H.L., Philadelphia.
>> "Jepson's note "Western School
>> very fair."
>> I enclose eighth bundle of Joyce [i.e., *Ulysses*]. Also
a skit by Huxley, do as you like about it. It may amuse you.
Not up to Laforgue. but still has its moments.

Huxley has shown a trace of intelligence in his last booklet of poems.

Only If you dont want the Huxley, please send it back at
once.

DeGourmont essay at typists, will send it in few days. In time for Feb.
number I should think.

Could use some more July, and more James numbers.

Enclose also a few lines of my own, put in fairly soon. let us say. Jan. ⟨It
don't need a signature.⟩

yours

E

Ezra Pound

*a skit by Huxley:* The *LR* did publish a playlet of Aldous Huxley entitled
"Happy Families," but not until its September 1919 issue (18–30).

*a few lines of my own:* The January issue contains nothing of EP's. Perhaps he
is referring to a short, unsigned article entitled "The Death of Vorticism,"
published in the February–March 1919 issue (45, 48).

**117. TLS–1.**   On stationery embossed: 5, Holland Place Chambers/ Kensington. W. [16 November 1918]

⟨16–11–1918⟩

Dear M.

> Subscription. (Beginning Sept. have sent Sept.
> and will send Oct.)
> Clement Shorter, "The Sphere",
> Great New St.
> Fetter Lane, E.C. 4.

I enclose two articles by Rodker. The Joyce seems to me very good. Can you get it into Jan. ? The De Gourmont, naturally goes into Feb.

/// 

Might be more criticism ⟨written⟩ in U.S.A.

Should announce. last vol. L.R. May 1917–18 at 12/–
> and special numbers. French number, and H. James number @ 2/6.
> 3 dollars, for vol. unbound. and 60 cents (or 50 cents, as you think best, for special numbers.)

/// 

Marsden Hartley, simply an ass, so far as the revelation has reached me. Have you any further data. Suppose it is as well to have him pickled and on view, but I would have had fewer people bothering me about "WHY the hell, he is printed" if you had put a few editorial asterisks after him. "Divagations" is all right, but the word has been dignified by J. Laforgue.

> (above reflection not for publication. Hartley is probably surrounded by barbarians among whom he is a beacon light of culture. Incident IV. being of course ample acquaintance etc. etc.)

[Max] Michelson says he is going to New York. He ought to write you some criticisms. He has an idea of qualitative criticism. Sherwood Anderson, [Ben] Hecht, Michelson, [William Carlos] Williams,

Oh hell, I dont know why they cant get together and rub off their corners and stir up some sort of vortex.

> yours Ezra Pound

*two articles by Rodker . . . :* The Joyce article, a discussion of *Exiles,* was published in the January 1919 issue along with discussions of *Exiles* by Israel Solon, Samuel A. Tannenbaum, and Jane Heap (20–22). "De Gourmont–Yank" was included in the February–March 1919 issue (29–32).

*Marsden Hartley:* Under the title "Divagations," the comments of the American painter Marsden Hartley (1877–1943) appeared in the "Reader Critic" of the September 1918 issue (59–62). Hartley's main point seems to be that the content of Joyce's *Ulysses* is too trivial to bear the style in which Joyce treats it:

> Jane Austen, Thomas Hardy, and Henry James are certainly various [stylists], but you get the sense of consequence in them. The Joyce species of entertainment is a restive feathering of the acid upon a not too expansive plate. You are fed with a fascination of little touches. It is Messionierism in words. Cross-hatching which has not the distinction of Rembrandt. There is a humoristic tracery in Joyce which will amuse any ardent lover of the touch. I wonder if we do not hear the strumming of the mosquitoe's [*sic*] wing a little excessively in Joyce. Does he care for entirety as much as the whimsie en passant? Is it not a too close relationship of tense values[?] I have only "Ulysses – Episode IV" to begin my premise. (60)

**118. TLS–1.** On stationery headed: THE LITTLE REVIEW/ London Office:—5, HOLLAND PLACE CHAMBERS, W.8. [1 January 1919]

⟨1 Jan 1919⟩

Dear M.

The Yeats play and the American number will throw the Chinese essay rather late, SO if Knopf wants it to set up my book from, please let him have the mss.

and in any case please get the original mss. back from the printer ⟨when done⟩ as Knopf will presumably want to begin printing before I can correct the Feb. Little Review, and the mss. (typescript) will be better for his printer than an uncorrected L.R.

No need to print the Chinese essay in the L.R. at all, if it doesn't suit the general condition.

///

Can you send me two or three copies of April. 1918; Sept. and Oct. '18; all gone.

///

Also, some verses signed "Crelos" of no particular interest.

Will you return mss. as author has had all own copies ⟨of all works⟩ destroyed by "over-zealous" (possibly divinely inspired) char woman.

>Happy New Year.
>
>E.P.
>
>E Pound

*The Yeats play:* i.e., "The Dreaming of the Bones," published in the January 1919 issue (1–14).

*the American number:* EP is referring to the second "American Number," the December 1918 issue.

*the Chinese essay:* i.e., "The Chinese Written Character as a Medium for Poetry" by Ernest Fenollosa and EP. EP was planning that this essay would be published by Knopf in the autumn of 1919 as a part of a collection of essays to be entitled *Instigations.* Knopf, however, rejected the book, and *Instigations* was not published until April 1920, when Boni and Liveright brought out the book. The *LR,* however, did publish the essay in four installments, September through December 1919.

*verses signed "Crelos":* See Letter 85n.

[In the spring of 1919, EP left his post as foreign editor of the *LR* and John Rodker replaced him. With the war over and travel on the Continent again possible, the Pounds left for Paris and the south of France in May of 1919, returning to London in September of that year. In March 1920, EP became foreign correspondent for *The Dial* (New York), which had recently been taken over by Scofield Thayer and James Sibley Watson, Jr. At the end of April or the beginning of May 1920, the Pounds again left London, this time for Italy. In June 1920, the Pounds returned to London by way of Paris, but by the end of 1920 EP had decided that London no longer was conducive to artistic creation and left to take up residence in Paris. From the spring of 1919 until April of 1921, when he again took up in an informal way with the *LR,* EP maintained only a loose connection with the magazine, publishing a few articles in its pages: a review of Douglas's *Economic Democracy* (April 1920); an article on W. H. Hudson, "Hudson: Poet Strayed into Science" (May-June 1920); a note attached to a Dadaist novel entitled "Bibi-la-Bibiste" (the "novel" also has the EP touch) in the September–December 1920 issue; and a satiric barb on the sculpture of George C. Barnard ("Sculpshure") in the January–March 1921 issue. After April 1921, EP's renewed connection with the *LR* lasted until the spring of 1923.]

**119. TLS–1.** On stationery headed: THE DIAL./ Edited by Scofield Thayer./ 152 W. 13th St. New York./ Agency—/ 5, Holland Place Chambers,/ London, W. 8. [26 October 1920]

26 Oct.

Not for publication.

Dear Maragret [*sic*]:

I cabled to Quinn when J[ohn].R[odker]. told me of the trouble; has been adumbrating an article on clause 211, which is, I take it, unconstitutional; at least [Thomas] Jefferson wd. have considered it so, but T.J. was a civilized person, long since forgotten in the U.S.; last Sat. I saw jh's [Jane Heap's] letter stating that the case was called for the 18th. as I believe John [Rodker] told me of the matter on the 19th. my cable will probably arrive only in time to irritate J.Q. . . . but it was sent as soon as possible, and the Jefferson angle may sometime be of use.

I agree with jh. that it is MUCH better the Ulysses shd. have appeared serially; much better. I dont, however, know that there is much use in being suppressed a fourth time. Q's plan for a private vol. now will serve.

Will even improve demand for vol. if the end of the book hasn't been printed in the L.R.

Article in Oct. Dial, a bit heavy, but timely, I take it.

I shall, in time, I hope, do my article on clause 211; but not until Q. has either used or rejected my suggestion of using point in court, in which case; if the matter isn't already finished (today, Oct. 26) the other side may just as well not be prepared[.]

H[ealth &?] luck.

E.

*the trouble:* The *LR* editors were once again facing legal difficulties. The July–August 1920 issue of the *LR,* containing the "Nausicaa" section of *Ulysses,* had been brought to the attention of John Sumner, the secretary of the New York Society for the Prevention of Vice. In late September, Sumner swore out a warrant against the proprietors of the Washington Square Bookshop, the store in which he had bought several copies. The issues that were to be mailed to subscribers were held up at the Post Office pending a hearing scheduled for October 4. When she heard of the trouble, MCA wrote John Quinn and he agreed to handle the case, largely because he was interested in seeing *Ulysses* published in book form and felt that unwarranted legal difficulties would jeopardize that venture.

Quinn managed to get the case against the Washington Square Bookshop dropped and the hearing for the *LR* editors was postponed until October 18. The hearing, however, did not take place until October 21, with Magistrate J. E. Corrigan presiding in a small Jefferson Market police court. Magistrate Corrigan, after reading the material in question, decided to hold the defendants over for trial in Special Sessions, the case to be heard by three judges— McInerney, Kerochan, and Moss. The trial took place in February 1921, and the *LR* lost. Each editor (MCA and Jane Heap) was fined fifty dollars and the *LR* was barred from publishing any further installments of the novel.

For a detailed explanation of the events surrounding this case, see Jackson R. Bryer's "Joyce, *Ulysses,* and the *Little Review*" in *South Atlantic Quarterly* 66 (Spring 1967): 148–64.

*suppressed a fourth time:* During its publication of twenty-three installments of *Ulysses* (between March 1918 and December 1920), the *LR* had been held up at the Post Office on three occasions other than this last: in January 1919, reacting to the first part of Episode VIII ("Lestrygonians"), the Post Office had forbidden MCA, who had already mailed copies to subscribers, to mail additional copies; in June 1919, the editors were informed that the May 1919 issue was unmailable, not only because of the *Ulysses* episode it contained but because of the whole tone of the magazine; and in January 1920, the issue was suppressed because of supposed disrespect for Victoria and Edward.

*Article in the Oct. Dial:* i.e., Evelyn Scott's "A Contemporary of the Future," published in the October 1920 issue (351–67). Scott's article praises *Ulysses* as a "slice of life in a new sense, a cross of the mind in action" (363), and maintains that Joyce "expresses more clearly than any other writer of English prose in this time, the conviction of modernity—a new and complex knowledge of self which has passed its period of racial gestation and is ready for birth in art" (367). To substantiate his claims on the literary merits of *Ulysses,* John Quinn had passed this article on to John Sumner at a luncheon meeting he had invited Sumner to prior to the preliminary hearing on the *LR* case. (See Bryer, "Joyce, *Ulysses,* and the *Little Review,*" 156.)

**120. ALS–1.** [?17 January 1921]

> 3 rue de Beaune
> (en passant)
> write via London

Dear M.:

As Romains ⟨⟨also all that lot are stuck about 1911–12)⟩ has never done anything I strongly suggest you ask Louis Aragon[.]
  (12 rue Ste. Pierre
    Neuilly/s/ Seine
      France[)]

to take on French editorship.

    Rodker left 2 days ago for Madrid[.]

———————

——————

———————

You might do worse than reproduce the manifesto enclosed issued at the contra-Marinetti demonstration yesterday.

            yours

              E.P.

*Romains:* Jules Romains was the nominal French editor of the *LR* (see Letter 95). With the Autumn 1921 issue, Romains' name is dropped and Francis Picabia's is listed as a part of the magazine's "Administration." (Other members of the "Administration" are MCA, Jane Heap, and EP.) John Rodker's name as editor last appears in the January–March 1921 issue.

*Louis Aragon:* (1897–1982), French novelist and poet and one of the early practitioners of Surrealism in literature. Aragon eventually broke with Surrealism when he joined the Communist Party. Regarding his editorship of the *LR,* see Letter 124.

*reproduce the manifesto:* The Dadaist manifesto was reproduced in the January–March 1921 issue ([62]–[63]).

*Marinetti:* Italian novelist, poet, and critic, Filippo Tommaso Marinetti (1878–1944), the founder of Futurism, a movement in art and literature which tried to reproduce the clamorousness and confusion of the machine age. The Futurists, generally, tended to glorify war, danger, and destruction.

**121. ALS–1.**  [2 February 1921]

                      St Raphael

                           Var.

                    2–Feb. 1921

Dear Margaret:

        I think you ought to print both of these documents—certainly & especially the CHUBB ——— otherwise some happy mortal who has left the country & forgotten what it is like might return to it ———
which — in view of the high cost of steamer tickets, wd. be rather a shame.

    ==

    I like especially Jerry talking about "Thee (the church)" =

              yours

               Ezra

*both of these documents:* We can find no trace of either of these "documents" in the *LR*.

**122. ALS–1.** [March? 1921]

Progress

Peoria and Pottstown papers please copy.

> [*Newspaper clipping follows:*]
>> For Paris Envoy
>> President Harding and Secretary of State Hughes are discussing diplomatic appointments and it is understood, unofficially, that Paris suggests an envoy able to speak French.

> [*Letter continues*]
>> Washington correspondent to Paris edtn. N.Y. Herald
>> 6 March 1921

P.S. Does this mean that we are about to have an "educational clause" relating to other "important appointments"? say elementary history, geography & economics.

> E.P.

**123. TLS–1.** [20 April 1921]

> Hotel du Pas de Calais
> 59 rue des Saints Peres
> Paris, VI.

(Private and
not for print)

Dear Margaret:

Neither Joyce nor I have had any direct news of the trial. However . . . necrology is not a necessity.

My connection with the Dial comes to an end on July 1st. I don't yet know what exterior (if any) activity I shall . . . . etc.

But I have a present for you in the form of Picabia, who doesn't contribute to reviews, but was interested in my statement that you wd. go the whole hog.

He ⟨is willing to⟩ take on the job that [Jules] Romains has never done anything with, and I believe he can give you some live stuff; at any rate he and Cocteau are intelligent, which a damn'd large number of Parisians aren't.

I dont know when you are going to "resume"; but it ought to be with a swish when it does occur. You can write your answer to this proposition either to me or to

Francis Picabia, 14 rue Emile Augier, Paris, XVI.

(F.P's painting is perhaps not convincing when reproduced, but the intelligence in his last book is another matter.)

[unreadable word]
Ezra Pound
20 April
'21

*news of the trial:* i.e., the trial over *Ulysses*. The case had been decided against the *LR* on 21 February 1921. See Letter 119n.

*My connection with the Dial:* In March 1920, EP had become foreign correspondent for *The Dial* (New York).

*Picabia:* French painter and poet, Francis Picabia (1879–1953). Picabia, who had been involved, both in Zurich and later in Paris, in the Dadaist revolt against artistic conventions, was, by the time of this letter, siding with André Breton against Dada in favor of Surrealism. EP's observation that Picabia "doesn't contribute to reviews" is not strictly accurate. In 1915, he had collaborated with Marcel Duchamp on the magazine *291*, and, in 1917, he had published his own review called *391*. Furthermore, in 1920, Picabia had published two issues of a review entitled *Cannibale*. Perhaps what EP meant was that Picabia was not eager to contribute to reviews over which he had no editorial control.

*on the job that Romains has never done anything with:* See Letter 120n.

*Cocteau:* well-known French writer Jean Cocteau (1891?–1963).

*his last book:* EP may be referring to either *Jésus-Christ Rastaquouère* or *Unique eunuque,* both of which Picabia had published in Paris in 1920. EP specifically mentions the former in the following letter.

**124. TLS–6.**  [22? April 1921]

⟨Private =
i.e. you can
read it to yr. friends
but its not for
print.

Hotel du Pas de Calais
59 rue des Saints Peres
PARIS VI.

---

  E.⟩
Dear Margaret:

  Your and jh's letter re/trial just here (Friday, April 22 or thereabouts, anyhow, Friday)[.] Just wrote you two days ago, re Picabia. I think you had better take him on, he is more active and executive, ⟨than Ar[a]gon⟩ and also a live animal.

  I also shall be here to prod him. I think one foreign editor is perhaps enough, at any rate London is dead to deadish. Eliot apparently giving way to the milieu.

  ///

  My connection with the Dial ends on July 1st. after which I have no means of support visible or predictable. A tepid review, but it will be written on Thayer's tomb stone that he paid my rent for 15 months and there are few of whom such virtue will be recorded.

  The L.R. accomplished more in six months than the Dial has in a year, en fait de literature.

  ///

As your ⟨letter⟩ accepts my ⟨earlier⟩ suggestion re/Aragon, and in view of the rest of your letter, I take it that I may tell Picabia on Sunday that he is practically their Foreign editor, and that he can blaze away when ready. I don't make much of his poems printed in 1918, but his "Jesus Christ Rastaquouere" hits, and hits all with a thud.

  In taking Picabia, I do NOT suggest that you take Dadaism and all "les petits dadas".

  Roughly speaking the men who matter, as far as my information at the moment goes, are Cocteau, Morand, Cros, Cendrars, Picabia (⟨P.⟩ more as anti-Socratic writer than as painter, though the pictures have in them things which dont show in reprods.[)]

In Painting: Picasso, and Marcoussis (unreproducable, looks like mere paper in photo).

[Constantin] Brancusi as sculptor.

I have on my desk Jean Hugo's translation of Cocteau's Cap de Bonne Esperance, it is 128 pages, but might be a damn good come back on Sumner etc. IF I can get it for nothing or for a small price. I cd. even spend a little time brushing up the thing IF you are ready to go it blind.

Mrs Alicia Frank (Kerr)
13 Charles St. ⟨N.Y.⟩

will receive a copy (uncorrected) sent off two days ago by Mme Picabia. You can confer with her. She has been told to place the mss in America.

I think Hugo's english extremely clean colour, but the poem needs pulling together a bit to make it a whole, and, chiefly a few erasures, cuts ⟨of pp.⟩ in preface which were o.k. in french WHEN written, but don't hold now, or don't apply to english version.

I will talk the matter over which [with] Hugo and Cocteau.

///
Will also try to place my say about the trial in the N.Y. Post, when I have next occasion to speak of "Ulysses". (god knows if I shall get the thing through . . .)
////
"Bibi" has I hear reached H.P. Chambers in safety.
///
I am tempted to offer you my name as Editor in partibus for one issue, just as manifest of the extent to which I regard Sumner and the N.Y. courts as the dung of ignoble animals.

But ⟨it is⟩, possibly better not to ⟨do so⟩ if I were to be there only for one issue, and Picabia is enough.

Point I never can seem to get you to take is that I have done more log rolling and attending to other people's affairs, Joyce, Lewis, Gaudier, etc. (dont regret it) But I am in my own small way, a writer myself, and as before stated. I shd. like (and wont in any case get) the chance of being considered as the author of my own poems rather than as ⟨literary politician, &⟩ a very active stage manager of rising talent. ⟨== at least during periods when I see nothing of 1st order in need of launching.⟩

It is bad enough to have to look forward to Christ knows what means of paying ⟨for⟩ precisely my (as jh puts it) cup of coffee and shoes (say rather re-soles).

Precisely! various french publications solicit my collaboration (gratis) others at 10 fr. per pages, "Lumur" of Prague desires the light in Czeco-Slovakkia, "Hermes" in Bilbao is charming and pays £2 / per article; the New Age £1/1; none of these things being sufficient to leave one extra time to work, and therefore being a waste of time and an interference with production. ⟨can't spend whole life jawing about other people's work⟩

Joyce has the sense, or grit, or sheer imbecility to DO nothing but his Ulysses and let the world go hang.

One thing to be said for Dial job is that it has let me have the last three months to myself; has permitted me a complete silence, first time in seven years, I shd. think,

///

Also why the HELL shd. I deform my bloomin thought by being reminded of the existence of the ang-sax race in any or either of its branches, both of which are probably superfluous.

If either or both nations were worth saving they wd. raise 1000 dollars per yr. for me, 2000 for Joyce, Eliot and Lewis (who have less practical sense or more expensive habits than I have.)

Let us put it that Picabia will be your foreign editor and that I will give a heave at the axle when my unspeakable temper (or whatever else you choose to call it) permits. ⟨⟨Send details re. available space, so we can plan thumping 1st Quarterly issue.⟩⟩

Do you honestly think that a serious writer OUGHT to be reminded of the United States ??

I put this question in all seriousness; architects, social reformers, liquor specialists, yes, but if it is one's job to erect the "oeuvre", the impeccable and immortal opus ???? Ought one to be distracted, ought one to be asked to address that perpetual mother's meeting, that chaste Chitaqua [sic]; that cradle of on-coming Amys [Lowell] ??? ⟨The Eunited, Eunu-chated States of America ??⟩

As a subject matter, it is all right; but as a receptacle for ones meditations, I ax you ????

What I will try to do (Note that Picabia is much better than Aragon) . . . (⟨I⟩ can't be bothered to go into details.) Voila, I will try to get a new line up of the best here (leaving aside Proust and the older men).

I will try to get, apart from Picabia, who asks nothing save that you go ahead hell fer leather.

Cocteau, Cros, Morand, Cendrars (who is now in Rome, and can't be counted on.) as a nucleus.

Leaving ⟨to⟩ the Dial, Anatole France, Thos Hardy, and the Yeats memories.

I shall also be able to send in up to date illustrations, as here I am not wholly dependent on Lewis for work of interest.

Better bring out first Quarterly number on July 4th to celebrate my release from the Dial.

yours.   EP.

⟨P. S.⟩

The reading of the foregoing somewhat exhilerates or exilerates or howthehellever you spell its, me.

I propose first number of Quarterly with this line up.

| Cocteau, | ourselves | illustrations of work by |
|---|---|---|
| Picabia, | W.c. Williams | Brancusi etc. |
| Cendrars | Marianne [Moore] | Picasso |
| Cros, | Mina [Loy] | Picabia |
| Morand. | | Lewis. |

Also possibly Gertrude Stein
        and any a.⟨1.⟩ stuff you can raise from Ben [Hecht], Sherwood [Anderson], or other top liners. ⟨and no idiots.⟩

I of course damblastit agree that there ought to be one decent magazine in this tepid and suffering planet.
        ⟨will think up a few [unreadable word] etc.⟩

*Friday, April 22 or thereabouts:* 22 April 1921 was a Friday.
*than Ar[a]gon:* Louis Aragon. See Letter 120n.
*Thayer:* Scofield Thayer, the editor of *The Dial.*
*his poems printed in 1918:* i.e., *Poèmes et dessins de la fille née sans mère,*
    *Rateliers platoniques: poème en deux chapitres,* and *L'Athlète des pompes*

*funèbres: poème en cinq chants,* all of which were published in 1918 in Lausanne (where Picabia was then living).

*Morand:* Paul Morand (1888–1976), a native of Russia, was a widely-traveled diplomat as well as a novelist. EP translated Morand's "Turkish Night" for the September 1921 issue of *The Dial* and, in the spring of 1923 when EP lost his post as Paris correspondent for that magazine and was replaced by Morand, the experience was a bitter one for EP. Morand's works include *Tendres Stocks* (1921), *Ouvert la nuit* (1922), *Fermé la nuit* (1923), *Lewis et Irène* (1924), and *Rien que la terre* (1926).

*Cendrars:* Swiss novelist and poet Blaise Cendrars (1887–1961), who was living in Paris at the time and who had been associated with the early Cubist movement.

*Cros:* EP is referring here to Guy Charles Cros, the son of the better known French poet Émile-Hortensius-Charles Cros (1842–88). The elder Cros, whose Bohemian life-style and sardonic wit made him after his death a figure of interest for the Surrealists, is remembered primarily for two collections of verse and prose poems: *Le Coffret de Santal* (1873; augmented edition, 1879) and *Le Collier de Griffes* (published posthumously by his son in 1908). Guy Charles Cros, himself a poet and translator of Scandinavian literature into French, published three collections of poetry: *Les fêtes quotidiennes* (1912); *Pastorales parisiennes* (1921), which EP reviewed in the July 1921 issue of *The Dial;* and *Avec des mots* (1927). The younger Cros was also a frequent contributor to the *Mercure de France.*

*Marcoussis:* Polish-French painter Louis Marcoussis (1878–1941).

*Jean Hugo's translation . . . . :* Jean Cocteau's poem "Le Cap de Bonne Espérance," translated by Jean Hugo into English under the title "The Cape of Good Hope," was published in the Autumn 1921 issue of the *LR* (43–96).

*"Bibi" has I hear . . . . :* A Dadaist "roman," "Bibi-la-Bibiste" by "Les Soeurs X" (EP?), was published in the September–December 1920 issue of the *LR* (24–29). The novel consists of five chapters ("Enfance," "Adolescence," "Amour," "Deception," and "Rideau"), each no more than several paragraphs long. EP's note to the novel points out that the "author (infant of I should think about eighteen, at any rate can't be over twenty) has managed to satirize french religious institutions, french scientific instruction, Brieux and three schools of modern art with remarkable economy of means. The book is a chef d'oeuvre, – it has all the virtues required by the academicians – absolute clarity, absolute form, beginning, middle, end."

"H. P. Chambers" is EP's London address, Holland Place Chambers.

*"Lumur" of Prague:* i.e., *Lumir: Literániho odboru Umělěcké besedy,* a journal published in Prague between 1851 and 1872 and, in its new series, 1873 to 1937. EP did not contribute to it.

*"Hermes" in Bilbao:* EP contributed three articles to the Spanish journal *Hermes: Revista del pais vasco* (published in Bilbao from January 1917 through July 1922): "El arte poético Inglaterra contemporánea" (August 1920: 447–50), "Some Notes on Francisco de Quevedo Villegas" (March 1921: 199–213), and a translation of an article originally printed in *The Dial,* "The Island of Paris: A Letter" (November 1920: 663–75).

*thumping 1st Quarterly issue:* i.e., the Autumn 1921 issue. In reality, the *LR* was already being issued on a quarterly basis. Only four issues were included in the seventh volume, but these are designated by months: May–June 1920, July–August 1920, September–December 1920, and January–March 1921. Following this last issue, the *LR* suspended publication until it was reorganized as a quarterly with seasonal designations.

**125. TLS–9.**   [29 April – 4 May 1921]

59 rue des Saints Peres
Paris VI.

Dear Margaret:

(Lets call it for brevity the "July number".) You can put me down on that number as "Collaborator", under you[r] own name and under that

FRANCIS PICABIA, foreign editor.

English Office,

"The Egoist" ⟨Publishing Co.⟩, 23 Adelphi Terrace House, Robert St. W.C. 2.

and

On sale with B.F. Newmayer 70 Charing Cross Rd. W.C.2.

///

Miss Weaver (Egoist) will send out announcement slips of the number when she sends out announcement of publication of Ulysses, so send her a packet when they are ready.

[*Crossout:* I have in hand 15 of the Brancusi] photos. ⟨vide further on.⟩ The Cocteau translation is coming up as if the [poem] had been written originally in english.

////

Have talked the year's issue over with Picabia.

Features offered are

BRANCUSI NUMBER (July) 20 illustrations, essay on the
                                sculptor by E.P.

| | |
|---|---|
| Picabia Number | ditto, essay on artist by E.P. |
| Lewis Number | == " " " " |
| Picasso number. | " " " " " " " " " " " |

Third number will contain a brief anthology of the best

french poetry published between 1918–1922
(continuation of my first
French anthology number)

////////

I think that is about enough out [of] me.  ⟨i.e. anthol.
4 essays on art
& aid of translator⟩
Picabia must have free hand and hell fer leather with the literary side of the thing.


Questions, have you any relations good or bad with Picabia's friends, Steiglitz, Mann Ray, Duchamp, or Arensberg ???? What about Carnevalli ???

&&&&&&&&&&&&&&&&&&&&&&&&&&&&&&&
[*Crossout:* Tuesday] ⟨Wed.⟩
N.B. that Brancusi (photos, posted today) has just refused "L amour de l'Art", L Esprit Nouveau and a "Lumur" of Prague, all of which noted art reviews want to pub. photos of his stuff.
////
So that you are free to consider this lot as both a scoop and an honour.
Re the Brancusi photos.
A. Please keep the order marked on back, print them as Plate I. Plate II. etc. without the concession of titles,
Keep the order so that ⟨in order that⟩ the references in my note on Branc. will make sense.


B. There are 22 photos here. It is worth while publishing them all, not as an expense but as an investment, this number shd. be a permanent bit of property for you and counts as my contribution to the upkeep of the L.R. for the year. I think it is perfectly solid investment for anybody's money. There are the photos, and the whole of the Cocteau "Cap," and supposedly other valuable items on the way.


⟨ _____
_____


my "most interesting" (incidentally about my only) note on sculpture since the Gaudier book⟩

B.1. In case you can't raise the cash necessary for production, I am writing Liveright suggesting that he publish the number. (That means you wd. sacrifice chance of profits, it is merely a measure to be resorted to if others fail.)

Still with the years programme I have outlined you might get a publisher IF you want one.

In case you can only do twenty reprods, cut out the last three, and GET from either Steiglitz or DeZayas the photo of the "PENGUINS" (of which my masterly (?) sketch appears on the back of the cardboard case holding the photos). ⟨Very important to have these penguins anyhow.⟩

The Dial will also have one photo of the bronze bust, which you might get from them if they aren't using it (, and add to your lot,) but this only in case you are using 24 or more photos.

DeZayas or Steiglitz has also a good photo of egg, of which Branc. hasn't print here.

That also might be added.

The more in [I] think of this number the more I think we shd. say nothing of the trial, save the announcement of publication of Ulysses, and recommendation that americans wishing to read it shd. winter abroad.

The first and most impressive and also most unexpected answer to the suppression wd. be simply bringing out a number such a damn sight better than any other magazine in or out of America.

(Then in the second quarterly number, you can let lose [loose] with ALL there is to say about the trial.)

I know this requires a hell of a lot of restraint, but in dealing with a herd of mad bulls, a little craft is not amiss.

Also I think the Branc. number shd. be free of lesser frivolity (,suppress for present Abel Sanders remarks on the spaghetti sculptor Bernard, and similar fireworks).

I think I can also "introduce" a new poet, (Considering he is trying to put on my "Noh" and that only in process of translation did I discover his vol. I don't imagine he will raise obstacles[.])

///

I can't over emphasize the importance of getting the best possible reprods. of the photos. and getting them as large as the page will hold. (Quarterly page, as you proposed, being larger than old L.R. pages.)

The ANSWER is to come out, at least in appearance three times as solid, complete new birth, full of guts.

In any case a "reply" to Judge Juggins is out of the question, one can't argue with a barn yard; anybody intelligent enough to understand one's objections to censorship by imbeciles, is capable of arriving at the conclusion without any remarks, and will be more interested in fresh outburst "somewhere else".

Answer being that Ulysses is being published, and that Parisians benefit, and that L.R. is going stronger than it ever was.

////

To avoid confusion: I am asking Picabia to write to his friends in N.Y.; but if they contribute mss. these are for Picabia's first number, not for "my" number[.] This leaves both Picabia and myself free from critical responsibilities in cases of stuff we don't know. He can't be committed to my selection of verse, nor can I to work by Mann Ray (whose stuff I dont sufficiently know).

Arensburg, Steiglitz etc. may be valuable allies, all I suggest is that you say (quite truly) that July number is arranged, that you will be delighted to have them in the autumn issue (exception made IF the July number isn't full, I take it it will be.).

Also, of course, with new solidity, one shd. try for regular appearance within at least a week of the dates announced.

Here endeth the letter of Ec[c]lesiastes[.]

[*The remainder of this letter is in longhand.*]

Wednesday 4th May.

Mary Butts just in, says again you have number at printers. = Can't be helped. =use it in bits = or chuck it = but this new Brancusi, Cocteau, Picabia, me. etc. number must be a clean break. = a wholly new burst of something the public don't expect. =otherwise all my push goes to waste. =

and Picabia's effort to get the number placed here in Paris will come to nothing.

=

I have told Mary we probably wont be able to use her novel =

Certainly we cant afford to be suppressed at any time during the coming year. =Cost of reprods. forbids. = also 5 times is enough. Let someone else come for'ard.

=if you want to do Mary's novel, it wd. mean 32 pages extra per number.= & corresponding increase in price. which wd. make it too high. The fighting minimum is 20 reprods. Preferably 24 or 25 for Brancusi. Possibly 16 for Lewis. Picasso. Picabia.——

---

and 96 pp. ⟨print.⟩ for July number
    64 "                    later " s.

---

Shd. keep to 20 reprods. 96pp. get s.v.p. printers estimate on that & figure possible sale price.

=

Reprods. must be really good. = Print merely as good as possible = AND. as it is a Quarterly it will save heartburn to send me a set of proofs. = this certainly necessary in case of Cocteau trans. & the stuff to be done in french. = Quarterly issue & peace time postal service makes this possible.

People here—[*crossout:* even less than people in London—will] wont put up with printers errors. — for the sake of Christ, Bacchus & the Virgin spare me that wear & tear.

yours<br>E.P.

*the "July number":* i.e., the Autumn 1921 number.

*publication of Ulysses:* Following the court's unfavorable decision regarding the *LR*'s publication of *Ulysses,* American publisher B. W. Huebsch decided he could not publish the work in book form, and Boni and Liveright also lost interest in publishing it. When Joyce explained the situation to Sylvia Beach at her Paris bookstore Shakespeare and Company, Beach asked if she could bring out *Ulysses.* Joyce was pleased with her offer and it was agreed between them that she would publish an edition of 1,000 copies, to be sold as far as possible by advance subscription. When she heard of the plan, Harriet Weaver in London gave her immediate support and promised to send Beach the names of people and shops in England that had shown interest in *Ulysses.* In addition, Weaver promised an English edition which the Egoist Press would bring out (using the plates from the first edition) and sent Joyce £200 as advance royalties. The Autumn 1921 issue of the *LR* carried the subscription announcement of Miss Beach's edition of the novel.

*The Cocteau translation:* i.e., Jean Hugo's English translation of Cocteau's "Le Cap de Bonne Espérance."

*Steiglitz:* American photographer Alfred Stieglitz (1864–1946), proprietor of the Camera Work (or Photo Secession) Gallery (later renamed "291") at 291 Fifth Avenue, New York. During the first decade of the twentieth century, Stieglitz's gallery had become a meeting place for European and American artists, and Stieglitz himself had participated in the organizing of the Armory Show of February–March 1913. Between 1915 and 1916, Stieglitz, with the aid of Francis Picabia, who was then in New York, had published twelve issues of a journal named *291*.

*Mann Ray:* Man Ray (1890–1976), well-known American Dadaist artist and photographer.

*Duchamp:* Marcel Duchamp (1887–1968). A native of France, Duchamp had settled in New York in 1915 and there, along with Man Ray and Picabia, became one of the founders of the New York Dada group.

*Arensberg:* Walter Conrad Arensberg (1878–1954), American author, poet, and art collector. In 1917, Arensberg had contributed a piece of automatic writing titled "Partie d'échecs entre Picabia et Roché" to Picabia's journal *391*. By this time, he had also published two collections of verse: *Poems* (1914) and *Idols* (1916).

*Carnevalli:* Emanuel Carnevali (1897–1940?), Italian-American prose writer, poet, and translator. Having emigrated from Italy, Carnevali served for a time as an editor on the staff of *Poetry* until his health forced him to resign. After his death, Kay Boyle collected his personal writings and published them as his *Autobiography* (1967). The *LR* had published a number of Carnevali's pieces between 1919 and 1920.

*"L amour de l'Art":* L'Amour de l'art* was a Parisian art journal which began publication in May 1920.

*L Esprit Nouveau:* L'Esprit Nouveau* was published in Paris from October 1920 through January 1925, edited for a time by Dadaist poet Paul Dermée.

*"Lumur" of Prague:* See Letter 124n.

*my "most interesting" . . . note on sculpture:* i.e., "Brancusi" *LR* (Autumn 1921): 3–7.

*the Gaudier book:* i.e., EP's *Gaudier-Brzeska: A Memoir.*

*DeZayas:* Mexican caricaturist and art theorist Marius de Zayas, a close associate of Alfred Stieglitz at 291.

*the "PENGUINS":* Brancusi's sculpture was entitled "Trois Pingouins" and is now a part of the Louise and Walter Arensberg Collection of the Philadelphia Museum of Art. The *LR* included a photo of this sculpture as Plate 15.

*we shd. say nothing of the trial:* Besides the *Ulysses* subscription announcement, the editors mentioned the *Ulysses* affair just twice: a statement on the second page read, "As PROTEST against the suppression of the Little Review containing various instalments of the 'Ulysses' of JAMES JOYCE, the following artists and writers of international reputation are collaborating in the autumn number of the Little Review: BRANCUSI, JEAN COCTEAU, JEAN HUGO, GUY CHARLES CROS, PAUL MORAND, FRANCIS PICABIA, EZRA POUND"; and at the end of the magazine, Jane Heap commented, "Before we could revive from our trial for Joyce's 'Ulysses' it was announced for publication in book form. We limp from the field" (112).

*with ALL there is to say about the trial:* EP had apparently not seen the January–March 1921 issue, as MCA had already "let loose" on the subject: see " 'Ulysses' in Court" (22–25).

*Abel Sanders remarks . . . Bernard:* Under the title "Sculpshure," "Abel Sanders" (EP's pseudonym) had already published his remarks on George C. Barnard in the January–March 1921 issue (47).

*a "reply" to Judge Juggins:* EP's sarcasm directed at the judges who presided at the *Ulysses* trial.

*Mary Butts:* English novelist (1892–1937). The serialization of Butts's novel *Ashe of Rings* had already begun in the January–March 1921 issue, but was dropped following the installments appearing in the Autumn 1921 number.

*fighting minimum is 20 reprods.:* The *LR* printed twenty-four plates.

**126. TLS–2.**   Plus Enclosure of EP's "Historical Survey." [21 May 1921]

⟨21 May⟩
59 rue des Saints Peres

Dear Jane an' Margaret

[John] Quinn will never forgive me for takin' up with you ⟨once more again⟩, and Marianne Moore is evidently an ass (don't count on any appui from that petticoat).

Morand has as you see, stumped up[.] I expect the Cocteau trans. clean typescript by Monday.

PLEASE KEEP the arrangement of print in the Morand, and the border lines of his Carte Postale. I enclose Pansaers ⟨also follow type⟩. Probably will include some Iwan Goll in the bosche languidge.

As Mary's novel has been commenced I suppose we'd better continue it, as rapidly as circumstances permit. Only the Cocteau must go in whole.

I think we can get some (at least moral) support for being the ONE place where a poem of "some length" can appear.

I want the Ad. of Joyce printed. Also, preferably fac simile as large, ⟨of Irish Times adv.⟩ [*crossout:* or better still, slightly larger of the Dublin Irish Times a̅d̅. .] No it is in large type, print it same size. It is the largest tribute to Joyce we have yet had. i.e. "popular tribute".

　　　　Irish Times for 4th May 1921.

And fer Gordsake, as we are a quarterly, do try to send me proofs, at least of french and foreign stuff, AND certainly of the Cocteau.

I enclose also my own declaration of independence ⟨"Historical Survey"⟩. It is important ⟨for me⟩ that this appear soon. If you aren't sure of getting it into the July number, send it back, s.v.p. at once, and I'll try it on Alfred [Orage]. ⟨It can very well go in small print.⟩

　　　　　　　　(I perhaps ought to anyhow. ; but the lone raft has charms.)

I think M.'s article on the trial DAMN good. I suspect the Sanders family of having a familiar alias. (If it aint so, dew tell. Have arrived at the point where gleam of sense in ANY uncharted Emmy seems noteworthy.)

Old Ford has done me proud in "Thus to Revisit"[.]

I think the Pansaers GOOD. He is a discovery of Picabias. Picabia has had a damn bad attack of near-pneumonia, but if he don't die I think we shall have his copy.

I am ruined if the July number aint a KORKER. And in anny case I have no prospects. There is no possibility of my paying my board unless I get a grant from the Nihon o̳f̳ Korea or the Boowahl of Nigonapuri. Son fritto, old bean, or rather old pod, since there are two blossoms on your ascending tendril.

Already more than enough subs. for "Ulysses" in Paris alone to pay for printing, and J.J. ⟨presumably⟩ assured a fat profit.

*Marianne Moore is evidently an ass:* In April 1921, EP had written to Moore asking for her help in providing a "proper list of new books of LITERARY interest" for the reorganized *LR* and, possibly, contributing some of her own verse to its pages (see Letter 179, Paige, 167–68). Moore, apparently, declined to help.

*Morand:* Four poems by Paul Morand were published in the Autumn 1921 issue: "Francisque fait la bulbate," "Spectacle effrayant," "Esprit d'enterprise [*sic*]," and "Carte postale express [*sic*]," this last printed as though it were a post card (20–23).

*Pansaers:* Belgian poet Clement Pansaers (1885–1922), whose "Bruxelles-Berlin Via Rotterdam" was published in the Autumn 1921 number (38).

*Iwan Goll:* pseudonym of novelist, poet, dramatist, and critic Isaac Lang (1891–1950). He provided the first German translation of *Ulysses* (1927). Goll's poem "Ein Gesang" was published in the Autumn 1921 issue (8–11).

*Irish Times adv.:* not printed in the *LR*.

*"Historical Survey":* EP's essay was published in the Autumn 1921 issue (39–42) and later reprinted as part of *Ezra Pound and the Visual Arts* (1980).

*M.'s article on the trial:* i.e., " 'Ulysses' in Court" in the January–March 1921 issue (22–25), MCA provided a summary of the trial along with her own reactions to the event ("the only farce I ever participated in with any pleasure").

*the Sanders family:* EP's reference is to an article by Emmy V. Sanders entitled "Apropos Art and Its Trials Legal and Spiritual" in the January–March 1921 number (40, 42–43). ("Abel Sanders" is, of course, one of EP's pseudonyms.) The article takes to task the "cultured philistine" who persists in making judgments about (and persecuting) art he doesn't understand. The only art he pronounces to be good is that which has been tamed, emasculated, or made safe through museum showings and the explanations of professors, art which is "of a date anterior to 1900."

*Old Ford . . . :* In "Mr. Pound, Mr. Flint, Some Imagists or Cubists, and the Poetic Vernacular," a chapter in his *Thus to Revisit* (1921; rpt. 1966), Ford has this to say about EP:

> For myself, I have always wished that I possessed some of the immense, human erudition of Mr. Pound. For the matter of that I have long, gradually, come to wish that I could put things so well—for then I could put things so much better. For Mr. Pound is a very great poet; but he approaches prose with the attack of a writer of dramatic fiction. He renders, that is to say, rather than commenting—and the business of Criticism being comment this gives to his critical works an atmosphere of restlessness. So that his critical writings are much more craftsman's notes than the balanced or the beautiful prose of the Born Critic and they are more to be appreciated by—they will be more useful to—the intelligent Craftsman than the Uninstructed Reader, however intelligent he may be. Compared with the tender, rather muted and persuasive prose of Mr. Flint, Mr. Pound's harsh aphorisms are like sharp splinters of granite struck off by a careless but violent chisel. (167)

**127. TLS–1.**    [31 May 1921]

⟨31 May⟩                                          59 rue des Sts Peres
                                                  Paris VI.

Dear MargaretanJane
                    Here is Cocteau's Cap de Bonne Esperance.
NOTE.
        In the revision pages 3 - 4 of introd have been cut. Thus it runs 1 2-5
etc., I have left the original numberings to save trouble.
                Roughly one shd. keep spacings as near as possible in present
proportion, trying to do two pages of type-script to one of L.R.
                (the little slips pasted on full pages are also marked as 11a.
in case they get unstuck.)

NOW IN THE NAME of all the Christs that have ever been, DEW for
Jheezus sake send me proofs. It dont matter a kuss whether a quarterly
appears in July or Aug., but it does matter, when one is getting ones mss.
free, to keep the authors interested and more satisfied than the London
gang used to be.

Sherwood Anderson is here, and promises something for coming year.

Must get whole of Cape of Good Hope, and ALL the Brancusi into summer number.

[Mary] Butts['] novel [*Ashe of Rings*] can be held over, or one can print
two or three pages of it.

F[rank]. Rummel painter brother of Walter R. has done some poems that
I think will do for the 2nd. number.
                        ///
I enclose also our ole friend Abel Sanderes [*sic*]. Keep his Dada in small-
est print, but end up as on typescript.

⟨Also keep his @¼ etc.
        line intact.⟩                                          E.P.

*Walter R.:* See Letter 48n.

                The poems of Abel Sanders
To Bill Williams and Else von Johann Wolfgang Loringhoven y
                        Fulano

Godsway bugwash
Bill's way backwash
FreytagElse ¾ arf an'arf
Billy⟨Sunday⟩ one harf Kaiser Bill one harf
            Elseharf Suntag, Billsharf Freitag
Brot wit thranen, con plaisir ou con patate    pomodoro

Bill dago resisting U.SAgo, Else ditto on the verb basis ⟨yunker⟩/, plus
Kaiser Bill reading ⟨to goddarnd stupid wife anbrats⟩ works of simple
domestic piety in Bleibtreu coner of Hockhoff's besitzendeecke before the
bottom fell out. Plus a little ⟨boiled⟩ Neitzsch on the sabath. Potsdam,
potsdorf potz gek und keine ende. Bad case, bad as fake southern gentleman tells you everymorn that he is gentleman, and that he is not black.
Chinesemandarinorlaundryman takes forgranted youwillsee he is not
BookerTWashington.
            :::::::

Poem No. 2.
   Able Abel
Mounts dernier bateau
@¼%&:/7½    @¾) (&7;¼% @&%&&&&¼ ¼ ¼ ¼ @¼%
            ;34%3
            [The following turned on its side.]
                        dada
                        deada
                        what is deader
                                    than dada

**128. TLS–2.**  Incomplete item: Page two of two-page letter. [January–
March 1922]

2.
I hope Picabia will get something from DE MASSOT.

As for L.R. ad. you might try the following. Filling in blanks that I cant,
not having files here.
////
WHAT THE LITTLE REVIEW

has done

It has printed all of ⟨JAMES JOYCE'S⟩ "Ulysses" that the U.S. posterior ⟨(we mean postal)⟩ authorities wd. permit.

It has printed FORD MADOX HUEFFER'S "Men and Women".

It has printed nearly all of the critical papers included in EZRA POUND'S "Instigations".

It has printed                    etc. by Sherwood Anderson . . . . . . . etc. by Wyndham Lewis; 30% of T.S. Eliot's poems; Poems, stories, plays by W.B. Yeats, Ben Hecht, May Sinclair, Djuna Barnes, Lady Gregory, John Rodker, ⟨W.C.W.⟩ etc.

⟨not too many more
names.   if there are too many
they won't be [read?]⟩

It has published the only single group of 24 reproductions of BRANCUSI'S sculpture, . . .

What other American publication old or new has done as much in equal or double for quintuple the number of pages? IS THE LITTLE REVIEW contributing to the mental upkeep of Columbia Jem of the Ocean?

yours
E.

*DE MASSOT:* French Surrealist Pierre de Massot, author of *De Mallarmé à 391* (1922). De Massot contributed three selections to the *LR:* "Conte pour la Comtesse de Noailles," (Autumn 1922: 24), "Theatre and Music-Hall" (Autumn–Winter 1923–24: 3–6), and "Soirée de Paris" (Autumn 1924–Winter 1925: 24–27).

*Filling in the blanks* . . . *:* The Spring 1922 *LR* ended with this announcement (65). MCA filled in the blanks as follows:

it has printed
the bulk of Sherwood Anderson's short stories
it has printed
"The Ideal Giant," "Cantleman's Spring Mate," etc.
Also reproductions of the work of Wyndham Lewis.
it has printed
30% of T. S. Eliot's poems; poems, stories, plays by W. B. Yeats; Ben Hecht, Emanuel Carnevali, W. C. Williams, Djuna Barnes, Dorothy Richardson, Aldous Huxley, Arthur Waley, John Rodker, Lady Gregory, Mary Butts, Jean Cocteau, Louis Aragon, P. Soupault, Francis Picabia

**129. TLS–1.**  [January–April 1922]

⟨address 70 bis rue Notre Dame des Champs
Paris VIe⟩

Dear M.

The Christian era came to an end at midnight of Oct 29-30.

I have had this new calendar lying round ever since, but my private life prevented my getting it off. I also intended manifesto. But think it better to print the simple statement, herein enclosed.

Print the calendar as frontispiece, also as back cover OR even better on separate semi-cardboard inset. With lower label LITTLE REVIEW CALENDAR. People will keep a calendar in sight for 12 months. And you shd. issue the new calendar with each autumn number hence forth.

We've had enough political and religious time divisions.

Give 'em the plain fact both barrels. I'm not enclosing ANY explanations even to you. That leaves you in position to make the statement, and no fuss about arguing. "The news has reached you." That's ALL.

Picabia wanted the announcement made here, but I crossed the channel on the day arranged for publication. U.S. correspondent also desirous for article on the subject. But I think statement shd. be made first in the L.R.

Note the designatio[n] of the age. p.s.U. y basta.
⟨only that isn't all of it.⟩        E.
⟨more depends on this than you might think. I will explain sometime. =
(you never do but still——)⟩


*midnight of Oct 29–30:* The significance of this date is that on 29 October 1921 James Joyce announced that he had completed *Ulysses* (see Ellmann 519). The "p. s. U." is most likely "post scriptum *Ulysses.*"
*this new calendar:* The first year of the calendar appeared on page two of the Spring 1922 issue and the following explanation was printed on page forty:

The Christian era came definitely to an END at midnight of the 29–30 of October (1921) old style.
There followed the Feast of Zagreus, and a Feast of PAN counted as of no era; the new year thus beginning on 1st November (old style), now HEPHAISTOS.
The new months replacing the old months: of cold months HEPHAISTOS (for November), and then in the following order ZEUS, SATURN, HERMES, MARS, PHOEBUS APOLLO; and the warm months; KUPRIS, JUNO,

ATHENE, HESTIA, ARTEMIS, and DEMETER, the male months being also under ISIS, and the female months, two by two, under PAN, POSEIDON and BACCHUS.

The following feasts are instituted, to ZAGREUS on the 30th Demeter; to PAN on the 31st Demeter; Feast of Figures on the 14th Hermes; Feast of Political Buncomb, ancient feast of fools or feast of the ass, Mort de Caesar, Jules, 15th Mars; PRIAPUS, 1st Kupris; EPITHALAMIUM, ancient Corpus Domini, 15th Juno; FAUNUS 6th Artemis; AUSTER and APELIOTA 14th Artemis.

The year turns upon HORUS.

---

**130. AC–1.**   On postcard postmarked: Siena/ 15.4.22 25. Addressed: Miss Margaret Anderson/ Little Review/ 27 W. 8th Street/ New York./ Stati Uniti America. [14 April 1922]

Siena.                                                    April 14 1922.

Dear Miss Anderson

   I have sent you the photos of Ezra's death-mask.
   There is nothing more to be said.

   Yours sincerely
      D. Pound.

The plaster mould of the features was taken by Mrs. [Nancy Cox] McCormack.

*photos of Ezra's death-mask:* Several photos purporting to be of EP's death mask were sent to the *LR* office. The *LR* did not publish the photos and the only mention of them in the Spring 1922 issue appeared in one of Jane Heap's comments: "Several weeks ago we received a note from Mrs. Ezra Pound (in Rodker's handwriting) announcing Ezra's death; also some phoney death masks. Whatever the hoax (?) as far as we are concerned Ezra will have to be satisfied to go on living" (60). EP was irritated with the editors for not publishing the photos (see Letter 134), and he expressed this irritation in a letter to Wyndham Lewis dated 14 July 1922: "They [MCA and Jane Heap] have bungled my death mask, sheer stupidity. I told 'em something was coming, and they hadn't sense enough to reprod. the documents. You have to guide 'em hand an foot" (Letter 110, *Pound/Lewis* 133).

**131. ALS–2.**    [? April 1922]

> address: Paris.
> 70 bis N.D. de C.

That's all very well but I'm not the apostle Paul. (Amy [Lowell] may be.).

I don't propose to die daily. I died once to satisfy the consolidated hecklery [?] assn.    that's enough.

Neither am I a yearly Adonis — tell the Ebullient Draper. That if she wants beauty she must apply to Ed. Pinaud.

also has she hit any of her toff friends for the Eliot (Bel Esprit) foundation. — or is she just another enthusiast ???

Re. dth masks. print a.b.d. [*crossout:* or procure the lovely people from W]
> "Start something" — morbus

americanus.
> Why not finish something. i.e.

complete something.
> or both.

Where are your poussins. where are the downy chicks. aint the little prairie flower growing wilder anny more ??

> What

about art in the middle south

=

If you have printed a number already and want (for any unfathomable reason) me to see it before May you'll have to send it to this address. as all printed matter is held for me in Paris. — Thus allowing one to breathe.

> ⟨Hotel Mignon.
> Rapallo
> Italy⟩

Who is Mr. Munson? (G.B.)

What about arboriculture. ? pruning the tree, in order that some of the pomegranites may come to maturity.

No. dont print calendar in middle of year. — Probably print the year II in autumn ==

you might note that Italy put up SOME celebration
on what used to be Oct. 31 == just to emphasize the feast as announced.

                          ETC
                          EP.

*the Ebullient Draper:* New York hostess, Muriel Gurdon Draper (1886–1952).
EP's comment in this letter may have been prompted by two of Draper's
poems which were printed in the Spring 1922 *LR:* "Loose Leaf Products"
and "America" (36–37). Ed Pinaud was a manufacturer of beauty products
and toiletries based in New York.

*Eliot (Bel Esprit) foundation:* During the spring of 1922, EP had worked out a
plan to allow T. S. Eliot to leave his job at Lloyds Bank in London and devote
all his time to his writing. The scheme called for locating thirty donors who
would guarantee Eliot £10 per year for life or for as long as he would need
assistance. Natalie Barney named the plan "Bel Esprit" and EP had circulars
printed to announce it. When Eliot refused to take the money, however, the
scheme collapsed. (See Stock 244–46).

*Mr. Munson (G. B.):* American critic Gorham Bert Munson (1896–1969). In
1922 Munson founded a review called *Secession,* which he edited for two
years with the aid of Matthew Josephson and Kenneth Burke.

**132. TLS–1.**   [April–May 1922]

                    70 bis rue Notre Dame des Champs
                                Paris VI

Dear M:

        Thanks for photos. Lewis says he is about to remit. Abel makes
herewith his usual bright contribution.

                                        yours
                    ABEL'S CONTRIBUTION
French School of Poesy, synthèse
                    En versant ces fleurs dans ce vin,
                    J'ai pense au veau marin.
        ⟨sic pensé⟩
WESTERN school of poesy, synthèse
                    Say, bo ! I heard that fourty-niner.
                    Say, Bo; I've heard erbout that Perarie Schooner!
                                SAY, BO !!

—'—'—'—'

⟨Abel Sanders⟩

paper dont hold ink, get acute accents on pense and grave accents on syn-
these.

*ABEL'S CONTRIBUTION:* This was published in the Spring 1922 issue (33).

**133. TLS–1.**   [April–May 1922]

70 bis, Notre Dame des Champs

Paris VI. e

Chere M and jh

Lewis ⟨writes that he⟩ will go to work and arrange a top-
notch number IF you will assure him that you mean business, and have the
cash to print the number.

I have written a certain number of letters stirring up
thing[s]. BUT, both you and he OUGHT to be able to get on without
clutching at my coat tails. It is just as simple for you to write to each other
as to write to me.

his address is

Lee Studio,

Adam and Eve Mews
Kensington High St. London W.8.

E

*I have written a certain number of letters . . . . :* See Letters 106, 107, and 110
(27 April 1921, Autumn 1921, and 14 July 1922) in *Pound/Lewis* (127–29,
131–33). As late as November of 1922, EP was still encouraging Lewis to
organize his selections for the proposed Lewis Number (see Letters 113 and
114—7 November and 11 November—in *Pound/Lewis*). Lewis never did so.

**134. TLS–1.**  [13 July 1922]

13 th Athene,
Annus Primus
70 bis, rue N.D. des C.

Really you are IMPOSSIBLE.

In response to repeated requests; requests for death, for crucifixion etc. etc. etc. etc. I finally die.

Why the hell shouldn't I vary the bowling, and give this small drop of liquid pleasure to a long parched, long exasperated public.

Why the hell shd.n't I die? what is, after all so incredible in my my [*sic*] coming to the fated end of all human perturbations? The comfortable cool of the sepulchre.

Also you have no respect for precedent. Look at the date of the letter (not this but D's [Dorothy Pound's])

from Siena

yours
Ezra

*I finally die:* See Letter 130. EP had, apparently, just received the Spring 1922 issue of the *LR* and had discovered the death-mask photos were not included. *date of the letter:* The card had been dated 14 April 1922, which was Good Friday.

**135. TLS–1.**  [7 November 1922]

7 Hephaistos
AN II
responsum est.

Chere jh:

My actions inactions etc. are as you know governed always by personal rage, spite, envy, malice, vainglorious contentiousness ⟨offness, onness, etc.⟩ etc. Never has it occurred to me to attend to my own affairs: i.e. to spend my time on my own job namely writing (Poetry, or something of that sort.)

However said defects of character have led me at last to cut AHT, (out) critical work, and write my own stuff. Personally and impersonally interruptors may got [go] to jhell [*sic*].

ALSO I thought [Wyndham] Lewis HAD sent you stuff for his number. If he hasn't sent enough, write to him for more.

When the number is actually ready I will try to send a brief Decalogue or Heptalog or some other Divine order to fall flat ye angels, archangels, Boobs, Mencks, etc.

In the meantime I am trying to start a symposium on W.L., inviting Wadsworth, Kreymborg, and Mathers to contribute.

You might call in a few other lights to write crits of W.L.'s books.

Let me know when the thing is ready, actually on the verge on [of] going to press.

E.

Further suggestions for future. (i.e. after the Lewis no. and proposed miscellaneous number.)
1. Marcel Duchamp number. IF you can get Duchamp to collaborate.
2. I still think a good group of [Charles] Demuths stuff ought to be collected. Perhaps a Demuth number.
   or at least group of ten, in mixed number.
3. Hueffer number, as thorough as my Henry James. weeding out his real stuff from the rest.
4.        Symposium on my death, and earlier actions.

I can't be bothered to rowt out the stuff for Picasso number. The Duchamp wd. do just as well, and has been less done.

The Duchamp and Demuth wd. be N.Y., possible adv. of not always IMporting stuff from abroad.

Also, [John] Storrs will be on the spot.

*I thought Lewis HAD sent you stuff:* EP's contention is corroborated by a letter he wrote to Lewis, also dated 7 November 1922 (Letter 113, *Pound/Lewis* 135): "Little Review pulluling to me about stuff for the W. L. number. Didn't you say you had sent them the photos? They seem ready for outburst. You might send em any instructions you think of."

*a symposium on W. L.:* EP's proposed Wyndham Lewis symposium involving
Edward Wadsworth, Alfred Kreymborg, and Edward Powys Mathers was
never put together.

*when the thing is ready:* The Winter 1922 number was not issued until spring
1923. The following note is included in the number: "The Post Office regulations make it impossible to call this number anything but Winter 1922.
Wyndham Lewis number [which had been announced in the previous issue]
postponed owing to delays on part of collaborators."

*Further suggestions:* MCA and Jane Heap followed none of these suggestions.

*Storrs:* See Letter 137.

---

**136. TLS–1.**   [28 December 1922]

28 Dec.

70 bis, N.D. de Champs

Paris VI.

Dear M:

Re miscellany number, to follow (or precede Lewis number) I enclose.

1. Three damnd interesting designs by Christian (want originals
back, with care, s.v.p.). Can you reprod the coloured one in colour[?] If
not state in letter press what the colours are.

2. Prose mss. by Christian, to be used IF you have careful proof-
reader; or translated IF you have good translator[.]

3. Two circulars to be reproduced, as you reproduced the Larionov
announcement. in Picabia number. "The news from Russia".

This series to be entitled

L'histoire morale contemporaine

4. "Re/Tarr"

quot from Paris N.Y. Herald

to be reprinted.

The priere pour la bonne prosse [presse] is a Gem.

yours

E.

*Christian:* pseudonym of French artist Georges Herbiet. A friend of Francis
   Picabia, Herbiet lived in St. Raphael and ran a bookstore there named Au
   Bel Exemplaire. One of the three designs EP refers to was included in the
   Winter 1922 issue along with a translation of Herbiet's story "In the Minor
   Key of an Epoch" (29–34).
*Two circulars:* Not included in the number.
*the Larionov announcement:* A reproduction of a Dadaist poster announcing a
   soirée to be held on behalf of Futurist painter Mikhail Larionov was included
   in the Spring 1922 issue (between pages 44 and 45). The note below the
   poster read: "Entitled 'The News from Russia' or 'We wonder what' Messrs.
   Kreymborg and Santayana 'think about it.' "
*"Re/ Tarr":* Not included in the number.
*priere pour la bonne prosse:* Never printed. See Letter 140.


**137. TLS–4.**   [29 December 1922]

70 bis, N.D. des C.

Paris VI e.

Dear M:

   Saw [John] Storrs yesterday. he is sending you ten or a dozen good
photos.

   I suggest you write to [Wyndham] Lewis, and that if he dont answer,
saying WHEN he will have this material ready[.]

                    THEN it seems to me you might as well go
ahead and do a miscellany number. With the Storrs photos. and the Rummel, impressions of Norway.

   Storrs gets to N.Y. in Feb. for a show, and a number of the L.R.
containing twelve reprods of his work, and possibly a crit. by JH. [Jane
Heap] cd. be sold at show.

Marcel Duchamp is in N.Y. ; he ought to collaborate, and if you cd. get
him interested he wd. probably draw in stuff from Man Ray (who is
here, but says publicity is no damn use). (neither it is), and others.

Any rate, Duchamp is intelligent and in touch with things.

Storrs more interesting as liaison between sculpture and architecture (vide
my next Dial letter, presumably Jan.), than for sheer sculptural sense.

Also he has, or says he has PASSED through the rodin and mestrovic phases. The Rodin (i mean his Rodin phase) was rather good. The mestrovic phase was muck. Mestrovic being muck. At present there is architectural interest. AND the photos I picked out yesterday happen to be interesting. (possibly more interesting than the original works.) Any how rather better to reproduce than were the larger part of the Picabia reprods. ⟨have not chosen photos of Mes. phase. but he may put some of it in his show.⟩

There is a german publication called GENIUS, that la baronne might review. If you can find a copy in N.Y. also the Quertschnitt [Querschnitt].

A real Lewis number wd. be more important. BUT if he dont get the stuff to you, SOON, bloody soon, Lewis number can wait till next time. Seems about time something occurred.

Brancusi wd. like a couple of copies of his number if you have them.
Constantin Brancusi, 8 Impasse Ronsin, rue Vaugirard
Paris XV.
Intelligent reviews of my last work, of Eliots Waste Land, and even of that olde classicke Ulysses wd. be suitable features for an up to date annual. However I have dwelt on this point before without much response.

A sottisier of the imbecilities uttered re/Ulysses wd. also employ some-one's spare time. Vide suprout, Noyes, Murry, the pink un, and Shane leslie in the Quarterly Review.

There ought to be some young talent left in america.

I wonder has jh any news of a damsel that used to be called Charlotte Teller, before she married a man named Hirsch (that was 'fo de woh), possibly sunk on the Lusitania; if not the family shd. have concentrated a reasonable amt. of intelligence.

There is also a pianist (whose book on music I do not approve of) K.R. Heyman (general address The Judson, 53 Washington Sq.) who might be of some use to the L.R. (not as a critic of literature.)

Duchamp wd. be the most valuable collaborator you cd. get IF you can get him[.]

Monroe Wheeler, 11 Kaiserplatz, Bonn, Germany, wd. probably send you german chronique, if you wrote to him saying I had suggested it. . You might even incorporate his monthly magazine. as the Eng. Rev. has incorporated Theatrecraft; saying that you assume no responsibility for its editorial judgement. .

Virgil Geddes, whom I know nothing of, and who writes atrociously, is the only sprout in U.S. who appears to have any good will toward me personally. I mention this because good will is a necessary ingredient in the make up of les jeunes who are ready to write unpaid criticism.

The Dial perhaps gives ample scope to les jeunes who want [to] cover ignorance by TREmendous, I might say Thrmenjus, smartness.

Geddes might do you a review of Waste Land. Or he might do a long article on J.J.[James Joyce,] Eliot and yrs. truly. There are several articles waiting for the analyst. Either on three moderns, or on T.S.E. and myself contrasted. (with dates)

One ought to distinguish between Carnevalli's [Emanuel Carnevali's] hate of [*crossout:* me, or rather] of my work, which is brisk, lively, real, and a puling idiot like E[dmund]. Wilson who is merely ignorant (of things which he perhaps cdnt. be expected to know.)

There ought to be some literate person to discuss the Propertius, either as poetry or as a contribution to critical understanding of the original latin.

Perhaps Bill Wms. [William Carlos Williams] wd. take a shot at a critical essay, on any of the three subjects. He seems cheered at prospect of 3 Mts. edtn.

ETC.

E.P.

I think you've been wrong not to take up with McAlmon, NOT as critic or poet, but as prosateur. Raw, raw, raw, but chance of something coming.

⟨29 Dec 1922⟩

Of course he was even rawer when you saw him. and less to be seen.

*Storrs:* American sculptor John Storrs (1885–1956). Storrs, who spent most of his adult life in France, had studied with Rodin from 1912 until Rodin's death in 1917. But by 1917, Storrs was abandoning traditional representation for modernist forms. The Winter 1922 *LR* published five photos of Storrs's sculpture.

*Rummel, impressions of Norway:* These were never published in the *LR.*

*my next Dial letter:* i.e., "Paris Letter, December 1922," *The Dial* (January 1923): 85–90. In the letter, EP maintains that "painting ought to be part of architecture," but he laments the fact that "there is no place for sculpture or painting in modern life." As a consequence, "painters make innumerable scraps of paper. . . . The stuff is vendible or non-vendible[;] it is scraps, knick-knacks, part of the disease that gives us museums instead of temples, curiosity shops instead of such rooms as the hall of the Palazzo Pubblico in Siena or the Sala di Notari in Perugia." Citing the Italian architect and painter Alberti, EP suggests that "the architect gets his *idea* from the painter, that the painter stirs the desire for beautiful building." But making beautiful buildings poses economic problems, EP concedes; but "if art schools set their infant sculptors to making columns instead of drawing-room ornaments" and if "a number of schools could agree on a uniform size or several sizes of columns, there would be a supply available, which could be sold at a possible commercial price; it would bring in something to the school or to the student instead of the usual nothing; and the town would have or could have a few agreeable facades."

*Mestrovic:* Yugoslavian sculptor Ivan Mestrovic (1883–1962), known primarily for his public monuments.

*GENIUS:* i.e., *Genius: Zeitschrift für Werdende und alte Kunst,* three numbers of which were published in Leipzig from 1919 through 1921.

*la baronne:* One of MCA and Jane Heap's friends, Baroness Else (Elsa) von Freytag (Freitag) Loringhoven, whose bizarre behavior and poetry evidently attracted the two editors. Her writing—poetry and prose—appeared frequently in the *LR.*

*Quertschnitt:* i.e., *Der Querschnitt,* published in Berlin from 1921 through 1936. EP contributed three articles to the magazine: "Le Prix Nobel" (in English with a German translation provided), Spring 1924: 41–44; "Law and the Merchant of Venice," Autumn 1924: 237–38; and "Definitions, etc.," January 1925: 54.

*my last work:* EP is referring either to his *Poems 1918–21* (1921) or to his translation of Remy de Gourmont's *The Natural Philosophy of Love* (1922).

*Vide suprout, Noyes . . . :* EP is referring to the following reviews of and articles on *Ulysses:* Alfred Noyes, "Rottenness in Literature," *Sunday Chronicle* (29 October 1922): 2; John M. Murry, Review, *Nation & Athenaeum* (22 April 1922): 124–25; a review by "Aramis" entitled "The Scandal of *Ulysses*" in the *Sporting Times (Pink 'Un),* (1 April 1922): 4; and Shane Leslie, Review, *Quarterly Review* (October 1922): 219–34. Pertinent extracts from each of these may be found in *James Joyce: The Critical Heritage,* vol. 1, 1902–1927, ed. Robert H. Deming.

*whose book on music:* i.e., Katherine Ruth Heyman's *The Relation of Ultramodern to Archaic Music* (Boston: Small, Maynard, 1921).

*Monroe Wheeler:* b. 1900, American book designer, publisher, and museum director, who, along with Barbara Harrison, founded Harrison of Paris, a publishing firm devoted to bringing out high-quality, limited editions. In 1923, Wheeler was publishing a magazine called *Manikin,* the three issues of which were published in Bonn, Germany, and in New York.

*Virgil Geddes:* b. 1897. Geddes, who had published poetry in a number of reviews and who was to become from 1924 through 1928 the financial editor of the Paris edition of the *Herald Tribune,* had written a complimentary article on EP entitled "Ezra Pound Today" in *Poetry* (November 1922): 95–100.

*the Propertius:* i.e., EP's "Homage to Sextus Propertius."

*prospect of 3 Mts. edtn.:* In 1923, William Bird of the Three Mountains Press in Paris published William Carlos Williams's *The Great American Novel.* This book was to be one of a series which William Bird had asked EP to supervise, and it was EP who had solicited the Williams volume for publication.

*McAlmon:* American writer and publisher Robert McAlmon (1896–1956). In 1920 and 1921 in New York, McAlmon and William Carlos Williams had published four issues of a magazine called *Contact* (a fifth issue came out in June 1923). In 1921, McAlmon married Annie Winifred Ellerman, who wrote under the name Bryher and was the daughter of one of England's richest men. Following their wedding, the couple left New York for Europe. By 1923, McAlmon was spending most of his time in Paris and there, with money he had obtained from his father-in-law, he established the Contact Publishing Company. In its first year of operation, Contact brought out two of McAlmon's own books (*A Companion Volume* and *Post-Adolescence*), Bryher's *Two Selves,* Marsden Hartley's *Twenty-five Poems,* Mina Loy's *Lunar Baedecker,* William Carlos Williams's *Spring and All,* and Hemingway's *Three Stories and Ten Poems.* On a number of occasions, McAlmon contributed to the *LR:* "Essentials" (September–December 1920): 69–71; "What Is Left Undone," (Spring 1923): 32–43; "Three Generations: The Same" (Spring 1924): 43–57; and three brief poems (Autumn 1923–Winter 1924): 3–9.

**138. ALS–2.**  On stationery headed: 109, RUE DU CHERCHE-MIDI. [December 1922–January 1923]

Dear M:

> Are you doing the Lewis Number – = ??
> If not = use these ⟨10 photos⟩ of J[ohn]. Storrs =
> & if you are doing the Lewis= I suggest you use the Storrs, later.

> > yours
> > E.P.

P.S. = If the Lewis stuff hasn't arrived— or don't arrive
SOON—

Better bring out miscellany
Storrs arrives N.Y.
    about Feb. 18.

[Sometime in 1922, EP had sent the following typescript to MCA, but she declined to print it in the *LR*.]

**Typescript–2.** [1922]

PROGRESS OF AMERICAN FICTION
1897
"The titmouse was twittering in the soft shadows of the cedars. (1860
"umbrage," Nat. H) A figure in clinging organdy . . . . . . . . . . . "
                    Hen Van Kyke

1900
"The magic of his touch"
                    Robt W. Clambers

1917 and after
"An opulent figure with an orange tummy-band she lurched heavily along under the gharish ghlare of the arc lights in the kaleidoscopic refraction of the sensuous broadway ; from the opposite direction a male in ill-fitting trousers with a peculiar hip-motion of the short legs and disproportionate trunk approached her clumsily ; he hooked arms with an affable roughness, and they lurched disappearingly round the corner."
              [*Crossout:* Hen Becht]

1919 and after
"and suddenly in open corn-field, she started running . . . . . . (variant: he started running)"
              Sherlock Sanderson

FOR SUCCESS: Make simple statement of above sort early, often and repeatedly, avoid brevity and aim at the Saturday Boast[.]

**139. TLS.1**   [4 January 1923]

4 Jan.

Dear M

Leaving Paris. Have asked M.G.HBishop to complete copy for Miscellany number.

Of course IF W.L. sends on his copy, his number shd. come first. Otherwise, do the Miscellany, and announce that Lewis copy and illustrations are ⟨actually⟩ on hand and will form basis for NEXT number.

Only dont, for peace' sake, mix the two numbers together.

E.P.

*M. G. HBishop:* Morris Gilbert Bishop? Bishop served as a professor of Romance languages at Cornell University from 1921 to 1960. We have not been able to establish, however, whether this is the person referred to here.

**140. TLS–4.**   [January–March 1923]

70 bis, rue Notre Dame des Champs
Paris VI

Dinsmore (Elsie), Hamsun & Co.

Messieurs:

Green number to hand. At any rate it isn't a mausoleum.
Expect to get a week off, sometime about the end of June.
Confound Wyndham ANYHOW ! ! ! !

Do you want me to arrange a number?

There are the following possibilities:
Brancusi . . . . . . . . just possible, but probably
⟨illustrations⟩ wd, have to be confined to him.

One couldn't do better, but there are various illustrations on hand, might be better to do a miscellany next (unless the Lewis stuff does arrive)[.]

and follow it by an ALL Brancusi.

The Leger comes up so damn well, I think we ought to use more of him.

% % % %

The people I could bulldoze into contributing are possibly Cocteau,
    B.M.G Adams
    Hemingway
    Christian [Georges Herbiet], if I can find him
    [Robert] MacAlmon and I suppose Mina L[oy].
Art: [Hilaire] Hyler
    Sandford.
        ⟨Orloff⟩
Art of book making : reproduce the best of the designs [by Dorothy
Pound] for [Windeler's] Elimus,
           (possibly the two best)
    cd, probably borrow the block from the Three Mts, Press.

---

E.P. available matter: Two of my friends have gone over my pseudonymous music and art crit, mostly New Age from 1915–20 or 17–20.
              and made selections,
                    about 40 typescript pages of music, and
    10 or 15 art.
I haven't read the selections. If you wanted to use 'em, wd, have to print
the lump. Otherwise nothing to it.

General design being to make sometime a book of paragraphs from my as
yet uncollected, and uncollectable outcries.

---

Price for my services:
        A. That you print that priere pour la bonne presse and other
fragments of the sottisier, I sent last winter.
        B, That you print full page ad, of Three MOUNTAINS PRESS
        C. publication of calendar. for the year III
(((((((
The damn trouble about my trying french anthology etc, is that it means
    so much work for me;
                interruption of
    KWREEATIV woik; and no rent paid. ⟨pure philanthropy & I've
done so much ⟨that⟩ am ready for a little variety⟩

I might however get someone to copy out a few poems, by [Guy Charles]
    Cros, [Maurice de] Vlaminck, Toulet, and [Jean] Cocteau (there are
some good things by Cocteau in '1917–20 volume). There again it means

taking the guts of what I ought to make into an article and sell for fifty bones.

     add 1000 words and serve.

    add words 1000, and serve recipt [*sic*] for polite essay on litterchure.

   ////

Re/ MacAlmon: worth notice; has come on a long way since relieved of ammospheric [*sic*] pressure of U.S.A.

N.B. These collaborators are problematic. I don't want to rush round (i,e, let em come here to tea and devour ten afternoons)

    UNTIL I hear from you that the programme is acceptable.

    % % % %

    P.S. have just looked at Mr Jitro's contribution. Why all this post-boche, post-Grosz bloody murther ??

    % % % %

Mind, I don't know that ANY of the above is feasible; don't want to thrust forward my services, till I know they are desired. And can not promise ANY thing.

    except the postage on items transmitted,

    % % %

On the whole better make miscellany; and consider an all Brancusi illustrated; for the second number. ⟨Subject to revision if B. shd. feel like disgorgin photos[.] The other artists cd. wait⟩

    B. may definitely refuse, any how. Especially as he is VERY bored at prospect of having to leave his studio in a years time; and has three or four years work that he wants to finish first.

       ETC.

       BLAST

      Commissioner Burke,

       Jitro

      Stephen Hudson

     Yvonne George

Bless

    The Baroness

     yrs

      E.

*Green number:* i.e., the Miscellany Number, Winter 1922.
*The Leger comes up:* The Miscellany Number printed a reproduction of a painting by French artist Fernand Léger. The following issue, the Exiles' Number

(Spring 1923), published seven more: "The Two Smokers" (1911), "Painting" (1912), "Landscape" (1921), "The Breakfast" (1921), "Curtain for the Ballet 'Skating Rink,' " "The Dish of Pears" (1923), and "The Bridge" (1923).

*B. M. G. Adams:* maiden name of EP's close friend Bride Scratton, a married woman he had met at Yeats's. She is the author of *England* (Paris: Three Mountains Press, 1923).

*Hyler:* EP is referring to American painter Hilaire Hiler (1896–1966), who was living in Paris at the time and who was, along with Wyn Holcombe, running Le Jockey, a nightclub.

*Orloff:* Russian-French sculptress Chana Orloff (1888–1968). Orloff had been in Paris since 1910.

*the best of the designs for Elimus:* The Three Mountains Press had published B. C. Windeler's *Elimus,* for which Dorothy Pound had made woodcuts. One of these was published in the Spring 1923 issue of the *LR* (44).

*Two of my friends . . . . :* English musician Agnes Bedford (1892–1969) and American pianist and composer George Antheil (1900–59). The two excerpted selections from EP's William Atheling articles on music in *The New Age.* These were eventually published, not in the *LR,* but in Ford Madox Ford's *Transatlantic Review:* February 1924: 109–15, May 1924: 370–73, and August 1924: 222–25. In October 1924, these were included in EP's *Antheil and the Treatise on Harmony,* published by Bird's Three Mountains Press.

*Price for my services:* Of the three conditions here set down, only the second was met by the editors.

*Toulet:* French journalist, poet, and novelist Paul-Jean Toulet (1867–1920), who was noted for the witty, cynical, ironic tales he wrote for *La Vie parisienne.* His verse was published posthumously in 1921 as *Les Contrerimes.*

*Mr. Jitro's contribution:* i.e., W. C. G. Jitro's "Spring Song: Night on the Fields," published in the Winter 1922 issue (5–16). The story is a gruesome account of the beating murder of "a tall bony youth" by a "fat man" and a "small withered man." "Post-Grosz" refers to German-American painter and caricaturist George Grosz (1893–1959), noted for his depictions of the horrors of war and the brutality of the military.

*Commissioner Burke:* i.e., Kenneth Burke, whose "The Death of Tragedy" had been included in the Autumn 1922 issue (9–17).

*Stephen Hudson [and] Yvonne George:* Stephen Hudson's story "Transmutation" and Yvonne George's "Notes: Parisienne, Americaine, Espagnole" had been published in the Winter 1922 number (35–39, 28–29).

*The Baroness:* Baroness Else von Freytag Loringhoven's poem "Affectionate" and a photo of her construction of cogs, sprockets, and feathers entitled "Portrait of Marcel Duchamp" were included in the Winter 1922 issue (40, facing page 40).

[In the spring of 1923, MCA, who had tired of editing the *LR,* and Jane Heap left New York for Paris, arriving there in May. In Paris they met EP for the first time. In her autobiography *My Thirty Years' War,*

MCA describes her reaction to the man she had known only through letters and his published writing: "He was totally unlike any picture I had formed of him. Photographs had given no idea of his height, his robustness, his red blondness—could have given no indication of his high Rooseveltian voice, his nervousness, his self-consciousness. After an hour in his studio I felt that I had been sitting through a human experiment in a behaviorist laboratory. Ezra's agitation was not of the type to which we were accustomed in America—excitement, pressure, life too high-geared. It gave me somehow the sensation of watching a large baby perform its repertoire of physical antics gravely, diffidently, without human responsibility for the performance. . . . I am very fond of Ezra. Only it will be more interesting to know him when he has grown up" (243–44).

During their stay, the editors became acquainted with many of the writers, sculptors, and artists whose work they had already presented in the *LR* and met others whom they were later to publish (René Crevel, Paul Eluard, Jacques Baron, Joseph Delteil, Tristan Tzara, Drieu la Rochelle, and Pierre Reverdy—all of whom were represented in the Autumn–Winter 1923–24 French Number). They also met Ernest Hemingway, whose poem "They All Made Peace—What Is Peace?" and short stories "Mr. and Mrs. Elliot" and "Banal Story" were later published in the *LR*.

MCA decided to stay on in Europe, but Jane Heap returned to New York where she carried on the managing of the *LR,* publishing six more numbers before the final issue. In 1929, the *LR* ceased publication. For its last number, MCA sent out a questionnaire to many of the authors who had contributed to the magazine, asking such questions as "What should you most like to do, to know, to be? Why wouldn't you change places with any other human being? What is your attitude toward art today? What is your world view? Why do you go on living?" etc. Fifty-two responses to the questionnaire were printed in the last issue, but EP sent the card which follows.]

**141. TC–1.**  On postcard postmarked: Rapallo/ 22 1. 2818. Addressed Mlle/ MARGARET ANDERSON/ 80 rue de l'/ UNIVERSITE/ PARIS VI/ FRANCIA [1928]

Print what you've got on hand.

E.P.

P.S. This refers to mss. of mine suppressed by you or "jh", when I last assisted you in preparing a number of the L.R., and never returned to the author.

[MCA wrote the following note, in pencil, over EP's typed message: "Suppressed by me, dear Ezra, and thrown in the waste basket; and a very good thing for you. Such a collection of stale witticisms it has rarely been my lot to receive. You couldnt really hope to get away with them in a magazine published in N.Y. in 1926."]

[In 1936, Jane Heap wrote EP to sound him out on the possibility of another little magazine venture, perhaps a revival of the *LR*. EP's reply follows.]

**142. TLS–2.** On stationery headed: ANNO XIV/ 1936/ VIA MARSALA 12–5/E. POUND    RAPALLO [26 May 1936]

26 May

Dear "jh"

Yes. A live mag/ wd. fill a G A P.
My letter to Stan[ley Nott] is intended CONstructively, not destructively. I don't know of anyone else who cd/ interest me in a noo mag//=
BUT it ought to be done REALLY or NOT. If you choose to write me seriously, go ahead. either LOGISTICO, re commisariat, or program.

It wont just drift into happening.

It is NOT impossible.

yrz
E.P.

⟨Prob. not what Stan. was driving at. BUT I don't need a printer to say what I mean.⟩
⟨No compromise with public. TASTE[.] [I]n England that means no compromise with dry rot & mouldiness.⟩
Official English crap is PRE/Hen = James / what wd. be the sense

in my pulling in my horns and trying to write something that Abercrumbie and Masefield wd/ approve of?

AND THAT is what the crab lice who run the british public demand.

No use using me as a lever to hoist up a few half baked[,] half energized unweaned wobblers.

     a sane program, contemporary with ???? ?? the Vou club of Tokio
         ???
or WHAT ?
and who is to WRITE the mag?
and how much have you to spend on ART ??!!! if any?
               NOT that I think writing can be hung up as letter press and mean anything.

If the bastards wont absorb the Ideogramic series/ already ten or 20 years old ???

             You've GOT to have a financial leverage ⟨for the mag// or it will be merely⟩ a shadow on the wall.

There IS money I F ( I F spelling IF)
     where wd/ you run it ?? London, Paris/ N.Y. or Denmark ??

                                 E

*Stan:* London publisher Stanley Nott, who in 1935 had published EP's *Alfred Venison's Poems* and *Social Credit: An Impact.*

*Vou club of Tokio:* a Japanese literary group whose magazine *Vou* was edited by the poet Kitasono Katue. Katue admired EP's work and between 1936 and 1940 published a number of translations of EP's poetry and essays.

*Ideogramic series:* Noel Stock explains the allusion: "In March 1936 Stanley Nott published Fenollosa's *The Chinese Written Character as a Medium for Poetry*, 'An Ars Poetica With Foreword and Notes by Ezra Pound'. After twenty years struggle, on and off, by Pound, this was the first separate publication in book-form. It included an appendix in which Pound ('a Very Ignorant Man', he said) commented on the meaning of certain Chinese characters. The Fenollosa was the first in a new 'Ideogramic Series' edited by Pound; the second was *Ta Hio, the Great Learning,* published in May 1936—an English edition of Pound's translation brought out in 1928 by Glenn Hughes in Seattle; the third volume in the 'Ideogramic Series' was to have been a reprint of William Carlos Williams's *In the American Grain* (first published in 1925), but Stanley Nott went out of business before it could be printed. At Pound's urging it was brought out by New Direction[s] in 1939" (338).

[In January 1953, Hermitage House of New York brought out *The Little Review Anthology,* a collection of pieces which had been published in the magazine. MCA edited the book, selecting the contents and providing introductory comments on her choices. To offer something of an historical perspective, she arranged the material chronologically. Gorham Munson (see Letter 131n) served as her editor at Hermitage House.

When EP saw the anthology, he wrote to MCA from St. Elizabeths. She had done a "good job," he admitted, but suggested that T. S. Eliot would be upset that "Eeldrop and Appleplex" had been included. Eliot, apparently, objected to having this singular bit of prose fiction reprinted. EP also offered to send a list of little magazines in which she might advertise the anthology.

The correspondence thus resumed lasted nearly a year. EP's letters are characteristic of those he wrote to others during this period: fragmentary, allusive (sometimes to the point of obscurity), written in a kind of personal shorthand. They are unsigned and undated. But because MCA's responses to EP (included in the Appendix) have survived and were for the most part dated, it has been possible to establish what seems to us a logical ordering and we have supplied approximate dates. (Some curious omissions and unexplained references in the correspondence suggest, however, that not all of the letters are present here.) EP's letters, although obscure, gain in clarity when read alongside the replies MCA sent; we have, when possible, indicated at the beginning of the Pound letter the number of the Anderson one which seems to respond to it. A1, for example, refers the reader to MCA's first letter in the Appendix. When references in a Pound letter are made clear by MCA's response, we have not supplied a footnote.]

**143. TL–1.** [?1–15 June 1953]. For MCA's response, see A1.

Marg[aret] AND[erson]

did good    job Lit/ Rev/ Anth/
question did her damPBRS [damn publishers] send it to the half doz li'l mags that are still fighting, and that wd/ be stiMUlated by it, and review it/ or only to the old sewers that hated it when it was, and still hate to hear it existed??

list of li'l mags that WERE alive last week, and may still be there when yu git this, CAN be supplied if yu and yr/ pbrs aint dead fr/ nekkk up.

Mr Elyump [T. S. Eliot] allus threateded AXshun if anybuddy reprinted Eeldrop ["Eeldrop and Appleplex"] but praps he wunt never found out yu dunnit.

It has entertained several readers unborn at date of initial pubctn.

yrs anonYmouse

**144. TL–1.**   [?16 June–?13 July 1953]. For MCA's response, see A2.

M.A.

if you're as near as awl that why the hell dont you come in fer a l'il intelligent conversation.

No I do NOT wish to communicate with Mr [Gorham] Munson DIrectly[;] genocide is impractical and wd/ be unjust[.]

I am not in the LEAST surprised at the pubrs/ actions. I spose yu spent so much time abroad that it surprises you.

M.A.

and as subject for meditation

不
靈
承
帝
矢

meaning, in its context: Our dynasty came in because of its great sensibility.

After 曰 made that remark the dynasty lasted 800 years.

*to communicate with Mr Munson:* MCA had suggested that EP send his list of little magazines directly to Munson. See Letter A1.

*pubrs/ actions:* MCA had complained of having to cut fifty pages from the page proofs and of the lack of advertising for the book. See Letter A1.

**145. TL–1.** [June–July 1953]

M/A

git off yr/ tuffet and stop
watching spiders/
Russel: (Pete not Bertie)

"Yes, we got Lit. Rev. anth. Anth absolutely magnificent. Whigham is in sort of 7th heaven raptures over it."

*Russel: (Pete not Bertie):* i.e., Peter Russell, not Bertrand Russell. During the early 1950s, Peter Russell's activities in England helped to keep EP's name before the public. Russell formed an "Ezra Pound Society" to work for EP's release from St. Elizabeths; used his magazine *Nine* to publish some of EP's work and to publicize some of EP's ideas; brought out a series entitled "Money Pamphlets of £"—reprints or translations of EP's writings on economics; and, with the assistance of Pound, established The Pound Press to publish a new edition of *ABC of Economics.*

*Whigham:* Poet, translator, and schoolteacher, Peter Whigham, one of EP's followers in England, wrote an account of EP's life and work which was privately printed. He was active in the "Ezra Pound Society."

**146. TL–1.** [June–July 1953]. For MCA's response, see A2.

M.A.

settin on yr/ hump and prob/ neglecting the air an the wypers/
Jedge Hand has been banned by the State Dept/

they hadn't the guts to hold it/ BUTTT

as I am in buGOUze, you had ought to let
out whoop.

# # #

Was it Rumbold the demon barber or some other stiffed shirt over jim's
[James Joyce's] grave "not only a grrreat oirishman but a grreat englishman."

I cant write to him [Judge Hand]/ BUT yu could/ time revenges.


*Jedge Hand:* On 25 June 1953, Judge Augustus N. Hand, who had presided
over the *LR*'s *Ulysses* trial (see Letter 67n), had written to President Eisenhower, notifying the president of his retirement from the Second Circuit
Court of Appeals, to be effective June 30. President Eisenhower did not accept the resignation, however, until 23 July 1953. News releases surrounding
the judge's retirement make no mention of his being "banned by the State
Dept," and MCA indicates her ignorance of what EP is referring to (see
Letter A2). EP's interpretation of Hand's retirement is, most likely, fanciful.
*Rumbold the demon barber:* EP's allusion here is to Sir Horace Rumbold, British minister to Switzerland in 1918 and later to Poland. Joyce had a grievance
against Rumbold and incorporated his name into the "Cyclops" episode of
*Ulysses* in which "H. Rumbold, Master Barber" offers his services as a
hangman.



**147. TL–3.** [15 July 1953]. For MCA's response, see A4.


S.Liz          15 Lug


Chere M/

The NEED is, that when the slogan "no comp/ wiff pub taste" was
lowered, neither printed nor observed

this desert went infor 30 years of sterility/

Carter is born/ the other mags/ ⟨some⟩ try to be respectable (from necessity) [Peter] Russel[l] trying to fill Criterion role/ European hedgin cause
its owner has POlitical or polecatical ambish/ Et/bloody cetera/

Some years ago ( about 5) Fr Moore [Marianne Moore?], said there
OUGHT to be 4 pages monthly, but there aren't.

Carters 16 p/ quarterly has now the necessary six guarantors for printing bill/

On which I offer my trans/ of Pea's "Moscardino" so he can run to 32 without putting in hoGWasch.

BUT I'm damned if I [will] pay for having it printed.

Did it in mid war in woptalia with NO chance of its being printed then. First time I ever wanted to trans a novel.

The universal corruption. Davenport howling re/ boycott of Frobenius, whom he IS, after 25 year time lag, translating.

No I haven't seen any revs/ of Lit/Rev/anth/ I do NOT see weekly slopliments etc/ or read bk/reviews, save when ole Vyoler [Viola Baxter Jordan?] (ef yu kno who that is) sends on N. Porker [*The New Yorker*], or clips/)

News this a.m. Dulac d[ied]. on Whit Monday (whenever that was) deBos[s]chere some months ago, also Walt. Rummel.

Bill Wms [William Carlos Williams] ½ paralyzed. H.D. very ill in Zurich.

Bro/ Eliot settin like a buzzard on the limb. W.L. totally blind as you prob/ know. But still more life than the lot uVUM.

Hv/ yu seen his [Wyndham Lewis's] "Rotting Hill"?

I dunno wot printed matter was sent/ all any can do is to get facts one at a time to honest auditors. Paige het up over Rosewater Benet printing three total lies in some "work of reference"

M.A.2 [page two]

returning to p/1. I shd/ say some AIM at respectability, merely wild with no knowledge inside 'em. others hedge.

Carter HAS, for first time in decades, the prospect of several, perhaps as much ⟨many⟩ as 8

                                        intelligent people into
one fasciculus.

      Fordie [Ford Madox Ford] started "transatlantic [review]" at a
time where there wasn't the stuff to fill it.

Dont talk of it as "MY" project. I dun't even know wot its name is.
'Martinsville' probably the best.
# # #
Who WOULD do a good review of L.R. anth?

                        Marianne [Moore]
probably PAINED. n.y. school-teachers TERRIFIED,
                   spectacle of
murkin⟨s⟩ living under terror is a NEW one,
                      there [they]
weren't scared in '39?

30 years of Dial fuss-budgets, preceded by [Edgar Lee] Masters who never
discovered he was Darrow's law partner, plus the wide open guitar players,
      commendable, but not a complEAT paideuma.

did I send you that ideogram/ from passage

Our dynasty came in because of a great sensibility.  

      that was the one that lasted 800 years

tell D.C. to accelerate recovery. We need able bodied scouts.

      Yes, re Horan. only trouble his line bumps, stops, and has to heave to
git goin again.

*Carter is born:* While a student at Washington and Lee University, Thomas H.
    Carter edited *Shenandoah* from 1951 through the summer of 1953. In the
    magazine, he published EP's "James Joyce and Pécuchet" (Autumn 1952)
    and several of his other short pieces. Following his graduation, he planned to
    begin a quarterly of his own, one which could publish Pound's work regu-
    larly. Whether he successfully launched a new little magazine is difficult to
    say as EP's translation of Enrico Pea's *Moscardino* (the first of Pea's four-
    volume *Il romanzo di Moscardino,* translated by EP in June and July 1941)
    was not published until it came out in the fifteenth volume of *New Directions
    in Prose and Poetry* (1955). Carter died at the age of thirty.
*Criterion role:* T. S. Eliot's *The Criterion* was published from October 1922
    through June 1939. Although the journal printed poetry and fiction, it is
    most notable for the criticism (Eliot's, in particular) it carried.

*Pea's "Moscardino":* See above note.

*Davenport:* Guy Davenport (b. 1927), currently professor of English at the
   University of Kentucky at Lexington, at the time of this letter was an instructor at Washington University in St. Louis. His essay "Pound and Frobenius"
   (the "translation" EP may be referring to in the letter) was published in
   *Motive and Method in* The Cantos *of Ezra Pound* (1954).

*Dulac:* Edmund Dulac (1882–1953)—artist, illustrator, and stage designer—died
   in London on May 29.

*deBoschere:* Jean de Bosschère. See Letter 1n.

*Walt. Rummel:* Composer and pianist Walter Morse Rummel (1887–1953) died
   May 2 in Bordeaux, France.

*W.L. totally blind:* By 1951, Wyndham Lewis had lost his eyesight, the result
   of a brain tumor.

*his "Rotting Hill":* Lewis's book of short stories *Rotting Hill* was published in
   London by Methuen in 1951.

*Paige het up over Rosewater Benet . . . :* D. D. Paige, editor of *The Letters
   of Ezra Pound 1907–1941,* objected to the Pound entry in William Rose
   Benét's *The Reader's Encyclopedia: An Encyclopedia of World Literature
   and the Arts,* the first edition of which was published in New York by Crowell
   in 1948. The entry states that EP's poetry had begun "in the school of Imagism," that EP "held an official position under Benito Mussolini," and that he
   had "broadcast the Fascist party line by short wave to America"—none of
   which is accurate. EP had, of course, been writing poetry for a number of
   years before the founding of Imagism. During the Second World War, he had
   no "official position" in Mussolini's government, and his broadcasts over
   Rome Radio (not short wave) ranged over a variety of topics, only some of
   which were directly within the "Fascist party line." The Pound entry in the
   second edition of *The Reader's Encyclopedia* was thoroughly rewritten.

*he was Darrow's law partner:* From 1903 to 1911, Masters and Clarence Seward
   Darrow (1857–1938) were law partners. Darrow is most remembered today
   for his role in the Tennessee evolution trial ("the Scopes Case") during the
   1920s.

*tell D.C. to accelerate recovery:* Dorothy Caruso, the widow of tenor Enrico
   Caruso, had become a close friend of MCA. See Letter A3.

*Yes, re Horan:* In addition to his contributions of poems to a variety of maga-
   zines, American poet Robert Horan (b. 1922) has published one book of
   verse entitled *The Beginning* (New Haven: Yale UP, 1948; vol. 46 of the
   Yale Series of Younger Poets), for which W. H. Auden wrote a foreword.
   For a number of years, Horan was a close friend of Gian Carlo Menotti and
   Samuel Barber, sharing a home with them outside of Mt. Kisco, New York.
   We are unable to identify the poem(s) to which EP and MCA refer.

**148. TL–2.**   [?15 July–20 July, 1953]. For MCA's response, see A4.

Chere M/

That yu shd/ write to me as if YU thought that I thought you a total idiot instead of the sole productress of, I will not say a spiritual home, but at least [the only] roof or awning ever provided me in this distressed and distressing country . . . .

NOR did I suggest yu DO [see Letter A3] anything[,] but the finer shades of karmic irony are (whatever damp cloud you are settin on) no more to be ignored than the marking on a blue jay's tail.

Hence that the old goat (Hand) shd have a book of HISN grabbed by the orthorities . . . .

AND that [Gorham] Munson shd/ be the instrument re/ the Possum's [T. S. Eliot's] unimportant but extant crimes [i.e., "Eeldrop and Appleplex"]

UGH.

Please thank D[orothy].C[aruso]. for sending me her book. Much to my surprise I have read it.

Bring her along when you come.

re/ end yrs/ curious details the same on both sides.
re/ hers cf/ past Fara Sabina between the two armies: "cosa vuole, non ci siamo che donne" (or "rimaste che donne")

*That yu shd/ write to me:* See Letter A3.
*old goat (Hand)* . . . : See Letter 146n.
*sending me her book:* i.e., *Dorothy Caruso, a Personal History* (1952).
*re/ end yrs/:* MCA had sent EP *The Fiery Fountains,* the continuation of her autobiography begun in *My Thirty Years' War.*
*Fara Sabina* . . . : EP's meaning is obscure here. Fara Sabina is a town in the province of Rieti, Italy, in which territory is found the Abbey of Farfa (founded in A.D. 680 and famous for an important codex). EP's Italian may be translated: " 'What do you want, we are merely women here?' (or 'there are only women left here')."

**149. TL–1.**  [?21 July–28 July 1953]. For MCA's response, see A5.

M.A.

    deah ole Bill the Ferdinand [William Carlos Williams]/ like the rest
ROTTED with Thoreau/ all they can do is to REtire into rural/
D[orothy]. C[aruso]. having seen ruling class may be able to translate
      se non fosse cive                            or look it up
                                                       in the
               for you.                             Paradiso
If I had time to teach a b AB, a, b, c, in 6000 pages to each of 'em.
           and then drag 'em to cooperate, or at least CONverse with
each other or ANY one . . .

On pol/ side Bridges, who seemed good human value[,] babbles of GOLD
like zif [as if] one advocated POLitically the paddle-wheel steamer for
atlantic transport/

and up to the level of the esteemed Marianne [Moore]/ stuffed to the gills
with the slicks[,] writes me TEXtually that Winston [Churchill] is "one of
the few men in public life who isn't a rogue".
           Note the terminology of refinement. says she wunt come to
Wash/ again IF I mention him.

Of course [Alfred] Kreymborg found Marianne informed re Christy Mat-
thiessen/ but if yu kno[w] any of the intelliGENTZZZZiaaaaaaa capable
of grasping anything more cosmopolite than the Bkln dodgers, GIVE!

thanks fer the Cocteau/ D[orothy] P[ound] sending the WynDAMMM [i.e.,
*Rotting Hill*]

*se non fosse cive:* EP is quoting Dante's *Paradiso* 8, the last half of line 116: "if
    he were not a citizen."
*Bridges:* EP is probably referring to Styles Bridges, U. S. Senator from New
    Hampshire, 1937 until 1961.
*Christy Matthiessen:* EP probably means Christy Matthewson (1880–1925),
    well-known pitcher for the New York Giants. Marianne Moore was an avid
    baseball fan.
*the Cocteau:* Cocteau's preface for Georgette Leblanc's *La Machine à Courage.*
    See Letter A4.

**150. TL–1.**   [15 August 1953]

                         15Ag
Chere M/

   Yu nvr DID inform me re/ sales of Lit/Rev.

No damage can be done by revelation NOW. This in lookin' for'ard / cause
a phrase in young [Thomas] Cart[er]'s le'r might lead one to believe that in
his immaturity he thinks he can SELL copies of a mag/ fit to read.

Whether there are 160 people now fit to READ anything of interest, is, in
my mind, an oPEN kQesschun.

BUT it is time something worth reading wuz PRinted.

**151. TL–1.**   [?August–September 1953]

   M.A.

            He [T. S. Eliot] d/n well OUGHT to like it/ considering the
dreary wastes of Criterion, Dial and other et/bloody/ceteraaaaa.
                  re/TSE.

I cd/ alZo lend you de Angulo's Indians in Overalls/ but it wd/ hv/ better
moral effect if you were to order a copy of the Hudson Review/ Autumn
1950/ 1950 **

got it into print just a few weeks before Jaime died.

How to get into 'em that there are TWO kinds of writing, the live an the
DEAD.
**

I mean damBit order diREKT from office, and say WHY yu want THAT
issue.

Goacher has a good note on W[yndham].L[ewis]. in current Social Crediter, several TR(bloody)rying to lift that sheet into kulchrl level

evr/ hear more of Richard (the virtuous) <u>Johns who ran Pagany</u> fer a year and prezombl[y] went broke?

the widdy Fletcher (J[ohn]. G[ould].) sez she is buying yr/ Anth.

<u>ring up another sale for E.P.</u>

*OUGHT to like it:* i.e., *The Little Review Anthology*. See Letter A6.

*de Angulo's Indians in Overalls:* Anthropologist Jaime de Angulo's "Indians in Overalls," a story set among the Pit River Indians, was published, at EP's urging, in *The Hudson Review* (Autumn 1950): [327]–79.

*Goacher:* Denis Goacher, a poet, and BBC actor. He was a Pound enthusiast, a member of the Ezra Pound Society, and (in 1955) wrote about EP's confinement in a foreword for the Neville Spearman edition of *The Women of Trachis.*

*Richard (the virtuous) Johns:* Richard Johns was the editor of *Pagany,* a little magazine published in Boston from 1930 to 1933. William Carlos Williams had a close association with the journal.

**152. TL–2.** [20 September 1953]. For MCA's response, see A8.

Chere M.

If yu wanna give me name AND cog/ ed ADDRESS of the Lunnon bloke, I might have a try.

BUTTT in yr/ youth an

inEgsperience of the London scene, as from 1908

yu NEGlect

certain factors/

London BOMbarded with mystics, Blavatsky, Quest Society, Echos from the Gnosis (GRS Mead) Wisdom of the East Series, [A. R.] Orage an the unreadable Mahabharatta, etc.

Yeats on W[yndham].L[ewis] as "poWWnd's zevil geenius"/ etc.

people been tryin to change WynDAMMn's KeraKter for some time.

Gurdieff I thot a man an a bruvver, but NObuddy is goin to swallow Ouspensky

or the periphery, Lady R/ etc.


There is nowt in yr/ ms [i.e., *The Fiery Fountains*]/ IN that form, general statement, that W.L. hasn't heard 400 times/


Some of it vorticism, some in Kung [i.e., K'ung-Fu-tzu, Confucius]. And W.L. wd/ first hv to respect the INDividual who told him

and the individ wd/

have to know something pretty goddam specific.

After all,

there wuz Dant[e] and R. St Victor, etc, to say nowt of a remark in D. Quixote

I fergit whether as from Sancho or from the author.

the umbrella and the rain pipe

IF yr/ denizen of Sodom on Thames wants to catch W.L.

attention

he (or she or it) wd/ hv/ to convince W.L. that sd/ Denizen is interested IN W.L. and wants to do something for him that W.L. wd/ be interested in having done for him.


Cant recall that W.L. has approved of any effort in his behalf for some time, save young [Thomas H.] Carter's.

I doubt if ⟨he⟩ still OWNS any of his own paintings or drawings/ so it is not as simple as wanting to buy one.


He is testardo come un mulo/ but not DEAD in the head like Joyce or the Rev. Eliot.

the question of printing, reprinting or whatso/ might be a lead

if used with TACT.


Kenner has done a bk/ on him, but doubts that W.L. will much like it. It is over 30 years since Orage pinted out that W.L. and yr/ anon[ymous]/ crspdt [correspondent] were NOT philosophically at one.


W.L.'s value being largely that he wasn't. i.e. with ANYone whatsodam.

Y'only see pipple's [people's] fyces [faces] when going' ⟨toward 'em⟩ tother way. on. (no that aint my original).

Ole Arriet W [Harriet Shaw Weaver]/ backed J.Jheezus [James Joyce],
Tinkabell boosted the Possum.

W.L. assist/ has been them less flavoured by forchoon.

AND ov course, he must hv/ some kind of inner accensio
to keep cheerful an chipper

AZ he indubitably
does, lemons being q[uite]. as useful as lollypops.

CONtemplatio.

an t'wold VORT[icism] is even old⟨er⟩ than I am.
benedictions, and saluti alla Gnt/S/a

D[orothy].C[aruso].

*of the Lunnon bloke:* The "Lunnon bloke" is Mme. Vera Daumal, widow of
French writer and poet René Daumal (1908–44). MCA was encouraging EP
to write Mme. Daumal, hoping that she could "help" Wyndham Lewis, specifically by talking to him of the spiritual insights of Gurdjieff. See Letter A8.

*Blavatsky:* Russian-born Helena Petrovna Hahn Blavatsky (1831–91) was a cofounder (with Colonel Henry S. Olcott) of the Theosophical Society. Her
published works include *Isis Unveiled* (1877) and the two-volume *The Secret
Doctrine* (1888), an exposition of Theosophy.

*Quest Society . . . :* George Robert Stow Mead (1863–1933) was the founder
of The Quest Society, which was devoted to the exploration of mysticism
and the occult. His published works include *Echoes from the Gnosis* (1907),
*The World Mystery* (1908), and *Some Mystical Adventures* (1910). Mead
edited the quarterly *The Quest*. See Letter 15n.

*Mahabharatta:* The Mahabharata is the great epic compendium which includes
much of the legendary tradition of India.

*Gurdjieff:* Georges Ivanovitch Gurdjieff (1872–1949), the founder of the Institute for the Harmonious Development of Man in Fontainebleau-Avon,
France. MCA stayed for a time at the Institute and was profoundly influenced
by Gurdjieff's teachings, which stressed the need for man to unite his intellectual, physical, and emotional faculties to effect a harmony between the
various facets of his nature. In 1962, she published *The Unknowable Gurdjieff*,
an exploration of the influence the teacher had on her and on others.

*Ouspensky:* P. D. Ouspensky (1878–1947), a native of Russia, came under the
influence of Gurdjieff (see above), whose thought he propagated in England,
where he settled in the early 1920s. His writings include *Tertium Organum*
(1920), *A New Model of the Universe* (1931), and a posthumously published novel, *The Strange Life of Ivan Osokin* (1947).

*Lady R:* Lady Rothermere, wife of the first Viscount Rothermere (Harold
Sydney Harmsworth), who was the owner of a number of newspapers. For

a time, Lady Rothermere was interested in Gurdjieff's thought, as expounded by Ouspensky, and offered financial assistance to both men.

*R. St Victor:* Richard St. Victor, twelfth-century mystic whose treatise on the degrees of love influenced Dante.

*save young Carter's:* EP is referring to the "Wyndham Lewis Number" of *Shenandoah* (Summer/Autumn 1953). Thomas H. Carter was the editor of the mazagine. See 147n.

*Kenner has done a bk/ on him:* Hugh Kenner's *Wyndham Lewis* was published by New Directions in 1954.

*Tinkabell boosted the Possum:* EP is probably referring to Lady Rothermere's support of T. S. Eliot's *The Criterion.* She was the sole owner and provided the chief subsidies for Eliot's journal from October 1922 to November 1925, at which time the magazine was incorporated with Eliot as a director as well as the editor.


**153. TL–1.**    [?10–14 October 1953] For MCA's response, see A9.

M.A.

WotCHU mean "IF possible"/ Yu are welcome any ole time/

"possible" applies only to yr/ git up an' git plus means of transport (alledged to eggzist.)

      ***

If Vera D[aumal]/ or any of her fambly or in-laws has or has had any connection with the stinckg of the n.r.f. the first step wd/ be to conceal that fact from W[yndham].L[ewis]. (as from me, fer that matter.). NOT that I insist on guilt by association[.]


How the h/l (blue, saffron or pink-shaded) do yu expect me to tell a goddam frogessa [i.e., Mme. Daumal] HOW to approach W.L. who has for 40 years been one of the most difficult animals to lead that I have encountered.

      AND the damn french are biologiquement fixes.

    If V.D. is an exception/ how t'll do I know wot KIND of a eggception??

      **

the word "nead" in yr/ epizl is puzzling. is it typographic head, read, need, all approx.

      banzai, alala, and saluti a D[orothy].C[aruso].


*WotCHU mean "IF possible":* See Letter A8, paragraph seven.

*the stinckg of the n.r.f.:* In 1943, *La Nouvelle Revue Française* ceased publication except for a special number ("Hommage à Gide"), which was brought out in the autumn of 1951. In 1953, the journal resumed publication under the title *La Nouvelle Nouvelle Revue Française*.

*the word "nead":* See Letter A8, paragraph five.

**154. ALS–2**   [22 December 1953]

|  |  |
|---|---|
| 22 | S. |
| DE | L |
|  | I |
|  | Z |

to

M[argaret] & D[orothy]

yuss. & don't that look JUST like the skuffchoor [sculpture] in the Lxbg Gdns [Luxembourg Gardens].

---

one comin' out ov a meal sock & one out of a bottle. & do the fraugs [the French] git sore when yu kid 'em 'bout scupchoor n archiTexchoor.

  luvv

   To yu both but nacherly more to M. ov whom I hv more definite image.

     E.P.

  a 'oss
  a 'orse
 my kingdumb
   fer a 'orsse.

accuse [?] (thankfully) reception of largest Xmas cawd ever seen — & mos' elegant.

best to yu both for '54

    E.P.

*& don't that look:* From Paris, MCA and Dorothy Caruso had sent EP a large Christmas card decorated with a drawing of a horse.

**155. TL–1.**   [? February 1954]

M.A.

Ole VYoler [Viola Baxter Jordan?] has sent on New Porker fer 23/ Jan. in which Lit/ Rev/ Anth/ is mentioned. Does M.A. know anything of Dwight Macdonald? Does Dwight know that NO pubr/ has ever accepted a book on E.P's recommendation?? Does he synchronize the STOP of conversational life with the day the Dial sacked grampaw [i.e., EP]?

IF he think⟨s⟩ Ez picked anything fer a series of mags/ beinging [beginning] with the Sewing Circle Gazette, visible in L.R. smorzato in Dial, (that ought to be spelled with a TR–)

DOES he note the date ⟨on⟩ which CONversation (a[n] idea he seems to hv/ COlected from M.A.) began to skid?

Of course gulph between Potry [*Poetry*] of Chi/ and L.R. was that Potry s'infischiava of the live mind (not merely mine, but ANYbuddy'z)

incidentally

Dwight dont seem to like W[yndham]. L[ewis]. You did see Shenandoah? what about Perspective (NOT to be confused with Pers/s in the PLUral) on W[illiam]. C[arlos]. W[illiams].

An CONsiderin how casual some folk are/ did YU ever read Fordie on Heart of the Country/ Soul of London/ Sperrit ov the Peepul?

ther Z item in current Hud/

and SO on

anonymously yrz

*New Porker fer 23/Jan . . . :* Dwight Macdonald's review of *The Little Review Anthology* and of *New Directions 14* appeared in the January 23, 1954, issue of *The New Yorker* (92–100) under the title "Two Acorns, One Oak," the oak being MCA's anthology. Macdonald points out that EP secured for the magazine some of its best contributions and that MCA's motivation for founding the *LR* in the first place was to encourage conversation: he quotes her comment, "The thing I wanted—would die without—was conversation. The only way to get it was to reach people with ideas." Although he gives for the most part a favorable review, Macdonald does complain that "such *Little Review* standbys as Wyndham Lewis and Ford Madox Hueffer (later

Ford) seem, at least in this anthology, as arid and contrived (*and* long-winded) as most of the New Directions people."

*the day the Dial sacked grampaw:* See Introduction and Letter 121n.

*You did see Shenandoah:* The Summer/Autumn 1953 issue of *Shenandoah* was devoted to Wyndham Lewis. The number included Lewis's story "The Rebellious Patient" and articles about Lewis by EP, Hugh Kenner, Marvin Mudrick, T. S. Eliot, Peter Russell, and Marshall McLuhan.

*Perspective . . . on W.C.W.: Perspective: A Quarterly of Literature and the Arts* devoted its Autumn/Winter 1953 number to William Carlos Williams.

*read Fordie on . . . :* The books to which EP refers are Ford Madox Ford's *The Heart of the Country* (1906), *The Soul of London: A Survey of a Modern City* (1905), and *The Spirit of the People: An Analysis of the English Mind* (1907), each published in London by A. Rivers.

*ther Z item in current Hud/:* i.e., EP's "The Women of Trachis" in *The Hudson Review* (Winter 1954): [487]–523.

**156. TL–1.**   [28 February 1954]. For MCA's response, see A10.

M.A.                   28 Feb

    As you are now in full ripe adolescence why don't yu turn in and do a job of work?

    Is there a proper and lively biography of Fanny Wright?

    ***

regards to D[orothy]. C[aruso].

    **

alZo Geof Moore has not selected badly in his damPenNGuin tho' he cd/ have avoided various minor inaccuracies.

yu wd/ be proper person to chew his ear for OOOOmission of Elsa vF. L.

*Fanny Wright:* Scottish-born reformer, free-thinker, and journalist, Frances Wright (1795–1852).

*Geof Moore . . . in his damPenNGuin:* i.e., *The Penguin Book of Modern American Verse* (1954), compiled by Geoffrey Moore.

*Elsa vF. L.:* eccentric (and possibly insane) poet, Baroness Elsa von Freytag-Loringhoven.

# Appendix

**A1. TLS–2.**  On stationery headed "Springhill"/ Riderwood, Maryland. [16 June 1953] MCA's response to 143.

June 16, 1953

Dear Ezra,

I was glad to have your letter, and glad that you thought the L.R. Anthology a good job. My own feeling about it was deep disappointment: first because my original conception was marred by being forced to cut 50 pages from the final page-proofs (at a minute's notice, with only a day to do it in); second because the publishers, for a reason still unknown to me, (since they refuse to explain) decided to do no advertising at all.

⟨Last⟩ summer, from France, I tried to withdraw the book when they backed down on using promised photographs and gave no assurances of decent publicity. They wouldn't let me, but promised "adequate advertising". You can imagine my consternation when they launched the book with just one ad (in any newspaper or magazine) — a small one in the N.Y. Times, completely invisible because of lack of spacings. Their ⟨only⟩ explanation is that they advertised in trade papers such as Publishers' Weekly.

There's nothing that I can do, apparently, in this lugubrious situation. But I'm sending them your suggestion about a list of little magazines and will keep after them until they ask ⟨you⟩ for it. Or would you rather send the list to me?

In any case their address is:

> Gorham Munson (whom you know?)
> Hermitage House, 8 West 13th St
> New York 11

I do wish I could hear more of your news. I've been in touch with Arthur Garfield Hays who tells me of some possible good news, and that has made me happy.

Always with affection, and with a lasting gratitude for all that you did for the L. R. Your Letters, published two (?) years ago, were magnificent.

Ever,

Margaret

*Arthur Garfield Hays:* A lawyer practicing in New York, Hays (1881–1954) was active in the American Civil Liberties Union, which was taking an interest in EP's situation.

*Your Letters: The Letters of Ezra Pound 1907–1941,* edited by D. D. Paige, was published in New York by Harcourt, Brace in October 1950 and in London by Faber and Faber in March 1951.

**A2. TLS–1.** On stationery headed "Springhill"/ Riderwood, Maryland. [?16 June—?13 July, 1953] MCA's response to 144–46.

Dear Ezra,

I wish I could run down to see you, but there's illness in "the family" and I can't get away even for a moment. Perhaps later.

If you hadn't written me about Eliot and "Eeldrop" ["Eeldrop and Appleplex"] I wouldn't have known anything about his objection to reprinting this fragment. You see, when [Gorham] Munson asked me to do the L.R. Anthology I consented on the condition that he would attend to all the business of it — copyrights, releases, etc. The boredom of that would have been so inconceivable to me that I wouldn't have attempted the thing.

I was in France for eight months and got back here just in time to read the page proofs. Munson never mentioned any of the business arrangements, except to say that it had been a maddening experience. I wrote him the other day, telling him what you had said about Eliot's attitude toward "Eeldrop". He has just answered:

"Eliot's story is in the public domain, according to the Library of Congress copyright office, and you were therefore free to use it. We sent him a courtesy payment which he returned with a stiff note saying that if he accepted this payment it could be construed as authorization to use his story".

This is consternating to me, as I'm writing to Eliot. Had I known how he felt I would never have used the story in the Anthology. Eliot was always wonderful to the L.R. — the least I could have done for him would have been to respect his wishes. I'm sorry that Munson didn't see fit to tell me.

I haven't the least idea what you're talking about as to Judge Hand, etc. But even if I had I wouldn't do anything about it. I've no longer any connection with, or interest in (never did have), these subjective worlds. Yes, I'd love to have some "intelligent conversation", but I'm convinced that my contribution to it might hold no interest for you. I'm sending you a book of mine which shows my "subjects", but I send it with no illusion that you'll care for it. Still, it's a beautifully organized book, and some of it is well-written.

I shall hope to get down to Washington as soon as possible. ⟨In the meantime, all my friendship & best wishes.⟩

Margaret

*a book of mine:* MCA sent EP *The Fiery Fountains,* the continuation of her autobiography begun in *My Thirty Years' War.* The book focuses primarily on her years in France (up to 1950), interest in Gurdjieff, and association with Georgette Leblanc.

**A3. TLS–2.**   On stationery headed "Springhill"/ Riderwood, Maryland. [14 July 1953] MCA's response to 144–146.

July 14

Dear Ezra,

I've "been serious" and answered T[homas]. H. Carter's letter; AND told him that I'd try to help with your new project. But one thing I've never been able to do is to raise money. I see and know no people with money today — in fact I see no people at all. I'm a happy recluse, and I can't think, seriously, of the need for any new little magazines. What I think there's a need for can't be stated without pomposity — at least by me, since I'm largely inexpressive (except with effort). To be really serious, I've seen one thing lately that impresses me with beauty — published, of all places, in Harper's Bazaar. You may not have seen — I enclose.

However, if the new magazine prints YOU, I'll be interested. Also I've told [Gorham] Munson to send Carter the Anthology, which for some unholy reason he refused to do, C. says.

Jarvis Thurston seems too unimportant to answer. He ought to send me a tribute for having had the sense to keep the "minor figures" out of the Anthology.

Yes, Dorothy Caruso and I shall descend on you one day. She's the one who's ill. Better soon.

In the meantime is there anything we can DO — à propos the printed matter you sent???

Hope New Directions will send me your "Selected Translations". You might ask them to put me on the list. I've bought all the other things of yours. Came across a translated phrase of yours the other day (in an article in the Paris Herald Tribune): "the turn of the wave". Marvelous.

Ever,
Margaret

*your new project:* Thomas H. Carter had hoped to start a little magazine which could become a Poundian vehicle. EP, however, objected to MCA's calling the attempt his (EP's) project. See Letter 147.

*Jarvis Thurston:* Jarvis A. Thurston, professor of English at Washington University in St. Louis, was an editor of *Perspective: A Quarterly Journal of Literature and the Arts.* We have been unable to locate his comment about *The Little Review Anthology,* an observation apparently about the absence of the works of "minor figures."

*your "Selected Translations":* MCA is referring to *The Translations of Ezra Pound,* published by New Directions in August 1953.

**A4. TL–1.**  [20 July 1953] MCA's response to 147.

July 20

Dear Ezra,

Would you be interested in looking at — and improving — a translation of Cocteau?

Before Georgette Leblanc died she had finished her second volume of "Souvenirs". She called it "La Machine à Courage". Cocteau wrote a preface for it — the book was published in 1947. ⟨In Paris, not yet over here.⟩

Several people have had a shot at the translation, including Lewis Gallantière.

---

No, I didn't know about Wyndham Lewis — how awful. Haven't seen, and would love to, "Rotting Hill". Who publishes? Yes, you're right about [Robert] Horan. But — BEAUTY. Ditto — the ideogram.

*Georgette Leblanc:* Singer Madame Georgette Leblanc (1869–1941), the widow of Maeterlinck, was an intimate friend of MCA. She is, in MCA's words, the "principal figure" in *The Fiery Fountains*. Leblanc's memoirs are included in *Souvenirs (1895–1918)* (Paris: B. Grasset, 1931) and *La Machine à Courage: Souvenirs* (Paris: J. B. Janin, 1947). The second volume contains a preface by Cocteau. An English translation of the first volume was done by Janet Flanner and published in New York by E. P. Dutton in 1932 under the title *Souvenirs: My Life with Maeterlinck*.

*Lewis Gallantiere:* Editor and translator Lewis Galantière (1895–1977) provided translations of *The Goncourt Journals 1851–70* (1937), Antoine de Saint-Exupéry's *Wind, Sand and Stars* (1939) and *Flight to Arras* (1942), and Jean Anouilh's *Antigone* (1951).

**A5. TLS–1.**  [29 July 1953] MCA's response to 149.

July 29

Dear Ezra,

Many thanks for the Lewis [i.e., *Rotting Hill*]. Will read quickly and return.

The esteemed Marianne [Moore] — "terminology of refinement" AND sterile opaque intellectualized "poetry" — always my special red flag.

As to the ruling classes . . . D[orothy]. C[aruso]. is trying but without much hope. Later about this.

Will you please return the Cocteau and the ⟨translation and⟩ press notices?? Thought it might amuse you to improve the translation. NO??

Always,<br>Margaret

## A6. TLS–1.   [11 August 1953]

<u>August 11</u>

Cher Ezra — What a master! — Lewis. Mental-center and emotional-center in absolute balance. Have ordered a copy from Methuen and will return yours soon. D[orothy]. C[aruso]. so crazy about it she can't put it down.

Unthinkable that a man with such an eye should be blind. Is there no hope? — an operation or something???

Did I tell you that Eliot wrote me a nice letter? No longer annoyed about Eeldrop ["Eeldrop and Appleplex"], and likes the Anthology.

Always,<br>M.

## A7. TLS–1.   [5 September 1953]

<u>September 5</u>

Dear Ezra,

    I'm in a fearful climax of work — will write you in a day or two.

Haunted by Wyndham Lewis's tragedy. Have the American edition of "Rotting Hill". Have you seen it? On the back cover: "Pushed into an un-lighted room, the door banged and locked forever" . . . etc.

More later.

Always

**M.**

*American edition of "Rotting Hill":* The book was published in Chicago by Regnery in 1952.

**A8. TLS–2.**   [9 October 1953] MCA's response to 152.

October 9

Ezra — you ARE nice — I loved your letter. Rather expected you to answer more negatively.

I'm not "too young and inexperienced" to know — as everyone does — that Los Angeles and London are hotbeds of crack-pot mystics. Also know that all literate persons have read all the great general statements 4000 times. All of which has nothing to do with Gurdjieff and autre chose.

There IS nothing "goddam specific" anywhere. In Confucius? the New Testament? Certainly not. It's all there — all but the specific. It was Gurd-jieff's function to be specific.

But no one will realize this until he gets into the thing, and no one gets into it without a NEED. Still . . . a great shock like blindness can create a need, and an unknown experience can begin.

Of course you're right about Joyce: Eliot a little less nead [*sic*], don't you think, because at least he wanted something — even if only what can be found in conventional religion. If Lewis has nothing but "young [Thomas] Carter's efforts on his behalf" it's too bad. What ⟨on earth⟩ can Carter do for him — except to publish him???

In any case, my bloke is not a man. Name is Mme. Vera Daumal—1, Square Delambre, Paris 14. Widow of René Daumal, whom the N[ouvelle].

R[evue].F[rançaise]. is still publishing. She has real intelligence, various cultures, can present Gurdjieff's "specific" decently, and can certainly match Lewis in ideas. Why don't you write to her? — but in English. I doubt whether she would understand your latest letter-prose.

We're going to try to see you in November. If possible?? D[orothy]. C[aruso]. very much wants to. She makes most effective speeches about you from time to time. The other day: "Ezra is one of the few people (lately) who has shown me how large the spirit of man can become".

Greetings from us both, au revoir et à bientôt.

                              M.

*Eliot a little less nead:* See EP's comment in Letter 153 about this typographic
    error.
*Mme. Vera Daumal:* See Letter 152n.

**A9. TLS–1.**   On stationery headed "Springhill"/ Riderwood, Maryland. [After 14 October 1953] MCA's response to 153.

Dear Ezra,

    See what happened to your last letter. No reason for it, except the usual one.

My word was n e e d. And I must stop my Wyndham Lewis solicitudes. Too naive of me to assume that he's a starving man. As you say, his inner accensio will probably keep him going. Too bad he doesn't NEED something more.

"Exceptional"?? I could never use the word, now, except in relation to someone who has gone up the scale to a "higher level of being".

(. . . with which vile and loose phrase I will close.)

(Not "possible" to see you very soon. I managed somehow to wrench my back and have been in bed for a week, unable to move without screams of pain).

Is there anything you want to read that we can find for you???

Always,

**M.**

*what happened to your last letter:* MCA enclosed the envelope of EP's last letter. It was postmarked "Oct. 14" and carried the message, "MISSENT TO UPPER MARYLAND, MD."
*his inner accensio:* See paragraph seven of Letter 153.
*"Exceptional"??:* See paragraph six of Letter 153.

**A10. TLS–1.**   [4 March 1954] MCA's response to 156.

RIDERWOOD, Md., March 4

Ezra dear — What possible interest can you imagine I take in Fanny Wright (the only one I know of) ??

As for Elsa von F[reytag-]. L[oringhoven]. — that must be left to Peter Whigham. I did all about her I could in the L. R.

And anyhow I ⟨know no⟩ one I would take up cudgels for at the moment except myself — depicted in the London Times of February 12 as "a genius without talent". Oh of course I'd fight for you at any time — except on the damned subject of your interest in economics, which I deplore.

I never see the Penguin. Where is it published?? — or can you send me the Geoffrey Moore article? Have you seen review of L. R. Anthology in Poetry? I've not yet, but have sent for it.

I've written for your Literary Essays. Hope it comes soon. Booksellers — and publishers — make one wait 2 or 3 weeks before filling any order.

⟨I'm doing a job of work that would repulse you as much as your economics do me. Well . . . ⟩

Ever

**M.**

*Peter Whigham:* See Letter 145n.

*see the Penguin:* Apparently MCA is under the impression "the Penguin" is a journal. See Letter 156n.

*review of L.R. Anthology in Poetry:* G. Robert Stange's review "The 'Lost' Renaissance" appeared in the February 1954 issue of *Poetry* (290–94). In it he provides a generally favorable commentary, but laments the fact that no anthology can provide for us what we really want ("the experience of reading new bits of Joyce or Eliot or Yeats in, say, 1918"). He does concede that the book is "pleasant to dip into" and "good to have" ("since copies of the *Little Review* are almost unprocurable").

*your Literary Essays:* i.e., *Literary Essays of Ezra Pound* (London: Faber and Faber; Norfolk, Conn.: New Directions, 1954).

# Selected Bibliography

(Including Works Cited in Notes)

## I. Ezra Pound's Contributions to *The Little Review* (arranged chronologically)

"A Letter from London." 3 (Apr. 1916): 7–8.

Letter. 3 (Apr. 1916): 36.

"Das schone [*sic*] Papier vergeudet." 3 (Nov. 1916): 16–17.

Editorial. 4 (May 1917): [3]–6.

"Pierrots: Scène courte mais typique (after the 'Pierrots' of Jules Laforgue)." 4 (May 1917): 11–12. Signed "John Hall."

"Jodindranath Mawhwor's Occupation." 4 (May 1917): 12–18.

"An Anachronism at Chinon." 4 (June 1917): 14–21.

"Aux étuves de Weisbaden [*sic*], A.D. 1451." 4 (July 1917): 12–16.

"List of Books: Comment by Ezra Pound." 4 (Aug. 1917): 6–11.

"Stark Realism: This Little Pig Went to Market (A Search for the National Type)." 4 (Aug. 1917): 16–17.

"[Editor's Note to] Inferior Religions [by] Wyndham Lewis." 4 (Sept. 1917): [3].

"L'Homme Moyen Sensuel." 4 (Sept. 1917): 8–16.

"Imaginary Letters. IV. (Walter Villerant to Mrs. Bland Burn)." 4 (Sept. 1917): 20–22.

"Imaginary Letters. V. (Walter Villerant to Mrs. Bland Burn)." 4 (Oct. 1917): 14–17.

"Editorial on Solicitous Doubt." 4 (Oct. 1917): 20–22.

"Letters from Ezra Pound." 4 (Oct. 1917): 37–39.

"This Approaches Literature!" 4 (Oct. 1917): 39. Signed "Abel Sanders."

"Imaginary Letters. VI. (Walter Villerant to Mrs. Bland Burn)." 4 (Nov. 1917): 39–40.

"A Letter from Remy de Gourmont." 4 (Dec. 1917): [5]–8.

"That Boston Paper Again." 4 (Dec. 1917): 22. Note from the "London Office."

"The Reader Critic." 4 (Dec. 1917): 55–56.

"Advice to a Young Poet." 4 (Dec. 1917): 58–59.

"America's Critic." 4 (Jan. 1918): 10–12. Signed "Raoul Root."

"Thoughts from a Country Vicarage." 4 (Jan. 1918): 52–53.

"Mr. Lindsay." 4 (Jan. 1918): 54–55. Signed "Abel Sanders."

"The Quintuple Effulgence or The Unapproachable Splendour." 4 (Jan. 1918): 56. Signed "S. O. S."

"A Study in French Poets." 4 (Feb. 1918): [3]–61.

"The Classics 'Escape.' " 4 (Mar. 1918): 32–34.

"Cantico del Sole." 4 (Mar. 1918): 35. Signed "Ezra I.Y.H.X."

"[A Review of] 'Tarr' by Wyndham Lewis." 4 (Mar. 1918): 35.

"A List of Books." 4 (Mar. 1918): 54–58.

"Astronomy." 4 (Mar. 1918): 59. Signed "X."

"Raymonde Collignon." 4 (Mar. 1918): 60.

"The Criterion." 4 (Apr. 1918): 11. Unsigned.

"Unanimism." 4 (Apr. 1918): 26–32.

"Poems." 5 (May 1918): 19–31. Includes "Homage à la langue d'Or [i.e., d'Oc. 'Alba'; I–V]"; "Moeurs contemporaines, I–IX."

"Imaginary Letters [X]. (W. Villerant to the ex-Mrs. Burn)." 5 (May 1918): 52–55.

"The Criterion." 5 (May 1918): 62.

"Ben Hecht." 5 (June 1918): 55.

"Our Tetrarchal Précieuse (A Divagation from Jules Laforgue)." 5 (July 1918): [3]–12. Signed "Thayer Exton."

"Our Contemporaries." 5 (July 1918): 35–37.

"Cooperation (A Note on the Volume Completed)." 5 (July 1918): 54–56.

"De Goncourt." 5 (July 1918): 56.

"The Recurrence." 5 (July 1918): 58. Unsigned. (Not listed in Gallup's bibliography.)

"From the Clergy." 5 (July 1918): 60.

"In Explanation." 5 (Aug. 1918): 5–9.

"A Shake Down." 5 (Aug. 1918): 9–39.

"The Notes to 'The Ivory Tower.' " 5 (Aug. 1918): 62–64.

"[Note to] The Western School [by] Edgar Jepson." 5 (Sept. 1918): 5.

"The Notes for 'The Ivory Tower.' " 5 (Sept. 1918): 50–53.

"On the American Number." 5 (Sept. 1918): 62–64.

"De Bosschère's Study of Elskamp." 5 (Oct. 1918): 5–8.

"Breviora." 5 (Oct. 1918): 23–24.

"Note upon Fashions in Criticism." 5 (Oct. 1918): 24–25. Signed "J. H. Le Monier," but almost certainly by EP. (Not listed in Gallup's bibliography.)

"Albert Mockel and 'La Wallonie.' " 5 (Oct. 1918): 51–64.

"The Audience." 5 (Oct. 1918): 64. Unsigned.

"Nine Poems." 5 (Nov. 1918): [1]–6. Includes "Cantus planus"; "Chanson arabe"; "Dawn on the Mountain" (Omakitsu); "Wine" (Rihaku); "φανοποεία" ["Phanopoeia"] (I. "Rose White, Yellow, Silver"; II. "Saltus"; III. "Concava Vallis"); "Glamour and Indigo: A Canzon from the Provençal of 'En Ar. Dan'el' "; and "Upon the Harps of Judea."

"Mr. Villerant's Morning Outburst. (Four Letters)." 5 (Nov. 1918): 7–12.

"H.D.'s Choruses from Euripides." 5 (Nov. 1918): 16–20.

"Tariff and Copyright." 5 (Nov. 1918): 21–25.
"Memorabilia." 5 (Nov. 1918): 26–27.
"The Disease of 'American' 'Criticism.' " 5 (Nov. 1918): 43–44.
"The Audience." 5 (Nov. 1918): 44. Unsigned.
"Genesis, or, The First Book in the Bible. ('Subject to Authority')." 5 (Nov. 1918): 50–64. A footnote identifies this as a translation "from an eighteenth century author."
"De Gourmont: A Distinction (Followed by Notes)." 5 (Feb./Mar. 1919): [1]–19.
"[Footnote to] M. de Gourmont and the Problem of Beauty [by] Frederic Manning." 5 (Feb./Mar. 1919): 26–27.
"[Footnote to] Remy de Gourmont, After the Interim [by] Richard Aldington." 5 (Feb./Mar. 1919): 34.
"The Death of Vorticism." 5 (Feb./Mar. 1919): 45, 48. Unsigned.
"Concerning Certain Effusions of the 'Chicago Daily News' Correspondent." 5 (Apr. 1919): 61.
"Avis." 6 (May 1919): 69–70.
"The Chinese Written Character as a Medium for Poetry, by Ernest Fenollosa and Ezra Pound." 6 (Sept. 1919): 62–64; 6 (Oct. 1919): 57–64; 6 (Nov. 1919): 55–60; 6 (Dec. 1919): 68–72.
"Hudson: Poet Strayed into Science." 7 (May/June 1920): 13–17.
"Bibi-la-Bibiste (roman) par les Soeurs X." 7 (Sept./Dec. 1920): [24]–[29]. Possibly by EP although not listed in Gallup's bibliography.
"[Note to] Bibi-la–Bibiste (roman) par les Soeurs X." 7 (Sept./Dec. 1920): [24].
"Sculpshure." 7 (Jan./Mar. 1921): 47. Signed "Abel Sanders."
"Brancusi." 8 (Autumn 1921): 3–7.
"Historical Survey." 8 (Autumn 1921): 39–42.
"The Poems of Abel Sanders: To Bill Williams and Else von Johann Wolfgang Loringhoven y Fulano." 8 (Autumn 1921): 111.
"The Little Review Calendar." 8 (Spring 1922): [2].
"Stop Press." 8 (Spring 1922): 33. Signed "Abel Sanders."
"French School of Poetry, Synthèse. Western School of Poetry, Synthèse." 8 (Spring 1922): 33.
"Suppressed Passage." 8 (Spring 1922): 34.
"Boll Weevil." 8 (Spring 1922): 34. Signed "Abel Sanders."
"From Ezra." 12 (May 1929): 41.

## II. General

Ackroyd, Peter. *Ezra Pound and His World*. London: Thames and Hudson, 1980.

Adler, Betty and Jane Wilhelm, comp. *H.L.M.: The Mencken Bibliography*. Baltimore: Johns Hopkins UP, 1961.

Aiken, Conrad. *A Reviewer's ABC: Collected Criticism of Conrad Aiken from 1916 to the Present*. London: W. H. Allen, 1961.

Aldington, Richard. *Life for Life's Sake*. New York: Viking, 1941.

Alpert, Barry S[tephen]. "Ezra Pound, John Price, and *The Exile*." *Paideuma* 2 (Winter 1973): 427–48.

———. "The Unexamined Art: Ezra Pound and the Aesthetic Mode of the Little Magazine." Diss. Stanford U, 1971.

Anderson, Margaret. *The Fiery Fountains: The Autobiography, Continuation and Crisis to 1950*. New York: Hermitage House, 1951.

———. ed. *The Little Review Anthology*. New York: Hermitage House, 1953.

———. *My Thirty Years' War: The Autobiography, Beginnings and Battles to 1930*. 1930. New York: Horizon, 1969.

———. *The Strange Necessity: The Autobiography, Resolutions and Reminiscence to 1969*. New York: Horizon, 1969.

———. *The Unknowable Gurdjieff*. New York: Weiser, 1962.

"Aramis." "The Scandal of *Ulysses*." Rev. of *Ulysses*, by James Joyce. *Sporting Times (Pink 'Un)* 1 Apr. 1922: 4.

Baker, Denys Val. *Little Reviews 1914–1943*. London: George Allen and Unwin, 1943.

Barry, Iris. "The Ezra Pound Period." *Bookman* (New York) 74 (Oct. 1931): 159–71.

Benstock, Shari. *Women of the Left Bank: Paris, 1900–1940*. Austin: U of Texas P, 1986.

*BLAST: Review of the Great English Vortex*, nos. 1 & 2 (June 1914, July 1915). Ed. Wyndham Lewis.

*BLAST 3*. Ed. Seamus Cooney. Santa Barbara: Black Sparrow Press, 1984.

Bonnefoy, Claude. *La Poésie française: Des origines à nos jours*. Paris: Éditions du Seuil, 1975.

Bosanquet, Theodora. "Henry James." *Fortnightly Review* ns 101 (June 1917): 995–1009; rpt. as "Henry James as Literary Artist." *Bookman* (New York) 45 (Aug. 1917): 571–81.

———. *Henry James at Work*. London: Hogarth, 1924.

Bosschère, Jean de. *Béâle-Gryne*. Paris: Occident, 1909.

———. *The Closed Door*. With Eng. trans. by F. S. Flint. London: John Lane, 1917.

———. *Dolorine et les ombres*. Paris: Occident, 1911.

———. *Métiers divins*. Paris: Occident, 1913.

———. *Twelve Occupations*. English prose translation by Ezra Pound, anonymously. London: Mathews, 1916.

*British Literary Magazines: The Victorian and Edwardian Age, 1837–1913*. Ed. Alvin Sullivan. Westport, CT: Greenwood, 1984.

Bryer, Jackson R[obert]. "Joyce, *Ulysses,* and the *Little Review.*" *South Atlantic Quarterly* 66 (Spring 1967): 148–64.

———. " 'A Trial-Track for Racers': Margaret Anderson and the *Little Review.*" Diss. U of Wisconsin, 1965.

Bynner, Witter. *The Works of Witter Bynner: Prose Pieces.* Ed. James Kraft. New York: Farrar, Straus & Giroux, 1979.

Cahill, Daniel J. *Harriet Monroe.* New York: Twayne, 1973.

Camfield, William A. *Francis Picabia: His Art, Life and Times.* Princeton: Princeton UP, 1979.

Carnevali, Emanuel. *The Autobiography of Emanuel Carnevali.* Comp. Kay Boyle. New York: Horizon, 1967.

Carswell, John. *Lives and Letters: A. R. Orage, Beatrice Hastings, Katherine Mansfield, John Middleton Murry, S. S. Koteliansky.* London: Faber and Faber; New York: New Directions, 1978.

Caruso, Dorothy. *Dorothy Caruso: A Personal History.* New York: Hermitage House, 1952.

*Catholic Anthology 1914–1915.* Ed. Ezra Pound. London: Elkin Mathews, 1915.

Chisholm, Anne. *Nancy Cunard.* London: Sidgwick and Jackson, 1979.

Coffman, Stanley K., Jr. *Imagism: A Chapter for the History of Modern Poetry.* 1951. New York: Octagon Books, 1972.

Connolly, Cyril. "Fifty Years of Little Magazines." *Art and Literature* 1 (March 1964): 95–109.

Cork, Richard. *Vorticism and Abstract Art in the First Machine Age.* 2 vols. Berkeley: U of California P, 1976.

Cornford, Leslie Cope. *William Ernest Henley.* London: Constable; Boston: Houghton Mifflin, 1913.

Couffignal, Robert. *Apollinaire.* Trans. Eda Mezer Levitine. (Studies in the Humanities 11: Literature.) University, AL: U of Alabama P, 1975.

Cournos, John. *Autobiography.* New York: Putnam's, 1935.

Cowley, Malcolm. *Exile's Return.* New York: Viking, 1951.

Crowley, Aleister. "Art in America." *English Review* 15 (Nov. 1913): 578–95.

Damon, S. Foster. *Amy Lowell: A Chronicle, with Extracts from Her Correspondence.* Boston: Riverside-Houghton Mifflin, 1935.

Davenport, Guy. "Pound and Frobenius" in *Motive and Method in* The Cantos *of Ezra Pound.* Ed. Lewis Leary. (*English Institute Essays,* 1953.) New York: Columbia UP, 1954, [33]–59.

Davie, Donald. *Ezra Pound: Poet as Sculptor.* New York: Oxford UP, 1964.

———. *Pound.* (Fontana Modern Masters, Frank Kermode, ed.) Fontana: Collins, 1975.

De Angulo, Jaime. "Indians in Overalls." *Hudson Review* (Autumn 1950): 327–77.

Delany, Paul. *D. H. Lawrence's Nightmare: The Writer and His Circle in the Years of the Great War.* New York: Basic Books, 1978.

Deming, Robert H., ed. *James Joyce: The Critical Heritage.* 2 vols. New York: Barnes and Noble, 1970.

*Des Imagistes: An Anthology.* Ed. Ezra Pound. London: Poetry Bookshop; New York: Albert and Charles Boni, 1914.

H.D. [Hilda Doolittle]. *Collected Poems, 1912–1914.* Ed. Louis L. Martz. New York: New Directions, 1983.

Duffey, Bernard. *The Chicago Renaissance in American Letters: A Critical History.* East Lansing: Michigan State College P, 1954.

Edelstein, J.M. "Exuberance and Ecstasy." *New Republic* 162 (13 June 1970): 19–22.

Ellmann, Richard. *James Joyce.* Rev. ed. New York: Oxford UP, 1982.

*The Exile.* Numbers 1–4, 1927/1928. Ed. Ezra Pound. New York: Johnson Reprint, 1967.

Feldman, Paula R. "Margaret Anderson." In *Dictionary of Literary Biography,* Vol. 4: *American Writers in Paris.* Ed. Karen Lane Rood. Detroit: Gale, 1980, 3–10.

Fielding, Daphne. *Those Remarkable Cunards: Emerald and Nancy.* New York: Atheneum, 1968.

Flanner, Janet. "Profiles: A Life on a Cloud." *The New Yorker* 50 (3 June 1974): 44–67.

Flora, Joseph M. *William Ernest Henley.* New York: Twayne, 1970.

Ford, Ford Madox. *Thus to Revisit.* 1921. New York: Octagon Books, 1966.

Ford, Hugh, ed. *Nancy Cunard: Brave Poet, Indomitable Rebel, 1896–1965.* Philadelphia: Chilton, 1968.

Friedman, Melvin J. "Lestrygonians" in *James Joyce's* Ulysses: *Critical Essays.* Ed. Clive Hart and David Hayman. Berkeley: U of California P, 1974, 131–48.

Gallup, Donald [Clifford]. *Ezra Pound: A Bibliography.* Charlottesville: UP of Virginia, 1983.

——. *T. S. Eliot: A Bibliography.* Rev. ed. New York: Harcourt, Brace, and World, 1969.

Geddes, Virgil. "Ezra Pound Today." Rev. of *Poems 1918–21,* by Ezra Pound. *Poetry: A Magazine of Verse* 21 (Nov. 1922): 95–100.

Goldring, Douglas. *The Last Pre-Raphaelite: A Record of the Life and Writings of Ford Madox Ford.* London: MacDonald, 1948.

——. *South Lodge: Reminiscences of Violet Hunt, Ford Madox Ford, and the English Review Circle, 1943.* London: Constable, 1943.

Goodwin, K. L. *The Influence of Ezra Pound.* London: Oxford UP, 1966.

Gordon, Lyndall. *Eliot's Early Years.* Oxford: Oxford UP, 1977.

Gould, Jean. *Amy: The World of Amy Lowell and the Imagist Movement.* New York: Dodd, Mead, 1975.

Gregory, Lady Isabella Augusta. *The Collected Plays, I: The Comedies.* Ed. Ann Saddlemeyer. Gerrards Cross, Eng.: Colin Smythe, 1970.

Grover, Philip, ed. *Ezra Pound: The London Years, 1908–1920*. New York: Ames Press, 1978.

Guggenheim, Peggy. *Out of this Century*. New York: Universe Books, 1979.

Harvey, David Dow. *Ford Madox Ford, 1873–1939: A Bibliography of Works and Criticism*. Princeton: Princeton UP, 1962.

Heymann, C. David. *Ezra Pound: The Last Rower*. New York: Viking; London: Faber and Faber, 1976.

Hoffman, Frederick J. *The Twenties: American Writing in the Postwar Decade*. New York: Viking, 1955.

——, Charles Allen, and Carolyn F. Ulrich. *The Little Magazine: A History and a Bibliography*. Princeton: Princeton UP, 1947.

Homberger, Eric, ed. *Ezra Pound: The Critical Heritage*. London: Routledge and Kegan Paul, 1972.

Howarth, Herbert. *Notes on Some Figures Behind T. S. Eliot*. Boston: Riverside-Houghton Mifflin, 1964.

Igly, France. *Troubadours et Trouvères*. Paris: Éditions Seghers, 1960.

"Japanese Mysteries." Rev. of *"Noh," Or Accomplishment: A Study of the Classical Stage of Japan*, by Ernest Fenollosa and Ezra Pound. *Times Literary Supplement* 25 Jan. 1917: 41.

Johns, Francis A. *A Bibliography of Arthur Waley*. New Brunswick, NJ: Rutgers UP, 1968.

Joost, Nicholas. *Scofield Thayer and* The Dial: *An Illustrated History*. Carbondale: Southern Illinois UP, 1964.

——. *Years of Transition:* The Dial, *1912–1920*. Barre, Mass.: Barre Publishers, 1967.

Josephson, Matthew. *Life among the Surrealists*. New York: Holt, 1962.

Joyce, James. *Letters of James Joyce*. Ed. Stuart Gilbert. London: Faber and Faber, 1957.

——. *Ulysses: A Critical and Synoptic Edition*. 3 vols. Prepared by Hans Walter Gabler with Wolfhard Steppe and Claus Melchior. New York and London: Garland, 1984.

Kenner, Hugh. *The Pound Era*. Berkeley: U of California P, 1971.

——. *Wyndham Lewis*. Norfolk, CT: New Directions, 1954.

Knapp, James F. *Ezra Pound*. Boston: Twayne, 1979.

Knoll, Robert E. *Robert McAlmon: Expatriate Publisher and Writer*. Lincoln: U of Nebraska P, 1959.

Kohfeldt, Mary Lou. *Lady Gregory: The Woman Behind the Irish Renaissance*. New York: Atheneum, 1985.

Kripalani, Krishna. *Tagore: A Life*. New Delhi: Malancha, 1961.

Laforgue, Jules. *Poems of Jules Laforgue*. Trans. Peter Dale. London: Anvil Press Poetry, 1986.

Lago, Mary. *Rabindranath Tagore*. Boston: Twayne, 1976.

Laughlin, James. "Solving the Ezragrams: Pound at 100." *New York Times Book Review* 10 Nov. 1985: 1+.

Lawrence, D. H. *The Collected Letters of D. H. Lawrence.* Ed. Harry T. Moore. New York: Viking, 1962.

——. "The Reality of Peace (i): The Transference." *English Review* 24 (May 1917): 415–22.

——. "The Reality of Peace (ii)." *English Review* 24 (June 1917): 516–23.

Leblanc, Georgette. *La Machine à Courage: Souvenirs.* Préf. de Jean Cocteau. Paris: J. B. Janin, 1947.

Leslie, Shane. Rev. of *Ulysses,* by James Joyce. *Quarterly Review* 238 (Oct. 1922): 219–34.

Levenson, Michael. *A Genealogy of Modernism: A Study of English Literary Doctrine 1908–1922.* Cambridge: Cambridge UP, 1984.

Levenson, Samuel. *Maud Gonne.* New York: Reader's Digest, 1976.

Lewis, Wyndham. *Blasting and Bombardiering.* London: Eyre and Spottiswoode, 1937.

——. *Collected Poems and Plays.* Ed. Alan Munton. Manchester, Eng.: Carcanet, 1979.

——. *The Ideal Giant.* London: Shield, 1917.

——. *The Letters of Wyndham Lewis.* Ed. W. K. Rose. Norfolk, CT: New Directions, 1963.

——. *Rotting Hill.* London: Methuen, 1951; Chicago: Regnery, 1952.

——. *Tarr.* New York: Knopf, 1918.

——. *The Wild Body: A Soldier of Humour and Other Stories.* New York: Harcourt, Brace, 1928.

Lhombreaud, Roger. *Arthur Symons: A Critical Biography.* Philadelphia: Dufour, 1964.

Lindsay, Jack. *The Troubadours and Their World.* London: Frederick Muller, 1976.

*The Little Magazine in America: A Modern Documentary History.* Ed. Elliott Anderson and Mary Kinzie. New York: Pushcart, 1978.

Lohf, Kenneth A., and Eugene P. Sheehy. *An Index to the Little Review, 1914–1929.* New York: New York Public Library, 1961.

Lowell, Amy. *Tendencies in Modern American Poetry.* New York: Macmillan, 1917.

——. *Six French Poets: Studies in Contemporary Literature.* New York: Macmillan, 1916.

*Lyrics of the Troubadours and Trouvères: An Anthology and a History.* Trans. Frederick Goldin. Garden City, NY: Anchor-Doubleday, 1973.

McAlmon, Robert. *Being Geniuses Together, 1920–1930.* Rev. and with supplementary chapters by Kay Boyle. Garden City, NY: Doubleday, 1968.

MacBride, Maud Gonne. *A Servant of the Queen: Reminiscences by Maud Gonne MacBride.* London: Victor Gollancz, 1974.

McColgan, Kristin Pruitt. *Henry James, 1917–1959: A Reference Guide*. Boston: G. K. Hall, 1979.

Macdonald, Dwight. "Two Acorns, One Oak." Rev. of *The Little Review Anthology* and *New Directions 14. The New Yorker* (Jan. 23, 1954): 92–100.

McDougal, Stuart. *Ezra Pound and the Troubadour Tradition*. Princeton: Princeton UP, 1973.

Mairet, Philip. *A. R. Orage: A Memoir*. New Hyde Park, NY: University Books, 1966.

Makin, Peter. *Provence and Pound*. Berkeley: U of California P, 1978.

Mariani, Paul. *William Carlos Williams: A New World Naked*. New York: McGraw-Hill, 1981.

Martin, Wallace. The New Age *Under Orage: Chapters in English Cultural History*. Manchester, Eng.: Manchester UP; New York: Barnes and Noble, 1967.

Massot, Pierre de. *De Mallarmé à 391*. Saint-Raphaël, Var: Au Bel exemplaire, 1922.

Masters, Edgar Lee. "Canticle of the Race." *Poetry* 11 (Oct. 1917): 1–5.

Matthews, Thomas Stanley. *Great Tom: Notes Towards the Definition of T. S. Eliot*. New York: Harper and Row, 1974.

May, Henry F. *The End of American Innocence*. New York: Knopf, 1959.

Mencken, Henry Lewis. *A Book of Prefaces*. 3rd ed. New York: Knopf, 1920.

Meyer, Michael Leverson. *Ibsen: A Biography*. Garden City, NY: Doubleday, 1971.

Meyers, Jeffrey. *The Enemy: A Biography of Wyndham Lewis*. London: Routledge and Kegan Paul, 1980.

Mizener, Arthur. *The Saddest Story: A Biography of Ford Madox Ford*. New York: World, 1971.

Monroe, Harriet. *A Poet's Life: Seventy Years in a Changing World*. New York: Macmillan, 1938.

Moore, Harry T. *The Priest of Love: A Life of D. H. Lawrence*. Rev. ed. New York: Farrar, Straus & Giroux, 1974.

Morrow, Bradford, and Bernard Lafourcade. *A Bibliography of the Writings of Wyndham Lewis*. Santa Barbara, CA: Black Sparrow Press, 1978.

Mullins, Eustace. *This Difficult Individual, Ezra Pound*. New York: Fleet, 1961.

Murry, John M[iddleton]. Rev. of *Ulysses*, by James Joyce. *Nation and Athenaeum* 31 (22 Apr. 1922): 124–25.

*The New Poetry: An Anthology*. Ed. Harriet Monroe and Alice Corbin Henderson. New York: Macmillan, 1917.

"The New Sculpture." Rev. of *Gaudier-Brzeska: A Memoir*, by Ezra Pound. *Times Literary Supplement* 27 Apr. 1916: 199.

Nolde, John J. *Blossoms from the East: The China Cantos of Ezra Pound*. Orono, ME: National Poetry Foundation, U of Maine, 1983.

Norman, Charles. *Ezra Pound*. Rev. ed. New York: Funk and Wagnalls, 1969.

Noyes, Alfred. "Rottenness in Literature." Rev. of *Ulysses,* by James Joyce. *Sunday Chronicle* 29 Oct. 1922: 2.

[Oppenheim, James.] "To the Friends of The Seven Arts." Editorial. *Seven Arts* 2 (Oct. 1917): 672a-d.

*Others: An Anthology of the New Verse.* Ed. Alfred Kreymborg. New York: Knopf, 1916.

Rev. of *Passages from the Letters of John Butler Yeats, Selected by Ezra Pound. Times Literary Supplement* 7 June 1917: 271.

Patmore, Brigit. *My Friends When Young: The Memoirs of Brigit Patmore.* Ed. Derek Patmore. London: Heinemann, 1968.

*The Penguin Book of Modern American Verse.* Comp. Geoffrey Moore. London: Penguin, 1954.

Peterson, Elmer. *Tristan Tzara: Dada and Surrational Theorist.* New Brunswick, NJ: Rutgers UP, 1971.

"Poems from Cathay." Rev. of *Cathay,* by Ezra Pound. *Times Literary Supplement* 29 Apr. 1915: 144.

"The Poems of Mr. Ezra Pound." Rev. of *Lustra,* by Ezra Pound. *Times Literary Supplement* 16 Nov. 1916: 545.

Pound, Ezra. *The Cantos.* Rev. ed., 3rd printing. New York: New Directions, 1972; London: Faber and Faber, 1975.

——. *Collected Early Poems of Ezra Pound.* Ed. Michael King. New York: New Directions, 1976; London: Faber and Faber, 1977.

——. *Ezra Pound and Music: The Complete Criticism.* Ed. R. Murray Schafer. New York: New Directions, 1977; London: Faber and Faber, 1978.

——. *Ezra Pound and the Visual Arts.* Ed. Harriet Zinnes. New York: New Directions, 1980.

——. "Ford Madox (Hueffer) Ford: Obit." *Nineteenth Century and After* 126 (Aug. 1939): 178–81.

——. *Gaudier-Brzeska: A Memoir.* 1916. New York: New Directions, 1970.

——. *Instigations.* 1920. Essay Index Reprint Series. Freeport, NY: Books for Libraries, 1967.

——. *The Letters of Ezra Pound, 1907–1941.* Ed. D. D. Paige. New York: Harcourt, Brace, 1950.

——. *Lustra.* London: Mathews, 1916; New York: Knopf, 1917.

——. *"Noh," or Accomplishment: A Study of the Classical Stage of Japan by Ernest Fenollosa and Ezra Pound.* London: Macmillan, 1916; New York: Knopf, 1917.

——. "Paris Letter, December 1922." *Dial* 74 (Jan. 1923): 85–90.

——. *Pavannes and Divisions.* New York: Knopf, 1918.

——. *Personae: Collected Shorter Poems.* New York: New Directions, 1949; London: Faber and Faber, 1952.

——. *Pound/Joyce: The Letters of Ezra Pound to James Joyce, with Pound's Essays on Joyce.* Ed. Forrest Read. New York: New Directions, 1967.

——. "Psychology and Troubadours." *Quest* (London) 4 (Oct. 1912): 37–53. Rpt. as Chapter V of *The Spirit of Romance* (in editions 1932 and later).

——. "Rabindranath Tagore: His Second Book into English." Rev. of *The Gardener*, by Rabindranath Tagore. *New Freewoman* 1 (Nov. 1913): 187–88.

——. "Remy de Gourmont [Part I]." *Fortnightly Review* ns 98 (1 Dec. 1915): [1159]–66.

——. "Remy de Gourmont [Part II]." *Poetry: A Magazine of Verse* 7 (Jan. 1916): 197–202.

——. *Selected Prose: 1909–1965.* Ed. William Cookson. New York: New Directions; London: Faber and Faber, 1973.

——. "Small Magazines." *English Journal* 19 (Nov. 1930): 689–704.

——. "Webster Ford." *Egoist* 2 (1 Jan. 1915): 11–12.

——, and Ford Madox Ford. *Pound/Ford, the Story of a Literary Friendship: The Correspondence Between Ezra Pound and Ford Madox Ford and Their Writings About Each Other.* Ed. Brita Lindberg-Seyersted. New York: New Directions, 1982.

——, and Wyndham Lewis. *Pound/Lewis: The Letters of Ezra Pound and Wyndham Lewis.* Ed. Timothy Materer. New York: New Directions, 1985.

——, and Dorothy Shakespear. *Ezra Pound and Dorothy Shakespear: Their Letters, 1909–1914.* Ed. Omar Pound and A. Walton Litz. New York: New Directions, 1984.

Pound, Omar, and Philip Grover. *Wyndham Lewis: A Descriptive Bibliography.* Folkestone, Kent, Eng.: Dawson, 1978.

Powys, John Cowper. *Letters of John Cowper Powys to Louis Wilkinson, 1935 to 1956.* London: Macdonald, 1958.

Putnam, Samuel. *Paris Was Our Mistress.* New York: Viking, 1947.

——. *The World of Jean de Bosschère.* N.p.: Fortune, 1932.

Reid, Benjamin Lawrence. *The Man from New York: John Quinn and His Friends.* New York: Oxford UP, 1968.

Ricks, Beatrice, comp. *Ezra Pound: A Bibliography of Secondary Works.* Metuchen, NJ: Scarecrow, 1986.

Rimbaud, Arthur. *Prose Poems from the Illuminations of Arthur Rimbaud.* Trans. Helen Rootham. Norfolk, CT: New Directions, 1943.

Roberts, Warren. *A Bibliography of D. H. Lawrence.* 2nd edn. Cambridge: Cambridge UP, 1982.

Robinson, Janice S. *H.D.: The Life and Work of an American Poet.* Boston: Houghton Mifflin, 1982.

Rothenstein, William. *Men and Memories: Reflections of William Rothenstein, 1900–1922.* New York: Coward-McCann, 1932.

Sencourt, Robert. *T. S. Eliot, A Memoir.* Ed. Donald Adamson. New York: Dodd, Mead, 1971.

Sinclair, May. "The Novels of Dorothy Richardson." *Egoist* 5 (Apr. 1918): 57–59; *Little Review* 4 (April 1918): 3–11.

——. "The Reputation of Ezra Pound." *English Review* 30 (Apr. 1920): 326–35.

Slocum, John J., and Herbert Cahoon. *A Bibliography of James Joyce.* New Haven: Yale UP, 1953.

Smoller, Sanford J. *Adrift among Geniuses: Robert McAlmon, Writer and Publisher of the Twenties.* University Park, PA: Pennsylvania State UP, 1975.

Stange, G. Robert. "The 'Lost' Renaissance." Rev. of *The Little Review Anthology. Poetry* (Feb. 1954): 290–94.

Stock, Noel. *The Life of Ezra Pound.* Expanded ed. San Francisco: North Point Press, 1982.

Symons, Arthur. *Poems by Arthur Symons.* 2 vols. London: Heinemann, 1909.

——. *Spiritual Adventures.* New York: Dutton, 1905.

——. *The Symbolist Movement in Literature.* London: Heinemann, 1899.

Symons, Julian. *Makers of the New: The Revolution in Literature, 1912–1939.* New York: Random House, 1987.

Taupin, René. *L'Influence du symbolisme français sur la poésie américaine (de 1910 à 1920).* Paris: Champion, 1929.

Troy, William. "The Story of the Little Magazines." *Bookman* (New York) 70 (Jan. 1930): 476–81.

Tytell, John. *Ezra Pound: The Solitary Volcano.* New York: Doubleday, 1987.

*The Vidas of the Troubadours.* Trans. Margarita Egan. Vol. 6, Series B. Garland Library of Medieval Literature. New York: Garland, 1984.

Viereck, Peter. "Pound at 100: Weighing the Art and the Evil." *New York Times Book Review* 29 Dec. 1985: 3.

W., S. "Our Contemporaries: A Modern French Anthology." *Poetry: A Magazine of Verse* 12 (Apr. 1918): 54–55.

Wagner, Geoffrey. "Wyndham Lewis and the Vorticist Aesthetic." *Journal of Aesthetics and Art Criticism* 13 (Sept. 1954): 1–17.

——. *Wyndham Lewis: A Portrait of the Artist as Enemy.* New Haven: Yale UP, 1957.

Waley, Arthur, trans. *A Hundred and Seventy Chinese Poems.* London: Constable, 1918.

Wees, William C. *Vorticism and the English Avant-Garde.* Toronto: U of Toronto P, 1972.

Wells, H. G. "James Joyce." *New Republic* (10 Mar. 1917): 158–60.

West, Herbert Faulkner. *Robert Bontine Cunninghame Graham: His Life and Works.* London: Cranley and Day, 1932.

Wilhelm, James J. *The American Roots of Ezra Pound.* New York: Garland, 1985.

Williams, Ellen. *Harriet Monroe and the Poetry Renaissance: The First Ten Years of Poetry, 1912–22.* Urbana: U of Illinois P, 1977.

Williams, William Carlos. *The Autobiography of William Carlos Williams.* New York: Random House, 1951.

——. *The Selected Letters of William Carlos Williams.* Ed. John C. Thirlwall. New York: McDowell, Obolensky, 1957.

Yeats, John Butler. *Letters to His Son W. B. Yeats and Others, 1869–1922.* Ed. Joseph Hone. London: Secker and Warburg, 1983.

——. *Passages from the Letters of John Butler Yeats: Selected by Ezra Pound.* Churchtown, Dundrum: Cuala, 1917.

Yeats, William Butler. *The Letters of W. B. Yeats.* Ed. Allan Wade. New York: Macmillan, 1955.

——. *Memoirs: Autobiography—First Draft, Journal.* Ed. Denis Donoghue. New York: Macmillan, 1973.

Young, Alan. *Dada and After: Extremist Modernism and English Literature.* Manchester, Eng.: Manchester UP, 1981.

# Index

A. E., *see* Russell, George William
"A Clair Matin" (Albert Mockel), 239n
*A Lume Spento* (1908; Ezra Pound),
  xv, 48n, 107n
Abbot, Lyman, 82n
Abbott, Ella, 39, 40n, 52, 215
*ABC of Economics* (1953; Ezra Pound),
  305n
*The Academy*, 19n
Adams, B. M. G., 297, 299n; *see also*
  Scratton, Bride
*The Adelphi*, 74n
Advertising, influence on the magazine
  industry [in Ezra Pound's view], xiv
"Affectionate" (1922; Baroness Else von
  Freytag-Loringhoven), 299n
"After Hafiz" (1918; Iris Barry), 198n
Aiken, Conrad, 5n, 33n, 96n, 180n
*Al Que Quiere!* (1917; William Carlos
  Williams), 255n
"Alba" (1918; Ezra Pound), 204n, 249n
"Albert Mockel and 'La Wallonie' "
  (1918; Ezra Pound), 136n, 238, 238n,
  240
Aldington, Richard, xvii, xxii–xxiii, 2n,
  5n, 10, 14n, 63–64, 82n, 92, 94n, 102n,
  173n, 191
*Alfred Venison's Poems* (1935; Ezra
  Pound), 302n
Allen, Charles, xiv, xxvi, 2n–3n, 105n
L'Alliance Française, 142
"America" (1922; Muriel Gurdon
  Draper), 285n
American Civil Liberties Union, 322n
*American Literature* (1915; Leon
  Kellner, translated by Julia Franklin),
  160n
*The American Monthly*, 146n
"American Numbers" of *The Little
  Review* [June 1918 and December
  1918 issues], 209n, 231n, 241n, 258,
  259n

*American Pewter* (1923; John Barrett
  Kerfoot), 113n
*L'Amour de l'art*, 271, 275n
"An Anachronism at Chinon" (1917;
  Ezra Pound), 21, 23, 23n, 25, 26, 27,
  27n, 45, 85, 86n, 93, 95n, 127
Anarchism, and social change, xxi–xxii
*Ancient Lights and Certain New Re-
  flections, Being the Memories of a
  Young Man* (1911; Ford Madox
  Ford), 65, 72n
"Ancient Music" (1915; Ezra Pound),
  48n
Anderson, Cornelia, xx
Anderson, Lois, xviii–xix
Anderson, Margaret C., administration
  of *The Little Review*, 171, 173n, 262n;
  anarchism, xxi–xxiii; areas of emphasis
  in *The Little Review*, xxi, xxiii–xxv;
  bookselling, 45, 47n–48n, 65, 69, 71n;
  collaboration with Jane Heap, xxiii;
  editorial relationship with Ezra Pound,
  xv, xxiv–xxv, xxviii, xxxiii, 3, 91–92,
  301n; impressions on first meeting
  Ezra Pound, 300n; influence of
  Gurdjieff, 315n; letters, located at the
  Beinecke Library, Yale University, xi;
  move to New York, 4, 5n; move to
  Paris, xxiii, 299n–300n; *My Thirty
  Years' War*, ix–xi, xviii–xix, xxxiv, 5n,
  15n, 299n; publication of *Ulysses* in
  *The Little Review*, xxxi–xxxii, 260n;
  *The Little Review Anthology*, 303,
  318n; *The Seven Arts*, 146n; theories
  concerning life, art, aesthetics, etc.,
  xxi; trial of *Ulysses* for obscenity, 15n,
  260n, 261n, 276n; views regarding
  Ezra Pound's economic ideas, 327
Anderson, Sherwood, xix–xx, 5n, 69, 249,
  257, 268, 279, 281, 281n, 295
*Anglo-Mongrels and the Rose* (1923;
  Mina Loy), 208n

*Année littéraire* (edited by Élie Fréron), 94n
Anouilh, Jean, 325n
*Antheil and the Treatise on Harmony* (1924; Ezra Pound), 299n
Antheil, George, 299n
*Anthology of Magazine Verse and Year Book of American Poetry* (edited by William Stanley Braithwaite), 179n, 180n
*Antigone* (1951; Jean Anouilh, translated by Lewis Galantière), 325n
Antonini, A. [printing firm, Venice], 48n
Apollinaire, Guillaume, 1, 126n, 140
*Apollon*, 85, 86n
"Apropos Art and Its Trials Legal and Spiritual" (1921; Emmy V. Sanders), 278n
Aragon, Louis, 261, 262n, 265, 267, 268n, 281n
Aramis [pseudonymous reviewer of *Ulysses*], 293n
Arcos, René, 125n
Arensberg, Walter Conrad, 271, 273, 275n
"Aria" (1911; Ezra Pound), 189n
Armory Show [1913], 53n, 275n
Arnold, Matthew, xix
"Art in America" (1913; Aleister Crowley), 159n
"El arte poético Inglaterra contemporánea" (1920; Ezra Pound), 269n
"The Ascension of Edward VII to Heaven" (translation of "Saptam Edoyarder Svargobohan" by Tarini Prasad Jyotishi), 199n
*Ashe of Rings* (1921; Mary Butts), 276n, 279
Ashleigh, Charles, xxii
Association of American Painters and Sculptors, 53n
"At the Hotel" (1917; Iris Barry), 47n
"At the Ministry: September 1916" (1917; Iris Barry), 47n
Atheling, William [pseudonym used by Ezra Pound], 188n, 204n, 221n, 299n
"L'Athlète des pompes funèbres: poème en cinq chants" (1918; Francis Picabia), 268n–269n
*The Atlantic*, xiv, xxviii, 4, 26, 82n, 162
"Au bal masque" (1911; Ezra Pound), 189n
Auden, W. H., 309n
"Audience" (1918; Ezra Pound), 240, 241n
Augener Ltd., London [publishing firm], 189n

Augustine, Saint, 187
Austen, Jane, 258n
Authors' League of America, 102n
*Autobiography* (1967; Emanuel Carnevali, edited by Kay Boyle), 275n
"Aux Étuves de Wiesbaden, A. D. 1451" (1917; Ezra Pound), 24n, 27, 27n, 49n, 54, 64, 85, 86n, 195
*Avec des mots* (1927; Guy Charles Cros), 269n
"Avril" (1918; Ezra Pound), 204n
*Azrael and Other Poems* (1925; Robert Gilbert Welsh), 114n

Bach, Johann Sebastian, 186
Bain, Francis William, see *Digit of the Moon*
Baker, Captain Guy, 43, 68, 73n, 248, 255
"Ballet" (Stuart Merrill), 239n
"Banal Story" (Ernest Hemingway), 300n
"Barbara Roscorla's Child" (1917; Arthur Symons), 98n, 103–04
"A Barbarian" (1919; John Rodker), 255n
Barber, Samuel, 309n
Barbusse, Henri, 241n
Barnard, George C., 259n, 272, 276n
Barnes, Djuna, 5n, 281, 281n
Barney, Natalie Clifford, xi, 32, 285n
Baron, Jacques, 300n
Barry, Iris, xv, xxix, 5n, 10, 14n, 21, 32, 44–45, 47n, 62–64, 67–68, 71n, 100, 197, 198n
"A Battery Shelled" [1918–1919; painting by Wyndham Lewis], 189n
Baudelaire, Charles, 219n
Baxter, Gwen, 31, 34
Bayle, Pierre, 217, 219n
Beach, Sylvia, 12n–13n, 274n–275n
*Béâle-Gryne* (1909; Jean de Bosschère), 2n
Beardsley, Aubrey, 73n, 100, 107n
Beardsley, Mabel, 73n
*Beasts and Men: Folk Tales Collected in Flanders and Illustrated by Jean de Bosschère* (1918; Jean de Bosschère), 72n
Bechhofer-Roberts, Carl Eric, 248, 250n
Bedford, Agnes, 299n
Beecham, Sir Thomas, 36, 149, 151, 153n; see also Thomas Beecham Opera Company
Beerbohm, Max, 107n
*The Beginning* (1948; Robert Horan:

Yale Series of Younger Poets, vol. 46), 309n
"Bel Esprit," 285n
Bell, Clive, 4, 5n
Benét, William Rose, 307, 309n
Bennett, Arnold, 82n, 181
Bennington, William, 17n
Bercovici, Konrad, 110, 113n
Bergson, Henri-Louis, 81, 83n
Berkman, Alexander, xxii–xxiii
Bernhard, Svea, 247n, 248, 250n
"Bertha" (1918; Arthur Symons), 206n
"Bibi-la-Bibiste" (1920; Ezra Pound?), 259n, 266, 269n
"Billet à Whistler" (Stéphane Mallarmé), 239n
Bird, William, 294n, 299n
Bishop, Morris Gilbert, 296, 296n
"The Black Fowl" (1917; Iris Barry), 47n
"Blamont" (1918; André Spire), 254n
*BLAST: A Review of the Great English Vortex,* xvi–xvii, 14n, 16n, 39, 40n, 65, 72n, 100, 102n, 193n
Blavatsky, Helena Petrovna Hahn, 313, 315n
*Bloomsbury* (1905; Charles Francis Keary), 168n
Blum, Jerome, xix
Blunt, Wilfrid Scawen, 36, 85
"The Boarding House" (1915; James Joyce), 160n
Bodenheim, Maxwell, 57n, 89–90, 92, 93n–94n, 106, 109, 185, 201, 202n, 207
*Le Boeuf sur le Toit* (Jean Cocteau), 200n
Bois, Jules, 239n, 240
"Le Bon Grain" (Edmond Hanton), 239n
Bonaparte, Napoleon, 219n
Boni, Albert, xxii
Boni and Liveright, 65, 259n, 272, 274n
Boni, Charles, xxii
*A Book of Famous Verse* (1892; compiled by Agnes Repplier), 107n
*A Book of Prefaces* (1917; H. L. Mencken), 154–159, 159n
*The Bookman* (New York), 173n
"Books" (1918; John Rodker), 215, 215n
Bosanquet, Theodora, 165, 166n, 171, 173n, 225, 226n
Bosschère, Jean de, xviii, xxiv–xxv, 1, 1n–2n, 28, 32, 38n, 41, 46, 64, 72n, 173, 238, 240, 241n, 243, 243n, 246, 247n, 307, 309n
*Boston Transcript,* 180n

Bourne, Randolph, 96n
Boyd, Ernest Augustus, 55, 57n, 162, 163n
Boyle, Kay, 275n
Bracciolini, Gian Francesco Poggio, 24n, 54, 64, 85, 86n
Braithwaite, William Stanley, 178, 179n–180n
"Brancusi" (1921; Ezra Pound), 275n
Brancusi, Constantin, xxxiii, 124, 126n, 145n, 266, 268, 270–74, 275n, 276n, 279, 281, 291, 296, 298
"Brancusi number" [proposed special issue of *The Little Review*], 270–74
Braque, Georges, 145n
"The Breakfast" [painting by Fernand Léger, 1921], 299n
Brebezieu, Richard de, 252, 252n
*The Breeder's Gazette,* xx
Brenner, Michael, 124, 126n
Breton, André, 264n
"The Bridge" [painting by Fernand Léger, 1923], 299n
Bridges, Robert, 78, 79n
Bridges, Styles, 311, 311n
"Brief Note" (1918; Ezra Pound), 223
British Academy, 116, 131, 132n
British Poetry Society, 251n
*Broadway* (1911; John Barrett Kerfoot), 113n
Brodzky, Horace, 17n
"Broken Dreams" (1915; William Butler Yeats), 26n
Brooke, Rupert, xv, 79n
Brooks, Van Wyck, 53n, 96n
Brown, Nicholas, 31, 45
Browne, Francis F., xix, 96n
Browning, Robert, 187, 195n
Bruncken, Herbert, 137, 138, 138n, 140
"Bruxelles-Berlin Via Rotterdam" (1921; Clement Pansaers), 278n
Bryan, William Jennings, 213n
Bryer, Jackson R., xxii, xxiv, 261n
Bryher [pseudonym of Annie Winifred Ellerman], 294n
Brzeska, Henri Gaudier, *see* Gaudier-Brzeska, Henri
Brzeska, Sophie, 16n, 17n, 53n
Bubb, Reverend C. C., 245, 246n, 254
*Bubu de Montparnasse* (1902; Charles-Louis Philippe), 255n
*Bulletin of the School of Oriental Studies,* 88n
Burke, Kenneth, 285n, 298, 299n
Butts, Mary, 133, 273–74, 276, 276n, 279, 281n
Bynner, Witter, 109, 111n, 112n, 148n

Byrne, Mrs. James, 13n
Byron, George Gordon, Lord, 186, 216–17, 219n, 222n


Camera Club, 17n
Camera Work Gallery (New York), 275n
Campion, Thomas, 187, 188n
"A Canadian Gun Pit" [1918–19; painting by Wyndham Lewis], 189n
*Candide* (1759; Voltaire), 94n
Cannan, Gilbert, xv, 63, 71n
Cannell, Skipwith, xxii
*Cannibale,* 264n
"Canticle of the Race" (1917; Edgar Lee Masters), 146n
"Cantico del Sole" (1918; Ezra Pound), xxx, 179, 180n, 183, 183n
"Cantleman's Spring-Mate" (1917; Wyndham Lewis), xxviii, 42n, 57n, 87n, 104, 167, 167n, 175n, 178, 281n
*Cantos* (Ezra Pound), xxvi, xxx, 82n, 188n
"Cantus Planus" (1918; Ezra Pound), 242n, 255n
"Canzon" (1918; Ezra Pound), 204n
*Canzoni* (1911; Ezra Pound), 189n
"Le Cap de Bonne Espérance" (Jean Cocteau; translated by Jean Hugo as "The Cape of Good Hope" in 1921), xxxiii, 266, 269n, 270, 271, 275n, 276, 277, 279
Carnevali, Emanuel, 271, 275n, 281n, 292
Carpenter, Edward, 99, 101n
Carr, Daphne, 249, 250n
Carson, Edward Henry, 144, 146n
Carswell, John, 201n, 204n
"Carte postale express" (1921; Paul Morand), 278n
Carter, Thomas H., 306–07, 308n, 312, 314, 316n, 323–24, 324n, 327
Carus, Paul, 206, 206n, 207, 208n, 209, 244–45, 245n
Caruso, Dorothy, 308, 309n, 310–11, 315–16, 317n, 319, 324, 326, 328
Caruso, Enrico, 309n
*Cathay* (1915; Ezra Pound), 16, 18n, 40n, 88, 88n
*Catholic Anthology: 1914–1915* (1915; edited by Ezra Pound), 65, 72n, 75
*Celtic Twilight* (1893; William Butler Yeats), 18n
*The Cenci* (1819; Percy Bysshe Shelley), 157
Cendrars, Blaise, 265, 268, 269n

*Century,* xiv, 9, 80, 82n, 103, 104, 105n, 123, 141, 215
"Certain Artists Bring Her Dolls and Drawings" (1917; William Butler Yeats), 47n
*Certain Noble Plays of Japan* (1916; Fenollosa/Pound), 13n
Cézanne, Paul, 145n
Chakravarty, Ajit [translator of Rabindranath Tagore], 59n
"The Challenge of Emma Goldman" (1914; Margaret C. Anderson), xxi
*Chamber Music* (1907; James Joyce), 65, 72n, 117
Chambers, Jessie, 71n
Chambers, Robert W., 295
"Chanson Arabe" (1918; Ezra Pound), 242n, 255n
*Charles Blanchard* (1913; Charles-Louis Philippe), 255n
"Chevaux de Diomedes" (Remy de Gourmont), 99
*Chicago Daily News,* 192n
*Chicago Evening Post,* xviii–xix
*Chicago Poems* (1916; Carl Sandburg), 48n
"Chicago Renaissance" writers, xix
"Le Chien domestique" (1918; Jean de Bosschère), 241n, 246
"The Children of Judas" (1917; Robert Alden Sanborn), 132n, 188n
*The Chinese Written Character as a Medium for Poetry* (1936; Fenollosa/Pound), 302n
"The Chinese Written Character as a Medium for Poetry, by Ernest Fenollosa and Ezra Pound" (1919; Fenollosa/Pound), 198, 199n, 206, 206n, 207, 208, 208n, 209, 212, 228, 233n, 239, 244, 248, 250n, 253, 254n, 258, 259n
"The Christening" (1914; D. H. Lawrence), 72n, 160n
Christian [pseudonym of Georges Herbiet], 289, 290n, 297
Christian era, end of [announced by Ezra Pound], 282, 282n
*Christmas Tales of Flanders* (1917; illustrated by Jean de Bosschère), 72n
Churchill, Winston, 311
*Cinderella* (opera by Massenet; libretto translated by Ezra Pound, 1916), 153n
*The City Curious: Illustrated by the Author and Retold in English by F. Tennyson Jesse* (1920; Jean de Bosschère), 72n
"Clara" (1918; Ezra Pound), 204n

*The Clarion,* 102n
"The Classical Stage of Japan: Ernest
Fenollosa's Work on the Japanese
'Noh' " (1915; Ezra Pound), 105n
"The Classics 'Escape' " (1918; Ezra
Pound), 175n, 180n
Claudel, Paul, 1n, 2n
Clayton, T. T., 173n
*The Clearer Vision* (1898; Ethel Colburn
Mayne), 107n
Clerk's Press [publishing firm], 188n,
245, 246n
Cline, Leonard, 191, 193n
*The Closed Door* (1917; Jean de
Bosschère), 2n, 3n
Clowes, William, *see* William Clowes
and Sons, Ltd.
Clutton-Brock, Arthur, 39, 40n, 231,
232n
Coady Gallery, New York, 123, 126n
Coady, R. J., 123, 126n
Coburn, Alvin Langdon, 16, 17n, 60,
86n, 215, 228
Cocteau, Jean, xxxiii, 200n, 264, 264n,
265, 266, 268, 269, 270–71, 273–74,
275n, 276, 276n, 277, 279, 281n, 297,
311, 311n, 325, 325n, 326
*Le Coffret de Santal* (1873; Émile-
Hortensius-Charles Cros), 269n
*The Collapse of the Penitent* (1900;
Frederick Wedmore), 107n
"The Collar-Bone of a Hare" (1915;
William Butler Yeats), 26n
*Collected Poems* (1913; Ford Madox
Ford), 65, 72n
*Le Collier de Griffes* (1908; Émile-
Hortensius-Charles Cros), 269n
Collignon, Raymonde, 180n, 186, 188n,
194, 195n
Colum, Padraic, 96n, 110, 113n
Colvin, Sir Sidney, 218, 219n
*A Companion Volume* (1923; Robert
McAlmon), 294n
*Les Complaintes* (1885; Jules Laforgue),
239n
*Complete Poetical Works* (1912; T. E.
Hulme [published as an appendix to
Ezra Pound's *Ripostes*]), 13n
"Compleynt of a Gentleman . . ."
(1918; Ezra Pound), 204n
Comstock Postal Act of 1873, 159n
"Concava Vallis" (1918; Ezra Pound),
242n, 255n
*Confessions* (1916; John Cowper
Powys), 48n
Confucius, 11, 314, 327
Conrad, Joseph, 38n, 42n, 159n, 181

*Contact,* 294n
Contact Publishing Company, 294n
"Conte pour la Comtesse de Noailles"
(1922; Pierre de Massot), 281, 281n
"Contemporania" (1913; Ezra Pound),
13n
"Contemporary French Poetry" (1912;
F. S. Flint), 135n
"A Contemporary of the Future" (1920;
Evelyn Scott), 261n
*The Contemporary Review,* 168, 169n
*Contemporary Verse,* 180n
*Contes d'Espagne et d'Italie* (1830;
Alfred de Musset), 219n
*Continent,* xix
*Les Contrerimes* (1921; Paul-Jean
Toulet), 299n
"The Convalescent in the South" (1918;
Jessica Dismorr), 193n
Cook, George Cram, xix
"Cooperation (A Note on the Volume
Completed)" (1918; Ezra Pound),
213n
Copeau, Jacques, 2n
Corbière, Tristan, 135n, 182, 219n
Corrigan, J. E., 261n
Cournos, John, xxii, 10, 14n, 34n
Crane, Hart, 185
"Le Crapaud" (Jules Laforgue), 239n
Crelos [pseudonymous author of the
poem "Whitehall"], 210, 210n–211n,
258, 259n
Crevel, René, 300n
*Crimes of Charity* (1917; Konrad
Bercovici), 110, 113n
Criminal Code, of the United States
(section 211), 173–74, 175n–176n
*The Criterion,* 306, 308n, 312, 316n
"The Criterion" (1918; Ezra Pound),
194, 195n, 240
*Croquignole* (1906; Charles-Louis
Philippe), 255n
Cros, Émile-Hortensius-Charles, 269n
Cros, Guy Charles, 125n, 265, 268,
269n, 276n, 297
Crowley, Aleister, 154, 159n
Crowley, Edward Alexander, *see*
Crowley, Aleister
Crump, Charles G., 219n
*A Crystal Age* (1887; W. H. Hudson),
48n
Cuala Press [publishing firm], Dublin,
13n, 28, 37, 39n, 63, 73n
Cubism, xxvi, 138n, 233n, 269n
Cunard, Lady, xi, 149, 150n, 151, 153n
Cunard, Nancy, 150n
Currey, Margery, xx

"Curtain for the Ballet 'Skating Rink' "
[painting by Fernand Léger, 1923],
299n
"Cyclops" [twelfth section of Joyce's
*Ulysses*], 306n


Da Vinci, Leonardo, xx
Dadaism in art and literature, 259n,
262n, 264n, 265, 269n, 275n, 279,
280, 290
"Dance Figure" (1916; Ezra Pound),
99, 101n
Daniel, Arnaut, 184, 187n, 246n, 254,
254n
"Dans l'eau" (1918; Max Michelson),
150n, 209n
"Dans le Restaurant" (1918; T. S. Eliot),
105n, 224n
Dante, 129, 159, 311n, 314, 316n
Darrow, Clarence Seward, 308, 309n
Daumal, René, 315n, 327
Daumal, Vera, 315n, 316, 327, 328n
Daumier, Honoré, 145n
Davenport, Guy, 307, 309n
Davies, Arthur B., 51, 53n, 123–24,
165n, 170
Davray, Henry D., 122, 125n, 140
"Dawn on the Mountain" (1918; Ezra
Pound [translated from Omakitsu]),
242n, 255n
de Angulo, Jaime, 312, 313n
de Bosschère, Jean, *see* Bosschère,
Jean de
"De Bosschère's Study of Elskamp"
(1918; Ezra Pound), 136n, 240
*De Dignitate* (Pico della Mirandola),
*see De Hominis Dignitate*
de Goncourt, brothers, *see* Goncourt,
Edmond de *and* Goncourt, Jules de
"De Gourmont: A Distinction" (1919;
Ezra Pound), 173n, 239n, 256, 257
de Gourmont, Remy, *see* Gourmont,
Remy de
"De Gourmont—Yank" (1919; John
Rodker), 173n, 258n
*De Hominis Dignitate* (Pico della
Mirandola), 10, 14n
de la Mare, Walter, xv
*De Mallarmé à 391* (1922; Pierre de
Massot), 281n
de Massot, *see* Massot, Pierre de
de Maupassant, Guy, *see* Maupassant,
Guy de
*De Vulgari Eloquentia* (Dante), 129
De Wolf, Richard C., 137, 138

de Zayas, *see* Zayas, Marius de
"Dear!" (1918; Jean de Bosschère),
241n
"The Death of Tragedy" (1922; Ken-
neth Burke), 299n
"The Death of Vorticism" [1919; un-
signed article, perhaps attributable to
Ezra Pound], 256n
"A Deep Sworn Vow" (1915; William
Butler Yeats), 25n, 26n
"Definitions, etc." (1925; Ezra Pound),
293n
*Deirdre* (1902; A. E.), 79n
Delaroche, Achille, 239n, 240
Delaunay, Robert, 124, 126n
Dell, Floyd, xix–xx
Delteil, Joseph, 300n
Demuth, Charles, 111, 113n, 124, 126n,
288
Derain, André, 123–24, 126n, 145n
Dermée, Paul, 275n
*Des Imagistes* (*Glebe,* no. 5, 1914, edited
by Ezra Pound), xxii, 14n, 65, 71n,
72n
*Des Imagistes: An Anthology* [1914; En-
glish edition of preceding title], 77n, 92
"Descant on a Theme by Clercamon [i. e.,
Cerclamon]" (1918; Ezra Pound),
204n
Deutsch, Babette, 249, 251n
*291* [i. e., *Deux cents quatre-vingt-onze*]
(Marcel Duchamp/Francis Picabia),
264n
*Devious Ways* (1910; Gilbert Cannan),
71n
"Devotion" (1918; Arthur Rimbaud,
translated by Helen Rootham), 208n
*The Dial*, xix, xxxii–xxxiii, 93, 96n, 189,
189n, 190, 209n, 259n, 260, 261n, 263,
264n, 265, 267–68, 268n, 269n, 272,
290, 292, 293n, 308, 312, 318, 319n
Dias, B. H. [pseudonym used by Ezra
Pound], 204n
Dickens, Charles, 217
*Dictionnaire historique et critique* (1697;
Pierre Bayle), 219n
*Dictionnaire philosophique portatif*
(1764; Voltaire), 174, 176n, 216–18,
218n
*Digit of the Moon: A Hindoo Love Story*
(1899, etc.: Francis William Bain
[translated from the Sanskrit]), 191,
193n
Dinsmore, Elsie, 296
"Le Directeur" (1917; T. S. Eliot), 29n,
49n

"The Dish of Pears" [1923; painting by Fernand Léger], 299n
Dismorr, Jessica, 16n, 127, 191, 193n
Dismorr, John, 55
"Divagations" (1918; Marsden Hartley), 257, 258n
Dolmetsch, Arnold, 110, 113n, 186, 188n
*Dolorine et les ombres* (1911; Jean de Bosschère), 2n
Donlin, George Bernard, 96n
Doolittle, Hilda, xvii, xxiii, 2n, 5n, 10, 14n, 33, 48n, 57n, 64, 74n, 82n, 85, 86n, 92, 94n, 95n, 99, 102n, 128, 159n, 307
Dore Galleries, London, 193n
*Dorothy Caruso, A Personal History* (1952; Dorothy Park Caruso), 310n
"Dostoevsky's Novels" (1914; Martin Lazar), xxi
Dostoievsky, Fyodor, 181
Douglas, Gavin, 134, 135n–136n
Douglas, Major C. H., xxxiii, 259n
Douglas, Norman, xv
*The Drama,* 103, 105n
Draper, Muriel Gurdon, 284, 285n
"The Dreaming of the Bones" (1919; William Butler Yeats), 259n
Dreiser, Theodore, xix, 100, 102n, 157, 159n
Drieu la Rochelle, Pierre, 300n
"The Drover" (Padraic Colum), 110
*Dubliners* (1914; James Joyce), 65, 72n, 128, 160n
Duchamp, Marcel, 264n, 271, 275n, 288, 290–91
Duckworth [publishing firm, London], 65, 72n, 121n
Dulac, Edmund, 32, 307, 309n

*Echoes from the Gnosis* (1907; George Robert Stow Mead), 313, 315n
*Economic Democracy* (1920; C. H. Douglas), 259n
*L'Écossaise* (1760; Voltaire), 94n
"Editorial on Solicitous Doubt" (1917; Ezra Pound), 173n
"Eeldrop and Appleplex" (1917; T. S. Eliot), 22n–23n, 24, 27n, 28, 45, 64, 74, 75n, 87n, 99, 129, 303n, 304, 310, 322, 326
*The Egoist: An Individualist Review,* xvi, xxx, 6, 10, 12, 12n, 14n, 20n, 33, 37, 45, 58, 59n, 61–62, 74n, 92, 95n, 102n, 119, 120, 121n, 122, 152, 177, 204n, 207, 223, 249, 270
The Egoist Press [publishing firm], xvi,

12n, 29n, 70n, 117, 121n, 122, 270, 275n
Eisenhower, Dwight David, 306n
"Elimus" (1918; B. Cyril Windeler), 183n, 191, 194n, 196, 229, 297, 299n
Eliot, Henry Ware, 70n
Eliot, T. S., xiii, xvii, xxv, xxvii–xxx, xxxiii, 2n, 5n, 6, 10, 12, 15, 19, 21, 22n, 23, 25, 26, 28, 32, 45, 49, 49n, 61, 66–68, 74, 81, 83n, 85, 87, 88, 92, 94n, 97, 105n, 106, 108, 115–17, 118n, 126, 127n, 135, 150, 150n, 152, 171, 173n, 187, 191, 194, 195n, 203, 213n, 223–24, 224n, 225n, 226, 228, 228n, 231–32, 232n, 233, 238, 253, 265, 267, 281, 281n, 284, 307, 308n, 310, 312, 314–15, 316n, 319n, 327, 330n; difficulties with deadlines, 64, 75, 78, 104, 129; influence of French poetry, 3n; influence of little magazines on his literary career, xiii; Pound's influence in obtaining Eliot an editorial position with *The Egoist,* xvi; reprint of "Eeldrop and Appleplex" in *The Little Review Anthology,* 303–04, 322–23, 326; work in banking, 83n, 187, 285n
"Elizabethan Classicists" (1917–18; Ezra Pound), 187n
Ellerman, Annie Winifred, *see* Bryher
Ellmann, Richard, 282
Elskamp, Max, 2n, 125n
*England* (1923; B. M. G. Adams), 299n
English Language Union, 204n
*The English Review,* xv, 38n, 41, 42n, 63, 71n, 100, 102n, 154, 159n, 224, 292
*Epochs of Chinese and Japanese Art* (1911; Ernest Fenollosa), 13n
Epstein, Jacob, xvi
"Esprit d'enterprise" [*sic*] (1921; Paul Morand), 277n, 278n
*L'Esprit Nouveau,* 271, 275n
"Essentials" (1920; Robert McAlmon), 294n
Etchells, Frederick, 16n, 58, 228
*Exiles* (1918; James Joyce), 258n
Exiles number [Spring 1923 "special issue" of *The Little Review*], 298n–299n
Exton, Thayer [pseudonym used by Ezra Pound], 206n, 209n
*Exultations* (1909; Ezra Pound), xvii, 67
*Ezra Pound and the Visual Arts* (1980; edited by Harriet Zinnes), 278n
*Ezra Pound: His Metric and Poetry* (1918; T. S. Eliot), 195n
Ezra Pound Society, 305n, 313n

"Ezra Pound Today" (1922; Virgil Geddes), 294n
*Ezra Pound: Translations* (1964; enlarged edition of *The Translations of Ezra Pound*), 71n

Fabian Society, 101n
Fascism, and Ezra Pound's World War II broadcasts from Rome, 309n
*The Fatherland*, 146n
"Fear" (1915; John Rodker), 75
Fenollosa, Ernest, xvii, 9, 13n, 88n, 105n, 198, 206–08, 208n, 212, 216, 224, 228, 239, 244, 302n
Fenollosa, Mary, 13n, 30, 36
*Fermé la nuit* (1923; Paul Morand), 269n
*Les fêtes quotidiennes* (1912; Guy Charles Cros), 269n
Ficke, Arthur Davison, xix–xx, 111n, 112n
*The Fiery Fountains: The Autobiography, Continuation and Crisis to 1950* (1951; Margaret Anderson), 310n, 314, 323n, 325n
"La Figlia che Piange" (T. S. Eliot), 225n
Fiske, Bertha, 129
Flanner, Janet, 325n
Flaubert, Gustave, 210, 211n
Fletcher, John Gould, xxiii, 14n, 82n, 92, 94n, 155, 159n–160n
*Flight to Arras* (1942; Antoine de Saint-Exupéry, translated by Lewis Galantière), 325n
Flint, F. S., xxii, 2n, 3n, 10, 14n, 64, 71n, 94n, 113n, 134, 135n, 155, 160n, 247n, 278n
Forbes, L. S., 124, 126n
Ford, Ford Madox (Hueffer), xv, xxii, xxx, 33, 37, 38n–39n, 41, 42n–43n, 46, 48n, 61, 63–64, 70n, 71n, 72n, 78, 89, 89n, 96, 97, 97n–98n, 98–100, 101n, 102n, 104–05, 108, 116, 152, 163, 166, 171, 179, 187, 192, 196, 213, 213n, 229, 231n, 255n, 277, 281, 299n, 308, 318, 318n–319n
Ford, Webster [pseudonym of Edgar Lee Masters], 59n
*Form: A Monthly Magazine Containing Poetry, Sketches, Essays of Literary and Critical Interest,* 99, 101n
Fort, Paul, 125n
*Fortnightly Review,* 5n, 171, 173n
*The Forum,* 19n, 74n, 112n
Foster, George Burnam, xx

*Four Masters of Etching* (1883; Frederick Wedmore), 107n
"Fragments" (1918; Ben Hecht), 222n
France, Anatole, xv, 63, 79, 79n, 268
"Francisque fait la bulbate" (1921; Paul Morand), 277n
Frank, Waldo, 53n
Franklin, Benjamin, 158
Fraser, *see* Frazer, Sir James
Frazer, Sir James, 216, 218n
Free verse, *see Vers libre*
Freitag-Loringhoven, Elsa von, *see* Freytag-Loringhoven, Baroness Else von
"French number" [February 1918 issue of *The Little Review*], 122, 130, 133–36, 137n, 162, 172, 182, 213n, 222n, 241n, 257
Fréron, Élie, 90, 94n, 117, 118n
Freud, Sigmund, 48n, 154
Freytag-Loringhoven, Baroness Else von, 291, 293n, 298, 299, 319, 319n, 329
Frobenius, Leo, 307, 309n
"From the Clergy" [1918; contribution to "Reader Critic" column in *The Little Review*], 232n–233n
Frost, Robert, xvi, 2n, 94n, 143–44, 146n, 159n, 224n
Fry, Roger, 5n
"Further Poems by Po Chü-I, and an Extract from His Prose Works . . ." (1918; translated by Arthur Waley), 88n
*Future,* 203, 204n
Futurism in art and literature, xxi, xxvi, 138n, 262n

Galantière, Lewis, 325, 325n
Gallup, Donald, xi, xiv, 47n, 48n, 148n, 189n, 222n
Galsworthy, John, xv, 131n
Garden, Mary, 241n
*The Gardener* (1913; Rabindranath Tagore), 59n
Gardner, Isabella Stewart, 34, 100, 101n–102n, 106, 107n
Garnett, Edward, 42n–43n
*Gaudier-Brzeska: A Memoir* (1916; edited by Ezra Pound), 17n, 40n, 48n, 271, 275n
Gaudier-Brzeska, Henri, xvi, xxii, xxvii, xxxii, 16, 16n–17n, 53n, 66, 85, 86n, 124, 164, 165n, 266
Gaudier-Brzeska, Sophie, *see* Brzeska, Sophie
Gauguin, Paul, 124
Gautier, Théophile, 219n, 222n

Geddes, Virgil, 292, 294n
"Genesis, or, The First Book of the Bible: ('Subject to Authority')" [1918; uncredited translation by Ezra Pound from Voltaire's *Dictionnaire philosophique portatif*], 218n
*The "Genius"* (1915; Theodore Dreiser), 102n
*Genius: Zeitschrift für Werdende und alte Kunst*, 291, 293n
"Gently-Drunk Woman" (poem by Li Po; translated by Sasaki and Maxwell Bodenheim), 94n–95n
George, Lloyd, 191
George, Yvonne, 298, 299n
*Germinie Lacerteux* (1864; Edmond and Jules de Goncourt), 226, 227n
"Ein Gesang" (1921; Iwan Goll), 278n
*Geshlecht und Charakter: eine prinzipielle Untersuchung* (1903; Otto Weininger), 101n
Gibson, Wilfred Wilson, 69, 74n
Gide, André, 2n, 317n
Gilder, Richard Watson, 82n
Gilmore, Louis, 90–91, 95n, 109, 111n–112n
*Gipsy, see Gypsy*
Giraudoux, Jean, 2n
*Gitanjali: Song-Offerings* (1913; Rabindranath Tagore), 16, 17n–18n, 59n
"Glamour and Indigo: A Canzon from the Provençal of 'En Ar. Dan'el' " (1918; Ezra Pound), 187n, 242n, 255n
Glaspell, Susan, xix
*Glebe*, xxii
Gleizes, Albert, 124, 126n
Goacher, Denis, 313, 313n
*The Golden Bough* (1890–1915; Sir James Frazer), 216, 218n
Goldman, Emma, xxi–xxiv, 95n
Goll, Iwan [pseudonym of Isaac Lang], 276, 278n
Goncourt, Edmond de, 227n
Goncourt, Jules de, 227n
*The Goncourt Journals 1851–70* (1937; translated by Lewis Galantière), 325n
Gonne, Iseult, 199n, 239n, 250n
Gonne, Maud, 199n
Gosse, Sir Edmund, 36, 107n, 131, 132n, 188n
Gourmont, Remy de, xxx, 4, 5n, 48n, 85, 86n, 99, 105n, 108, 121–22, 125n, 130, 135n, 150, 150n, 152, 171, 173n, 208, 228, 238–40
"Gourmont number" [February–March 1919 issue of *The Little Review*, de-voted to Remy de Gourmont], 173n, 188n, 192, 195–96, 196n, 206, 208, 213n, 217, 228, 248, 254, 257
Graham, Stephen, 248, 250n
Grant, General Ulysses S., xiv
Granville, Charles, 204n
*The Great American Novel* (1923; William Carlos Williams), 294n
*Green Mansions* (1904; W. H. Hudson), 48n
Gregg, Frances, 74n
Gregory, Lady Isabella Augusta, xxix, 38, 54–55, 56n, 62, 71n, 75, 77n, 78–79, 80, 88, 89, 93, 96, 99, 108, 118, 150, 150n, 164, 168, 179, 237, 237n, 281, 281n
Gris, Juan, 124, 126n
Groff, Alice, 249, 250n
Grosz, George, 298, 299n
Gurdjieff, Georges Ivanovitch, 314, 315n, 316n, 323n, 327–328
Gyldendal, Copenhagen [publishing firm], 204n
*The Gypsy*, 99, 101n

H. D., *see* Doolittle, Hilda
Haigh, Emily Alice, *see* Hastings, Beatrice
Hale, Gardner, 124, 126n
Hall, John [pseudonym used by Ezra Pound], 22n, 44–45, 63, 71n
Halpert, Samuel, 124, 126n
Hand, Judge Augustus N., 172, 174, 175n, 176n, 188n, 305, 306n, 310, 310n, 323
"Hanrahan's Oath" (1917; Lady Gregory), xxix, 54, 56n, 62, 71n, 76, 77n, 78, 89, 93, 96, 99, 108, 118, 150n, 164, 293n
Hanton, Edmond, 239n, 240
"Happy Families" (1919; Aldous Huxley), 256n
Harding, Warren G., 263
Hardy, Thomas, xv, 38n, 46, 63, 79, 96, 98, 99, 101n, 103, 258n, 268
"The Harper of Chao" (1917; translated by Arthur Waley), 117, 119n
*Harper's*, xiv, 4, 9, 103
*Harper's Bazaar*, 324
Harrison, Barbara, 293n
Harrison of Paris [publishing firm], 293n–294n
Hartley, Marsden, 124, 126n, 257, 258n, 294n
*Harvard Advocate*, xviii, 34
Harvey, David Dow, 39n

Hastings, Beatrice [pseudonym of Emily Alice Haigh], 200n–201n
Hatteras, Owen [pseudonym of H. L. Mencken and George Jean Nathan], 106, 107n, 131, 155, 159n, 201, 202n
"The Hawthorne Aspect" (1918; T. S. Eliot), 233n
Hawthorne, Nathaniel, 295
Hays, Arthur Garfield, 321, 322n
Heap, Jane, xiii, xxiii–xxiv, xxxi–xxxiii, 13n, 53n, 54, 57n, 66, 69, 71n, 89, 91–92, 95n, 101, 110, 116, 122, 123–24, 128, 131n–132n, 133, 135, 136, 141, 149, 154–55, 159n, 163, 169, 172n–173n, 186, 188n, 196, 199, 213, 217, 258n, 260, 261n, 262n, 267, 283n, 290, 299n, 301, 301n; return to New York, 300n; *Ulysses* obscenity trial, 15n, 265, 276n
Hearst, William Randolph, 176n
*The Heart of the Country* (1911; Ford Madox Ford), 65, 72n, 318, 319n
Hecht, Ben, 190, 192n–193n, 201, 202n, 220, 222n, 248, 257, 268, 281, 281n, 295
Heinemann, W. H. [publishing firm], 64, 71n, 72n, 105n
"Hélène" (Francis Vielé-Griffin), 239n
Hemholtz, Baptiste von [pseudonym used by Ezra Pound], xvi
Hemholtz, Bastien von [pseudonym used by Ezra Pound], xvi
Hemingway, Ernest, 294n, 297, 300n
Henderson, Alice Corbin, 2n, 69, 74n, 100, 102n, 136, 142
Henley, G., *see* William Ernest Henley
Henley, William Ernest, 91, 95n, 232, 232n
"Henry James" (1917; Theodora Bosanquet), 173n, 225
"Henry James and the Ghostly" (1918; A. R. Orage), 204n, 209n
"Henry James as Expositor" (1918; Ezra Pound), 204n
"Henry James as Literary Artist" (1917; Theodora Bosanquet), 173n
*Henry James at Work* (1924; Theodora Bosanquet), 167n
"Henry James" issue of *The Little Review, see* "James number"
"Her Friends Bring Her a Christmas Tree" (1917; William Butler Yeats), 47n
*Herald Tribune* (Paris), 294n
*Herbert Vanlennert* (1895; Charles Francis Keary), 168n
Herbiet, Georges, *see* Christian

Heredia, José-Maria de, 219n
Herford, Oliver, 59n
*Hermes: Revista del pais vasco* [Bilbao], 267, 269n
Hermitage House [publishing firm], 303n
"Hérodias" (1877; Gustave Flaubert), 210, 211n
Herrick, Robert, 188n
Hewlett, Maurice Henry, 32, 48n, 69, 74n
Heyman, Katherine Ruth, 31, 114, 114n, 291, 293n
*High Policy* (1902; Charles Francis Keary), 168n
Hiler, Hilaire, 297, 299n
Hinckley, Theodore Ballou, 105n
"The Hippopotamus" (1917; T. S. Eliot), 29n, 49, 117, 118n
Hirsch, Charlotte Teller, *see* Teller, Charlotte
Hirsch, Gilbert, 30, 114, 291
"His Girl" (1917; Iris Barry), 47n
"Historical Survey" (1921; Ezra Pound), 276, 277, 278n
Hoffman, Frederick J., xiv, xxvi, 2n–3n, 105n
Holcombe, Wyn, 299n
"Homage à la langue d'or" [i. e., langue d'oc] (1918; Ezra Pound), xxx, 187n, 204n, 230, 231n
"Homage to Sextus Propertius" (1919; Ezra Pound), xxvi, 292, 294n
Homer, 230
"Homer Marsh Dwells In His House of Planks" (translation by F. S. Flint of Jean de Bosschère's poem "Homère Mere Habite Sa Maison des Planches"), 3n
"Homère Mere Habite Sa Maison des Planches" (Jean de Bosschère), 3n
"L'Homme Moyen Sensuel" (1917; Ezra Pound), xxx, 73n, 75, 80–81, 82n, 85, 86n–87n, 99, 104, 129–31, 132n, 179
Horace, 94n
Horan, Robert, 308, 309n, 325
House of Books [Philadelphia], 45
*The House of Prophecy* (1924; Gilbert Cannan), 71n
Housman, Lawrence, 148n
"How I Came to Know Renoir" (1917; Ambrose Vollard), 126n
*How to Read* (1916; John Barrett Kerfoot), 113n
Howells, William Dean, 158, 159n, 195n
Hoyt, Helen, 2n, 57n
"Hudson: Poet Strayed into Science" (1920; Ezra Pound), 259n

*Hudson Review,* 313n, 318, 319n
Hudson, Stephen, 298, 299n
Hudson, W. H., xv, 46, 48n, 259n
Huebsch, W. B. [publishing firm], 12n–13n, 65, 72n, 73n, 110, 121n, 274n
Hueffer, Ford Madox, *see* Ford, Ford Madox
Hueffer, Francis (Franz Carl Christoph Johannes Hüffer), 231n
*Hugh Selwyn Mauberley* (1920; Ezra Pound), xxvi
Hugo, Jean, xxxiii, 266, 269n, 275n, 276n
Hulme, T. E., xv, 13n, 79n, 83n, 155, 160n
*A Hundred and Seventy Chinese Poems* (1918; translated by Arthur Waley), 29n
Huneker, James Gibbons, 52, 53n, 159n
Hunt, Violet, 102n–103n, 106
Huntley, Francis E. [pseudonym of Ethel Colburn Mayne], 107n
Huxley, Aldous, 255n, 256, 256n, 281n

Ibsen, Henrik, 203, 204n
"The Ideal Giant" (1918; Wyndham Lewis), 115n, 168, 168n, 179, 183, 183n, 192, 194n, 196, 281n
*The Ideal Giant* (1917; Wyndham Lewis), 167n
*Idols* (1916; Walter Conrad Arensberg), 275n
Igly, France, 252n
*Les Illuminations* (1873–75; Arthur Rimbaud), 208n
*The Image and Other Plays* (1922; Lady Gregory), 56n
"Images of Friendship" (1917; Maxwell Bodenheim), 57n
*Images of Good and Evil* (1899; Arthur Symons), 105n
*Imaginary Conversations* (1891 edition; Walter Savage Landor), 218, 219n
"Imaginary Letters" (Wyndham Lewis), xxix, 21, 22n, 23–24, 26, 27n, 45, 49, 96n, 115, 177, 178n, 192, 195–96, 196n, 197, 197n, 198, 251n
"Imaginary Letters" (Ezra Pound), xxx, 78, 80–82, 99, 104, 108, 115, 118, 170, 173n, 178n, 192, 196, 208
Imagism in literature, xvii, xxii–xxiii, 13n, 14n, 64–65, 80, 109, 113n, 138n, 155, 160n, 180n, 255n, 309n
"Imagisme" (1913; Ezra Pound/F. S. Flint), 113n
"Improvisations" (1917; Louis Gilmore), 95n, 111n–112n

"Improvisations" (1918; William Carlos Williams), 192n
"In Explanation" (1918; Ezra Pound), 223
"In Memory" (1917; William Butler Yeats), 26n
"In Memory of Robert Gregory" (1918; William Butler Yeats), 223n, 237n, 238n, 240
*In the American Grain* (1925; William Carlos Williams), 302n
"Incidents in the Life of a Poet" (1918; John Rodker), 47n, 73n, 183, 192n, 215, 215n
*The Independent,* 124
"Indians in Overalls" (1950; Jaime de Angulo), 312, 313n
"Indissoluble Marriage" (1914; Rebecca West), 102n
"Inferior Religions" (1917; Wyndham Lewis), 42n, 64, 75, 76n, 80–82, 99, 130
*L'Influence du symbolisme français sur la poésie américaine (de 1910 à 1920)* (1929; René Taupin), 2n
Innes, George, 124
*Instigations* (1920; Ezra Pound), xxix, 136n, 206n, 250n, 259n, 281
Institute for the Harmonious Development of Man, Fontainebleau-Avon, France, 315n
*Interior,* xix
*The Interpretation of the Music of the XVIIth and XVIIIth Century Revealed by Contemporary Evidence* (1915; Arnold Dolmetsch), 110, 113n
*The Irish Homestead,* 79n
Irish National Theatre, 56n
*The Irish Statesman,* 79n
*Irish Times,* 277, 278n
*Isis Unveiled* (1877; Helena Petrovna Hahn Blavatsky), 315n
"The Island of Paris: A Letter" (1920; Ezra Pound), 269n


Jackson, Holbrook, 66
James, Henry, xv, xxix–xxx, 38n, 63, 107n, 154, 158, 159n, 165, 167n, 169, 171–72, 173n, 184, 188n, 203, 208, 209, 209n, 212, 224n, 225, 228, 258n, 301
"James Huneker" (1917; essay included in *A Book of Prefaces,* by H. L. Mencken), 159n
"James Joyce and Pecuchet" (1952; Ezra Pound), 308n

"James number" [August 1918 issue of *The Little Review,* devoted to Henry James], 173n, 184, 187n, 195, 196, 204n, 206, 208, 209n, 212, 213n, 214, 217, 220–21, 223–24, 226n, 228, 230, 233, 238, 256, 257, 288

Jammes, Francis, 2n, 125n, 135n, 219n

Jefferson, Thomas, 158, 260

Jepson, Edgar Alfred, 36, 52, 106, 107n, 223, 224n–225n, 225, 226n, 256

Jesse, F. Tennyson, 72n

*Jésus-Christ Rastaquouère* (1920; Francis Picabia), 264, 264n, 265

Jesus Maria, Hermann Karl Georg [pseudonym used by Ezra Pound], xvi

Jitro, W. C. G., 298, 299n

"Jodindranath Mawhwor's Occupation" (1917; Ezra Pound), 9, 13n, 21, 22n, 44, 47, 65, 68–69, 73n, 74n, 198, 199n

John, Augustus, 124, 169

"John Rodker's Frog" (1920; Mina Loy), 209n

Johns, Orrick, 94n

Johns, Richard, 313, 313n

Johnson, Martyn, 96n

*Jonah* (1917; Aldous Huxley), 255n

Jones, Llewellyn, xix, xx

"Jongleuses" [painting by Pierre Auguste Renoir, reproduced in *The Soil,* 1917], 124, 126n

Jordan, Viola Scott Baxter, 30, 100, 102n, 113, 114n, 307, 318

"Joseph Conrad" (1917; essay included in *A Book of Prefaces,* by H. L. Mencken), 159n

Josephson, Matthew, 285n

Jourdain, P. E. B., 207, 208n, 244

*The Journal of the Society for Psychical Research,* 166n

*The Journalist* (1898; Charles Francis Keary), 168n

Joyce, James, xiii, xiv, xxii, xxv, xxvii–xxviii, xxxii, 6, 10, 15, 19, 22n, 28, 32, 37, 53n, 55, 61, 62, 64, 66, 68, 69, 70n, 72n, 74n, 93n, 108, 116, 117, 157, 160n, 161, 165, 166, 171, 181, 184, 186, 189, 213n, 226, 228, 258n, 266, 267, 277, 282n, 292, 314, 315, 327, 330n; influence of little magazines on his literary career, xiii, xiv; *A Portrait of the Artist as a Young Man,* xvi, 19, 48n, 57n, 70n, 73n, 120, 166n, 181; publication of *Ulysses* in *The Little Review,* xxv, xxix, xxxi–xxxii, 20n, 42n, 46, 122, 139, 171, 174, 177, 179, 189, 190, 196, 212, 223, 256, 257, 261n, 263, 275n–276n, 277, 281; medi-

cal problems, 19, 21, 29n, 37, 38n, 64, 78, 79n, 130, 132n, 226

Joyce, Nora Barnacle, 130

"Judicial Opinion: (Our Suppressed October Issue)" (1917; Margaret C. Anderson), 175n

Jung, C. G., 48n

Jyotishi, Tarini Prasad, 199n

Kahn, Gustave, 140, 142n

Kahn, Otto, 13n

Katue, Kitasono, 302n

Keary, Charles Francis, 168, 168n–169n, 184–86, 188n, 190, 196, 200

Keats, John, 188n

Kellner, Leon, 156, 160n

Kenner, Hugh, xxvi–xxvii, 314, 319n

Kennerly, Mitchell, 19n

Kenton, Edna, xix

Kerfoot, John Barrett, 109, 113n

Kipling, Rudyard, 79, 95n, 198

Knish, Anne [pseudonym of Witter Bynner and Arthur Davison Ficke], *see* Bynner, Witter; *and see* Ficke, Arthur Davison

Knopf, Alfred A. [publishing firm], xxvii, 13n, 45, 48n, 50, 50n, 51n, 54, 56n, 65, 70n, 72n, 80, 82n, 85, 86n, 110, 113n, 129–30, 156, 180–81, 190n, 193n, 194, 195n, 258, 259n

Kreymborg, Alfred, xxii, 5n, 17n, 80, 82n, 141, 185, 208n, 288, 289n, 290n, 311

Kuhn, Walt, 51, 53n, 62, 70n–71n, 123, 124, 165n, 170

Kung, *see* Confucius

K'ung-Fu-tzu, *see* Confucius

Kyle, Galloway, 251n

*Ladies' Home Journal,* 176n

Laforgue, Jules, xxviii–xxix, 21, 22n, 62, 63, 68–69, 71n, 73n, 77, 99, 135n, 206, 206n, 208, 209, 209n, 210, 219n, 224, 225n, 239n, 249, 257

"The Lake Isle" (1916; Ezra Pound), 48n

Landor, Walter Savage, 218, 219n

"Landscape" [painting by Fernand Léger, 1921], 299n

Lane, John, 2n, 17n, 72n, 107n

Lang, Isaac, *see* Goll, Iwan

Larionov, Mikhail, 289, 290n

"Le Latin Mystique" (1919; T. T. Clayton), 173n

Laurencin, Marie, 165n

Laurie, T. W. [publishing firm], 58, 59n, 121n

"Law and the Merchant of Venice"
(1924; Ezra Pound), 293n
Lawes, Henry, 186, 188n
Lawrence, D. H., xv, 10, 14n, 38n, 48n,
63, 64, 71n, 72n, 75, 94n, 100, 102n,
157, 160n
Lazar, Martin, xxi
Le Monier, J. H. [pseudonym used by
Ezra Pound], 222n
Léautaud, Paul, 134, 135n
Leblanc, Georgette, 311n, 323n, 325,
325n
Léger, Fernand, 296, 298n–299n
Lencour, Vail de, *see* Patmore,
Brigit
Leslie, Shane, 149, 291, 293n
"Lestrygonians" [eighth section of Joyce's
*Ulysses*], 261n
*Letters of Ezra Pound, 1907–1941* (1950;
edited by D. D. Paige), xi, 34n, 309n,
322, 322n
*Letters of John Cowper Powys to Louis
Wilkinson, 1935 to 1956* (1958; edited
by Louis Wilkinson), 74n
"La Lettre" (1895; Henri Barbusse),
241n
*Lettres philosophiques* (1734; Voltaire),
176n
*Lettres sur quelques écrits de ce temps*
(edited by Élie Fréron), 94n
*Lewis et Irène* (1924; Paul Morand),
269n
"Lewis number" [proposed special issue
of *The Little Review*], 270, 274, 286,
286n, 288, 289, 291, 294
Lewis, Wyndham, xv, xvi, xxii, xxv,
xxvii–xxx, xxxii–xxxiii, 6, 7, 10, 14n,
16n, 19, 21, 22n, 23–24, 26, 27n, 28,
32, 38n, 40, 40n, 41, 42n, 45, 53n, 56,
57n, 61, 63–64, 66, 67–68, 70n, 72n,
73n, 75, 76n, 78, 79n, 80–81, 85, 87–
88, 93, 96, 96n, 98n, 104, 108, 115,
115n, 116, 122–24, 130–31, 150,
150n, 152, 163, 164, 165n, 167n, 168,
168n, 169, 177, 179, 181, 182, 183n,
186, 187, 189n, 191, 192–93, 193n,
194n, 195–97, 197n, 198, 213n, 223,
228–29, 235, 266–68, 274, 281, 281n,
283n, 285–86, 286n, 288, 288n, 289n,
290, 296, 307, 311, 313–15, 315n, 316,
318, 318n, 319n, 325–26, 327–28
Li Po, 94n, 242n
*Life,* 109, 113n
*Life of Algernon Charles Swinburne*
(1917; Edmund Gosse), 188n
*The Life of Ezra Pound* (expanded edition, 1982; Noel Stock), xvii

*The Life of Lope de Vega* (1904; Hugo
Albert Rennert), 185, 188n
*Life of Père Marquette* (1929; Agnes
Repplier), 107n
Lindsay, Vachel, xx, 2n, 147, 148n, 224n
"Lion's Jaws" (1920; Mina Loy), 209n
Lippmann, Walter, 30, 33n–34n
"List of Books" (1918; John Rodker),
255n
"A Little Cloud" (1915; James Joyce),
160n
*The Little Magazine: A History and a
Bibliography* (1946; Frederick J. Hoff-
man, Charles Allen, and Carolyn F.
Ulrich), xiv, xxvi, 2n–3n, 105n
*The Little Review Anthology,* xxxiv, 22n,
23n, 303n, 307–08, 312, 313n, 318,
318n–319n, 321–24, 324n, 326, 329,
330n
"The Little Review Calendar" (1922),
282n–283n, 284–85, 297
*Livelihood: Dramatic Reveries* (1917;
Wilfred Wilson Gibson), 74n
"The Living Beauty" (1918; William
Butler Yeats), 223n
Longfellow, Henry Wadsworth, 179,
180n, 216, 218
"Loose Leaf Products" (1922; Muriel
Gurdon Draper), 285n
Loringhoven, Baroness Elsa von Freytag,
*see* Freytag-Loringhoven, Baroness
Else von
"The 'Lost' Renaissance" (1954; G. Rob-
ert Stange), 330n
"The Love Song of J. Alfred Prufrock"
(1915; T. S. Eliot), xviii
Lowell, Amy, xxii–xxiii, xxix–xxx, 5n, 10,
14n, 64, 82n, 91–92, 94n, 109, 116,
118n, 122, 125n, 135n, 139–41, 148n,
151, 154, 159n–160n, 162, 178, 180n,
190, 216, 267, 284
Lowell, Percy, 116
Loy, Mina, 207, 208n–209n, 255n, 268,
294n, 297
*Lumir: Literániho odboru Umelecké
besedy* [Prague], 267, 269n, 271, 275n
*Lunar Baedeker* (1923; Mina Loy),
294n
"Lune de Miel" (1917; T. S. Eliot), 29n
*Lustra* (1916; Ezra Pound), xxvii, 16,
17n, 40n, 46, 48n, 85, 86n, 99, 101n,
249
*Lustra of Ezra Pound with Earlier Poems*
(1917) [American edition of preceding title], 50n, 51n, 56n, 65, 72n, 80,
82n, 103n, 189, 190, 190n, 193n
*Lyrics* (1903; Arthur Symons), 113n

Mabie, Hamilton, 82n, 195n
Macdonald, Dwight, 318, 318n–319n
MacDougall, Allan Ross, xxiv
*La Machine à Courage: Souvenirs* (1947; Georgette Leblanc), 311n, 325, 325n
Macmillan [publishing firm], 13n, 58, 59n, 72n, 190, 190n, 203, 228n
Macy, John, 96n
"Madrigale" (1911; Ezra Pound), 189n
Maeterlinck, Maurice, 325n
*The Mahabharata*, 313, 315n
Makovski, Sergei Konstantinovich, 86n
Mallarmé, Stéphane, 219n, 239n, 240
Manet, Edouard, 144
*Manikin*, 294n
Manning, Frederic, 65, 72n, 173n
Mansfield, Katherine, xvi, 79n, 201n
Marcoussis, Louis, 265, 269n
Mare, Walter de la, *see* de la Mare, Walter
*A Mariage de Convenance* (1899; Charles Francis Keary), 168n
*Marie Donadieu* (1904; Charles-Louis Philippe), 255n
Marin, John, 124, 126n
Marinetti, Filippo Tommaso, 262, 262n
Markham, Edwin, 148n
Marsden, Dora, xvi, 20n, 152
Marshall, John, 17n, 246n
Marwood, Arthur, 43n
Masefield, John, 148n, 302
Massot, Pierre de, 280, 281n
*The Master Poisoner* (1918; Ben Hecht/ Maxwell Bodenheim), 202n
Masters, Edgar Lee, xvi, 5n, 56n, 58, 59n, 80, 90, 94n, 143–44, 146n, 159n, 224n, 308, 309n
Materer, Timothy, *Pound/Lewis: The Letters of Ezra Pound and Wyndham Lewis* (1985), ix
Mathers, Edward Powys, 288, 289n
Mathews, Elkin [publishing firm], 17n, 18n, 48n, 65, 72n, 86n, 88n, 103, 105n, 117, 166, 235
Matthewson, Christy, 311n
Matuce, H. Ogram [pseudonym of Charles Francis Keary], 168n
Maupassant, Guy de, 190, 220
Maxim, Hiram, 82n
Mayne, Ethel Colburn, 35, 106, 107n, 173n, 197, 223–25, 231
McAlmon, Robert, 292, 294n, 297, 298
McClure, J., 109
McLuhan, Marshall, 319n
Mead, George Robert Stow, 36, 38n, 313, 315n

"Mélange adultère de tout" (1917; T. S. Eliot), 3n, 29n, 49n
*Memories and Impressions, A Study in Atmosphere* (1911; Ford Madox Ford), 72n
*Men and Memories: Recollections of William Rothenstein, 1900–1922* (1932), 59n
"Men Improve with the Years" (1916; William Butler Yeats), 25n
Mencken, H. L., 31, 107n, 154, 155–56, 159n, 160n, 178, 193n, 199, 201
*Mendel* (1916; Gilbert Cannan), 71n
Menotti, Gian Carlo, 309n
*Mercure de France*, xxix, 5n, 32, 46, 48n, 78, 123, 125n, 135, 135n, 137, 139–40, 213n, 220, 222n, 238, 269n
*Mère Marie: of the Ursulines* (1931; Agnes Repplier), 107n
Merrill, Stuart, 135n, 239n, 240
"Mesopotamia" (1917; Rudyard Kipling), 90, 95n
Mestrovic, Ivan, 291, 293n
*Métiers divins* (1913; Jean de Bosschère), 1, 2n
Metzinger, Jean, 124, 126n
Michelson, Max, 150, 150n, 207–208, 209n, 242, 257
"The Middle Years" (1918; Ezra Pound), 203, 204n, 223
Milton, John, 90, 188n
*Minaret*, 137, 138, 138n, 142n, 151, 153n
*Minna and Myself* (1918; Maxwell Bodenheim), 202n
Minor, Robert, xxiv
Mirandola, Giovanni Pico della, *see* Pico della Mirandola, Giovanni
"Miscellany Number" [Winter 1922 special number of *The Little Review*], 296, 298n
"Mr. and Mrs. Elliot" (1924–25; Ernest Hemingway), 300n
"Mr. Eliot's Sunday Morning Service" (1918; T. S. Eliot), 105n, 224n
"Mr. James Joyce and the Modern Stage" (1916; Ezra Pound), 105n
"Mr. Lindsay" (1918; by Ezra Pound, writing pseudonymously as Abel Sanders), 148n
"Mr. Mencken, Philistine" (1918; Jane Heap), 159n
"Mr. Mencken's Truism" (1918; Margaret C. Anderson), 159n
"Mr. Pound, Mr. Flint, Some Imagists or Cubists, and the Poetic Vernacular"

[chapter in *Thus to Revisit*] (1921; Ford Madox Ford), 278n
"Mr. Styrax" (1918; Ezra Pound), 204n
Mithouard, Adrien, 1n
Mizener, Arthur, 38n
Mockel, Albert, 220, 222n, 238, 238n, 239n, 240
"Modern Beauty" (1899; Arthur Symons), 105n
Modern Gallery, New York, 142, 145n
*The Modern Review*, 59n
"Moeurs contemporaines" (1918; Ezra Pound), xxx, 204n
Molière, 96n
"Momie" (1918; Jean de Bosschère), 241n
"Money Pamphlets of £" [series of pamphlets reprinting Ezra Pound's writings on economics], 305n
Monier, J. H. Le, *see* Le Monier, J. H.
*The Monist: A Quarterly Magazine Devoted to the Philosophy of Science*, 198, 199n, 206, 206n, 208n, 244, 245n
Monro, Harold, xxii, 134, 135n, 247, 247n, 251n
Monroe, Harriet, xvii–xviii, xxiv–xxv, 1, 2n–3n, 17n, 40, 127, 136, 142, 143, 185, 188n, 203, 223, 225n
"M. De Gourmont and the Problem of Beauty" (1919; Frederic Manning), 173n
(*Monthly*) *Chapbook*, 247n
Montross Gallery, New York, 16n–17n
Moody, William Vaughn, 216, 219n
Moore, Geoffrey, 319, 319n, 329
Moore, Marianne, 5n, 82n, 207, 209n, 255n, 268, 276, 277n, 306, 308, 311, 311n, 326
Moore, T. Sturge, xv, 36, 79n
Morales, Tomás, 203, 204n–205n
Morand, Paul, xxxiii, 265, 268, 269n, 276, 276n, 277n–278n
Moréas, Jean, 135n, 219n
Morgan, Emmanuel [pseudonym of Witter Bynner], *see* Bynner, Witter
Morgan, Evan Frederic, 39, 97, 235n
Morrison-Scott, Ethel Elizabeth, *see* Patmore, Brigit
*Moscardino* (1955; Enrico Pea, translated by Ezra Pound), 307, 308n, 309n; *see also Il Romanzo di Moscardino*
Mosher, Thomas Bird [publishing firm], 82n, 106, 107n, 111, 113n
*Motive and Method in* The Cantos *of Ezra Pound* (1954; Guy Davenport), 309n

*The Mount* (1909; Charles Francis Keary), 168n
Mudrick, Marvin, 319n
Munson, Gorham Bert, 284, 285n, 303n, 304, 305n, 310, 321–24
Murray, John [publishing firm], 65, 72n
Murry, John Middleton, xvi, 79n, 291, 293n
Musset, Alfred de, 216, 219n, 222n
Mussolini, Benito, 309n
*My Friends When Young* (1965; Brigit Patmore), 102n–103n
*My Thirty Years' War: The Autobiography, Beginnings and Battles to 1930* (1969; Margaret Anderson), ix, xviii–xx, xxiii, 5n, 15n, 299n–300n, 310n, 323n

Nast, Condé [publishing firm], xiv
Nathan, George Jean, 107n, 202n
*Nation*, London, 166n
*Nation & Athenaeum*, 293n
*National Observer*, 91, 95n
*The Natural Philosophy of Love* (1922; Remy de Gourmont, translated by Ezra Pound), 293n
"Nausicaa" [thirteenth section of Joyce's *Ulysses*], xxxi, 260n
"Nausikaa," *see* "Nausicaa"
Nevinson, S. R. W., 124
*The New Age: A Democratic Review of Politics, Religion, and Literature*, xv–xvi, xxx, 70n, 74n, 79n, 83n, 110, 185, 187n, 188n, 191, 199–200, 200n–201n, 203, 204n, 207, 221n, 250n, 267, 297, 299n
*New Directions 14* (1953), 318n
*New Directions in Prose and Poetry* (1955), 308n
*New Directions: Number Seven* (1942), 39n
New Directions [publishing firm], 208n, 302n, 316n, 324, 324n
*The New Freewoman: An Individualist Review*, xvi, 14n, 59n, 74n
*New Ireland*, 57n
*A New Model of the Universe* (1931; P. D. Ouspensky), 315n
*The New Republic*, 30, 33n, 34n, 52, 65, 72n, 93, 138, 166n, 180n
*New Statesman*, 5n, 73n, 93, 102n
New York Post Office, and literary censorship, xxv, 42n, 57n, 88n, 119n, 172n, 173n, 260n–261n
New York Society for Suppression of Vice, xxxii, 82n, 159n, 260n

*The New Yorker,* 307, 318, 318n
Nietzsche, Friedrich, xx, 280
*Nine,* 305n
*Nineteenth Century and After,* 39n
"Nishi Hongwanji" (1918; Iris Barry),
 198n
"Nodier Raconte" (1918; Ezra Pound),
 204n
*"Noh" Or Accomplishment: A Study of
 the Classical Stage by Ernest
 Fenollosa and Ezra Pound* (1917;
 Fenollosa/Pound), 13n, 17n, 40n,
 56n, 65, 72n, 75, 272
*North of Boston* (1914; Robert Frost),
 143, 144
*Norway and the Norwegians* (1893;
 Charles Francis Keary), 168n
"Note upon Fashions in Criticism"
 (1918; Ezra Pound), 222n
"Notes on Elizabethan Classicists"
 (1918; Ezra Pound), 187n
"The Notes on Novelists" (1918; John
 Rodker), 183n
"Notes: Parisienne, Americaine, Espag-
 nole" (1922; Yvonne George), 299n
"The Notes to 'The Ivory Tower' "
 (1918; Ezra Pound), 204n, 224n
Nott, Stanley [publisher], 301, 302n
*La Nouvelle Nouvelle Revue Française,*
 2n, 316, 317n
*La Nouvelle Revue Française: revue
 mensuelle de littérature et de critique,*
 1, 2n, 316, 316n–317n, 327–28
"The Novels of Dorothy Richardson"
 (1918; May Sinclair), 178n
*The Novels of Henry James* (1908;
 Macmillan edition), 228n
Noyes, Alfred, 82n, 148n, 291, 293n

*L'Occident,* 1n
Occident Press [publishing firm], 2n
"Odour of Chrysanthemums" (1911;
 D. H. Lawrence), 71n
"L'Offre de Plebs" (1916; Jean de
 Bosschère), 2n
Olcott, Colonel Henry S., 315n
*On Heaven* (1918; Ford Madox Ford),
 255n
"On the Way to Hangchow: Anchored
 on the River at Night" (1917; trans-
 lated by Arthur Waley), 117, 119n
*Open Court,* 206n, 244, 245n
Open Court Publishing Company, 206n,
 244
Oppenheim, James, 53n, 72n, 143–44,
 145n, 146n

Orage, Alfred Richard, xv–xvi, 77, 79n,
 173n, 185, 199, 200n, 203, 204n, 207,
 209n, 221n, 223–24, 225, 250n, 277,
 313–14
Orloff, Chana, 297, 299n
"Osiris" (1912; Ezra Pound), xxvi
*Others: A Magazine of New Verse,* 4,
 5n, 74n, 82n, 141, 142n, 208n
*"Others" Anthology,* 255n
"Our Contemporaries: A Modern French
 Anthology" (1918), 218n–219n, 222n
"Our Tetrarchal Précieuse (A Divaga-
 tion from Jules Laforgue)" (1918;
 Ezra Pound [published under the
 pseudonym Thayer Exton]), 206n,
 209, 209n, 224, 225n, 238, 239n, 249
Ouspensky, P. D., 314, 315, 316n
*The Outlook,* 74n
*Ouvert la nuit* (1922; Paul Morand),
 269n
"Ozymandias" (1817; Percy Bysshe
 Shelley), 157

"Pagani's November 8" (1916; Ezra
 Pound), 48n
*Pagany,* 313, 313n
Paige, D. D., 307, 309n, and inclusion
 of Ezra Pound's letters to Margaret
 Anderson in *The Letters of Ezra
 Pound, 1907–1941,* xi
"Painting" [painting by Fernand Léger,
 1912], 299n
Pam, Max, 13n
Pansaers, Clement, xxxiii, 276, 277, 278n
*Il Paradiso* (Dante), 311n
*Paris Herald Tribune, see Herald
 Tribune* (Paris)
"Paris Letter, December 1922" (1923;
 Ezra Pound), 293n
"Partie d'échecs entre Picabia et Roché"
 (1917; Walter Conrad Arensberg),
 275n
Pascin, Jules, 165n
*Passages from the Letters of John
 Butler Yeats: Selected by Ezra Pound*
 (1917), 28, 29n, 37, 39n, 56n, 63,
 71n, 77, 79n
*Pastorales parisiennes* (1921; Guy
 Charles Cros), 269n
*Pastorals of France* (1877; Frederick
 Wedmore), 107n
Pater, Walter, xx
*The Pathfinder,* 139, 142n
Patmore, Brigit ["Vail de Lencour"], 55,
 100, 102n–103n, 193n, 243
Patmore, John Deighton, 55, 102n, 246

*Le Pauvre Diable* (1760; Voltaire), 94n
*Pavannes and Divagations* (1958; Ezra Pound), 23n, 24n, 57n
*Pavannes and Divisions* (1918; Ezra Pound), 13n, 23n, 24n, 57n, 71n, 132n, 187n, 249
"Paysages Souffrants, II" (Georges Rodenbach), 239n
Pea, Enrico, 307, 308n, 309n
Péguy, Charles, 2n
*The Penguin Book of Modern American Verse* (1954; compiled by Geoffrey Moore), 319, 319n, 329, 330n
Penguin Club, New York, 17n, 53n, 71n
"Penguins," *see* "Trois Pingouins"
*Le Père Perdrix* (1903; Charles-Louis Philippe), 255n
*Personae: The Collected Shorter Poems of Ezra Pound* (1909; Ezra Pound), xv, xvii, 67, 71n
*Personality* (1917; Rabindranath Tagore), 48n
*Perspective: A Quarterly Journal of Literature and the Arts,* 318, 319n, 324n
"Pétales de Nacre" (Albert Saint-Paul), 239n
*Peter Homunculus* (1909; Gilbert Cannan), 71n
*La Phalange,* 1n
Philippe, Charles-Louis, 255, 255n
Phillips, David Graham, 155, 157, 159n
Phillips, Stephen, 251n
Photo Secession Gallery [New York], 275n
Photo-Secession group [New York], 17n
*Physique de l'Amour; essai sur l'instinct sexuel* (1903; Remy de Gourmont), 99
Picabia, Francis, xxxiii, 124, 145n, 262n, 264, 264n, 265–68, 270–71, 273–74, 275n, 276n, 277, 280, 281n, 282, 290n, 291
"Picabia Number" [proposed special issue of *The Little Review*], 270, 274, 289
Picasso, Pablo, 124, 126n, 142, 145n, 265, 268, 274
"Picasso Number" [proposed special issue of *The Little Review*], 270, 274, 288
Pico della Mirandola, Giovanni, 10, 14n
"Pierrots: Scène courte mais typique (After the 'Pierrots' of Jules Laforgue)" (1917; Jules Laforgue, translated by Ezra Pound), xxix, 21, 22n, 62, 68, 71n
Pinaud, Ed, 284, 285n

*Pink 'Un, see Sporting Times* (*Pink 'Un*)
*Pistols for Two* (1917; H. L. Mencken/ George Jean Nathan) [pseudonymous work, under the name of Owen Hatteras], 202n
"The Place of Imagism" (1915; Conrad Aiken), 180n
*La Pléiade,* 48n
*Pleureuses* (1895; Henri Barbusse), 241n
Po Chü-I, 87, 88n, 104, 119n, 173n
Po, Li, *see* Li Po
Poe, Edgar Allan, 160n, 225n
*Poema del Cid* [*ca.* 1140], 245, 245n, 246n
*Poemas de la Gloria, del Amor y del Mar* (1908; Tomás Morales), 205n
"Poèmes et dessins de la fille née sans mère" (1918; Francis Picabia), 268n
*Poems* (1914; Walter Conrad Arensberg), 275n
*Poems* (1920; T. S. Eliot), 70n
*Poems and Plays* (1912; William Vaughn Moody), 219n
*Poems by Arthur Symons* (1909), 105n
*Poems, 1918–21* (1921; Ezra Pound), 293n
*Poems of Today* [anthology], 255n
*Poètes d'aujourd'hui, 1880–1900: morceaux choisis accompagnés de notices biographiques et d'un essai de bibliographie* (1900; Adolphe Van Bever and Paul Léautaud), 135n
*Poetical Works of Gavin Douglas, Bishop of Dunkeld, with a Memoir, Notes, and Glossary* (1874; edited by John Small), 135n–136n
*Poetry: A Magazine of Verse,* xvii–xviii, xxii, xxiv, xxv, xxix–xxx, 1, 2n, 3, 5n, 6–7, 12, 13n, 16, 17n, 22n, 25, 28, 32, 35, 40, 54, 56n, 67, 74n, 80, 82n, 86, 94n, 100, 102n, 113n, 140, 142–44, 146n, 185, 188n, 203, 204n, 212, 215, 216, 218n, 220, 222n, 225n, 275n, 294n, 318, 329, 330n
*Poetry and Drama,* 14n
Poetry Book Shop, London, xxii, 77, 77n, 128, 132, 247n
*The Poetry Review,* 135n, 155, 160n, 247n, 249, 251n
*The Poetry Review of America,* 180n
Poggio, *see* Bracciolini, Gian Francesco Poggio
"Portrait of Marcel Duchamp" (1922; Baroness Else von Freytag-Loringhoven), 229

*A Portrait of the Artist as a Young Man* 1916; James Joyce), xvi, 12n, 19, 48n, 56n, 57n, 70n, 73n, 120, 121n, 151, 174

"Possum" [T. S. Eliot's nickname], 310, 315

*Post*, New York, 266

*Post-Adolescence* (1923; Robert McAlmon), 294n

"Postlude" (William Carlos Williams), 92

Pound, Dorothy Shakespear, xxxi, 76, 153, 162, 183n, 253n, 283, 283n, 287, 297, 299n, 311

Pound, Ezra, broadcasts from Rome during the Second World War, 309n; censorship, 155, 173–74, 175n; criticized by readers, 113n, 192n–193n, 251n; Dorothy Caruso, 328; editorial involvement with Harriet Monroe, xvii–xviii, 3n; editorial involvement with *The Little Review*, xxiv–xxxiv, 3, 6–12, 75, 113n, 141, 259n, 280–81; editorial involvement with *Poetry*, xvii–xviii, 2n; *The Egoist*, xvi; financial relationship with John Quinn, 7–9, 11–12, 13n, 23, 28, 34–35, 51–52, 60–61, 139, 198; financial relationship with *The Little Review*, xxv, xxx–xxxi, 8–9, 11, 27–28, 162, 169–71, 194, 198; fraudulent death mask, xxxiii, 283, 283n; influence of little magazines on his literary career, xiv–xix; music, 186, 188n–189n; opinions about World War I and Kaiser Wilhelm, 92–93, 98, 144–45; personal finances, xxx–xxxi, 7, 213n–214n, 277; *Ulysses,* xxxi–xxxii, 189; use of pseudonyms by, xvi, 22n, 45, 63, 71n, 147, 148n, 159n, 171, 172n, 188n, 191, 199, 200n, 204n, 206n, 209n, 221n, 222n, 272, 276n, 278n, 279, 285–86, 286n, 299n [some references above are to individual pseudonyms or pseudonymous works by Pound; see also Atheling, William; "Bibi-la-Bibiste"; Dias, B. H.; Exton, Thayer; Hall, John; Hemholtz, Baptiste von; Hemholtz, Bastien von; Jesus Maria, Hermann Karl Georg; Le Monier, J. H.; "Our Tetrarchal Précieuse"; Root, Raoul; S. O. S.; and Sanders, Abel]; views regarding import tariffs on books, xxiv, 9–10; Vorticism, xvi–xvii, xxii, xxiv, xxvi–xxvii, 13n–14n, 16, 17n

Pound, Homer Loomis, 29, 163

Pound, Omar, 167n

"Pound and Frobenius" (1954; Guy Davenport), 309n

*The Pound Era* (1971; Hugh Kenner), xxvi, xxviii

*Pound/Lewis: The Letters of Ezra Pound and Wyndham Lewis* (1985; edited by Timothy Materer), ix, 283n, 286n

Pound Press, 305n

"Pour la Démone" (Jules Bois), 239n

"Pour la Démone, V" (Jules Bois), 239n

Powys, John Cowper, xix, 11, 15n, 48n, 70, 100

Powys, Llewellyn, xvi, 79n

"A Prayer on Going into My House" (1918; William Butler Yeats), 223n

"Presences" (1915; William Butler Yeats), 25n

"Le Prix Nobel" (1924; Ezra Pound), 293n

*Profiles from China: Sketches in Verse of People and Things in the Interior* (1917; Eunice Tietjens), 132n

"Progress of American Fiction" (1922; Ezra Pound [rejected by *The Little Review*]), 295

"Promontory" (1918; Arthur Rimbaud, translated by Helen Rootham), 208n

*Prose Poems from the Illuminations of Arthur Rimbaud, translated into English by Helen Rootham* (1932), 208n

Prothero, Sir George Walter, xvii, 37, 175n

Proust, Marcel, 83n, 267n

*Provença: Poems Selected from Personae, Exultations, and Canzionere of Ezra Pound* (1910; Ezra Pound), 65, 67, 72n

*Prufrock and Other Observations* (1917: T. S. Eliot), 29n, 45, 61, 70n, 117

*Prufrock and Other Observations* (1917; (1917; May Sinclair), 107n, 109, 125n, 126–27, 127n, 150n

"Psycho-Democracy: A Movement to Focus Human Reason on the Conscious Direction of Evolution" (1921; Mina Loy), 209n

"Psychology and Troubadours" (1912; Ezra Pound), 38n

*Publishers Weekly*, 321

*La Pucelle* (Voltaire), 94n

*Pugs and Peacocks* (1920; Gilbert Cannan), 71n

"Puritanism as a Literary Force" (1917;

[essay included in *A Book of Prefaces,*
by H. L. Mencken]), 154, 159n
*The Purple Land* (1885; W. H. Hudson),
48n
*The Pursuit of Reason* (1910; Charles
Francis Keary), 168n
"Push-Face" (1917; Jane Heap), 95n,
186, 188n
Puteklis, Louis, 110, 113n, 250n, 251,
252n

*The Quarterly Review,* xvii, 37, 122,
173, 175n, 291, 293n
*Der Querschnitt,* 291, 293n
*The Quest,* 36, 38n, 315n
The Quest Society, 313, 315n
Quinn, John, xxv, xxvii, xxx–xxxii, 13n,
14n, 15, 15n, 16n, 17n, 19, 19n, 20,
20n, 23, 27, 28, 31, 34n, 35, 40, 44,
47, 48n, 50n, 51, 53, 53n, 58, 60–62,
66, 70n, 71n, 79, 81, 84, 84n, 99, 114,
123, 125, 130, 132, 135n, 139, 142,
143, 161, 166, 169–72, 172n, 173n,
178, 179, 183, 186, 190n, 195, 197,
198, 202, 206, 221, 260, 260n, 261n,
276
"The Quintuple Effulgence or the Unapproachable Splendour" (1918;
attributed to Ezra Pound), 148n, 193n
*A Quinzaine for This Yule* (1908; Ezra
Pound), xv
"Quis multa gracilis?" (1918; Ezra
Pound), 204n

R. H. C., *see* Orage, Alfred Richard
Rabelais, François, 96n
"Rabindranath Tagore: His Second
Book into English" (1913; Ezra
Pound), 59n
*The Rainbow* (1916; D. H. Lawrence),
48n
Randall, A. E., xvi, 79n
Rasputin, Grigori Yefimovich, 248, 250n
"Rateliers platoniques: poème en deux
chapitres" (1918; Francis Picabia),
268n
Ray, Man, 271, 273, 275n, 290
Read, Herbert, 236
"The Reader Critic" [column in *The
Little Review*], xxiv, 93n, 113n, 148n,
162, 172n, 180n, 192n, 193n, 222n,
232, 232n, 241n, 248, 250n–251n, 256,
258n
*The Reader's Encyclopedia: An Ency-
clopedia of World Literature and the
Arts* (1948; William Rose Benét),
309n

"A Real Magazine" (1916; Margaret C.
Anderson), xxiii
"The Reality of Peace" (1917; D. H.
Lawrence), 102n
Rebel Art Centre [London], 14n
"The Rebellious Patient" (1953;
Wyndham Lewis), 319n
"The Recurrence" (1918; Ezra Pound),
210n
*Reedy's Mirror,* 249, 251n
Régnier, Henri de, 36, 125n, 135n, 219n
Reid, B. L., 53n, 70n
*The Relation of Ultramodern to Archaic
Music* (1921; Katherine Ruth Hey-
man), 293n
*Religious Hours* (1916; Charles Francis
Keary), 188n
Rembrandt, 70n, 258n
*Reminiscences* (1916; Rabindranath
Tagore), 48n
"Remy de Gourmont, After the Interim"
(1919; Richard Aldington), 173n
"Remy de Gourmont issue" [special
issue of *The Little Review*], *see*
"Gourmont number"
La Renaissance du Livre [publishing
firm], 222n
Rennert, Hugo Albert, 30, 185, 188n
Renoir, Pierre, 124, 126n
*Réponses aux questions d'un provincial*
(1704–1706; Pierre Bayle), 219n
Repplier, Agnes, 106, 107n, 131
"The Return" (1912; Ezra Pound), 187,
189n
Reverdy, Pierre, 300n
"The Rev. G. Crabbe, LL. B." (1917;
Ezra Pound), 204n
Rice, Cale Young, 148n
Richard Saint Victor, 314, 316n
Richards, Grant [publishing firm], 37,
65, 72n, 121n
Richardson, Dorothy, 174, 177, 178n,
281n
Richardson, Mary, 255n
*Rien que la terre* (1926; Paul Morand),
269n
Rihaku, *see* Li Po
Rimbaud, Arthur, 135n, 155, 159n–160n,
207, 208n, 216, 219n
*Riposte* (1912; Ezra Pound), 13n
"Ritratto" (1918; Ezra Pound), 204n
Rivera, Diego M., 124, 126n, 145n
Robinson, Edwin Arlington, 159n
Rochelle, Drieu la, Pierre, *see* Drieu la
Rochelle, Pierre
Rodenbach, Georges, 239n, 240
Rodin, Auguste, 291, 292n

Rodker, John, xv, xxix, xxxi, 5n, 10, 14n, 21, 25, 26, 26n, 27, 27n, 32, 38n, 44–45, 47n, 62–64, 67–68, 71n, 73n, 74–75, 76, 77, 99–100, 109, 142, 162, 171, 173, 173n, 182, 183n, 190, 192n, 214–15, 215n, 224, 255, 255n, 257, 258n, 259n, 260, 262, 262n, 281, 281n, 283n

*Rolla* (1833; Alfred de Musset), 219n

Romains, Jules, 46, 48n, 135n, 192, 194n, 196, 219n, 220–21, 227, 228n, 229, 253, 261, 262n, 264, 264n

"Romance" (Iris Barry; manuscript work, rejected by Ezra Pound in 1918), 197

*Il Romanzo di Moscardino* (Enrico Pea), 308n; *see also Moscardino*

Root, Raoul [pseudonym used by Ezra Pound], 159n, 191, 193n, 199, 200n

Rootham, Helen, 207, 208n

*Las Rosas de Hércules* (1919, 1922; Tomás Morales), 205n

"Rose White, Yellow, Silver" (1918; Ezra Pound), 242n, 255n

Rothenstein, Sir William, 58, 59n

Rothermere, Lady, 314, 315n–316n

Rothermere, Viscount Harold Sydney Harmsworth, 315n

"Rottenness in Literature" (1922; Alfred Noyes), 293n

*Rotting Hill* (1951; Wyndham Lewis), 307, 309n, 311, 325–27, 327n

*Round the Corner* (1913; Gilbert Cannan), 71n

Rumbold, Sir Horace, 306, 306n

Rummel, Frank, 32, 279, 290, 293n

Rummel, Walter Morse, 130, 132n, 180n, 186–87, 188n–189n, 279, 279n, 307, 309n

Russell, Bertrand, 305, 305n

Russell, George William ("A. E."), 77, 79n

Russell, Peter, 305, 305n, 306, 319n

*Russia in 1916* (1917; Stephen Graham), 250n

S. O. S. [pseudonym used by Ezra Pound], 147, 148n

Saint-Exupéry, Antoine de, 325n

"Saint-Moritz" (1918; André Spire), 254n

Saint-Paul, Albert, 239n, 240

Saint Victor, Richard, *see* Richard Saint Victor

"Sainte-Anne" (1918; Tristan Corbière), 182

*Salammbô* (1862; Gustave Flaubert), 210, 211n

"Saltus" (1918; Ezra Pound), 242n, 255n

Samain, Albert, 125n, 219n

Sanborn, Robert Alden, 129, 132n, 188n

Sandburg, Carl, 5n, 48n, 58, 90, 94n, 159n

Sanders, Abel [pseudonym used by Ezra Pound], 148n, 171, 172n, 272, 276n, 278n, 279, 285–86, 286n

Sanders, Emmy V., 277, 278n

Saphier, William, 5n

"Saptam Edoyarder Svargobohan" (1918; Tarini Prasad Jyotishi, translated into English by Iseult Gonne as "The Ascension of Edward VII to Heaven"), 198, 199n, 238, 239n, 248, 250n

Saunders, Helen, 16n, 50

*The Savoy,* 197

"The Scandal of *Ulysses*" (1922; Aramis [pseudonym]), 293n

"Scenes and Portraits" (1909; Frederic Manning), 65, 72n

Schelling, Felix Emmanuel, 185, 188n

Schlumberger, Jean, 2n

"Das Schone [*sic*] Papier Vergeudet" (1916; Ezra Pound), xxiv

Schopenhauer, Arthur, 82, 83n

*The Scots Observer,* 95n

Scott, Evelyn, 261n

Scratton, Bride, 297, 299n

*Scribner's Monthly,* xiv, 80, 105n; *see also Century*

"Sculpshure" (1921; Ezra Pound), 259n, 272, 276n

*Sea Garden* (1916; Hilda Doolittle), 48n

"Sea Poppies" (1917; Hilda Doolittle), 57n, 86n

*Secession,* 285n

Martin Secker [publishing firm], 121n

*The Secret Doctrine* (1888; Helena Petrovna Hahn Blavatsky), 315n

Segonzac, André, 165n

"The Sensitive Plant" (Percy Bysshe Shelley), 157

"Sestina: Altaforte" (1909; Ezra Pound), xv

*The Seven Arts,* 52, 53n, 65, 72n, 138, 143, 145n–146n

*Sex and Character* (1906; Otto Weininger), 101n

"The Shadow in the Rose Garden" (1914; D. H. Lawrence), 72n, 160n

"Shake Down" (1918; Ezra Pound), 224

Shakespeare and Company [booksellers], Paris, 274n

"Shapes" (1918; Mark Turbyfill), 241n
Shaw, George Bernard, 17n, 37, 81, 98
"She Goes to Pisa" (1918; Mark
   Turbyfill), 241n
"She Turns the Dolls' Faces to the
   Walls" (1917; William Butler Yeats),
   47n
Shelley, Percy Bysshe, 157, 188n
*Shenandoah,* 308n, 316n, 318, 319n
Shorter, Clement, 257
Sickert, Walter, 107n
Signac, Paul, 124, 126n
"Silence" (1918; Jean de Bosschère),
   241n
*Silhouettes* (1909; Arthur Symons),
   113n
Sinclair, May, 2n, 32, 55, 77, 106, 107n,
   109, 122, 125n, 126–27, 127n, 150,
   150n, 152, 161–62, 165, 172, 174, 177,
   178n, 203, 204n, 221, 281
Sinn Fein, 144
*Sister Carrie* (1900; Theodore Dreiser),
   xix
Sitwell, Edith, 208n
Sitwell, Sacheverell, 136, 221
*Six French Poets: Studies in Contem-
   porary Literature* (1915; Amy Lowell),
   xxix, 122, 125n
"Sketch 48b.11" (1918; Ezra Pound),
   204n
Sloan, John, 70n
"Small Magazines" (1930; Ezra Pound),
   xiv, xxxiv
Small, Maynard [publishing firm], 65,
   67, 72n, 293n
*The Smart Set,* 31, 72n, 74n, 107n, 109,
   156–57, 160n, 164, 201–02
*A Snapt Gold Ring* (1871; Frederick
   Wedmore), 107n
*Social Credit: An Impact* (1935; Ezra
   Pound), 302n
Society of Independent Artists, 126n
Society to Maintain Public Decency, 82n
Les Soeurs X [pseudonym associated
   with the Dadaist work "Bibi-la-
   Bibiste"], 269n
*The Soil: A Magazine of Art,* 99, 101n,
   122, 123, 124, 126n
"Soir Historique" (1918; Arthur Rim-
   baud, translated by Helen Rootham),
   208n
"Soirée" (1918; Ezra Pound), 204n
"Soirée de Paris" (1924–25; Pierre de
   Massot), 281n
*Les Soirées de Paris,* 123, 126n
"A Soldier of Humour" (1917–18;

Wyndham Lewis), 42n, 96, 98n, 108,
   150, 150n, 182, 191, 193n
"Solomon to Sheba" (1918; William
   Butler Yeats), 223n
Solon, Israel, 241n, 258n
*Some Imagist Poets* (1915/1916/1917;
   edited by Amy Lowell), 14n, 94n
*Some Mystical Adventures* (1910;
   George Robert Stow Mead), 315n
"Some Notes on Francisco de Quevedo
   Villegas" (1921; Ezra Pound), 269n
"A Song" (1918; William Butler Yeats),
   223n
"Sonnet" (Stéphane Mallarmé), 239n
"Sonnets Symphoniques" (Achille
   Delaroche), 239n
*Sordello* (1840, etc.; Robert Browning),
   195n
*The Soul of London: A Survey of a
   Modern City* (1905/1911; Ford Madox
   Ford), 65, 72n, 318, 319n
Soule, George, xx
Soupault, Philippe, 281n
*South Atlantic Quarterly,* 261n
*Souvenirs (1895–1918)* (1931; Georgette
   Leblanc), 325n
*Souvenirs: My Life with Maeterlinck*
   (1932; Georgette Leblanc, translated
   by Janet Flanner), 325n
"Spanish Number" [proposed special
   issue of *The Little Review*], 203, 213n
Spearman, Neville, 313n
"Spectacle effrayant" (1921; Paul
   Morand), 277n
*The Spectator,* 144, 146n
*Spectra* (1916; Witter Bynner and
   Arthur Davison Ficke), 111n
Spectrist hoax, 111n, 112n–113n
"Spectrum: Opus 96" (Witter Bynner
   and Arthur Davison Ficke), 111n
*The Sphere,* 257
Spire, André, 135n, 219n, 253, 254n
*The Spirit of Romance: An Attempt to
   Define Somewhat the Charm of the
   Pre-Renaissance Literature of Latin
   Europe* (1910, etc.; Ezra Pound), 38n,
   65, 72n
*The Spirit of the People: An Analysis
   of the English Mind* (1907; Ford
   Madox Ford), 318, 319n
*Spiritual Adventures* (1905; Arthur
   Symons), 103, 105n
*Splashing into Society* (1923; Iris Barry),
   63, 71n
*The Spoon River Anthology* (1915;
   Edgar Lee Masters), 56n, 59n

*Sporting Times* (*Pink 'Un*), 291, 293n
*Spring and All* (1923; William Carlos Williams), 294n
"Spring Song: Night on the Field" (1922; W. C. G. Jitro), 299n
"The Stage" (1918; Arthur Rimbaud, translated by Helen Rootham), 208n
Stanton, Theodore, 140, 220, 222n
*The Star,* 102n
"Stark Realism: This Little Pig Went to Market (A Search for the National Type)" (1917; Ezra Pound), 55, 57n, 75, 75n
"The Starry Sky" (1917; Wyndham Lewis), 164, 165n
Stein, Gertrude, 268
"Stele" (1918; Ezra Pound), 204n, 230, 231n
Stella, Joseph, 124, 126n
Stephen, Vanessa, 5n
Stevens, Wallace, 2n, 5n, 82n
Stieglitz, Alfred, 113n, 271–73, 275n
Stock, Noel, xvi–xvii, xxxi, 5n, 13n, 72n, 114n, 302n
Stork, Charles Wharton, 178, 180n, 195n, 247
Storrs, John, 288, 290, 292n–293n, 294–95
Strachey, Lytton, 144, 146n, 231
Strachey, St. Loe, 146n
*The Strange Life of Ivan Osokin* (1947; P. D. Ouspensky), 315n
*Studies in English Art* (1876; Frederick Wedmore), 107n
"A Study of French Poets" (1918; Ezra Pound), xxix, 136n
Stuhlmann, Frank, 249, 251n
Suarès, André, 1n
Sullivan, John L., 172
Sumner, John Saxton, xxxiii, 81, 82n, 260n, 261n, 266
*Sunday Chronicle,* 293n
*Suspended Judgments: Essays on Books and Sensations* (1916; John Cowper Powys), 48n
"Sweeney Among the Nightingales" (1918; T. S. Eliot), 105n, 224n
Swiggett, Glen Levin, 139, 142n
Swinburne, Algernon Charles, xv, 63, 90, 185, 187, 188n, 203, 219n, 222n
"Swinburne versus Biographers" (1918; Ezra Pound), 188n, 203, 204n
*Sword Blades and Poppy Seed* (1914; Amy Lowell), 180n
*The Symbolist Movement in Literature* (1899; Arthur Symons), 160n
Symons, Arthur, 96–97, 98, 98n, 103–05, 105n, 111, 113n, 133, 139, 156, 160n, 179, 205, 206n
Synge, John Millington, 110
Szukalski, Stanislaw, 241n

*Ta Hio, the Great Learning* (1936; translated by Ezra Pound), 302n
Tagore, Rabindranath, xvii, 16, 17n–18n, 48n, 56n, 58, 59n, 128, 131n–132n, 198
Tailhade, Laurent, 135n, 219n
*The Tale of Genji* (Murasaki Shikibu), 29n
Tannenbaum, Samuel A., 258n
*Tarr* (1916; Wyndham Lewis), xvi, 73n, 180–81, 181n, 213n, 289, 290n
Taupin, René, 2n, 3n
Teller, Charlotte, 30, 114, 291
"The Temperaments" (1917; Ezra Pound), 48n
*Tendencies in Modern American Poetry* (1917; Amy Lowell), 154, 159n
*Tendres Stocks* (1921; Paul Morand), 269n
*Tertium Organum* (1920; P. D. Ouspensky), 315n
Thayer, Scofield, xxxii, 259n, 260, 265, 268n
"Theatre and Music-Hall" (1923/1924; Pierre de Massot), 281n
"Theatre Muet" (1917; John Rodker), 27, 27n, 47n, 73n, 74–75
"Theodore Dreiser" (1917; essay included in *A Book of Prefaces,* by H. L. Mencken), 159n
The Theosophical Society, 315n
"They All Made Peace—What Is Peace?" (Ernest Hemingway), 300n
"Thirty-eight Poems by Po Chü-I" (1917; translated by Arthur Waley), 88n
*This Generation* [1915–17; proposed work (never published) by Ezra Pound], 16, 17n
Thomas Beecham Opera Company, 153n
Thoreau, Henry David, 311
*Thorgils* (1917; Maurice Henry Hewlett), 48n, 74n
"Thoughts from a Country Vicarage" (1918), 125n–126n
"Three Cantos" (1917/1918; Ezra Pound), 16, 17n, 54, 56n, 80, 82n, 86
"Three Generations: The Same" (1924; Robert McAlmon), 294n
Three Mountains Press, 39n, 98n, 183n, 292, 294n, 297, 299n
"Three Nightpieces" (1917; John Rodker), 26n, 27n, 47n, 73n, 76n

"Three Songs of Ezra Pound for a Voice with Instrumental Accompaniment by Walter Morse Rummel" (1911; Rummel/Pound), 188n–189n

*Three Stories and Ten Poems* (1923; Ernest Hemingway), 294n

*Through Russian Central Asia* (1916; Stephen Graham), 250n

Thurston, Jarvis A., 324, 324n

*Thus to Revisit* (1921; Ford Madox Ford), 277, 278n

Tietjens, Eunice, xx, 2n, 57n, 131, 132n

*Time and Eternity* (1919; Gilbert Cannan), 71n

*Times* (London), 39, 40n, 77, 250n, 329

*Times Literary Supplement,* 13n, 39, 40n, 79n, 231

Tina, Beatrice, *see* Hastings, Beatrice

"To a Young Girl" (1918; William Butler Yeats), 223n

*To-Day,* 66

"Toilers" (1918; Arthur Rimbaud, translated by Helen Rootham), 208n

"Tom O'Roughley" (1918; William Butler Yeats), 223n

Toulet, Paul-Jean, 297, 299n

Toulouse-Lautrec, Henri de, 145n

"Towards the End" (1917; Iris Barry), 47n

Towne, Charles Hanson, 114n

*A Tramp's Sketches* (1912; Stephen Graham), 250n

*Transatlantic Review,* 299n, 308

*The Translations of Ezra Pound* (1953), 324, 324n

"Transmutation" (1922; Stephen Hudson), 299n

Tredegar, Lady Katherine Agnes Blanche Carnegie, xi, 97, 234, 235n

Tredegar Memorial Lecture Royal Society of Literature, 235n

" 'A Trial-Track for Racers': Margaret Anderson and *The Little Review*" (Jackson R. Bryer), xxii, xxiv

*Tribune* (Berlin), 222n

*391* [i.e., *Trois cents quatre-vingt-onze*] (edited by Francis Picabia), 264n, 275n

*Trois Contes* (1877; Gustave Flaubert), 211n

"Trois Pingouins" [sculpture by Constantin Brancusi], 272, 275n

Turbyfill, Mark, 241n

Turgenev, Ivan S., 96n

"Turkish Night" (1921; Paul Morand; translated by Ezra Pound), 269n

Twain, Mark, 156

*Twelve Occupations* (1916; version of Jean de Bosschère's *Métiers divins,* translated into English by Ezra Pound), 2n

*Twenty-five Poems* (1923; Marsden Hartley), 294n

"Two Acorns, One Oak" (1954; Dwight Macdonald), 318n–319n

*Two Girls* (1874; Frederick Wedmore), 107n

*291* (edited by Francis Picabia and Alfred Stieglitz), 264n, 275n

291 Gallery, New York, 275n

*The Two Lancrofts* (1893; Charles Francis Keary), 168n

*Two Selves* (1923; Bryher), 294n

"The Two Smokers" [painting by Fernand Léger, 1911], 299n

Tzara, Tristan, 300n

Ulrich, Carolyn F., xiv, xxvi, 2n–3n, 105n

"Ulysse Fait Son Lit" (1916; Jean de Bosschère), 2n

*Ulysses* (1918–20; James Joyce), xxv, xxix, xxxi–xxxii, 13n, 28, 37, 46, 122, 139, 166, 167, 171, 174, 176n, 189, 190, 196, 212, 223, 248, 251n, 256, 258n, 260, 270, 272–73, 274n–275n, 277, 278n, 281, 282, 282n, 306, 306n; and censorship, xxv, xxxi–xxxii, 260n–261n, 264n, 266, 267, 274n–275n, 276n, 306n; contemporary reviews of, 291, 293n

" 'Ulysses' in Court" (1921; Margaret C. Anderson), 276n, 277, 278n

"Unanimisme" (1918; Ezra Pound), 136n, 194n, 196

"Under the Round Tower" (1918; William Butler Yeats), 223n, 236

*Undiscovered Russia* (1911; Stephen Graham), 250n

*Unique eunuque* (1920; Francis Picabia), 264n

*The Unknowable Gurdjieff* (1952; Margaret C. Anderson), 315n

Untermeyer, Louis, 143, 146n, 148n

"Upon a Dying Lady" (1917; William Butler Yeats), 47n, 73n, 76n

"Upon the Harps of Judea" (1918; Ezra Pound), 242n, 255n

Upward, Allen, xvi, xxvi, 79n

*A Vagabond in the Caucasus* (1910; Stephen Graham), 250n

"Vagabonds" (1918; Arthur Rimbaud, translated by Helen Rootham), 208n

Vail de Lencour, *see* Patmore, Brigit
Valéry, Paul, 2n
Vallette, Alfred, xxix, 5n, 48n, 122, 125n
Van Bever, Adolphe, 134, 135n
Van Dine, S. S., *see* Wright, Willard Huntington
Van Dyke, Henry, 82n, 216, 219n, 295
Van Gogh, Vincent, 124, 145n
Vanderpyl, Fritz-René, 32, 46, 48n
*Vanity Fair,* 99, 101n, 107n
"I Vecchii" (1918; Ezra Pound), 204n
Verdi, Giuseppe, 231n
"Vergier" (1918; Ezra Pound), 204n
Verhaeren, Émile, 125n, 135n, 219n, 220, 222n
Verlaine, Paul, 219n
*Vers et Prose,* 1n
*Vers libre,* 22n, 73n, 80, 86n, 109, 142n, 160n, 180n
Veselofskii, Aleksei Nikolaevich, 1, 3n
Victor, Richard Saint, *see* Richard Saint Victor
*La Vie parisienne,* 299n
Vielé-Griffin, Francis, 135n, 239n, 240
Viereck, George Sylvester, 144, 146n
*The Vikings in Western Civilization* (1890; Charles Francis Keary), 168n
Vildrac, Charles, 32, 135n, 219n
Villon, François, 59n
Vittorio Emmanuele, king of Italy, 230, 231n
Vlaminck, Maurice de, 124, 126n, 145n, 297
*Vogue,* 3, 8
Vollard, Ambrose, 126n
Voltaire, François-Marie Arouet, 52, 94n, 176n, 216–17, 218n
Von Freitag Loringhoven, Baroness Else, *see* Freytag-Loringhoven, Baroness Else von
Vorticism in art and literature, xxii, xxvi–xxvii, 13n–14n, 16, 17n, 72n, 123, 193n, 314–15
Vorticist Show (New York, 1916), xxvii, 15, 16, 16n–17n, 53n, 70n
Vortoscope [invention of Ezra Pound and Alvin Langdon Coburn], 16, 17n
*Vou* [Japanese literary magazine], 302n
"The Vowels" (John Gould Fletcher), 159n
"Voyelles" (Arthur Rimbaud), 159n

Wadsworth, Edward, 16n, 248, 255, 288, 289n
Waley, Arthur David, 28, 29n, 41, 42n,

68, 73n, 87–88, 88n, 97, 104, 108, 115, 118, 119n, 120, 121n, 173n, 281n
Walkowitz, A., 124, 126n
Waller, Edmund, 187, 188n
*La Wallonie,* 238, 238n, 239n
Walpole, Hugh, 211, 215, 231
*The Wanderer* (1888; Charles Francis Keary), 168n
Washington, George, 158
Washington Square Bookshop, 260n
*The Waste Land* (1922; T. S. Eliot), 291–92
Watson, James Sibley, Jr., 259n
Weaver, Harriet Shaw, xvi, 6, 12n–13n, 20n, 37, 120, 121n, 270, 274n–275n, 315
Webb, Beatrice Potter, 98, 101n
Webb, Sidney, 98, 101n
Weber, Max, 124, 126n, 165n
Wedmore, Frederick, 106, 107n
Weininger, Otto, 99, 101n
Wells, H. G., 100, 165, 166n, 181
Welsh, Robert Gilbert, 114, 114n
West, Dame Rebecca, 100, 102n
Wharton, Edith, 106, 131, 132n, 165, 169, 172, 184, 203, 205, 207, 224
"What Is Left Undone" (1923; Robert McAlmon), 294n
Wheeler, Monroe, 292, 293n–294n
Whigham, Peter, 305, 305n, 329, 330n
"Whispers of Immortality" (1918; T. S. Eliot), 105n, 224n
White, J. R., 118, 119n
*The White Peacock* (1911; D. H. Lawrence), 71n
"The White Stocking" (1914; D. H. Lawrence), 72n, 160n
"Whitehall" (1919; published under the pseudonym "Crelos"), 210, 210n–211n, 258–59, 259n
Whitman, Walt, 7, 13n, 101n, 160n, 180n
Whitney, Mrs. Harry Payne, 124, 126n
"Widow" (1917; Iris Barry), 47n
*The Wild Body* (1927; Wyndham Lewis), 98n
*The Wild Earth* (1916; Padraic Colum), 110, 113n
"The Wild Swans at Coole" (1916; William Butler Yeats), 25n
*The Wild Swans at Coole, Other Verses and a Play* (1917; William Butler Yeats), 73n
*Wilderness Love Songs* (Mary Richardson), 255n
Wilkinson, Louis Umfreville, 70, 74n, 191

William Clowes and Sons, Ltd, London [publishing firm], 48n
Williams, Edgar, 111, 113n, 141, 142n
Williams, William Carlos, xxii, 2n, 5n, 30, 33, 55–56, 57n, 82n, 92, 94n, 111, 113n, 114, 141, 172, 190, 192n, 204n, 241n, 255n, 257, 268, 279, 281, 281n, 292, 294n, 302n, 307, 311, 313n, 318, 319n
Wilson, Edmund, 292
Wilson, Henry Lane, 245, 245n–246n
Wilson, Woodrow, 172
*Wind Among the Reeds* (1899; William Butler Yeats), 213n
*Wind, Sand and Stars* (1939; Antoine de Saint-Exupéry, translated by Lewis Galantière), 325n
Windeler, B. Cyril, 148, 151, 183, 183n, 184, 188n, 191–92, 194n, 196, 204, 221, 223, 229, 229n, 234, 235n, 297, 299n
"Wine" (1918; Ezra Pound), 242n, 255n
Wing, DeWitt C., xx
Wisdom of the East Series [series of translations published by J. Murray, London], 313
*With Poor Immigrants to America* (1914; Stephen Graham), 250n
*With the Russian Pilgrims to Jerusalem* (1913; Stephen Graham), 250n
"Woman Shapely as a Swan" (Padraic Colum), 110
"A Woman Tramp" (1918; Max Michelson), 150n, 209n
*Women & Men* (1918; Ford Madox Ford), xxix, 38n–39n, 70n, 78, 89n, 96, 97n–98n, 101n, 152, 163, 166, 171, 192, 196, 213, 281
"The Women of Trachis" (1954; Sophocles, translated by Ezra Pound), 319n
*Women of Trachis: A Version by Ezra Pound* (1956; Sophocles, translated by Ezra Pound), 313n

Woodberry, George, 82n
Woolf, Virginia, 5n, 83n
*The World as Will and Idea* (1883; Arthur Schopenhauer), 83n
*The World Mystery* (1908; George Robert Stow Mead), 315n
Wright, Fanny, *see* Wright, Frances
Wright, Frances, 319, 319n, 329
Wright, Frank Lloyd, xix
Wright, Willard Huntington, 157, 160n, 202, 202n
"The Writer and His Job" (1918; Israel Solon), 241n
*Wyndham Lewis* (1954; Hugh Kenner), 316n
*Wyndham Lewis: A Descriptive Bibliography* (1978; Omar Pound and Philip Grover), 167n
"Wyndham Lewis Number" [of *Shenandoah*] (1953), 316n

*Years of Transition: The Dial, 1912–1920* (1967; Nicholas Joost), 96n
Yeats, John Butler, 28, 29n, 31, 37, 39n, 63, 70n, 77, 79n, 170
Yeats, William Butler, xv, xvii, xxviii, xxix, 18n, 23, 24, 24n, 25, 25n–26n, 26, 27, 27n, 28, 29, 32, 37, 40, 40n, 41, 44–45, 47, 47n, 49, 52, 53, 54, 55, 56n, 57n, 58, 59n, 63–64, 67, 68, 73n, 75, 76, 76n, 78, 79, 80, 93, 116, 129, 136, 147, 167, 186, 213n, 221, 223n, 228, 228n, 232, 233, 235, 235n, 236, 237, 237n, 238, 238n, 240, 242, 258, 259n, 268, 281, 281n, 313, 330n
*The Yellow Book*, 106, 107n, 197, 197n
"You Say You Said" (1918; Marianne Moore), 209n

Zayas, Marius de, 272, 275n